618· 97689 /AGE

Ageing and Older Adult Mental Health

This book examines the issues and implications tha᙮ ᴍᴇntal hᴇ..ᴉth professionals face when dealing with ageing and older adults. The book focuses on the biological, psychological and cultural influences that impact on the work of mental health practitioners who work with this client group.

Based on current empirical research and evidence-based practical issues this book explores topics including:

- ageing and dementia
- elder abuse
- caring for older adults
- depression and ageing
- the paradox of ageing
- how older adults are key to the success of future gener᙮ ᵢons.

Throughout the book the contributors emphasise the r᷄ ᵢon of 'healthy ageing', and the importance and significance of this cᴏ᷄ ᵗ as part of the life-cycle process. As such *Ageing and Older Adulᴛ Mᴇ. ᴉl Health* will be key reading not only for mental health professionals ᴜut also for those involved in policy making for older adults.

Patrick Ryan is a Senior Lecturer and Director of the Doctoral Programme in Clinical Psychology at the University of Limerick, Ireland. He has been involved in the training of clinical psychologists, psychotherapists and counsellors for ten years with a particular interest in the area of lifespan development and its contribution to understanding family relations.

Barry J. Coughlan is Senior Lecturer and Assistant Director of Clinical Psychology at the University of Limerick, and Senior Clinical Psychologist with the Brothers of Charity Services, Limerick, Ireland. His clinical/ research focus includes mental health and emotional well-being in intellectual disability, ageing and disability. He holds an international publications profile and is in regular demand for international workshops and symposia in his field.

Ageing and Older Adult Mental Health

Issues and Implications for Practice

Edited by Patrick Ryan and
Barry J. Coughlan

Routledge
Taylor & Francis Group

LONDON AND NEW YORK

First published 2011 by Routledge
27 Church Road, Hove, East Sussex BN3 2FA

Simultaneously published in the USA and Canada
by Routledge
270 Madison Avenue, New York NY 10016

Routledge is an imprint of the Taylor & Francis Group, an Informa business

Typeset in Times by Garfield Morgan, Swansea, West Glamorgan
Printed and bound in Great Britain by TJ International Ltd, Padstow,
Cornwall
Paperback cover design by Andrew Ward

British Library Cataloguing in Publication Data
A catalogue record for this book is available from the British Library

Library of Congress Cataloging-in-Publication Data
Ageing and older adult mental health : issues and implications for practice /
edited by Patrick Ryan & Barry J. Coughlan.
     p. ; cm.
   Includes bibliographical references.
   ISBN 978-0-415-58289-6 (hardback) – ISBN 978-0-415-58290-2 (pbk.) 1.
Older people–Mental health. 2. Older people–Health and hygiene. 3. Aging.
I. Ryan, Patrick, 1969- II. Coughlan, Barry J. (Barry John), 1974-
   [DNLM: 1. Aging. 2. Aged. WT 104]
   RC451.4.A5A345 2010
   618.97'689–dc22
                                                                    2010029253

ISBN: 978–0–415–58289–6 (hbk)
ISBN: 978–0–415–58290–2 (pbk)

Contents

Tables

Figure

Contributors

Cian Aherne, BA, is a Masters student at the University of Limerick. He works as a research assistant in the Oakwood Counselling practice in Castletroy, Limerick and in the University of Limerick counselling department.

Maja Barker, BA, MSc, PhD, DClinPsych, is a clinical psychologist with the Health Service Executive in Ireland. Previously, she worked as a researcher on a large-scale 'Aging, Health and Healthcare' programme and through this work, she also completed a PhD in the psychology of ageing. Maja has authored several research articles and books.

Alison Bonham, BA, BSc Psych, MSc Forens Psych, DClinPsych, is working as a clinical psychologist at the Brothers of Charity, Ennis, County Clare. Her experience includes working with older adults at St Andrews Hospital, Northampton, UK in 2004, and working in the HSE Older Adult Services at Camillus' Hospital, Limerick, Ireland from 2007 to 2008.

Barry J. Coughlan, BA, PhD, DPsychSc (Clin Psych) is a Senior Lecturer and Assistant Director of Clinical Psychology at the University of Limerick and a Senior Clinical Psychologist with the Brothers of Charity Services, Limerick. His clinical/research focus includes mental health and emotional well-being in intellectual disability, ageing and disability. He holds an international publications profile and is in regular demand for international workshops and symposia in his field.

Helen Dempsey, RGN, BA(Psych), MPsychSc (Health Psychology), is completing a doctoral programme in clinical psychology. Her experience includes working in health care settings with older adults with both medical and mental health needs and in a residential community setting with older adults with intellectual disability and mental health difficulties.

Jessica Dudley, BA, MSc (Health Psychology), DClinPsych, works as a clinical psychologist with the Health Service Executive South in the North Lee Primary Care Clinical Psychology Service, Ireland where her work includes providing a service to older adults in the assessment of cognitive function, support for carers and psychotherapy for adjustment difficulties.

Lorraine Feeney, BSc, MSc, DClinPsych, is a clinical psychologist who works in child and family community services in the Irish Health Service Executive. She has previous experience working with older adults presenting with Alzheimer's disease and other neurological disorders and also has worked with older adults in intellectual disability settings.

Emma Flynn, BA (Early Childhood Studies), HDip (Psychology), MSc (Applied Psychology), is completing a PhD in Clinical Psychology. She has previous experience with older adults in a support service for individuals with dementia in Northern Ireland, and also in the learning disability field as both a support worker and a psychologist in clinical training.

Jutta Roisín Greve, BA, MPsychSc (Health Psychology), DClinPsych, has been involved in various research projects in relation to older adults. These explored subjects such as attitudes toward older people, carers' needs and the role of various psychosocial constructs in adaptation outcomes for older hip fracture patients.

John Lalor, BSc, MSc, is completing his DClinPsych at the University of Limerick and is employed by the Irish Health Service Executive. He has experience in working with elderly people within the general population and within intellectual disability services.

Deirbhile Lavin, BA, MPsychSc (Health Psychology), PhD (Clinical Psychology), works as a clinical psychologist in the Health Services Executive in Ireland and has previously worked in research in Australia in the area of older adult physical health.

Niamh Maria Long, BSc (Applied Psychology), MSc (Work & Organisational Psychology) DClinPsych, has a background in intellectual disability and organisational psychology prior to her clinical psychology training. She is currently employed by the Health Service Executive South, working in adult mental health.

Colum MacMahon, BA, HDipEd, BSc, MSc, DClinPsych, works as a clinical psychologist for the Health Service Executive in Longford, Westmeath, Ireland. He is employed as the primary care psychologist for County Longford where he frequently works with older adults presenting with anxiety, depression and bereavement issues.

Denise O'Connell-Kehoe, BSc (Hons) Psychology, PGradDip Statistics, MSc Applied Psychology, is currently completing the doctoral programme in clinical psychology at the University of Limerick. She works in the Limerick Mental Health Services for Older People. Her research interests include older adult service users' understanding of diagnosis and treatment plans.

Mary O'Donoghue, BA, PhD (Clinical Psychology), works as a clinical psychologist with the Brothers of Charity Services in Limerick, Ireland and has previous experience of working in paediatric care and care for elderly people with intellectual disabilities.

Olive O'Reilly, BEd, HDip ICT & Ed, DClinPsych, is currently working in the Department of Education and Science and private clinical practice catering for children and adolescents with learning, intellectual, social, emotional and behavioural difficulties. She has experience in working with older adults in community and residential care settings addressing educational, occupational and mental health needs.

Lena O'Rourke, BA (Psych), MA (Counselling Psychology), is a counselling psychologist who is currently completing her doctoral studies in clinical psychology at the University of Limerick. Prior to this, she worked as a counselling psychologist with the Alzheimer's Society of Ireland and is currently engaged in a specialist placement in older adult mental health.

Claire O'Sullivan, holds a BA and Masters in Psychology from University College Cork. Having worked for over 16 years in rehabilitation/disability services, she is currently completing her doctorate in clinical psychology with the University of Limerick and has a keen interest in the application of positive psychology in clinical practice.

Patrick Ryan, BA, DClinPsych, is a Senior Lecturer and Director of the Doctoral Programme in Clinical Psychology at the University of Limerick. In clinical practice, he specialises in the application of lifespan developmental psychology to mental health problems.

Zarqa Shahid, BSc, Dip (TCO3) in Counselling and Therapeutic Skills, MSc Appl Psy, PhD, is currently working in the National Health Service with clients with terminal illness, disability and loss issues, recovering or going through treatments for cancer, diabetes and renal failure.

Elaine Smith, BSc (Psych), PGDip (Stats), PhD, DClinPsych, currently works for the Health Service Executive, Dublin South West, Early Intervention/School Age teams. Her doctoral thesis in clinical psychology explored challenging behaviour in elderly people and how such behaviour is understood and managed by staff working alongside them.

Lucy Smith, BSc (Psychology), MSc (Applied Psychology), PhD (Psychology), is currently employed by the Health Service Executive working with adults of all ages who have experienced abuse throughout their childhood. She is due to complete her doctorate in clinical psychology in September 2010 at the University of Limerick.

Mairead Smyth, BA (Hons Psych) Hip Dip ABA, MSc Applied Psych, is currently completing her PhD in Clinical Psychology at the University of Limerick. She works with the Irish Health Services Executive, in Beaumont Hospital, Dublin in the field of neuropsychology with adults and older adults.

Marcia Ward, BA (Applied Psychology), PGDip (Mental Health), MA (Behavioural and Cognitive Psychotherapies), Board Certified Behaviour Analyst (BCBA), is currently completing her Doctorate in Clinical Psychology (University of Limerick). She is working in an acquired brain injury service and has experience working with older adults in both acquired brain injury and adult mental health services.

Anna Wroblewska, BSc, MPsychSc, is a counselling psychologist with 10 years of experience addressing mental health difficulties. She is currently completing her final placement of her Doctorate in Clinical Psychology with the Health Services Executive in Kerry Adult Mental Health Services providing services for older adults. Her main research interests are cultural aspects of clinical psychology.

Acknowledgements

We would like to acknowledge the support and work of the team at, and associated with, Routledge. In particular we are grateful for the guidance and support of Jane Harris, Kate Moysen and Erasmis Kidd for their commitment to this project and their patience with us.

We would also like to acknowledge the support of our colleagues in the Department of Education and Professional Studies at the University of Limerick who have helped to create a work and learning environment that made it possible for us to further our development as academic and clinical practitioners.

Introduction

Patrick Ryan and Barry J. Coughlan

Ageing and Older Adult Mental Health: Issues and Implications for Practice offers health practitioners, educators and students an introduction to the area of normal and differentiated ageing. It has a deliberate emphasis on the biological, psychological and cultural influences that have an impact on the work of mental health professionals while also addressing the explicit and implicit value systems that underpin much of this work. Given this, the book is also of relevance and interest to those involved in strategy and policy development with regard to the provision of mental health services for older adults.

We discuss up-to-date, empirical, evidence-based practice issues, where the focus is not just on the deficit-model of understanding ageing, but on the normative processes and influences associated with it. Throughout the fifteen chapters of this book, the editors and contributors emphasise the notion of 'healthy ageing', and the importance and significance of this concept, as part of the life-cycle process. It is argued that for too long there has been a stigma associated with growing old, and one of the aims of this volume is to dispel this stigma and challenge many of the common myths associated with it. One of the key arguments outlined is that older adults and their life experience is the key to the success of future generations. Hence as individuals, practitioners and citizens, we need to grasp and value this notion, but more importantly we need to continue to learn from our elders, in all aspects of life.

We aim to provide the reader with appropriate and relevant theoretical foundations, many derived from a developmental psychology perspective, and critically apply these to the ageing process. Each chapter provides the most recent research evidence pertaining to that topic, with a particular emphasis on issues relating to practice, where appropriate. Within each chapter, while the contributors have taken a broad holistic perspective on the topic, the importance of the individual person at the centre of a confluence of interacting variables and systems is emphasised.

The book divides into three parts. First there is an examination of the normative ageing processes. Chapters 1 and 2 introduce the reader to the importance of developmental, psychosocial and biological perspectives on ageing and to the challenge of integrating these into a coherent formulation of understanding so that best practice places the individual at the centre of clinical work. Chapter 3 targets ageism and challenges the reader to question many of the underlying assumptions associated with how we view ageing and opens the debate with regard to critical issues when addressing this question.

Next, in Chapters 4–10, there follows discussion of issues that pertain to the assessment and intervention of a range of presentations that may have an impact on this population. Chapter 4 outlines evidence-based approaches and frameworks that contribute to our understanding of how to appropriately assess for any underlying mental health issues that may exist. Chapter 5 outlines important treatment considerations when treating such difficulties. Chapter 6 examines assessment and intervention issues with regard to dementia while Chapter 7 highlights discourse relevant to the experience of loss, bereavement and grief. This is examined separately from the assessment and treatment of depression, which is dealt with in Chapter 8, as a way of exemplifying the normal experiences of loss and grief; which if not managed in a psychologically efficient manner become an abnormal response of depression. The issue of elder abuse is considered and discussed within the next two chapters of the book; these address the context within which abuse occurs and the possible preventative measures that can be taken to reduce its incidence and prevalence. Chapter 9 outlines three individual case studies, as a means of deepening our knowledge of this topic, while Chapter 10 describes relevant preventative techniques, with a view to minimising level of risk.

The final five chapters provide the reader with an insight into topics such as attachment, caring, well-being and sexuality. The emphasis in these chapters is one of a strengths-based view of the ageing process and ultimately the reader is encouraged to view older adults as a positive resource both for themselves and for the younger generations.

With these considerations in mind, *Ageing and Older Adult Mental Health: Issues and Implications for Practice* aims to provide the reader with a detailed account of some of the critical issues, arguments and debates that surround the importance and significance of growing old. It also aims to remind professionals of the hope, joy and continued opportunity for positive development that can be associated with this phase of life and of their responsibility to comprehensively assess and intervene in a manner that captures this as much as the negative, deficit-oriented data that traditionally form our views of the life and times of older people.

Chapter 1

Ageing

Historical and current perspectives

Patrick Ryan, Lena O'Rourke, Marcia Ward and Cian Aherne

Introduction

Many authoritative accounts of the process of working therapeutically with older people have been generated, debated, agreed and argued over. The aim of this chapter is to orientate the reader to various influences on the construct of ageing that are fundamental in understanding how this group is viewed in modern thinking. Such components will include current demographic changes in society, different forms of ageing and relevant theories that have evolved from both a historical and current understanding of what the term ageing actually refers to.

What is ageing?

Ageing may be viewed as the accumulation of changes in an organism or object over time. Biologically, ageing is defined as a deteriorative process, a fact that has almost become the very definition of ageing in current thinking. In humans though, ageing refers to a multidimensional process of physical, psychological and social change. Some dimensions of ageing grow and expand over time; whereas others decline, e.g. reaction time may slow with age whereas knowledge and wisdom may increase. Research shows that late in life potential exists for physical, mental and social growth and development. This could be termed as 'successful ageing' as it refers to optimal physical, psychological and social possibilities for living. It points to an experience of ageing where health, activity and role fulfilment are better than supposedly found within the population generally (Rowe & Kahn, 1997). Ageing therefore is part of what makes up society and it captures not just biological changes that occur across the lifespan for people but also reflects the prevailing cultural and societal conventions related to growth and development that a particular person experiences at a given time.

Demographic changes in society

We are led to believe that we live in an ageing society and actuarially this seems to be the case. In the developed and developing world, people are living longer, and increasing longevity across societies is both a major societal achievement, and a challenge (World Health Organization [WHO], 2002). A combination of low fertility rates and increased life expectancy has resulted in the relative ageing of societies worldwide. The United Nations Department of Economic and Social Affairs (2004) reported that 5.2 per cent of the world's population was over the age of 65 in 1950, and that this had risen to 6.9 per cent by 2000. Furthermore, it predicted that this percentage would reach 15.9 per cent by 2050 and 24.4 per cent by 2100. Overall, a 238.4 per cent increase in the number of older adults globally is projected between 2000 and 2050. In more developed regions, people over the age of 65 make up 14.3 per cent of the population in 2000 and this will increase to 25.9 per cent by 2050. In Ireland, the Central Statistics Office (2004) predicted that the population would grow from approximately 430,000 in 2001 to between 1.119 and 1.146 million in 2036 – thus more than doubling in size over a space of 35 years. In the UK, the Office for National Statistics (2009) found that the percentage of the population aged 65 and over increased from 15 per cent in 1983 to 16 per cent in 2008, an increase of 1.5 million people in this age group. It also predicted that by 2033, 23 per cent of the population will be in this age group. In the European Union (EU), Giannakouris (2008) found that the percentage of the population aged 65 and over is projected to increase from 17.1 per cent (84.6 million) to 30 per cent (151.5 million) by 2060. Statistics also show that in developing countries the demographic transition occurred much faster than developed countries. In France, it took 120 years for the pro- portion of elderly people to increase from 7 to 14 per cent. Developing countries like China, Malaysia, Jamaica, Brazil and Thailand will have had a doubling of their older adults from 7 to 14 per cent in less than 30 years (Global Health through Education Training and Service, 2005).

It is the oldest old segment of society (people aged 85 years plus) that shows the most dramatic increase in numbers with a five-fold increase from 69 million in 2000 to 379 million older people in 2050. It is estimated that over the next 50 years the numbers of people aged 90 and above will show an eight-fold increase, but the number of centenarians will show the greatest increase in numbers as the number of people aged 100 and above in 2050 will be 18 times greater than the numbers in 2000. The fastest population increase, in the UK, has been in the number of those aged 85 and over. Since 1983, the number of people in this age group has more than doubled from 600,000 to 1.3 million. By 2033 the number of people aged 85 and over is projected to more than double again to reach 3.2 million, and to account for 5 per cent of the total population (Office for National Statistics,

2009). The number of people aged 80 years or over in the EU is projected to almost triple from 21.8 million in 2008 to 61.4 million in 2060 (Giannakouris, 2008). Interestingly, the growth of the oldest-old section of society is also a feature in developing countries and the absolute numbers of older people in developing countries is increasingly marked (WHO, 2002). So the concept of the ageing society seems valid but somehow is also presented as having problematic resonances that society will struggle with. Why that is and how it influences working with this age group will be a question that permeates the chapters that are to follow.

Chronological ageing

Chronological ageing, referring to how old a person is, is arguably the most straight forward definition of ageing. The differentiation between middle age and old age at the age of 65 was first postulated by Bismarck in Germany in the 1880s, when formulating social policy for the country (Butler & Lewis, 1973). It has since been used as a benchmark for the age of retirement and eligibility for social benefits. Levinson (1978) identified the early sixties as the period when middle adulthood ends and late adulthood begins. Bromley (1988) distinguished between the 'young-old' (65–74 years) and the 'old-old' (75 plus years). A different perspective of ageing was proposed by Birren and Schaie (1977) who introduced the concept of functional age as an individual's level of capacity to fulfil given roles relative to others of similar chronological age. However, the age of 65 has limited, if any, relevance as an indicator of functioning, such as general health, mental capacity, psychological or physical endurance or creativity (Butler & Lewis, 1982). Western society assumes that there is general deterioration in adults in all of these areas of life once the demarcation age of 65 has been reached. This assumption is so thoroughly embedded in popular thinking that it rebuffs the daily living evidence that undermines it with ease. Such an assumption does not serve Western society well as it builds itself on the distorted notion that all that is good and desirable is only to be found in young people. Ageing has become almost solely defined as a negative, wearisome process that drains from the good in society when in fact it is the only developmental process that people experience from the moment of conception. From that moment, we are all ageing.

Biological ageing

Victor (1987) outlines that biological ageing is an estimate of the impact of ageing upon physiological systems. It provides a physical basis for ageing. Similarly, Aiken (1999) postulated that biological age is the anatomical or physiological age as determined by changes in organismic structure and function (encompassing structures such as skin texture, hair colour, mobility, etc).

Various hypotheses have been proposed to account for biological ageing such as wear and tear theories (Perlmutter & Hall, 1992). The three most common are the deoxyribonucleic acid (DNA) repair theory (Perlmutter & Hall, 1992), the cross linkage theory (Bjorksten, 1974) and the free radical theory (Harman, 1968). The DNA repair theory proposes that repair of DNA cannot keep up with the damage from metabolism, radiation or contact with pollutants. The cross linkage theory holds that the cross linking of large intracellular and extracellular molecules causes connective tissue to stiffen. These highly reactive molecules, or parts of molecules, may connect with and damage other molecules. The free radical theory is based on the fact that free radicals damage membranes by working on unstructured fat in them.[1]

Four other theories of ageing are also proposed (Busse & Blazer, 1989). These include the immunological theory, the exhaustion theory, the ageing clock theory and the biological programming theory. The immunological theory suggests that with time there is a waning level of immunoglobin in the body that results in lowering the older adults' immunity and makes them more susceptible to disease and infection. The exhaustion theory proposes that a definite amount of energy is available to the body and that this eventually becomes exhausted. The ageing clock theory, as the name suggests, posits that a 'clock' resides in the hypothalamus in the brain and cell loss in this area results in a decline of homoeostatic mechanisms with age. Finally, the biological programming theory suggests that cells are genetically programmed to have a certain lifespan. However, it must be concluded, as posited by Busse and Blazer (1989), that a convincing and empirically validated theory of old age simply does not exist.

Regardless of the underlying cause, certain biological changes occur in specific systems in old age. These include the changes in the skeletomuscular system that result in a general decline in strength. Muscle cells are replaced by fat cells and bones become thinner. Height can be reduced due to atrophy of the discs between the spinal vertebrae, a general atrophy of bones and skeletal atrophy. Changes occur in the skin due to loss of hydration and are often the most obvious manifestations of the ageing process. Metabolic and structural changes occur in the eyes, which lead to a deterioration in vision and eyeball mobility. The ability to focus at different distances may be reduced owing to loss of lens elasticity (Stuart-Hamilton, 1994) and the pupil decreases in size (Perlmutter & Hall, 1992). Such changes are evidenced in behavioural manifestations. For example, impaired vision affects driving. The American Psychological Association (1994) found that impaired vision affects driving and driving is often seen as the primary source of mobility for older adults. Therefore maintenance of driving becomes a primary mediator in the focus to maintain independent functioning. It is proposed here that rural populations in general share this belief but unfortunately it is well-known that transport links and infrastructure is indeed limited and inadequate in rural parts of even the most developed countries, thus decreasing social interaction.

Increased physical incapacity and hearing loss also appear common in old age. However, the effects of decreased physical incapacities are not as difficult in familiar surroundings. Older people with failing eyesight are less likely to be afraid when they know the layout of a house and where assistance may be maintained. It is also easier to engage in an activity if it has been established as a routine. Hence, the effects of decreasing physical capabilities may be lessened in a familiar and appropriate environment. Hayflick (1977) and Gueli *et al.* (2005) concluded that disease rather than biological ageing is the more common cause of deterioration in old age. As a direct result, the older adult population will require access and increased input from both primary and secondary care services.

Although much of the discussion thus far considers particular difficulties that emerge in old age, the general picture is bright, with four out of five older adults being fully mobile. The overall physical health of the body plays a critical role in determining energies and adaptive capacities of older people. Adults in later life are not as anxious, depressed or fearful as might have been expected (Kunzman *et al.*, 2000; Thompson *et al.*, 1990) and as such have much to offer to the generations coming behind, a theme explored in Chapter 15.

Sexual ageing

Renshaw (1996) noted that disbelief, humour and neglect have all been associated with the expression of sexuality in the older adult. In the famous Kinsey reports (Kinsey & Pomeroy, 1948; Kinsey & Gebhard, 1953), only two references address issues with men over 60, whereas women over 60 are mentioned in a meagre half a page. Belsky (1990) observed that negative stereotyping of older adults includes an evaluation of the unattractiveness and inappropriateness of sexual behaviour within this age group. This may prevent older adults disclosing information on their sexual lives. Another possible reason for non-disclosure may be that older adults may not be accustomed to speaking about their sexual lives given that they grew up in an era where such matters were not freely discussed (Stuart-Hamilton, 1994).

Sexual desire remains active throughout life, even if only expressed in fantasy. Winn and Newton (1982) found that in over two-thirds of 106 different societies, older males had a negligible loss of sexual interest, with the figure for continued interest for females (84 per cent) even higher. This view was initially reported by Pfeiffer (1974) who purported that sexual capacity continues for the majority until extreme old age, and in some individuals can continue into the nineties. Masters and Johnson (1966), imminent sexologists, found that although sexual responsiveness weakens in the male after the age of 60 years, regularity of arousal, adequate physical well-being and a healthy mental orientation to the ageing process provide a climate conducive to sexual performance that may extend up to and beyond the age of 80 years. Chew and colleagues (2009) found that one-third of men above 65 years of age and one-eighth of men above 80 years of age, in an Australian sample, had experienced sexual activity in the preceding 12 months; 11 per cent and 3 per cent of these, respectively, experienced sexual intercourse on a regular basis. However, 50 per cent of these sexually active men had erectile dysfunction problems.

Lidz (1983) confirmed that older people remain sexually active into advanced old age. The male becomes less potent but not impotent. There is a difference of opinion regarding female sexual response. Corby and Solnick (1980) concluded that female sexual response did not change with age. Masters and Johnson (1966) found that the intensity of physiological reaction and response to sexual stimulation were both reduced with advancing years. The value of seeing sexual experience as more than just sexual behaviour was highlighted by Butler and Lewis (1982) when they broadened sexual activity to include the opportunity to explore personal value systems in relation to loyalty, passion, self-affirmation and relationship with the physical self.

Psychological ageing

Psychological ageing is the capacity of individuals to respond and adapt to their changing environment. Birren and Schaie (1977) asserted that psychological ageing involves the study of memory, learning, intelligence, skills, motivation, emotion and feeling. Psychological developmental theories seek a greater understanding of the life course, how it unfolds and the meaning that can be assigned to the many aspects and dimensions of that process (Clark & Cafferella, 1999). Various concepts form the foundation for the study of psychological development in older adulthood; cognitive/intellectual development, memory, sensation, ego development, moral development, faith/ spiritual development, life events, transitions and relational development among others. In addition, psychological theories of development also concern themselves with context or how the environment may shape this internal sense of self.

Cognitive and intellectual functioning in older adulthood

Individual differences in performance on most cognitive tasks including those of learning, memory, problem solving and intelligence are debated in cognitive ageing research in terms of the extent to which age-related decrements in performance reflect normative changes in ability and/or the extent to which they can be accounted for by motivational or contextual processes (Birren & Schaie, 1990).

Findings of normative patterns of age-related change are important contributors to a general understanding of cognitive ageing. Cross-sectional studies typically provide a pattern confirming the stereotypical view of ageing as reflecting general decline in most cognitive abilities (Woods & Clare, 2008). In the 65 to 75-year-old cohort changes in cognitive abilities appear to be small with tasks such as vocabulary/knowledge demonstrating little or no decline. Whereas among the 75 years and older cohort there are average declines on virtually all measures of intellectual skill, with the largest declines on measures that require speed/processing abilities (Bee, 1994).

Longitudinal studies of adult development have implicated a number of factors in reducing risk of cognitive decline in old age including: (1) absence of cardiovascular and other chronic diseases; (2) favourable environment mediated by high social economic status; (3) involvement in a complex and intellectually stimulating environment; (4) flexible personality style at midlife; (5) high cognitive status of spouse; (6) maintenance of high levels of perceptual processing speed; and (7) the remediatory effects of cognitive training interventions (Schaie, 1998).

Schaie *et al.* (1994) posited that the observed cognitive decline in many older people is likely to be a function of disuse and thus may be reversible. In their research they focused on training specific reasoning, memory and processing skills in older adults. Approximately two-thirds of their experimental participants showed considerable improvement with about 40 per cent of those who had demonstrated significant decline over the previous 14 years returning to their predecline level. Training effects were found to be long lasting with the trained participants still at an advantage over their controls 7 and 14 years later (Schaie *et al.*, 1994). Carlson *et al.* (2008) conducted a randomised controlled trial study based upon cognitive training in older adults. Their results found intervention-specific improvements in executive function and memory among those with borderline to impaired executive functioning at baseline. These findings appear to support the assertion that older adults with the most to lose or at greatest risk for health disparities have the most to gain from cognitive training interventions (Carlson *et al.*, 2008).

However, there still remains so much variability regarding cognitive abilities in older adulthood that researchers have pointed to the usefulness of a multidimensional and multidirectional conception of development such as that embodied by Horn's theory of 'fluid' and 'crystallised' abilities (Horn & Stankov, 1982; Woods & Clare, 2008).

Horn and Stankov (1982) forwarded a theory based upon the distinction between fluid and crystallised abilities. Fluid abilities involve the cognitive processes concerned in identifying complex relations among stimulus patterns and drawing inferences based on the comprehension of more complex relationships. Fluid abilities are typically measured by tests of logical reasoning, figural and spatial relations. In contrast, crystallised abilities refer to the lifelong cumulative product of information acquired mainly through interaction with the environment. Broadly speaking fluid intelligence has been proven to decline in older adulthood whereas crystallised intelligence can continue to strengthen. Women may decline earlier on fluid abilities, whereas men do so on crystallised abilities with the latter showing steeper decremental loss once the late seventies are reached (Schaie, 1996; Horn & Stankov, 1982). This suggestion of a system of abilities is an example of multidimensionality with these multiple-ability components theorised as differing in the trajectory of their development (Woods & Clare, 2008).

The results of the Seattle Longitudinal Study of Adult Intelligence (Schaie, 2005) supports a multidimensional, multidirectional view of cognitive ability in ageing. This study beginning in 1956 has measured intra-individual changes in cognitive ability in over 5000 people. It focused on demonstrating the presence or absence of age-related changes and differences and also attended to the magnitude and relative importance of the observed phenomena. The results detected the earliest reliable decline for cognitive abilities in perceptual speed and numerical ability from age 60; inductive reasoning and spatial orientation from age 67 whereas fluid ability remained reasonably stable and declined only after age 80 (Birren & Schaie, 1990). Even by 81 years, fewer than half of participants had demonstrated reliable decremental change on a particular ability over the preceding 7 years (Schaie, 2005). Furthermore the authors illustrated that the size of the decline in intellectual functioning was significantly reduced when processing speed is taken in to account (Schaie, 2005). The substantial discrepancies evident in these findings highlight the need for caution when interpreting theories that simplify abilities into broad categories such as fluid and crystallised abilities and/or attempt to forward homogenous theories of cognitive/intellectual functioning in older adulthood.

The area of intellectual functioning is probably the best studied domain of lifespan developmental psychology (Baltes, 1987). Nevertheless, research studies have shown that there is no uniform pattern of age-related changes across all intellectual abilities, and that studies of an overall index of intellectual ability (IQ)/or categories of abilities do not suffice to monitor age changes and age differences in intellectual functioning for either individuals or groups.

Affective ageing

Emotional adjustment is of paramount importance in old age, as change in many different forms becomes a reality for the older adult. Given the physical and cognitive declines in ageing, it is heartening that emotional experience improves with age. Generally, older adults are better at regulating their emotions and experience negative affect less frequently than younger adults and show a positivity effect in their attention and memory. The emotional improvements have been found in longitudinal studies as well as in cross-sectional studies (Strawbridge *et al.*, 2002). Affective ageing according to Woodruff and Birren (1975) depends on the interaction between the individual and the culture that influences him.

Social ageing

Social ageing may be defined as the changing pattern of interaction in relation to other members of the community (Wienclaw, 2009a). Social ageing is determined by the social activities of the individual and whether society considers these to be appropriate or inappropriate at a particular age or stage of maturity. Role theory holds that successful ageing is dependent on appropriate role transitions and substitutions. The taking on of new roles in old age may occur when the support network of friends is diminished by death and physical incapacities. Although the circumstances underlying this change can be viewed as negative, what is important to remember is that the capacity to engage with new roles remains available and intact regardless of chronological age.

The symbolic interaction approach holds that older people create their own age (Marshall, 1980). Individuals interact with the social world to construct and develop their own self-concept. As with psychological ageing, there tends to be continuity in a person's social activities from middle adulthood to old age. Rose and Peterson (1965) suggested that social adjustment is easier by maintaining effective relationships within one's group. However, social class may influence the experience of the ageing process. For example major events such as parenthood and grandparenthood tend to occur at earlier chronological ages in the lower socioeconomic classes than members of the middle and upper classes. Furthermore, older adults from lower socioeconomic classes are less likely to be involved in community activities and more likely to live with their children than the middle social classes. Cutler, as far back as 1977, found that older people in the middle and upper social classes have more friends outside the family than older people of lower class status. They also take a more active part in social organisations.

It is important to acknowledge that most of the changes and difficulties associated with old age have social implications. Chronological ageing brings with it new experiences such as being a grandparent, and other changes in social roles. A loss of social identity can occur as a result of forced retirement and death. Long cultivated patterns of interactions with work colleagues and friends can disappear completely without an active commitment to maintaining them. Retirement from paid work is often forced upon older adults in such a way that it weakens not only their financial and social status, but also their emotional and psychological well-being. The loss of a spouse also involves loss of a significant role within the family not to mention the actual spousal relationship itself. Older individuals can find themselves in a vacuum when these life events occur.

The capacity to develop and maintain social roles may serve as substitutions for the individual and may assist them to cope and adapt to some of the inevitable changes. Such formal substitution may include political involvement, voluntary organisation involvement and religious participation. Similarly, friendship networks and family support systems are sources of informal social participation.

Theoretical paradigms

Given the outline of the practical and functional changes above it is useful to consider if theoretical paradigms have contributed to our understanding of ageing. What follows is a description of some of the theories that are associated with ageing. These include disengagement theory, activity theory, subculture theory, phenomenological and lifespan developmental approaches.

Disengagement theory

This theory proposes that the process of disengagement is a mutual one between the person and society and may be initiated by the older individual or others. It was proposed by Cumming and colleagues (1960) and Cumming and Henry (1961), and argues that old people voluntarily withdraw from many of the connections and obligations that they were previously engaged in. It is believed that the process of growing old alters the manner in which individuals view themselves and this arises from a lessening of responsibility and participation owing to the presumed decrease in physical and psychic energy. Berger (1994) outlined four steps in the process of disengagement.[2] However, disengagement can be viewed in a positive light if it is something *desired*. It can bring renewed energy from pressures such as work productivity. Such withdrawal may open the doors to other forms of social engagement, such as development of new interests, roles and relationships. The process can be good for individuals because it allows them to refocus considerations in later life and helps prepare them for death and it can be beneficial for society because it enables the smooth transition of social roles from one generation to the next (Wienclaw, 2009b).

Havighurst *et al.* (1968) asserted that disengagement is often forced on older adults as a result of society's failure to enable them to continue making a positive contribution. It may also be a response to the constraints imposed by society through stereotyping. Disengagement does not take into account individual and cultural differences and the variations that occur as a result of old age. Rather than being a natural part of ageing, disengagement is only one of the many possible reactions to it. Mandatory retirement for a 65-year-old does not necessarily lead to disengagement, but may lead to uncertainty and insecurity. Although retirement from work is frequently determined by chronological age, preparation for this event can significantly change its impact on the individual. Psychological growth can occur if it is viewed as part of the older person's continuing emotional and social development. Adams (2001) found that 60 per cent of a sample of people aged 75 and over were found to have moderate levels of disengagement without depression.

Activity theory

Activity theory directly contrasts disengagement theory. It was proposed by Havighurst (1961) and it views older adults as active and involved even when their major work role has been lost. It is a symbolic interactionist perspective on ageing that posits that those elderly individuals who remain active will be the most well adjusted. The activities that are considered helpful under this theory include informal activities (e.g. social interaction with family and friends), formal activities (e.g. participation in group functions), and solitary activities (e.g. reading, watching television). Older individuals who are active using the above criteria tend to be happier, have higher self-esteem, and a better quality of life than their peers (Wienclaw, 2009c).

This theory assumes that active, productive people are happiest in old age. Continued productivity and social interaction are essential to satisfaction and a sense of well-being. This theory corresponds closely to that of successful ageing. Activity theory has been supported by anecdotal and empirical evidence and has been made the basis for many programmes in nursing homes for older adults (Wienclaw, 2009c) However, the major difficulty with this theory is that it does not take into account the need for reduced activity among some of the aged, particularly those affected by declining health.[3]

Subculture theory

Subculture theory was developed by Rose and Peterson (1965). This theory of ageing shows how ageing is viewed from the conflict perspective. This perspective asserts that elderly people compete with younger members of society for the same resources and social rewards and suffer a variety of disadvantages because of their lack of social power.

The subculture theory of ageing states that older persons form subcultures in order to interact with others with similar backgrounds, experiences, attitudes, values, beliefs and lifestyles. This happens not only by choice but because of segregation, social differentiation and discrimination based on age. This theory assumes that aged people sever social ties with people from other age cohorts and increase them with others of similar age. These result in intensified age consciousness, creating social bonds based on age that become more important than other variables that differentiate people. Studies on subculture theory indicate that primary social isolation is a group phenomenon (Rutzen, 1980).

Lifespan approaches

The focus of lifespan approaches is on the challenges and changes that occur throughout adulthood. Danish (1981) outlined four basic suppositions in the lifespan developmental approach:

1   development is a continual process – not limited to any one stage of life;
2   change occurs in various social, psychological and biological areas of human development that are inter-related;
3   change is sequential and therefore it is necessary to place any 'stage' of life within the context of that which preceded and followed it;
4   changes in individuals must be considered within the framework of the norms of the day, as well as the *historical* time within which one lives.

Within the developmental perspective, the tasks of one stage must be completed before individuals can move to those of the next stage. The lifespan approach challenges the negatives and stereotypes associated with old age. Although it acknowledges changes and losses it emphasises the ability of the individual to change and develop. This approach connects current behaviour to past development and views old age as a continuing development based on previous experiences. Hence, older adults will not deal with old age in a uniform manner, rather with a variety of responses that depend on their personality and previous experiences. However, the developmental perspective does not consider fully what happens to those who were unable to progress through developmental tasks of previous stages successfully. Furthermore, the developmental perspective on ageing tends to underestimate individual variations. It stresses general developmental trends that are believed to refer to most people, but which do not apply equally to everyone. However, once the developmental themes are recognised, individual variations may then be considered to allow concentration on a particular individual, in a specific place, at a specific time. Such theorists of lifespan psychology include Jung, Adler, Erikson, Peck,

Neugarten and Havighurst. Each suggests different methods through which older adults may attain full potential.

The Jungian approach

Jung described the age of 40 as the 'noon of life' and stressed the importance of understanding the afternoon and evening of life in their own right. A key concept in the Jungian approach was that of balance. He distinguished between two major orientations: towards the external world or towards inner subjective experience. He believed that in the first phase of life individuals learn to deal with instinctual drives and are caught up in the emotional involvement of childhood and adolescence. As young adults they focus largely on the outside world as they cope with the demands of family, work and society as well as establishing an identity. However, their need for balance emerges as they approach middle age. In the second phase of life they assess their lives and develop an increasing awareness of the self and inner life. The search for meaning takes place in the face of inevitable death. Coming to terms with the end of life on earth is part of the task of the older adult. The process through which this is achieved is called individuation, in which individuals become conscious of the other. Older adults turn their energy towards the undeveloped aspects of their personality, which are usually the neglected intrapsychic realities (Moraglia, 1994).

Jungian theory proposes that there is a tendency in old age for men to attend to the more feminine side of the personality, and for women to concentrate on their more masculine characteristics. This allows a greater sense of balance to develop. Jung used the term self-actualisation to express the ability of individuals to enrich their inner lives and to better their appreciation and understanding of themselves (Oxidine, 2001). Accepting death and living life as fully as possible are the two major tasks of the older adult.

The Adlerian approach

Adler's work did not deal extensively with old age and he primarily considered the younger old, whom he believed would be content if they had an opportunity to work. Adler believed that mental health depended on social involvement and satisfactory lifestyle. He believed that people define themselves in relation to other people. Decreased social involvement can occur as a result of retirement, loss of spouse and friends and lack of mobility. He also believed that both community feeling and social interest were central to the solution of difficulties in old age. His approach closely resembles activity theory in that it stresses the impact of social involvement and meaningful lifestyle.

The Eriksonian approach

Erikson (1963) highlighted the developmental conflict of old age as ego integrity versus despair. Ego integrity is the acceptance of one's life and responsibilities, whereas despair derives from non-acceptance and the feeling that it is too late to make up for missed opportunities. Erikson held the belief that right up to the end of life individuals either grow and develop or stagnate and wither. The manner in which individuals deal with this depends on their personality development throughout life. The awareness that little time remains and death is approaching heightens the basic conflict. Ego integrity involves an emotional integration of all that has gone before, whereas loss of this integration results in fear of death. In ego integrity, this despair is integrated into the life of the older adult as a component of old age. Butler (1982) advocated caution in accepting Erikson's theoretical framework highlighting that sampling problems weakened the applicability of Erikson's conclusions to older adults. Stuart-Hamilton (1994) held that successful ageing, according to Erikson's theory, may be seen as a passive preparation for death, whereas Erikson's emphasis was on learning in such a manner that individuals were able to deal with death from the standpoint of integrating all that has gone before. By using the polarity of ego integrity versus despair, Erikson heightened the positive and negative aspects of old age.

The approach of Peck

Peck (1968) developed Erikson's thinking by distinguishing three stages of old age:

1   ego differentiation versus work role preoccupation;
2   body transcendence versus body preoccupation;
3   ego transcendence versus ego involvement.

The process of ego differentiation is likely to emerge at retirement. Ego differentiation involves the acquisition of a range of valued self-attributes that relate to alternatives other than the work role. Body transcendence reflects the older adult's capacity to invest energy in human relationships and creative mental activities despite physical deterioration. Where there is a greater emphasis on bodily preoccupation during early life, the less likely it is that body transcendence will be achieved. Body transcendence is most likely to occur in individuals who have invested time and energy into mental activities, relationships and community endeavours. Although physical powers may decrease, emotional and social powers may increase. Ego transcendence means that older adults transcend self-concerns and accept that they will eventually die (Cook-Greuter, 2000). Peck (1968) suggested that success in ego transcendence is measured by the degree of contentment or stress experienced by the older adult and its impact on others, whether constructive or stress inducing. Ego transcendence has been found to correlate highly with psychological well-being and quality of life (Zappala, 2008).

The approach of Neugarten

Neugarten (1964) stated that the development of the ego is for the first two-thirds of the lifespan outward toward the environment and for the final one-third inward toward the self. He believed that in old age there is a withdrawal from the outer world and a new preoccupation with the inner self. This process is referred to as the 'interiority' of the personality. Neugarten held that the individual's social framework is important for understanding the older adult. The age structure of a society, the internalisation of age norms and age-group identifications are dimensions of the environment within which the individual life must be placed. Neugarten and Peterson (1957) found that adulthood was seen in terms of transition points, namely young adulthood, maturity, middle age and old age. Each period has distinctive characteristics. In a study carried out by Dalakishvili and colleagues (1989), a group of adults over the age of 90 showed signs of growing excitability and decreasing stability, including high emotional excitability, superficially explosive reactions and lability of motives when compared to a group of adults under the age of 90. In terms of mental condition, this old age sample exhibited high ability for adaptation to the environment; which is seen as a crucial factor for longevity. Progression from one period to another was seen to be related to social and psychological changes as opposed to biological changes.

The approach of Havighurst

Havighurst (1972) viewed the developmental task of old age as involving change in a social–psychological context. He stated that neither activity theory nor disengagement theory was sufficient for explaining patterns of ageing, and proposed that personality organisation and coping style were the main factors involved in adjustment to old age. Three adjustments that might have to be made consisted of the following: (1) decreasing physical strength and health; (2) retirement and reduced income; and (3) death of one's spouse.

He believed that these three factors were important in predicting life satisfaction, but one must also take into account the norms and expectations of the subculture in which the person lives, economic security and societal provisions to assist adaptation. Furthermore, he believed that the following three tasks are necessary in old age: (1) establishing an explicit affiliation with one's age group; (2) adopting and adapting social roles in a flexible manner; (3) establishing satisfactory living.

Association with one's own age group can occur through engaging in a new hobby or social and political group participation. Furthermore, people may expand their social roles through involvement in community or church activities. Finally, it is important that older adults live in an environment that enables access to shops, etc. The key to development then is adaptation to changes in structure and functions of the body and changes in the social environment.

The adjustments and tasks outlined by Havighurst (1972) are more or less relevant to older adults, depending on whether they are young-old or old-old. The healthy old-old will have adjusted to retirement and reduced income almost a decade previously, However, financial difficulties may become the focus of concern, such as the ability to pay for nursing home care (given that many older adults are no longer cared for by their children as may have been previously). Physical decline is more likely to occur among the old-old than the young-old. Given that old age can span a period of 30 years or more, the adjustments and tasks outlined by Havighurst could be considered more meaningful if viewed within the two different contexts of the young-old and the old-old.

Many of the associated myths of ageing (time of negative change, loss of independence, etc.) may have originated as a direct result of social policy that shares a long-standing history with ageing. However, the next step is to recognise the potential of this cohort and place resources within the communities and local settings to encourage and assist with 'successful ageing' and view this period of life as one of hope, change and growth.

As population demographics change, social policy as it relates to the problems of ageing has moved to the front line of policy debates. However, social policy as it relates to older people is not simply a response to the problems of ageing and old age. The notion pervades that the lives of older people and the problems of ageing continue to be constructed and reconstructed through social policies (Estes *et al.*, 2003) rather than psychological evidence. The political economy of ageing perspective, which takes up aspects of Marxism, emphasises macro-level influences on the state and economy on the experience of ageing and the conditions of old age (Estes *et al.*, 2003). A key assumption of the political economy of ageing is that ageing and old age 'cannot be considered or analysed in isolation from other societal forces and phenomena' (Estes *et al.*, 2003: 638). These other forces and phenomena lie within each individual in the form of our prejudices, views and values that we place on our ageing population.

Conclusion

The current understanding of what it is to be an older adult is still coloured by traditional metrics that lie in the use of chronological ageing, measurement of loss of functional capacity and cost to the economy. Outside of advocacy groups or specialist research interest groups, there seems to be little capacity in Western thinking for the added value that the experience and knowledge of the older generation imbues in society. As a consequence, a negative, deficit model of thinking, talking and working with older people permeates services to them. Much work is to be executed in order to comprehensively and accurately reflect the true nature of this generational cohort and to ensure that the distorted societal view of the ageing process is amended to properly reflect the true nature of being an elder in society.

Notes

1 Free radicals are created by various foods and tobacco smoke, whose formation is accelerated through radiation and inhibited by antioxidants. Both free radical and cross linkage theories focus on changes that occur in the proteins of cells after they have been formed.
2 The four steps in the process of disengagement are: (1) the social sphere of individuals' contracts owing to a variety of factors (death of relatives, spouses, friends and changing parental and work roles); (2) individuals accept this change in their social interactions; (3) their interactions become more passive; (4) as a result of this passivity, it is less probable that they will be offered new roles, hence, disengagement is more likely.
3 An interesting variation of activity theory was the consolidation approach, proposed by Atchley (1976). This approach stated that older adults who are involved in a variety of roles may not need to find new roles when they lose some. Rather, they can redistribute their energy and time across the remaining activities. However, the consolidation approach is not applicable if an individual has so few roles.

References

Adams, K. (2001). Depressive symptoms, depletion or developmental change? Multidimensionality in the geriatric depression scale according to contemporary interpretations of the Disengagement Theory of ageing. *Dissertation Abstracts International* Section A, 61.
Aiken, L. (1999). *Human Differences*. Mahwah, NJ: Lawrence Erlbaum Associates, Inc.
American Psychological Association. (1994). *Vitality for Life: Psychological Research for Productive Aging*. Washington, DC: American Psychological Association.
Atchley, R. (1976). *The Sociology of Retirement*. Chichester, UK: Wiley.
Baltes, P. (1987). Theoretical propositions of life-span developmental psychology: On the dynamics between growth and decline. *Developmental Psychology*, 23(5), 611–26.
Bee, H. (1994). *Lifespan Development*. New York: HarperCollins.
Belsky, J. (1990). *The Psychology of Aging: Theory, Research and Interventions*. Florence, KY: Brooks Cole.
Berger, K. (1994). *The Developing Person through the Lifespan*. New York: North.

Birren, J. E., & Schaie, K. W. (1977). *Handbook of the Psychology of Aging*. San Diego, CA: Academic Press.

Birren, J. E., & Schaie, K. W. (1990). *Handbook of the Psychology of Aging, 3rd ed.* San Diego, CA: Academic Press.

Bjorksten, J. (1974). Crosslinkage and the aging process. In Rockstein, C., & Sussman, M., eds., *Theoretical Aspects of Aging*. New York: Academic Press.

Bromley, D. B. (1988). *Human Ageing, 3rd ed.* London: Penguin Books.

Busse, E. W., & Blazer, D. G. (1989). *Handbook of Geriatric Psychiatry*. Washington, DC: American Psychiatric Association.

Butler, R. N. (1982). The life review: An interpretation of reminiscence in the aged. In Allman, R. L., & Jaffe, D. T., eds., *Readings in Adult Psychology*. New York: Harper & Row, pp. 87–94.

Butler, R., & Lewis, M. (1973). *Aging and Mental Health: Positive Psychosocial Approaches*. St Louis, MO: C. V. Mosby.

Butler, R. N., & Lewis, M. I. (1982). *Aging and Mental Health, 3rd ed.* St Louis, MO: C. V. Mosby.

Carlson, N., Moore, M., Dame, A., Howieson, D., Silbert, L., Quinn, J., et al. (2008). Trajectories of brain loss in aging and the development of cognitive impairment. *Neurology*, 70(11), 828–33.

Central Statistics Office (2004). *Population and Labour Force Projections: 2006–2036*. Dublin: Stationery Office.

Chew, K., Bremner, A., Stuckey, B., Earle, C., & Jamrozik, K. (2009). Sex life after 65: How does erectile dysfunction affect ageing and elderly men? *The Aging Male*, 12(2/3), 41–6.

Clark, M. C., & Cafferella, R. S. (1999). Theorizing adult development. *New Directions for Adult and Continuing Education*, 84, 3–8.

Cook-Greuter, S. (2000). Mature ego development: A gateway to ego transcendence? *Journal of Adult Development*, 7(4), 227–40.

Corby, N., & Solnick, R. L. (1980). Psychosocial and physiological influences on sexuality in the older adult. In Birren, J. E., & Sloane, B., eds., *Handbook of Mental Health and Aging*. Englewood Cliffs, NJ: Prentice-Hall.

Cumming, E., & Henry, W. E. (1961). *Growing Old: The Process of Disengagement*. New York: Basic Books.

Cumming, E., Dean, L. R., Newell, D. S., & McCaffrey, I. (1960). Disengagement: A tentative theory of aging. *Sociometry*, 23, 23–35.

Cutler, S. J. (1977). Aging and voluntary association participation. *Journal of Gerontology*, 32, 470–9.

Dalakishvili, S., Bakhtadze, I., & Nikuradze, M. (1989). A study of personality traits in old age. *Soviet Journal of Psychology*, 10(4), 80–9.

Danish, S. J. (1981). Life span human development and intervention: A necessary link. *Counselling Psychologist*, 9, 40–3.

Erikson, E. H. (1963). *Children and Society, 2nd ed.* New York: W. W. Norton & Co.

Estes, D., Chandler, M., Horvath, K., & Backus, D. (2003). American and British college students' epistemological beliefs about research on psychological and biological development. *Journal of Applied Developmental Psychology*, 23(6), 625–42.

Giannakouris, K. (2008). *Ageing Characterises the Demographic Perspectives of the European Societies. Population and Social Conditions. Statistics in Focus, Eurostat,*

72/2008. Luxembourg: Eurostat. (Retrieved 25 July 2010 from http://epp.eurostat. ec.europa.eu/cache/ITY_OFFPUB/KS-SF-08-072/EN/KS-SF-08-072-EN.PDF)

Global Health through Education Training and Service. (2005). *Support for the Development of the Network: TUFH (Towards Unity for Health) Elderly Care Taskforce Community-Based Care for Older Adults Position Paper*. November 2005. (Retrieved 25 March 2009 from www.the-networktufh.org/publications_ resources/positionpapers.asp)

Gueli, N., Piccirillo, G., Troisi, G., Cicconetti, P., Meloni, F., Ettorre, E., *et al.* (2005). The influence of lifestyle on cardiovascular risk factors: Analysis using a neural network. *Archives of Gerontology and Geriatrics*, 40(2), 157–72.

Harman, D. (1968). Free radical theory of aging: effect of free radical reaction inhibitors on the mortality rate of male LAF_1 mice. *Journal of Gerontology*, 23, 476–82.

Havighurst, R. (1961). Successful aging. *The Gerontologist*, 1, 8–13.

Havighurst, R. (1972). Nurturing the cognitive skills in health. *Journal of School Health*, 42(2), 73–6.

Havighurst, R. J., Neugarten, B. L., & Tobin, S. S. (1968). Disengagement and patterns of aging. In Neugarten, B. L., ed., *Middle Age and Aging*. Chicago, IL: University of Chicago Press.

Hayflick, L. (1977). The cellular basis for biological aging. In Finch, C. E., & Hayflick, L., eds., *Handbook of the Biology of Aging*. New York: Academic Press, pp. 207–18.

Horn, J., & Stankov, L. (1982). Auditory and visual factors of intelligence. *Intelligence*, 6(2), 165–85.

Kinsey, A. C., & Pomeroy, W. B. (1948). *Sexual Behaviour in the Human Male*. Philadelphia, PA: W. B. Saunders.

Kinsey, A. C., & Gebhard, P. H. (1953). *Sexual Behaviour in the Human Female*. Philadelphia, PA: W. B. Saunders.

Kunzman, U., Little, T. D., & Smith, J. (2000). Is age-related stability of subjective well-being a paradox? Cross-sectional and longitudinal evidence from the Berlin Aging Study. *Psychology and Aging*, 15, 511–26.

Levinson, D. J. (1978). *The Seasons of a Man's Life*. New York: Ballantine Books.

Lidz, T. (1983). *The Person: His and Her Development Throughout the Life Cycle*. New York: Basic Books.

Marshall, V. (1980). Dominant and emerging paradigms in the social psychology of aging. In Marshall, V., ed., *The Social Psychology of Aging, Later Life*. Beverly Hills, CA: Sage, pp. 104–27.

Masters, W. J., & Johnson, V. E. (1966). *Human Sexual Response*. Boston, MA: Little, Brown.

Moraglia, G. (1994). C. G. Jung and the psychology of adult development. *Journal of Analytical Psychology*, 39(1), 55–75.

Neugarten, B. (1964). *Personality in Middle and Late Life: Empirical Studies*. Oxford, UK: Atherton Press.

Neugarten, B. L., & Peterson, W. A. (1957). A study of the American age-grade system. *Proceedings of the 4th Congress of the International Association of Gerontology*, 3, 497–502.

Office for National Statistics. (2009). *Mid-year Population Estimates: Office for*

National Statistics, General Register Office for Scotland, Northern Ireland Statistics and Research Agency. Newport: Stationery Office.

Oxidine, S. (2001). Healing into death: How does individuation as described by C. G. Jung unfold in adults age 65 and over who perceive themselves to be nearing death? *Dissertation Abstracts International*, 62.

Peck, R. (1968). Psychological developments in the second half of life. In Neugarten, B. L., ed., *Middle Age and Aging*. Chicago, IL: The University of Chicago Press.

Perlmutter, M., & Hall, E. (1992). *Adult Development and Ageing, 2nd ed.* Oxford: John Wiley & Sons.

Pfeiffer, E. (1974). Sexuality in the aging individual. *Journal of the American Geriatrics Society*, 22(11), 481–4.

Renshaw, D. (1996). *Sexuality and Aging. Comprehensive Review of Geriatric Psychiatry—II, 2nd ed.* Washington, DC: American Psychiatric Association, pp. 713–29.

Rose, A., & Peterson, W. (1965). *Older People and Their Social World.* Philadelphia, PA: Davis.

Rowe, J., & Kahn, R. (1997). Successful aging. *The Gerontologist*, 37(4), 433–40.

Rutzen, S. (1980). The social distribution of primary social isolation among the aged: A subcultural approach. *International Journal of Aging & Human Development*, 11(1), 77–87.

Schaie, K. (1996). Intellectual development in adulthood. *Handbook of the Psychology of Aging, 4th ed.* San Diego, CA: Academic Press, pp. 266–86.

Schaie, K. (1998). The Seattle Longitudinal Studies of adult intelligence. In Salthouse, T. A., & Lawton, M., eds., *Essential Papers on the Psychology of Aging.* New York: New York University Press, pp. 263–71.

Schaie, K. W. (2005). *Developmental Influences on Adult Intelligence: The Seattle Longitudinal Study.* New York: Oxford University Press.

Schaie, K., Willis, S., & O'Hanlon, A. (1994). Perceived intellectual performance change over seven years. *Journal of Gerontology*, 49(3), 108–18.

Strawbridge, W. J., Wallhagen, M. I., & Cohen, R. D. (2002). Successful aging and well-being: Self-rated compared with Rowe and Kahn. *The Gerontologist*, 42(6), 66–72.

Stuart-Hamilton, I. (1994). *The Psychology of Ageing.* London: Jessica Kingsley.

Thompson, P., Itzin, C., & Abdenstern, M. (1990). *I Don't Feel Old: The Experience in Later Life.* Oxford: Oxford University Press.

United Nations Department of Economic and Social Affairs, Population Division. (2004). *World Population to 2300.* New York: United Nations.

Victor, C. R. (1987). *Old Age in the Modern Society: A Textbook in Gerontology.* London: Croom Helm.

Wienclaw, R. (2009a). Growing old: Social ageing. *Research Starters Sociology*, 1, 1–6.

Wienclaw, R. (2009b). The functionalist perspective: Disengagement theory. *Research Starters Sociology*, 1, 1–5.

Wienclaw, R. (2009c). Symbolic interaction analysis: Activity theory. *Research Starters Sociology*, 1, 1–5.

Winn, R. L., & Newton, N. (1982). Sexuality in aging: a study of 106 cultures. *Archives of Sexual Behaviour*, 11, 283–98.

Woods, R., & Clare, L. (2008). *Handbook of the Clinical Psychology of Aging, 2nd ed.* New York: John Wiley & Sons Ltd.

Woodruff, D. S., & Birren, J. E. (1975). *Aging: Scientific Perspectives and Social Issues.* New York: Van Nostrand.

World Health Organization. (2002). *Active Ageing: A Policy Framework.* Geneva: World Health Organization.

Zappala, C. (2008). Well-being: The correlation between self-transcendence and psychological and subjective well-being. *Dissertation Abstracts International, 69.*

Chapter 2

The biology of ageing
What works, what slows, what stops?

Emma Flynn and Patrick Ryan

Introduction

We have seen significant advances in our understanding of the ageing process during the last two decades. Our burgeoning knowledge informs us that there appears to be no such thing as a 'normal' ageing process. People age in unique ways depending on a multiplicity of factors including gender, ethnicity and cultural background, living in industrialised versus developing countries, in urban or rural settings. Climate, family size, life skills and experience are all variables that make people more and more diverse as they progress in age (World Health Organization [WHO], 1999).

To further add to the complexity, ageing also has a clear genetic heritability, which most likely is dependent on multiple genes. In genetic research it has been found that the lifespans of human monozygotic twin pairs are statistically more similar to each other than the lifespans of dizygotic twins, the extent of this difference indicates that around 25 to 33 per cent of what determines lifespan is genetic (Kirkwood, 2002). However, non-genetic factors are vital too. Therefore, there is significant interest not only in relation to identifying genes influencing human ageing but also in exploring gene–environment interactions.

There are, however, certain biases evident in research on the ageing process. The gerontologist Richard Atchley has written of researchers who focus on sickness, poverty, isolation and demoralisation in older people. Such researchers develop theories that seek to explain how people end up in such an unhappy state. They also tend to see ageing as a social problem according to Atchley (1982). Indeed, many studies involving older adults are conducted in clinics where only 'sick' people come. These individuals are often eager to participate in studies but healthy older people are rarely seen by doctors or researchers.

Conversely, Atchley credited other researchers who injected more positivity into their work: 'They look at the elderly and see that most have good health, frequent contact with family members, adequate incomes, and a high degree of satisfaction with life' (1982: 268). The well-being and general health of the older person are not wholly determined by the biological changes and functional changes to which they are unavoidably subject. 'For the fact of the matter is that in old age the individual's powers of adaptation and compensation are quite as influential in matters of health as are involutive changes and functional disturbances' (Vischer, 1966: 12). Indubitably, biological and psychological processes in ageing are inextricably linked.

It is therefore vital to view ageing from multiple perspectives, because if we only look through the lens of the deficit model of ageing we run the risk of neglecting the very real potential for compensation, adaptation, creativity and growth in old age. As Carlsen (1991: 18) points out; age is a tangle of complexity and 'there are as many opinions and reactions as there are individuals'.

Ergo, while discussing the statement 'Biology of ageing: What works, what slows, what stops?' it is necessary to be cognisant at all times of the following principles.

1   There is no such thing as a 'normal' ageing process due to increased individual variability as we age.
2   Biological, psychological and social factors are inextricably linked in the ageing process.

Keeping such principles in mind, this chapter aims to challenge certain assumptions or myths around the ageing process. First, physical functioning in ageing will be explored, within which, the assumption that every organ and function fails will be challenged. Second, illness and disease in ageing will be discussed, examining evidence for and against the inevitability of illness and disease in old age. Third, cognitive functioning in ageing will be dissected, attempting to answer such questions as 'Do all older people necessarily develop memory problems?' Other topics to be discussed include sexuality in ageing and the menopause. Sexuality in ageing is very much a neglected subject in the extant literature, and it is an area that has been blighted by myth and misunderstanding. Of course, the menopause is closely tied up with a woman's sexuality from a biological and indeed psychological perspective. A more complete discussion of sexuality will be offered in Chapter 12.

The biology of ageing

Before considering physical function in ageing it would be fruitful to examine the biological processes involved in ageing. As previously suggested, ageing has a strong heritability that most likely is dependent on multiple genes. Evolutionary theory posits that ageing is not programmed, like development, but rather is the result of an 'inevitable decline in cellular repair and maintenance functions accompanied by stochastic accumulation of damage and decline in function' (Larsson, 2008: 114). Nevertheless, evolutionary theorists argue vehemently that organisms are programmed for survival, not death.

The central tenet of the disposable soma theory suggests that our body is merely a disposable vehicle for transmitting the genetic material to the next generation. Hamilton (1966) and Charlesworth (1980) developed a mathematical evolutionary theory of ageing. They argued that ageing can arise through two possible mechanisms that are not mutually exclusive. First, deleterious types of genes with late ages-of-action rise to higher frequencies than deleterious gene types with early ages-of-action, 'This is an inevitable consequence of the declining force of natural selection with increasing age' (Phelan & Rose, 1997: 65). The second hypothesis is that ageing arises from selection for individual genes if those genes have both positive effects with an early age of action and negative effects with a later age of action. This mechanism is known as antagonistic pleiotropy (Phelan & Rose, 1997). There are of course a plethora of biological theories of ageing that include:

- altered proteins (Levine & Stadtman, 1996);
- deoxyribonucleic acid (DNA) damage and less efficient DNA repair (Harley, 1991);
- inappropriate cross-linking of proteins, DNA and other structural molecules (Bjorksten, 1974);
- a failure of neuroendocrine secretion (Mobbs, 1996);
- cellular senescence in the cell culture system (Hayflick, 1965);
- an increase in free radical-mediated oxidative stress (Harman, 1981);
- and changes in the order of gene expression (Helfand & Rogina, 2000).

Keeping such biological theories of ageing in mind, ageing is therefore expected to be expressed as a large number of diverse, often unrelated mechanisms. Some individuals, therefore, will succumb to cardiovascular disease, others to cancer and others will experience complications arising from Alzheimer's disease (Phelan & Rose, 1997).

Physical function, illness and disease in ageing

Plato once said that 'we are bound to our bodies like an oyster is to its shell' (cited in Cash, 2004: 1). Hence, our life experiences are unavoidably influenced by the body we inhabit. Decline in physical function is commonly observed in older age and has important outcomes with regard to quality of life, falls, health care use, admission to residential care and mortality (Sibbritt *et al.*, 2007). Nevertheless, 'among individuals of similar chronological age some individuals appear to be resistant to decline in physical function while others appear more vulnerable' (2007: 382). There is now a general consensus that decline in physical functioning in older adults is dependent on a range of diverse factors, not just age. For instance, Stuck and colleagues (1993) conducted a systematic review of 78 studies and found that increased risk of functional decline among community-living older people was associated with cognitive impairment, depression, multiple morbidity, increased and decreased body mass index, low frequency of social contacts, low level of physical activity, no alcohol use compared with moderate use, poor self-perceived health, smoking and vision impairment.

As people age they are at higher risk of developing chronic diseases, which in turn may result in disability. Indeed, chronic diseases such as cardiovascular diseases, diabetes and cancer are predicted to be the main contributors to the burden of disease in developing countries by 2020 (WHO, 1999). As Vischer (1966: 19) suggests 'we can only ever hope to understand old age if we also take the preceding period of life with its inner experiences, its various stages of internal and external development, its physical and psychic occurrences into account'. Therefore, from a lifespan perspective, research has found that foetuses undernourished in the womb grow up to be adults more likely to suffer from a variety of diseases, including coronary heart disease and diabetes. They also seem to age faster than people who receive good nutrition during early life.

Malnutrition, particularly during the first year of life, childhood infections such as polio and rheumatic fever, and exposure to accidents and injuries all make chronic and sometimes disabling diseases more likely in adult life. Undoubtedly, lifestyle factors in adolescence and adulthood such as smoking, excessive alcohol consumption, lack of exercise, inadequate nutrition or obesity, greatly add to disease and disability at any age in adulthood (WHO, 1999).

There is, however, in the extant literature a struggle to distinguish between 'normal ageing' and disease. J. Grimley Evans once stated that 'in fact, to draw a distinction between disease and normal ageing is to attempt to separate the undefined from the indefinable' (Grimley Evans, 1988: 40).

The ageing process in terms of physical functioning is also influenced by gender. Women live longer than men and this advantage in life expectancy is very much biological. Women appear to be more resilient than men at all ages but particularly during infancy. In adulthood a biological advantage remains, at least until menopause, for instance, hormones protect women from ischaemic heart disease (WHO, 1999). Conversely, longevity makes women more likely to suffer from chronic diseases commonly associated with old age. For example, research shows that women are more likely to suffer from osteoporosis, diabetes, hypertension, incontinence and arthritis than men (WHO, 1999).

In general, the capacity of our biological systems (e.g. cardiac capacity, muscular strength) improves during the first years of life, reaches its peak in early adulthood and declines thereafter. The rate of decline is mostly determined by external factors relating to adult lifestyle: smoking, alcohol intake, diet and social class. To illustrate, the natural decline in cardiac function can be accelerated by smoking, with the result that the person will have a much lower functional capacity than would normally be expected for his or her age, indeed 'the gradient of decline may become so steep as to result in disability' (WHO, 1999: 14).

It is crucial to note that contrary to common opinion, the majority of individuals remain fit and able to care for themselves in later life. A small minority of old people, mostly the very old, become disabled to the point that they need care and assistance with activities of daily living. 'The most recent findings for developed countries show that severe disability is declining in older people at a rate of 1.5% per year' (WHO, 1999: 15).

It is important to be cognisant of the many cognitive, emotional and social factors that have been found to moderate the negative effects of illness. For instance, perceived personal control is tied up with notions such as mastery, hardiness, or self-efficacy. It is generally accepted that people differ in the extent to which they believe they can deal with or manage aspects of their life. Perceived internal control over health or illness has been associated with a range of positive outcomes in older populations, e.g. psychosocial adjustment and improved quality of life (Kempen et al., 1997, cited in Woods & Clare, 2008: 58). Johnston et al. (1999, cited in Woods & Clare, 2008: 55) found that perceptions of control over recovery significantly predicted recovery from disability 6 months following an acute stroke (mean age 69 years). Fisher and Johnston (1998) demonstrated that perceived control beliefs can influence pain-related behaviours.

With regards to physical health outcomes such as management of symptoms, recovery, or even survival, much research has focused on identifying coping strategies that can be considered 'adaptive'. Problem-focused coping has been shown to be more adaptive when there is something to be done to alter or control the stressor event. Conversely, emotion-focused coping is more likely to be adaptive where the person has little control over the event or if his or her resources to deal with it are diminished. Likewise, with regard to social support, there is a large body of evidence that suggests that social support effectively reduces distress during times of stress (e.g. Cutrona & Russell, 1990; Taylor, 2007). Social isolation has been associated with poorer survival and reduced quality of life among older populations (Woods & Clare, 2008). For instance, Evers et al. (2003) found that patients with rheumatoid arthritis (mean age 57 years) who had good social support reported less pain and better physical functioning than those who were less well supported.

Cognitive function in ageing: myths and science

Rabbitt (1977, cited in Salthouse, 1990: 323) once stated:

> In view of the deterioration of memory and perceptual motor perform-
> ance with advancing age, the right kind of question may well be not
> 'why are old people so bad at cognitive tasks' but rather 'how, in spite
> of growing disabilities, do old people preserve such relatively good
> performance?'

For the purposes of this discussion a distinction should be made between
cognitive ability that can be defined as the person's intellectual level as
measured by conventional tests of intelligence and cognitive functioning.
Cognitive competence is not as easy to define. Salthouse (1990) suggests
that it can be interpreted as the utilisation of one's abilities – cognitive,
interpersonal and others in adapting to particular situations. Therefore,
keeping this distinction in mind, it may be possible for an individual with a
low level of cognitive ability to achieve a high level of competence by
maximising his or her usage of available abilities for functioning in specific
situations (Salthouse, 1990).

A common finding arising from laboratory studies and psychometric
investigations is that although increased age appears to be associated with
lower levels of cognitive functioning, observations of the same middle-aged
and older adults outside of the laboratory environment generally demonstrate that they perform occupational and daily activities quite successfully
(Hess et al., 2003). Such discrepancies in age-related trends in cognitive
ability and cognitive competence have been attributed to differences in (1)
the type of cognition being examined; (2) the representativeness of either
the behavioural observations, or the samples of individuals; (3) the sensitivity of the measurement or evaluation; and (4) the amount of relevant
experience (Salthouse, 1990). Therefore, research on cognitive functioning
in older adults has been wanting thus far because of such methodological
limitations.

However, compelling new evidence from functional neuroimaging forces
us to reconsider the rather pessimistic view of recent times which assumed
that cognitive ageing is a process of progressive mental loss (Reuter-Lorenz,
2002). It has been discovered for example that in the domains of working
memory and episodic memory, older adults recruit different brain regions
from those recruited by younger adults when performing the same tasks.
'. . .older adults show prominent changes in the recruitment of prefrontal
regions, and a conspicuous increase in the extent to which activation
patterns are bilateral' (Reuter-Lorenz, 2002: 394). Results such as these are
generating new hypotheses about the processes underlying age-related
cognitive declines and the exciting potential for compensation.

Until relatively recent times, the lesion model was the prevailing approach to the neuropsychology of ageing. This approach explicitly described ageing as a 'deficit-laden trajectory where cognitive abilities and their neural substrates decline progressively' (Reuter-Lorenz, 2002: 394). However, neuroimaging findings have allowed us to see that the older brain is complexly different to the younger brain rather than a reduced, inferior brain as the older research, and indeed common perception, would have us believe. For instance, even when behavioural performance is matched younger and older adults demonstrate different brain activation patterns; this implies that they engage different brain areas to accomplish the same tasks. Additionally, some senior-specific activation patterns are associated with optimal performance, thus suggesting compensatory potential in the ageing brain (Reuter-Lorenz, 2002).

Fergus Craik and his colleagues proposed the resource-reduction hypothesis that suggests that the appropriate cognitive strategies could recruit enough resources to improve the effects of ageing (Craik, 1986). Some behavioural evidence backs this claim up. For example, engaging in elaborative encoding e.g. making animacy judgements improves ageing memory and can occasionally reduce age differences in performance. Also, facilitating this kind of 'environmental support' for ageing memory can result in greater activation of prefrontal regions, leading to near age-equivalent activation levels in some studies. 'Thus, older adults can activate the requisite brain regions and engage in effective semantic processing when given the appropriate strategies' (Reuter-Lorenz, 2002: 395). However, such compensatory strategies do not simply make brain activity young again. Under conditions that equate younger and older adults' performance, age differences in brain activity are still evident (Reuter-Lorenz, 2002). The compensatory-recruitment hypothesis highlights the potential for brain plasticity over the lifespan.

If we accept that cognitive performance declines with increasing age in elderly people, a question that continues to confound neuroscientists is to what extent this decline is the consequence of 'normal' or non-pathological ageing as opposed to neurodegenerative disease such as Alzheimer's disease (Anderton, 2002). Evidence from autopsy studies and recent magnetic resonance imaging have shown that at a gross level, there is a decrease in brain volume and weight in individuals over the age of 60 years. The brain regions most affected are the hippocampus and frontal lobes. However, as Anderton (2002) points out, it has been proven that genetic factors such as *ApoE4* and other unidentified genes contribute risk for developing Alzheimer's disease. It is perhaps more likely that the combination of genetic and environmental factors will determine whether individuals suffer this disease or escape, regardless of the age they live to (Anderton, 2002).

The appearance of numerous plaques and tangles with concomitant Alzheimer's dementia is the most common form of pathological ageing.

The question as to whether Alzheimer's disease is pathological in the sense that it is a disease or alternatively is just accelerated normal ageing remains because the characteristic lesions are present in small numbers in the brains of intellectually normal old people (Anderton, 2002).

Emerging evidence suggests that exercise and general fitness has a significant influence on cognitive functioning in old age. Churchill *et al.* (2002) suggest that a lifetime of exercise can result in enhancements in a number of aspects of cognition. Cross-sectional studies have reported benefits of aerobic exercise on both peripheral and central components of reaction time. Also, exercisers have been shown to outperform non-exercisers on tasks such as reasoning, working memory, Stroop, Trails-B, Symbol Digit, vigilance monitoring, and fluid intelligence tests. Undoubtedly, lifestyle differences (e.g. diet, smoking, nutrition) co-vary with exercise, therefore these variables may also account for part of the relationship between fitness and cognition (Churchill *et al.*, 2002).

Focus on the menopause

When exploring 'The biology of ageing: What works, what slows, what stops?' the menopause is a particularly relevant topic, because for a woman it signals the end of an important part of her life. The consequent infertility means she can no longer bear any more children. In many ways the menopause is an excellent representation of how ageing is a bio–psycho–social phenomenon where one domain cannot be fully appreciated without the other.

From an evolutionary perspective, the menopause is paradoxical because it appears to contradict Darwinian principles, closing down reproductive capacity long before ageing in other body functions is very far advanced (Kirkwood, 2002). Symptoms associated with menopause include an increase in somatic and psychological complaints. Approximately 75–80 per cent of women experience vasomotor symptoms. Other reported symptoms include forgetfulness, fatigue, problems concentrating, irritability, depressed mood, decrease in libido, mood swings and sleep disorder (Sjöberg *et al.*, 1997). Research on menopause has mostly come from the disciplines of psychiatry, gynaecology and endocrinology. Therefore, the biomedical view has prevailed in the last decade. A consequence of the biomedical view has been the promotion of hormone replacement therapy (HRT) as a treatment for all menopausal symptoms – '. . . a trend which has been conceptualised as the "medicalization" of the menopause' (Sjöberg *et al.*, 1997: 61).

A further consequence of the biomedical view is the dearth of research on women's psychological experiences of menopause. Controversy continues as to whether depressed mood is more common among menopausal women. Some studies have found that dysphoric mood is related to menopausal status and the biological changes associated with menopause

(Freeman *et al.*, 2004). Others would argue that the changes in social roles and family are more important in determining mood changes rather than changes in hormone levels. It is therefore assumed that those women who have invested the most in motherhood and childrearing will grieve the loss of reproductive ability the most (Sjöberg *et al.*, 1997). However, others have failed to find evidence that the empty nest period is a time of crisis. It has been found in fact that women become more reflective and more willing to satisfy egoistic impulses during this transition. For many menopause is viewed more as a new lease of life (Sjöberg *et al.*, 1997).

Indubitably, interaction of psychological and biological factors is vital in determining women's reactions to hormonal changes. As with many aspects of ageing, early experience, personality, earlier coping style and acquired behavioural patterns will all colour individual reactions to the menopause. For instance, stressful life events such as bereavement and divorce are correlated with more severe symptoms. Social support is another important variable. With regard to personality, a strong association between personality traits and psychological symptoms has been found during menopause. Women with more severe symptoms had lower self-esteem, were more emotionally dependent and had a more negative attitude to menopause. 'It is suggested that an integration of disciplines into an interactive approach to menopause be allocated, one that recognizes the interplay between the individual woman and her psychosocial environment' (Sjöberg *et al.*, 1997: 64). It is proposed here that much more research, particularly of a qualitative nature, into women's experience of the menopause would not just help to balance the medicalised view of the subject but also give important insight into the reality of the experience for women.

Conclusion

This chapter has sought to provide a balanced view of the biology of ageing. Although certain physiological changes are inevitable in ageing, it is clear that age is just one variable in a very complex equation that determines capacity, functionality and ability. For example, the decline in physical function is dependent on a range of diverse factors, not just age; e.g. exercise, mental health and social support to name but a few.

With regard to new scientific advances in the biology of ageing, due to genetic complexity a variety of drug targets may become available for 'treating' ageing. However, the same complexity may make it very difficult to predict the action of different anti-ageing drugs (Larsson, 2008). Scientists are currently exploring the control of ageing in laboratory animals and they are very close to applying this knowledge to human subjects. Phonetic engineering may be one such application, this involves taking cells from a person's body, altering them genetically so as to ameliorate ageing mechanisms, and then re-planting those cells to the person of origin (Phelan & Rose, 1997).

Indeed, scientists have already created longer-living mice. Mice are closely related to humans; with many of the same genes, cell types, organs and diseases (Phelan & Rose, 1997). These scientific advances have obvious positive implications regarding the possibility of slowing down or even in some cases preventing the onset of neurodegenerative disease such as Alzheimer's disease. However, as the reader can imagine, there are unavoidable ethical dilemmas inherent in any attempt to alter a person's genetic composition.

With regard to cognitive functioning, new evidence from functional neuroimaging has forced us to reconsider the pessimistic assumption that cognitive ageing is a process of progressive mental loss. Other research suggests compensatory potential in the ageing brain. It has also been found that exercise and general fitness has a significant influence on cognitive functioning in old age.

The menopause has been explored and viewed as an excellent representation of how ageing is a bio–psycho–social phenomenon. However, research has failed to highlight the importance of the psycho–social realm with an overemphasis on the biomedical view. Although the menopause is often associated with a decline in sexual interest or functioning, research evidence has been contradictory in this area. Indeed, new research challenges the assumption that ageing and sexuality are mutually exclusive while accepting that certain physiological changes are normal – issues that will be dealt with more comprehensively in Chapter 12.

Evidence is emerging from research that appears to challenge the assumption that the process of ageing is all about dysfunction, disability and despair. Flanagan's study (1978) investigated the lives of three cohorts of participants, aged 30, 50 and 70, with 1000 participants in each cohort. The results of this study demonstrated that three factors were especially important in maintaining quality of life: (1) material comforts, work and health; (2) intimacy, close friends and opportunities for socialising; and (3) ongoing opportunity to exercise cognitive capacities and creative expression. Birren (1983) reported that the majority of individuals in this study described their lives as 'good, very good, or excellent'.

> Is it not easy to criticise those who voice their despair? To turn our backs as we search for nuggets of hope and alternatives to the darker side of our last years? I think so: Isn't this our dilemma? Which way to look, what to believe, what to hope for.
>
> (Carlsen, 1991: 18)

This quote perfectly encompasses the quandary we face as social scientists, indeed as humans; do we dwell on our biological limitations or do we seek to vanquish them? Because although this chapter has shown that certain biological changes are inevitable, indubitably how a person adapts, copes and compensates for these changes will ultimately determine 'what works, what slows and what stops' as we age.

References

Anderton, B. H. (2002). Ageing of the brain. *Mechanisms of Ageing and Development*, 123, 811–17.

Atchley, R. (1982). Retirement as a social institution. *Annual Review of Sociology*, 8, 263–87.

Birren, J. E. (1983). Aging in America: Roles of psychology. *American Psychologist*, 38(3), 298–99.

Bjorksten, J. (1974). Cross linkage and the ageing process. In Rockstein, M., ed., *Theoretical Aspects of Ageing*. New York: Academic Press, pp. 43–60.

Carlsen, M. B. (1991). *Creative Aging: A Meaning Making Perspective*. New York: W. W. Norton & Company.

Cash, T. F. (2004). Body image: Past, present and future. *Body Image*, 1, 1–5.

Charlesworth, B. (1980). *Evolution in Age-Structured Populations*. Cambridge: Cambridge University Press.

Churchill, J. D., Galvez, R., Colcombe, S., Swain, R. A., Kramer, A. F., & Greenough, W. T. (2002). Exercise, experience and the aging brain. *Neurobiology of Aging*, 23, 941–55.

Craik, F. I. M. (1986). A functional account of age differences in memory. In Klix, F., & Hagendorf, H., eds., *Human Memory and Cognitive Capabilities: Mechanisms and Performances*. Amersterdam: Elsevier, pp. 409–22.

Cutrona, C. E., & Russell, D. W. (1990). Type of social support and specific stress: Toward a theory of optimal matching. In Woods, B., & Clare, L., eds., *Handbook of the Clinical Psychology of Ageing*. London: John Wiley & Sons, pp. 51–69.

Evers, A., Kraaimaat, F., Geenen, R., Jacobs, J., & Bijlsma, J. (2003). Pain coping and social support as predictors of long-term functional disability and pain in early rheumatoid arthritis. *Behaviour Research and Therapy*, 41(11), 1295–1310.

Fisher, K., & Johnston, M. (1998). Emotional distress and control cognitions as mediators of the impact of chronic pain on disability. *British Journal of Health Psychology*, 3, 225–236.

Flanagan, J. C. (1978). A research approach to improving our quality of life. *American Psychologist*, 33, 138–147.

Freeman, E., Sammel, M., Liu, L., Gracia, C., Nelson, D., & Hollander, L. (2004). Hormones and menopausal status as predictors of depression in women in transition to menopause. *Archives of General Psychiatry*, 61(1), 62–70.

Grimley Evans, J. (1988). Ageing and disease. In Evered, D., & Whelan, J., eds., *Research and the Ageing Population*. New York: Wiley, pp. 38–57.

Hamilton, W. D. (1966). The moulding of senescence by natural selection. *Journal of Theoretical Biology*, 12, 12–45.

Harley, C. B. (1991). Telomere loss: mitotic clock or genetic time bomb? *Mutation Research*, 256, 271–82.

Harman, D. (1981). The aging process. *Proceedings of the National Academy of Sciences of the USA*, 78, 7124–8.

Hayflick, L. (1965). The limited in vitro lifetime of human diploid cell strains. *Experiments in Cell Research*, 37, 614–36.

Helfand, S. L., & Rogina, B. (2000). Regulation of gene expression during aging. In Hekimi, S., ed., *The Molecular Genetics of Aging, Vol. 29*. Germany: Springer Verlag, pp. 67–80.

Hess, T. M., Auman, C., Colcombe, S. J., & Rahhal, T. (2003). The impact of stereotype threat on age differences in memory performance. *Journal of Gerontology: Psychological Sciences*, 58, 3–11.

Kirkwood, T. B. L. (2002). Evolution of ageing. *Mechanisms of Ageing and Development*, 123, 737–45.

Larsson, N. G. (2008). Introduction: Biology of ageing. *Journal of Internal Medicine*, 263, 114–16.

Levine, R. L., & Stadtman, E. R. (1996). Protein modifications with aging. In Schneider, E. L., & Rowe, J. W., eds., *Handbook of the Biology of Aging*. San Diego, CA: Academic Press, pp. 184–97.

Mobbs, C. V. (1996). Neuroendocrinology of aging. In Schneider, E. L., & Rowe, J. W., eds., *Handbook of the Biology of Aging*. San Diego: Academic Press, pp. 234–82.

Phelan, J. P., & Rose, M. R. (1997). Progress report: Research in the biology of ageing. *Ageing & Society*, 17, 65–74.

Reuter-Lorenz, P. A. (2002). New visions of the aging mind and brain. *Trends in Cognitive Sciences*, 6(9), 394–400.

Salthouse, T. A. (1990). Cognitive competence and expertise in aging. In Birren, J. E., & Schaie, K. W., eds., *Handbook of the Psychology of Aging, 3rd ed.* San Diego: Academic Press, pp. 311–23.

Sibbritt, D. W., Byles, J. E., & Regan, C. (2007). Factors associated with decline in physical functional health in a cohort of older women. *Age and Ageing*, 36, 382–8.

Sjöberg, N. O., Berg, G., Hammar, M., & Mattson, L. A. (1997). *The Climacteric and its Treatment*. New York: Taylor & Francis.

Stuck, A. E., Siu, A. L., Wieland, G. D., Adams, J., & Rubenstein, L. Z. (1993). Comprehensive geriatric assessment: A meta-analysis of controlled trials. *Lancet*, 342, 1032–6.

Taylor, S. E. (2007). Social support. In Friedman, H. S., & Silver, R. C., eds., *Foundations of Health Psychology*. New York: Oxford University Press, pp. 145–71.

Woods, B., & Clare, L. (2008). *Handbook of the Clinical Psychology of Ageing*. London: John Wiley & Sons.

World Health Organization. (1999). *Ageing: Exploding the Myths*. Geneva: World Health Organization.

Vischer, A. L. (1966). *On Growing Old*. London: George Allen & Unwin Ltd.

Chapter 3

Ageism

Myth or fact?

John Lalor and Patrick Ryan

Introduction

At the outset, it is useful to establish what is meant by the notion of ageism. Like any other emotive issue, the very use of the concept can offer it a face validity, particularly when it becomes part of the vocabulary of the general population. Those who are exposed to it argue strongly for its endemic presence in society whereas sceptics might argue that the concept can be applied to all ages at all stages in life if we simply listen to how people cope with the human condition as it develops from conception to death. The use of age to separate different cohorts of society is not unusual, so why make this a particular issue when dealing with older adults?

Ageism can be seen as a 'process of systematic stereotyping of and discrimination against people because they are old, just as racism and sexism accomplish this for skin colour and gender' (Butler & Lewis, 1973: 30). The Charter of Fundamental Rights of the European Union (2000: Chapter III, Article 21(1)), asserts that 'Any discrimination based on any ground such as sex, race, colour, ethnic or social origin, genetic features, language, religion or belief, political or any other opinion, membership of a national minority, property, birth, disability, age or sexual orientation shall be prohibited'. So clearly, there exists a philosophy that to make older adults vulnerable on the basis of age is inherently wrong. But how is the concept managed in critical thinking?

Clarity of definition

There are two differing issues to be addressed. First, does ageism exist? Second, if yes, what is the basis for it? This is an important distinction: often, so averse are we to countenance any 'ism', we automatically discount the possibility that there is any validity whatsoever to the 'ism'. Returning to the chapter title, more must be achieved than simply investigating the existence of ageism. Should ageism exist, it is necessary to examine whether or not it is wrong to hold, and act upon, the beliefs that form its premise.

After all, if it was entirely unjust and immoral to practice sexism in its purest form, there could be no barrier to women and men competing side-by-side in Olympic weight lifting. If this logic was practised in terms of physical ability, we could not prevent the legally blind from driving and flying aeroplanes. Or how about at the other end of the age spectrum: should not we include children and adolescents of all ages in the same pool for examinations and sports? So, are there inherent differences related to being aged? If so, is it not entirely ethical to hold ageist views, and to practice their consequences?

Economics and Utilitarianism

> The creed which accepts as the foundation of morals, Utility, or the Greatest-Happiness Principle, holds that actions are right in proportion as they tend to promote happiness, wrong as they tend to produce the reverse of happiness.
>
> (Mill, 1863/1972: 6)

The historical context to our concept of 'old age' must be understood to further understand the concept of ageism. A quick examination of Britain and the USA during their respective Industrial Revolutions offers useful insight. England's population in 1750 was 6 million, rising to 9 million in 1800, and to 12 million by 1820. A proportion of this increase can be attributed to a decrease in infant mortality rates, which fell from about three in every four in 1730–1749, to three in every ten by 1810–1829 (Buer, 1926). However, quite striking were the improvements in life expectancy: in the USA, this has effectively doubled during the past 200 years; in the nineteenth century it increased by 15 years, and it has increased by another 25 years since 1900 (Smith, 1993). In other words, for someone to be 'old' in the year 1800 would have meant they had lived beyond the age of 40 years.

Writing in the early 1800s John Stuart Mill followed in the footsteps of Jeremy Bentham as an advocate of Utilitarianism, which he defines in the quotation above. By way of offering reassurance to those who might accuse him of advocating a selfish individualism, Mill explained that his philosophical creed was actually a 'standard of morality' that uses happiness of the greater number of people as its ultimate goal. His formulation of the 'Greatest-Happiness Principle' encompassed intellectual as well as sensual pleasures.

Despite his efforts to guard against abuse, Mill failed to foresee the potential consequences of pursuing the happiness of the greater number of people. Being a Classical–Liberal, Mill should have foreseen that, to maintain the principle of 'the greater good', one must, as a consequence, sacrifice the remainder; 'the lesser good', so to speak. To paraphrase Norman Cohn (1967), this ethical principle was to become a warrant for the inhumanity of Leninist–Marxism, Maoism, Naziism and Fascism. A principle must be judged not on its 'intentions' but on the consequences of its completed execution. In terms of how we treat our elderly, how might a Utilitarianism framework be evidenced?

First, we need to consider that conscious thoughts, and the basis by which we live our lives, do not necessarily coincide; praxis need not be so obvious. How our beliefs lead to behaviours becomes more obvious, however, when we face difficulties. For instance, what happens to people's careers as unemployment rises? How do we allocate finite resources in our heath service – especially as tax revenues fall, putting further pressure on the system? Again, we return to economics.

In terms of Utilitarianism, people ask a simple question: who gets what? Or, as Friedrich Hayek (1944) asked, 'Who, Whom?': who decides what action to take, and who is the beneficiary. As will evolve in this chapter, Utilitarianism, couched in the fuzzy language of the 'Greatest-Happiness Principle', utterly fails to protect those who do not fall within the parameters of Mill's 'greater number of people'. What guarantees are there for them?

Health service provision

Utilitarianism within a socialised health system does something quite pernicious. Given the pyramid scheme-like nature of any publicly funded system (Borden, 1995), the unfunded liabilities of a health service ensure that some will lose out. And those who have ceased to contribute to the tax-net – *irrespective* of their contributions throughout their working years – will always lose out to those who have their working days ahead of them.

How might a Utilitarian ideology affect the health and well being of our aged? Rathmore and colleagues (2003) found that elderly patients are less likely to receive guideline-indicated therapies when hospitalised with myocardial infarction. Indeed, research in the USA suggests that, due to the pressure placed on physicians by health maintenance organisations (HMOs) and medical centres, less time is being spent with elderly patients (Levy & Banaji, 2002). Robb and colleagues detail more specific ways in which differential medical treatment exists for older adults (Robb *et al.*, 2002), citing physician–patient interaction, the use of screening procedures and treatment of varied medical problems.

But sometimes it is not simply economic rationing; sometimes a deciding factor is the health service provider's concept of the place that older adults occupy in society. In an Australian study comparing nurses' attitudes towards ageing with those of other health professionals, nurses were found to have less accurate knowledge of ageing than other health professionals. In particular, nurses expressed higher anxiety about ageing and were more likely to believe working with older adults was associated with low esteem in the profession. Interestingly, nurses were more likely to hold positive attitudes if they had received gerontology education, and worked outside the residential care sector (Wells *et al.*, 2004).

The frustration within the editorial board of the *British Medical Journal* is palpable. In their article entitled 'A new beginning for care for elderly people? Not if the psychopathology of this national service framework gets in the way', Grimley Evans and Tallis (2001: 807) unleash their fury at the bureaucracy within Britain's National Health Service (NHS). Concerning The National Service Framework for Older People, the authors lament the 'split personality' between the desires of an 'external reference group' of experts brought in to advise on policy, and an 'in group' of civil servants that 'subserves a political agenda', and write their own policy, anyway. From the point of view of these civil servants, care in 'proper hospitals' is too expensive when it needs to be delivered to older people.

Just in case the hoops through which a doctor must jump are lost on the public, Leonard Peikoff (1985: 420–1) demonstrated the effects of the multiple steps of government intervention:

> In medicine, above all, the mind must be left free. . . . The DRG administrator [in effect, the hospital or HMO man trying to control costs] will raise hell if I operate, but the malpractice attorney will have a field day if I don't – and my rival down the street, who heads the local PRO [Peer Review Organization], favours a CAT scan in these cases. I can't afford to antagonize him, but the CON boys disagree and they won't authorize a CAT scanner for our hospital – and besides, the FDA prohibits the drug I should be prescribing, even though it is widely used in Europe. And the IRS might not allow the patient a tax deduction for it, anyhow. And I can't get a specialist's advice because the latest Medicare rules prohibit a consultation with this diagnosis. And maybe I shouldn't even take this patient, he's so sick – after all, some doctors are manipulating their slate of patients, they accept only the healthiest ones, so their average costs are coming in lower than mine, and it looks bad for my staff privileges.

Again, although the bureaucracy within medicine so reviled by Grimley Evans and Tallis (2001) and Peikoff (1985) may delay, irritate and upset the otherwise able-bodied, consider what it does to those more infirm and vulnerable. Consider, as has been done here, the effects that Utilitarian principles have on Hayek's 'Who, Whom?' (1944): the eternal rationing decision that so often goes against the aged. As Peikoff (1985) points out, with the mounting pressure of litigation on the doctor's shoulders, would it not ease his worries to simply fob off some of his older clients? Sadly, in a climate of increased litigation and regulation, this is a logical proposition.

The ultimate Utilitarian sacrifice

Taking the Utilitarian argument to its natural consequence, we are forced to deal with the arguments for and against euthanasia. Although it is a brave doctor or judge or family member who argues that the elder patient in question must continue to live as he or she suffers from an agonising, terminal illness, does the individual not have ultimate property rights over his or her own life? What about the traditional demand that someone is proven *compos mentis* before their decisions are considered?

So, let the unmentionable be mentioned: more euthanasia relieves pressure on finite resources; remembering the tenets of Utilitarianism, this makes perfect sense. The Australian philosopher, and Princeton University professor, Peter Singer (2009: para 23) writes:

> When a human being once had a sense of the future, but has now lost it, we should be guided by what he or she would have wanted to happen in these circumstances. So if someone would not have wanted to be kept alive after losing their awareness of their future, we may be justified in ending their life; but if they would not have wanted to be killed under these circumstances, that is an important reason why we should not do so.

At first glance, there is reason here. It would be remiss to suggest that the current authors can ever know the desires of an unconscious or senile, elderly cancer patient or stroke victim. Bearing Singer's view in mind, recall the case of Terri Schiavo, the American woman who, in 1990 at the age of 26, suffered respiratory and cardiac arrest, resulting in extensive brain damage, and a diagnosis of 'persistent vegetative state'. There being no living will, her husband, Michael, testified that Ms Schiavo had stated previously that she would not wish to be kept alive, should there be no hope of recovery. Despite continuous protestations from Ms Schiavo's parents, a local Florida court ruling in favour of Michael Schiavo, allowed Ms Schiavo's life-support to be disconnected on 18 March 2005. She died almost 2 weeks later.

Next, consider the view of Britain's National Institute for Health and Clinical Excellence (NICE), which recently stated that 'patients should not expect the NHS to save their life if it costs too much' (cited in Winnett, 2008). NICE has now rejected the so-called 'rule of rescue' that stipulates that people facing death should be treated regardless of the costs. In a report on 'social values judgement', the regulator explained: 'When there are limited resources for healthcare, applying the "rule of rescue" may mean that other people will not be able to have the care or treatment they need' (cited in Winnett, 2008: para 5) . Further, the ruling contradicts the advice of NICE's Citizens' Council, which said that a rule of rescue was an essential mark of a humane society. NICE's defence was that its role was to determine how best to allocate the health service's limited resources.

Finally, still considering Singer's proposition, it must be asked what else he believes, as context will assist our understanding. ArcLink, an American online advocacy group for people with developmental disabilities would not quite support Singer's views (ArcLink, 2009). It cites Singer's claims that society cannot bear the economic burden of treating people with significant cognitive disabilities as full members of society, as well as Singer's erosion or outright denial of civil rights to members of society who are seen as less valuable than those in power. After all, Singer believes that not all humans are 'persons', as to qualify as such, and to deserve the subsequent moral consideration, beings must be self-aware, and capable of perceiving themselves as individuals through time. Singer claims that some people with life-long cognitive disabilities never become 'persons' at any time throughout their lives. He claims that some people who acquire cognitive disabilities cease to be 'persons'. For example, Singer writes:

> This means that to end the lives of people, against their will, is different from ending the lives of beings who are not people. Indeed, strictly speaking, in the case of those who are not people, we cannot talk of ending their lives against or in accordance with their will, because they are not capable of having a will on such a matter.
>
> (Singer, 1995: 197–8)

Whereas ArcLink's focus is people with developmental disabilities, Singer nicely expands the argument for the current topic by discussing people who *acquire* cognitive disabilities. Substitute a child with developmental disabilities with an elderly patient in the later stages of dementia, and the consequences of a moral position become clear. As stated above, a principle must be judged not on its 'intentions' but on the consequences of its completed execution.

Those who would accuse Michael Schiavo's opponents of intervening in the life of a private individual need to consider what they are supporting, and the principles they will be propagating. The room for manipulation of the medical system – stemming from ageism, economic difficulty, or otherwise – is vast. Ms Schiavo's life ended purely on unsubstantiated evidence of her wishes, coupled with the views of healthy human beings observing the incomprehensible state of Ms Schiavo's life.

What about those people, for example, who suffer from acute pain caused by terminal cancer and who wish to die by euthanasia? Many will likely be *compos mentis*. Conversely, elderly people who are *non compos mentis* cannot reassess their earlier desires – stated during full health – that they would never wish 'to be a burden'. Finally, such deliberations by those within the medical and legal profession do not begin at a persistent vegetative state. What about at the inability to recognise one's children? Or having to live in a dark, unkempt nursing home, with nobody visiting?

When does the undeniably severe persistent vegetative state become 'nothing to live for'? Combine Singerian disregard for diminished cognitive abilities, with a creaking, unfunded health system and the arguments in favour of euthanasia become more appealing. After all, you might think, *I* wouldn't want to live like that.

Economic necessity and justice?

The demographic decline of European economies is significant. Consider that the fertility rate of 2.1 children per woman is a requirement for a population to remain stable (Eurostat, 2004). Those nations around the 1.3 mark – i.e. almost all of the 10 of the 2004 EU accession states, as well as Germany, Spain, Italy and Greece – can, by the end of the century, expect a population of one-quarter of today's figure (European Commission, 2007). Even Ireland, at a comparatively high 1.99, lies below the optimal, population-stabilising level of 2.1.

What does this mean to the older adult cohort of the population? Given that there are a decreasing number of workers per pensioner, a real and substantial fiscal headache is on the way. Using figures from the United Nations (2003) and Eurostat (2004) it can be established that, in 1950, in those nations that are now in the European Union, less than 10 per cent of the population was 65 years of age or older. Back then, 66 per cent of the population were working and therefore tax-contributing. By 2050, we can expect the figure for those contributing to the tax-net to reach an absolute maximum of 50 per cent – but, in reality, some amount less, because of individual choices, childrearing, illness, etc. Almost one-fifth of society will be 65–79 years of age, and almost 12 per cent will be over 80 years of age – and these figures, in which the majority will have some form of state stipend, are certain. According to the United Nations World Youth Report, life expectancy in Europe will have risen from the 1950–1955 level of 66 years of age, to 83 years of age by 2050 (United Nations, 2005). To be blunt: someone born in the late 1800s had likely been working since their mid-teens, and, after retiring, had enjoyed the state pension for a couple of years, tops. In 2050, things will be very different.

Taking this into account, returning to the subject of work and the taxes that one pays, it might be a good idea for our elderly to continue in employment beyond their mid-sixties. Indeed, the various governmental departments of finance would thank them for it. But that simple solution is not generally available to state institutes as:

> At the moment it is legal in Britain to force a worker to retire after the age of 65 . . . [M]any workers who don't want to leave their jobs will be out of them anyway on their 65th birthday, with little more than a

carriage clock and a few kind words to speed them on their way. Or as Age Concern head Gordon Lishman more poetically puts it: "The Government continues to consign tens of thousands of willing and able older workers to the scrap-heap".

(Murray-West, 2009: para 1)

Age Concern, an advocacy group for the aged in the UK, along with Help the Aged, have responded with justified outrage (Age Concern, 2009). Although this case will continue for some time, at present, the European Court of Justice has given older British workers a stay of execution. European judges have confirmed that the UK government has to overcome a high hurdle to justify forced retirement and so will struggle to show that its national default retirement age of 65 satisfies European Union age discrimination rules when the case returns to the British courts. Age Concern and Help the Aged have condemned British ministers for 'sending mixed messages' to older workers by encouraging people to work beyond the age of 65 yet keeping legislation that prevents many from doing so (Age Concern, 2009: para 4).

This sort of legislation is baffling. Joerres (2009), writing in the *Wall Street Journal Europe*, reports that one of the biggest mistakes companies make is to alienate employees aged 50 and older by assuming they are no longer interested in training and career development. Consider the irony: chief executive officers (CEO) and other senior executives tend to be in their fifties or sixties, yet it is regularly assumed that middle managers of the same age are no longer interested in challenging work and development. If a former CEO is qualified to serve on a Fortune 500 firm's board of directors in his seventies, why would a manager not, at a comparable skill and experience level, be just as capable of working in another capacity at the same age?

So, who is pushing for these laws? Who stands to gain from barring the so-called elderly from the workplace? Still, do we not have a *responsibility* to our elderly population, so as not to pressurise them into working into their twilight years, seeing as their mental abilities will apparently be diminishing from their sixties?

The evidence is compelling that receiving a good education in the first two decades of life reduces the risk of developing dementia later on (De Ronchi, 2005; Butcher, 2008). In particular, low education is a known risk factor for Alzheimer's disease (Hall *et al.*, 2007). Using the Buschke Selective Reminding Test, researchers have reported that each additional year of formal education delayed the time of accelerated decline by the equivalent of 0.21 years. Moreover, whereas one's chances of developing dementia after the age of 85 is between 40 and 50 per cent, for those 65 years of age and older, it is between 5 and 10 per cent (Levine, 2006) – likely far less than the general public would have estimated.

Still, severe cognitive decline does not appear to be an inevitable process (Franco *et al.*, 2007). They report that Alzheimer's disease is only genetically determined to a small extent. Significantly – given this age of increasing awareness of health and self-care – many modifiable environmental and lifestyle factors (e.g. smoking, nutrition, physical inactivity and low social activity) are thought to play a key role in its development (Blennow *et al.*, 2006; Briones, 2006; Harman, 2006). So, with increased longevity, accompanied by increased health span, significant numbers of the labour force reaching a fixed retirement age will likely still have a full or considerable capacity for production (Franco *et al.*, 2007).

Now, given the evidence for the power that the individual has to protect against dementia, should society not respond accordingly? Given that there is far weaker evidence for ageist policies – after all, what other reason is there for expelling the over-sixty-fives from the workplace? – than many would assume, why is it still prevalent?

Politics

It would appear, then, that driving elderly people out of the workforce is founded more out of political necessity than neuro–psychological evidence. We return to economic necessity – and especially in these times of sharply rising unemployment, where there is an excess of labour supply over demand.

It is politically more advantageous to see a man in his mid-sixties 'offered' early retirement, thus freeing up capital to employ a college graduate, than have the latter be added to the live register. The myth that in their twilight years people get a little slow and lose their sharpness is indeed useful. The national debt to gross national product ratio is on an upward slope, but, it is the future generations that will have to solve that problem. As for the unions and Leftist commentators and advocates, it is a 65-year-old's right to retire. We are not in the Dickensian nineteenth century anymore; the days of people worrying about employment and living standards in their sixties is a vestige of greedier, grubbier times. And, as for the employer, early retirement just makes sense. You don't exactly have time to research the latest edition of *Neurology* or the *BMJ* to find out that cognitive decline is not what you assume. Anyway, some have the attitude that these third-level graduates have far better comprehension of computers, technology, and all that.

If we consider that there is finite employment at any one time, to maintain low levels of unemployment, sacrifices will be made. Witness the rationale behind the enactment of the 35-hour week in France – introduced by the former Socialist Prime Minister, Lionel Jospin, in 2000, and scrapped in 2008 – where people were forced by law to work less hours, thus, in theory, freeing extra hours for others to complete. So, although it would make no sense to disbar large portions of people from the workforce because of their sex or sexuality, those who must be sacrificed tend to be the older workers. (It should be added that any reluctance to employ women due to the affordability of maternity leave or childcare does not imply a reluctance to employ women *per se*, unlike being unwilling to employ an older adult purely because of their age.) And one cannot but get a sense that elderly people are seen as expendable in a rigid, highly regulated economy. Afflicting also the young, France's employment laws create bars to entry for the older generation wishing to return to the workforce (Hayden, 2006).

According to Joerres (2009: para 2), chairman and CEO of Manpower Inc., 'The loss of productivity and intellectual capital as baby boomers leave the work force could devastate some businesses'. ('Baby Boomers' are those within the glut of children who were born soon after the Second World War, and therefore all reaching retirement – and in search of their social security payments – over the next few years.) Joerres (2009: para 1) warns about 'the inadequate pool of younger workers to fill those roles' left by the Baby Boomers. Indeed, although income deficits to fund the retirements of the Baby Boomers is an imminent problem, Joerres touches on the oft-neglected aspect of the loss of these people to the workforce: their knowledge and accrued wisdom of years of problem solving and to some degree 'having seen it all before'.

A bizarre contradiction exists. Conventional wisdom points towards the retirement of the sixty-somethings as being something of a logical response to deficits in cognitive and physical abilities. However, Joerres (2009: para 4) points to employers' viewing coming retirements as cost-saving opportunities with trepidation, considering it 'dangerous and shortsighted'. Perhaps too much faith is put in the idea that employers know who benefits their business, and in what way. Joerres explains that many employers assume that all employees want to exit the workforce as soon as they are financially able.

Conclusion

The situation of how older adults are treated is rife with contradictions. Work, in place of retirement, has been shown to be detrimental to one's health but forced retirement is also detrimental to one's health (Donahue, 2007). However, retirement can bring health improvements (Siegrist & Wahrendorf, 2009). Our pensions are about as stable and guaranteed as the economic boom that underwrote them. We are not having nearly enough children, who, in time, would be paying the taxes to fund the health, welfare and pension services required by the older generation. There is a cognitive loss – but not in the assumed neuro–psychological sense. It is in the workplace, where able-minded workers are leaving, or, more accurately, being forced to leave and taking with them years of useful and useable knowledge and skill.

If these points appear challenging in their contradictory, self-defeating nature, that is because they are simply *that* illogical and futile. How ironic that, as the world gets richer – yes, even when you take into account the present economic crisis – our treatment of elderly people remains inconsistent at best.

It seems contradictory to many, but the mental health of the aged and our pension systems can both be better 'cared for' by allowing the aged the dignity of working until such time as they genuinely desire retirement. How sad that *any*one needs to be 'allowed' to work. How sad that, after having ended slavery, enacted suffrage, and normalised to an encouraging extent the differing sexualities within society, we are still at this point in terms of dealing with age. In short, this 'ism' is still alive and well.

How ironic, when we consider the evidence. We find that the age of retirement has a significant influence on remaining life expectancy (Franco *et al.*, 2007). Tsai *et al.* (2005) reported an improvement of mortality with increasing age at retirement, independent of socioeconomic status. Life expectancy for those retiring at age 55 was found to be 5 years shorter compared with those who retired at age 65. This is supported by a Danish study, which found that the increasing mortality of early retirement recipients is consistent with the adverse effect on health, due to the retirement process itself (Quaade *et al.*, 2002).

As Murray-West (2009: para 3) reported, concerning the upholding of the law enforcing retirement at 65, 'this decision is all the more poignant in the light of research this week from Prudential, showing that workers are delaying retirement because of the poor state of their investments and fears over the direction of the economy'. The Prudential report went on to explain that many who would have retired this year do not expect to be able to leave their jobs until 2012 or later. Further, about a quarter of those who are delaying drawing their pension this year believe that they will never be able to afford to retire. It begs the question as to if it is possible to get any more benevolent towards the aged than granting them the freedoms that bring about, as a consequence, increased life expectancy, financial security, dignity, a sense of purpose and good mental health.

Work is not solely seen as a means to an end; selling one's labour for an adequate sum is not the only purpose of working. Likewise, the desire to have children is not simply because of some evolutionary, animalistic concern for the continuation of the species. We are social beings who need the benefits of social interaction. And maybe sitting in a day centre surrounded only by others their age, or staring out a window in a nursing home, is not the best place to enhance your development as an older adult. As asked above, is 'old age' not a continually shifting, relative term, anyway, given our expanding life expectancy? Think how much more knowledge, wisdom, experiences and skills one can have acquired since the age at which one's 'elderly' predecessors would have passed away in the 1800s. Indeed, if more care were taken to *not* obstruct those who are in their sixties from reaching, and continuing in, their potential, maybe we might see even less cognitive decline thereafter. Science indicates that this is indeed the case.

Given that our affluence will enable many of us to reach our ninth decade, it makes sense to give ourselves the freedom to make those last decades as independent, comfortable, mentally sharp, and, above all else, as *dignified* as possible. It also offers the opportunity to tackle and undermine yet another 'ism' in society.

References

Age Concern. (2009). *We're Fighting on to Scrap Forced Retirement say Age Concern and Help the Aged*. London: Age Concern. (Retrieved 26 July 2010 from http://www.cardi.ie/?q=news/werefightingontoscrapforcedretirement%E2%80%9Asay ageconcernandhelptheaged)

ArcLink. (2009). *Against the Philosophy of Peter Singer from DREDF*. ArcLink.org (Retrieved 5 April 2009 from http://www.thearclink.org/news/article.asp?ID=426)

Blennow, K., de Leon, M. J., & Zetterberg, H. (2006). Alzheimer's disease. *Lancet*, 368, 387–403.

Borden, K. (1995). Dismantling the pyramid: The how & why of privitizing social security. *The Cato Project on Social Security Privatization*, 1(14 Aug): 1. (Retrieved 4 April 2009 from http://www.cato.org/pubs/ssps/ssp1es.html)

Briones, T. L. (2006). Environment, physical activity, and neurogenesis: implications for prevention and treatment of Alzheimer's disease. *Current Alzheimer Research*, 3, 49–54.

Buer, M. C. (1926). *Health, Wealth and Population in the Early Days of the Industrial Revolution, 1760–1815*. London: George Routledge & Sons.

Butcher, J. (2008). Mind games: Do they work? *British Medical Journal*, 336, 246–8.

Butler, R. N., & Lewis, M. I. (1973). *Aging and Mental Health*. St Louis, MO: Mosby.

Cohn, N. (1967). *Warrant for Genocide: The Myth of the Jewish World Conspiracy and the Protocols of the Elders of Zion*. London: Eyre & Spottiswoode.

De Ronchi, D. (2005). *Education and Dementing Disorders: The Role of Schooling in Dementia and Cognitive Impairment*. Stockholm: Ageing Research Center, Sektionen för Geriatrisk Epidemiologi, Instituten Neurotec, Karolinska Institutet.

Donahue, P. (2007). Retirement reconceptualised: Forced retirement and its relationship to health. *Dissertation Abstracts International Section A*, 67.

European Commission. (2007). *Europe's Demographic Future: Facts and Figures*. Brussels: European Commission.

European Union. (2000). Charter of Fundamental Rights of the European Union. *Official Journal of the European Communities*, C 364/1, 1–22.

Eurostat. (2004). *2004-Based Eurostat Population Projections and European Union Labour Force Survey* (*LFS*). Luxembourg, Eurostat. (Retrieved 4 April 2009 from http://epp.eurostat.ec.europa.eu)

Franco, O. H., Kirkwood, T. B. L., Powell, J. R., Catt, M., Goodwin, J., Ordovas, J. M., *et al.* (2007). Ten commandments for the future of ageing research in the UK: A vision for action. *BMC Geriatrics*, 7, 10. (Retrieved 4 April 2009 from http://ukpmc.ac.uk/articlerender.cgi?artid=952495#B15)

Grimley Evans, J., & Tallis, R. C. (2001). A new beginning for care for elderly people? *British Medical Journal*, 322, 807–8.

Hall, C. B., Derby, C., LeValley, A., Katz, M. J., Verghese, J., & Lipton, R. B. (2007). Education delays accelerated decline on a memory test in persons who develop dementia. *Neurology*, 69, 1657–64.

Harman, D. (2006). Alzheimer's disease pathogenesis: role of aging. *Annals of the New York Academy of Sciences*, 1067, 454–60.

Hayden, A. (2006). France's 35-hour week: Attack on business? Win–win reform? Or betrayal of disadvantaged workers? *Politics & Society*, 34(4), 503–42.

Hayek, F. A. (1944). *The Road to Serfdom*. London: Routledge Press.

Joerres, J. (2009). Ageing your workforce. *Wall Street Journal Europe*, 9 April 2009. (Retrieved 14 April 2009 from http://online.wsj.com/article/SB123923040617102 867.html)

Levine, R. (2006). *Defying Dementia: Understanding and Preventing Alzheimer's and Related Disorders*. Oxford: Greenwood World Publishing.

Levy, B. R., & Banaji, M. R. (2002). Implicit ageism. In Nelson, T. D., (ed.), *Ageism, Stereotyping and Prejudice Against Older Persons*. Cambridge, MA: MIT Press.

Mill, J. S. (1972). *Utilitarianism*. London: J. M. Dent & Sons, Ltd., p. 6. (Original publication 1863.)

Murray-West, R. (2009). Work may not be an option for pension victims. *Daily Telegraph*, 9 March 2009. (Retrieved 15 March 2009 from http://www.telegraph. co.uk/finance/personalfinance/comment/4961100/Comment-Work-may-not-be-an-option-for-pension-victims.html)

Peikoff, L. (1985). Medicine: The death of a profession. *Arizona Medicine*, 42(7), 420–8.

Quaade, T., Engholm, G., Johansen, A. M. T., & Møller, H. (2002). Mortality in relation to early retirement in Denmark: A population-based study. *Scandinavian Journal of Public Health*, 30(3), 216–22.

Rathmore, S. S., Mehta, R. H., Wang, Y., Radford, M. J., & Krumholz, H. M. (2003). Effects of age on the quality of care provided to older patients with acute myocardial infarction. *American Journal of Medicine*, 114(4), 307–15.

Robb, C., Chen, H., & Haley, W. E. (2002). Ageism in mental health and health care: A critical review. *Journal of Clinical Geropsychology*, 8(1), 1–12.

Siegrist, J., & Wahrendorf, M. (2009). Quality of work, health, and retirement. *Lancet*, 374(9705), 1872–3.

Singer, P. (1995). *Rethinking Life and Death*. New York: St. Martin's Press.

Singer, P. (2009). *Peter Singer: FAQ: III. The Sanctity of Human Life*. Princeton, NJ: Princeton University Department of Philosophy. (Retrieved 5 April 2009 from http://www.princeton.edu/~psinger/faq.html)

Smith, L. H. (1993). The environment since the Industrial Revolution. The future of freedom foundation. *Freedom Daily*, September 1993. (Retrieved 2 April 2009 from http://www.fff.org/freedom/0993d.asp)

Tsai, S. P., Wendt, J. K., Donnelly, R. P., de Jong, G., & Ahmed, F. S. (2005). Age at retirement and long term survival of an industrial population: Prospective cohort study. *British Medical Journal*, 331, 995.

United Nations. (2003). *World Population Prospects. The 2002 Revision*. New York: United Nations Population Division. (Retrieved 5 April 2009 from http://www.un.org/esa/population/publications/wpp2002/WPP2002-HIGHLIGHTSrev1.PDF)

United Nations. (2005). *World Youth Report 2005. Young People Today, and in 2015*. New York: Department of Economic and Social Affairs.

Wells, Y., Foreman, P., Gething, L., & Petralia, W. (2004). Nurses' attitudes toward aging and older adults – examining attitudes and practices among health services providers in Australia. *Journal of Gerontological Nursing*, 30(9), 5–13.

Winnett, R. (2008). Patients 'should not expect NHS to save their life if it costs too much'. *Daily Telegraph*, 12 August 2008. (Retrieved 5 April 2009 from http://www.telegraph.co.uk/news/2547393/Patients-should-not-expect-NHS-to-save-their-life-if-it-costs-too-much.html)

Chapter 4

Assessment of mental health issues[1]
Approaches and frameworks

Denise O'Connell-Kehoe and Barry J. Coughlan

Introduction

Although the rate of mental health difficulties is lower in the older adult population[2] when compared with earlier adult stages, it remains a significant issue for this group (Smyer & Qualls, 1999; Gatz *et al.*, 1997). There are many factors that may complicate the assessment and intervention process (Stanley, 2001). In addition, the literature suggests that many older adults with mental health difficulties are not getting the treatment that they require (Nordhus *et al.*, 1998). The remit of the present chapter is to consider the assessment of mental health issues, other than depression and dementia that appear to dominate the geropsychology literature. Within this chapter, we visit the various approaches and frameworks relevant to the assessment of mental health difficulties in older adults, and examine the contextual factors that are of significance in their assessment. Issues of effective evidence-based practice and service provision will be considered.

In the UK, the British Psychological Society (2006) advised that in a typical district population of 45,000 older people between 10 and 15 per cent will have depression; 13 per cent will have anxiety related disorders and 2 per cent will have a psychosis-related disorder. Some 5 per cent of the older adult population will be experiencing some form of dementia. It is estimated that approximately 20–25 per cent of the older adult population in Ireland are experiencing a mental health disorder at any one time (Keogh & Roche, 1996; Reidy & Kirby, 2008). Approximately one-fifth of this group are recognised as living with some form of dementia, while the remainder of this group experience other types of mental health issues (Keogh & Roche, 1996; Wrigley *et al.*, 2006a). The most common of these mental health difficulties being depression (e.g. Reynolds & Kupfer, 1999; Kaplan & Sadock, 1998). Approximately 1 per cent of the older adult population experience schizophrenia (Browne *et al.*, 2000). Keogh and Roche (1996) and Kelly (2004) estimated that 1–4 per cent of the older adult population experience a neurosis that requires some form of clinical intervention. Zweig (2008) reported that the incidence of personality disorders in later life may be more of an issue than previously believed. It is of note that 23 per cent of older adults in the community may experience psychological distress (Fahey & Murray, 1994).

Current assessment status

Many older adults that present to services have 'complex needs that span many domains' (Little & Doherty, 2008: 385). However, in mental health practice clinicians most commonly see the assessment of cognitive function, despite the identification of several contributory domains to the health and well-being of older adults. The World Health Organization identified that the health and well-being of older adults was influenced by factors in seven domains (cited in Little & Doherty, 2008). These domains are:

- physical health;
- cognition and mood;
- activities of daily living;
- independent activities of daily living;
- social;
- environmental; and
- economic.

Although mental health refers to the domains of cognition and mood, there is no doubt as to the inter-relatedness of all domains. The American Psychological Association highlights that a thorough assessment of the older adult needs to be interdisciplinary, and should take the variety of possible contributory factors into account (American Psychological Association, 2004).

Even though standardised measures exist to assess individuals in each of the seven domains outlined above, the current literature indicates that few are routinely used in older adult practice (see Burns et al., 2002; Reilly et al., 2004). Typically, cognitive function is routinely assessed, however the measures used to do so vary considerably (Little & Doherty, 2008). The most commonly used measure appears to be the Mini-Mental State Examination (MMSE) (Folstein et al., 1975). This ignites another issue pertaining to the known weaknesses therein. For example, the tendency of the measure to produce false positives for those with fewer years schooling is a significant difficulty (Anthony et al., 1982). Likewise, the measure may produce false negatives among well-educated individuals (Zarit & Zarit, 1998). As a result of these weaknesses the MMSE should not be used in isolation, and should only form part of the assessment process.

It is vital that all practitioners and clinicians alike develop an awareness of the issues regarding the use of standardised assessment measures in older adult practice. One must be aware that many current assessment tools may not be valid or suitable for use with older adults (e.g. Zweig, 2008) and one needs to critically evaluate the strengths and weakness of each tool, prior to its use. It is necessary that the measures employed are designed for use with the older adult population and that the psychometric properties are relevant to the older adult population (Nordhus, 2008). Nordhus noted that anxiety and depression measures that have been developed specifically for use with older adults 'typically have excellent norms' (2008: 99). It is therefore important to be clear regarding why tests are being included in the assessment process and if they fit the purpose for which they were intended.

There is little doubt in the literature regarding the influence of self-care on quality of life. Although there is some association between measures of cognitive function and self-care, it is only a modest correlation (Little & Doherty, 2008). Cognitive assessment has shown to be a poor predictor 'of real life performance' of tasks (Stuart-Hamilton, 2006: 237). Therefore one has to ask if we can justifiably infer a client's level of adaptive functioning and requirement for support from the results of cognitive testing. In this respect much of the current research would suggest decisions are being made on this basis, given that routine assessment appears to occur predominantly in the cognitive domain (Pachur et al., 2009).

Little and Doherty (2008) highlight an important consideration in relation to this point – that self-care measures do not take into account the impact of life experience or the lifestyle choices of the individual in question. They outline an occupational therapy framework that facilitates the client or carer identifying those areas that are personal priorities. Such a 'person-centred' approach returns the client to the centre of the assessment, where he or she belongs.

The use of behavioural measures in the assessment process allows the clinician to identify a client's strengths and weaknesses. In addition these measures facilitate the targeting of areas in which to strengthen adaptive behaviour (American Psychological Association, 1998). Adopting an approach that would take these issues into account may not always be the most cost-effective approach, and the most convenient option given the level of resources that may be required. However the appropriateness of the intervention would be related to the accuracy of the assessment, which underpins the notion of evidence-based practice. This is a critical issue with respect to positive outcomes for the individual.

An issue that arises when considering the assessment of mental health difficulties is the limitations of the *Diagnostic and Statistical Manual* (DSM), now in its fourth edition (DSM–IV; American Psychiatric Association, 2000). This classification framework does not have a specific section for older adult disorders, as it does for both child and adult disorders. In addition, conditions other than depression and anxiety are not served well by the DSM framework (Nordhus, 2008). It is vital that professionals are aware of this shortcoming. Stuart-Hamilton provides an interesting

comment by noting that that research has been limited by the perception that old age is 'a testing ground for how senescence or dementia affects models of memory, intelligence, personality or caregiver stress' (2006: 233). We believe this appropriately highlights how the older adult, with his or her unique experience of well-being and quality of life (impaired or otherwise), has been lost in the literature.

Lifespan disorders

Older adults may present with reoccurring mental health difficulties that they experienced earlier in life (Bonwick & Morris, 1996; Hyer & Sohnle, 2001; Hyer et al., 2004). They may also begin to experience mental health difficulties for the first time in their lives (Wrigley et al., 2006b). Both instances will undoubtedly be influenced by their own unique life experience, with applying predisposing, precipitating, maintaining and protective factors to be gleamed from their narrative. Therefore, difficulties are not limited to one domain but expanded to several domains. As such, the assessment should not be limited to specific symptoms but also include a consideration of the many factors that may influence the client's presentation (e.g. Light & Lebowitz, 1991; Meeks & Murrell, 1997; Rosowsky et al., 1999).

Nordhus (2008) highlights the relevance of a needs-focused approach in dealing with the older adult population. Thereby, taking the meaning of the experience for the individual into account and acknowledging that the significance of any experience will vary from person to person. It is clear that to date not enough is known about the mental health issues of the older adult lifestage, specifically conditions other than depression and dementia. This lack of knowledge pertains to the manifestation, experience and trajectory of all aspects of mental health conditions in the older adult population. Anxiety disorders, adjustment difficulties and difficulties relating to the misuse of prescription medication are common phenomena among older adults (Fisher & Noll, 1996; Gallo & Lebowitz, 1999; Reynolds & Charney, 2002), and deserve further consideration in terms of clinical practice and evidence-based research.

It is therefore imperative that the experience of impaired well-being or quality of life should not be dismissed as a normal part of the ageing process. It has been suggested that mental health difficulties may be under-diagnosed and hence not appropriately treated as a result of the myth that these difficulties are a 'normal' part of the ageing process (Department of Health, 2001; Prettyman, 2004). A comprehensive assessment is required in the event of impairment in functioning. Every opportunity should be made to facilitate the early identification and assessment of all difficulties, and not just limited to mental health difficulties. It is necessary that appropriate means of assessment are employed in this regard.

The assessment of factors in the resource domains, namely social, environmental and economic, necessitates a number of considerations. There is a vast body of research concerning the connection regarding social relationships and psychological difficulties (Schön *et al.*, 2009). The literature highlights the relationship between mental health difficulties and perceived social support (Barry *et al.*, 2002).

Due to the increased likelihood of reduced physical health, mental capacity and independence, older adults have particular vulnerability to all forms of abuse (National Strategy on Domestic, Sexual and Gender-based Violence, 2008). Therefore, elder abuse is an important consideration in the assessment of the older adult. There is also evidence for low levels of disclosure or reporting of abuse (National Strategy on Domestic, Sexual and Gender-based Violence, 2008). This would suggest the inclusion of questions facilitating the disclosure of abuse in clinical practice is warranted.

It has also been recognised that older adults may not provide accurate reports of their environment (Carter *et al.*, 1997). Therefore, home visits may provide a reliable addition to the assessment of the resource domains (Ramsdell *et al.*, 1989). Furthermore, they may be useful in order to complement the investigation of the nature of relationships in the home (Denton *et al.*, 2009).

Socioenvironmental factors

It is widely recognised that in times of economic downturn, people with mental health difficulties require additional support. In the current economic climate, it is likely that many older adults are experiencing financial worries due to a reduction in social welfare or loss of capital on investments. Therefore, it seems logical that the older adults should be asked about any financial concerns and given the opportunity to speak to someone about their financial situation, including social welfare entitlements. In order to facilitate the provision of a holistic service, coordination and communication between services and relevant agencies is fundamental.

It has been suggested that a measurement of quality of life should target what can be influenced by a health care intervention rather than adopting a more global stance (Little & Doherty, 2008; Herrman & Chopra, 2009). However, we suggest that we are limiting the potential of improvement in terms of service provision and therefore as well as stifling the potential for improvement of quality of life, one would also be stifling potential service development. Although there is agreement regarding the importance of a comprehensive evaluation of well-being, there is little consensus regarding what should be included in such an evaluation (Little & Doherty, 2008).

There has also been debate regarding the degree to which the person's subjective experience should be included in the assessment framework. Woods (2008: 418) highlights the consideration that phenomenological approaches 'do not lend themselves to a normative, standardized approach, which allows comparisons between individuals and groups and has been favoured in many research studies'.

Professional best practice

Zarit and Zarit (1998) highlight a number of ways in which any professional should endeavour to adapt his or her practice in order to facilitate the appropriate and effective clinical assessment of an older adult. The importance of building rapport with the individual should always be highlighted in an effort to alleviate the anxiety that may be experienced (Tedeschi & Kilmer, 2005).

We would like to highlight the need to be wary of expectations regarding the reaction time and the performance speed of the older adult being assessed. Zarit and Zarit (1998) highlight that both of these decrease with age, and the clinician should also consider the potential side-effects of prescribed medication (Darowski et al., 2009). This presents a need for the clinicians' expectations to be grounded in reality, at all times, while undertaking such assessments. In addition, practice should be adapted hence taking these factors into consideration, while also being aware of practical issues such as being mindful to read out questions slowly and clearly (Zarit & Zarit, 1998).

It is also the responsibility of the psychologist (or indeed any practitioner) to monitor fatigue in the client given the effect that this may have on performance and presentation (Zarit & Zarit, 1998; Östlund et al., 2005). In addition, the time of assessment is yet another important consideration, given the effect that this may have on performance and presentation. A further consideration in the adaptation of our practice refers to the development of awareness regarding the influence of sensory problems. One reason for this is to prevent sensory difficulties from being confused with cognitive impairments. Also, as Vernon (1989) and Horwitz et al. (2002) highlighted, background noise can be a distraction for those with hearing difficulties. The client's presentation and his or her performance on assessment tasks may also be influenced by test anxiety. The assessment procedure and the setting of the assessment may have particular meanings and significance for clients and it may be beneficial to consider these issues given the possible impact they may have on the outcome (Verheul et al., 1998).

Developmental issues of later life such as an increased likelihood of physical health difficulties present another important consideration in the assessment process (Lebowitz & Niederehe, 1992; Préville et al., 2005). It is also more likely that the individuals may be taking prescription medication and this may interfere with the expected clinical presentation of a particular condition. For a number of reasons, the effect of substance abuse can have 'a more profound effect on attention, concentration and general cognition than it would have at a younger age' (Goudie, 2002: 31). It has been linked with poor eating habits and confusion (Goudie, 2002). Given the increased likelihood that an older adult may be taking medication there is an increased risk of side-effects that represent mental health symptomotology or an interaction between medications (Stuart-Hamilton, 2006). There is also greater potential for medication misuse (American Psychological Association, 2004).

Earlier in the chapter, we noted that the most commonly used measure in routine mental health assessments and screenings appears to be the MMSE (Folstein *et al.*, 1975). Although the MMSE offers a brief assessment of mood, a more in-depth assessment of mood is often required in the older adult. It is vital that professional judgement is used so as to meet the potential needs of an older person at assessment and beyond. It is clear that this may require increased flexibility and innovation in clinical practice (Sanderson, 2006).

There is a need to employ measures that are specifically designed for use with the older adult population (Little & Doherty, 2008). It is also of note that self-report measures used in isolation may not be an appropriate measure of symptomotology including anxiety among the older adult population. It has been acknowledged that older adults may be 'loath to report' some symptoms of psychological distress and therefore may 'mini-mise' the effect that they have on their well-being and quality of life (Nordhus, 2008: 107). This is an important consideration in terms of clinical practice.

It is plausible that older adults may have a fear of what may happen if they admit to having psychological difficulties. For example, losing their independence or being stigmatised as a result of having mental health difficulties (Gamliel & Hazan, 2006). Such fears may be maintained by myths regarding older adults that pervade in our society such as that next of kin are entitled to make decisions for relatives, including financial deci-sions (National Strategy on Domestic, Sexual and Gender-based Violence, 2008).

One may choose to interview a third party regarding information across domains for a number of reasons including the inability of the individual to complete the measure or as part of collecting collateral information. It is important to consider how to interpret that information in relation to other evidence gathered (e.g. Teri & Wagner, 1991; Otto *et al.*, 2007).

The American Psychological Association (1998) produced a document entitled 'What are the essentials of a good psychological testing report on an older adult?'. The document highlights the need to consider psycho-logical findings in terms of their relationship with medical and social variables. It also highlighted the need to document the variables that may have had an impact on test scores. According to the American Psycho-logical Association, the recommendations made should aim to 'enhance or maintain the older client's cognitive and psychological well-being and independence' (1998: 22). There is a clear recommendation for the relevant referrals to be made to other professionals outside psychology given the complex biopsychosocial nature of needs. This recognises that difficulties often span many domains and need to be addressed as such. It may also be the case that further assessment and retesting is recommended in order to follow up with an individual or to evaluate an intervention. Finally, the report highlights that 'clear and timely communication of test findings and recommendations to all treatment team members, family caregivers, and especially to the older person is essential' (1998: 23).

Assessment protocols

A consideration of the larger context in which the assessment of mental health issues takes part, logically follows such recommendations. There are a variety of frameworks and approaches used within this milieu (Bledsoe *et al.*, 2008). The literature highlights the variation among these. Methods tend to be based upon what is required for the person to experience an acceptable[3] standard of living or the particular demands of a patient's presentation. They may also consider both of these issues in addition to the consideration of service provision (Little & Doherty, 2008). The latter frameworks feature structured survey interviews, goal planning, needs assessment tools and single assessment process tools.

Structured survey interviews were designed for use in profiling and identification of conditions in the serviced population (Little & Doherty, 2008). There are a number of pitfalls inherent in such an approach. First, they are not suitable for universal administration. In addition, they rely mainly on self-report and are by no means in-depth assessments of need across those domains known to contribute to well-being and quality of life. Therefore, although convenient it is important to remember the limitations of their usefulness in contributing to a detailed and appropriate assessment of need (Brugha *et al.*, 1999).

Appropriate goal planning refers to a constructional framework that takes both strengths and needs into account. Information is gathered from relevant sources across many areas of functioning. Similar frameworks are presented by Harding *et al.* (1987) and Smith (1998); the multi-level needs assessment and the DISC (Developing Individual Services in the Community framework) respectively. The latter provides a structured framework to facilitate the extensive information to be gathered as well as highlighting how a service can meet the client's needs. As such it is not limited by what is available in terms of resources and provides useful information in relation to the planning of services.

The Elderly Psychiatric Needs Schedule (EPNS) was developed and applied to older people with enduring mental illness in contact with the old age and general adult components of an inner-city mental health service (Abdul-Hamid *et al.*, 2009). Needs assessment tools may present yet another framework with which to establish the needs of an older adult. They examine the older adult's level of functioning and the support he or she receives. Not all of these tools are relevant to the older adult population however but some like the Camberwell Assessment of Need for the Elderly (CANE) have been cultivated for that purpose (University College London, 2009). The CANE identifies both met and unmet needs and highlights areas of risk. A need is defined as 'a problem with a potential remedy or worthwhile intervention' (University College London, n.d.: para 3). Facilitating the gathering of information from a variety of sources, the CANE covers multiple areas of functioning and is suitable for those with long-term mental illness (Vassilas, 2006).

A further advantage of the CANE is that it allows for the evaluation of outcomes through a follow-up assessment. With increasing economic uncertainty, there is a greater need for outcomes to be evaluated and to show effectiveness. This can be done on an individual, group, programme or systems level (American Psychological Association, 2004). In addition, it facilitates the recognition of remaining needs. The measurements of outcome support service development – for example they may highlight gaps in service provision or identify training needs, thereby facilitating the improvement of older adult services. The literature highlights two means by which to evaluate interventions. The first refers to specific measures of change for example an improvement in a specific area of functioning using a specific measure (Maguire *et al.*, 2010). The second refers to taking a broader measure of functioning (Hadley *et al.*, 1999). Little and Doherty (2008) highlight the Health of the Nation targets in this regard (Department of Health, 1992). However, this is not without its limitations. They offer the Canadian Occupational Performance Measure (COPM; Law *et al.*, 1990) as a client-focused measure of outcome. This needs assessment framework refers to the Single Assessment Process tools that include the Care Programme Approach (Jones, 2009). This allows for the assessment of need as well as the planning of care. Needs are identified with a view to implementing appropriate interventions. This framework encapsulates four levels of assessment that correspond to the older person's need. Like other frameworks, no tool should act as a substitute for professional judgement and must be used appropriately with due consideration (Horwath, 2007).

Little and Doherty (2008) highlight that while government policy in the UK stipulates that the needs of older people must provide the basis for the services they are offered, there is no authoritative definition of need. As clients live longer the potential level of need required is also increasing; which highlights the necessity of methods that can not only identify need but also the level of need required (Tennessee Mental Health Planning Council Older Adult Committee, 2000).

In the UK, it is stipulated under the Community Care Act (Department of Health, 1990) that all domains of a person's life must be considered in an assessment of need (Little & Doherty, 2008; Drukker *et al.*, 2008). There is a requirement for the consideration of the client's views in addition to those of professionals and carer's (Little & Doherty, 2008; Gibbons *et al.*, 2005). It has been highlighted that professionals often view themselves as occupying the best position to evaluate the needs of clients (Arvidsson, 2001). It has been suggested that this is often driven by a desire to prevent undue strain on themselves and the client (Arvidsson, 2001). It has also been reported that there is fear among professionals regarding the possibility of a client requesting something that may not benefit them; which would have a negative effect on already stretched resources (Stevens & Gabbay, 1991; Walters *et al.*, 2001). It is important therefore to consider what may benefit the client, what the client's perspective is and also what is available to meet that need in terms of service provision. Although there may be incongruence between professional perception of need, service provision and client demand, one cannot ignore the marked difference between the perspectives of client, carer and professional (Gannon *et al.*, 2000; Gibbons *et al.*, 2005). Hancock and colleagues (2003) highlighted evidence to suggest that fears regarding client demand burdening resources are not justified and concluded that users perspectives should be given high priority in an assessment of need.

From an Irish perspective, *A Vision for Change*, produced by the Expert Group on Mental Health Policy (2006), highlights a move towards a community-based approach offering holistic services. The criteria for accessing mental health services in Ireland are provided in Recommendation 13.1 which states: 'Any person, aged 65 years or over, with primary mental health disorders or with secondary behavioural and affective problems arising from experience of dementia, has the right to be cared for by mental health services for older people' (Expert Group on Mental Health Policy, 2006: 115).

While *A Vision for Change* is currently under implementation it is of note that many of the teams that provide mental health services for older people are understaffed when reality is compared with the document's requirements for these teams. Undoubtedly, this is preventing many older adults from receiving the services they require.

Conclusion

Within the present chapter, we undertook to consider the current topography of the approaches and frameworks within older adult assessment and the wider context of which they are part. In doing so, many issues arose.

Mental health problems, for example, affect one in four of the Irish population at some point in their lives (Expert Group on Mental Health

Policy, 2006). Mental health difficulties do not discriminate against the older adult population. However, there is a disproportionate amount of attention paid to and, research regarding the older population and that which exists is limited and often biased towards depression and dementia.

An appropriate assessment of need, that takes the complex biopsycho-social factors into account, is where we must begin in order to deliver acceptable, appropriate and effective intervention to the older adult population. Taking a person-centred holistic approach to assessment is a positive proactive step and preferable to the more traditional reactive one. As a result, society will be better able to plan appropriate, effective services rather than disregarding the goal of achieving the highest level of independence and quality of life. This level should not be restricted by the perception that limitations are something inherent in the health and social services. These issues should be challenges that we as a profession, as well as a society, should endeavour to overcome.

Notes

1 Other than depression/dementia.
2 Population aged 65 years and over.
3 'The Social Services Inspectorate (1991) describes a need as that which is required for a person to achieve, maintain or restore an acceptable level of independence and quality of life' (Little & Doherty, 2008: 398).

References

Abdul-Hamid, W., Lewis-Cole, K., Holloway, F., & Silverman, M. (2009). Older people with enduring mental illness: A needs assessment tool. *Psychiatric Bulletin*, 33(3), 91–5.

American Psychiatric Association. (2000). *Diagnostic and Statistical Manual of Mental Disorders, 4th ed., Text Revision*. Washington, DC: American Psychiatric Association.

American Psychological Association. (1998). *What are the Essentials of a Good Psychological Testing Report on an Older Adult?* Washington, DC: American Psychological Association. (Retrieved 27 July 2010 from http://www.apa.org/pi/aging/resources/guides/practitioners.pdf)

American Psychological Association. (2004). Report of the Association: Guidelines for psychological practice with older adults. *American Psychologist*, 59(4), 236–60.

Anthony, J. C., LeResche, L., Niaz, U., Von Korff, M. R., & Folstein, M. F. (1982). Limits of the 'Mini-Mental State' as a screening test for dementia and delirium among hospital patients. *Psychological Medicine*, 12, 397–408.

Arvidsson, H. (2001). Needs assessed by patients and staff in a Swedish sample of severely mentally ill subjects. *Nordic Journal of Psychiatry*, 55(5), 311–17.

Barry, M., Friel, S., Dempsey, C., Avalos, G., & Clarke, P. (2002). *A Report for the Centre for Cross Border Studies & the Institute of Public Health in Ireland.*

Promoting Mental Health and Social Well-Being: Cross-Border Opportunities and Challenges. Galway: Centre for Health Promotion Studies, National University of Ireland.

Bledsoe, S., Lukens, E., Onken, S., Bellamy, J., & Cardillo-Geller, L. (2008). Mental illness, evidence-based practice, and recovery: Is there compatibility between service-user-identified recovery-facilitating and -hindering factors and empirically supported interventions? *Best Practice in Mental Health: An International Journal*, 4(2), 34–58.

Bonwick, R. J., & Morris, P. L. P. (1996). Post-traumatic stress disorder in elderly war veterans. *International Journal of Geriatric Psychiatry*, 11, 1071–6.

British Psychological Society (2006). *Commissioning Clinical Psychology Services for Older People, their Families and Other Carers.* Leicester: BPS.

Browne, C., Daly, A., & Walsh, D. (2000). *Irish Psychiatric Services Activities 1998.* Dublin: Health Research Board.

Brugha, T., Bebbington, P., & Jenkins, R. (1999). A difference that matters: Comparisons of structured and semi-structured psychiatric diagnostic interviews in the general population. *Psychological Medicine*, 29(5), 1013–20.

Burns, A., Lawlor, B., & Craig, S. (2002). *Assessment Scales in Old Age Psychiatry, 2nd ed.* London: Martin Dunitz.

Carter, S. E., Campbell, E. M., Sanson-Fisher, R. W., Redman, S., & Gillespie, W. J. (1997). Environmental hazards in the homes of older people. *Age and Ageing*, 26, 195–202.

Darowski, A., Chambers, S., & Chambers, D. (2009). Antidepressants and falls in the elderly. *Drugs & Aging*, 26(5), 381–94.

Denton, G., Rodriguez, R., Hemmer, P., Harder, J., Short, P., & Hanson, J. (2009). A prospective controlled trial of the influence of a geriatrics home visit program on medical student knowledge, skills, and attitudes towards care of the elderly. *Journal of General Internal Medicine*, 24(5), 599–605.

Department of Health. (1990). *Caring for People: Community Care in the Next Decade and Beyond.* London: HMSO.

Department of Health. (1992). *Introduction to Inequalities in Health: The Black Report.* London: HMSO.

Department of Health. (2001). *National Service Framework for Older People.* London: HMSO.

Drukker, M., Dillen, K. van, Bak, M., Mengelers, R. van, Os, J., & Delespaul, P. (2008). The use of the Camberwell Assessment of Need in treatment: What unmet needs can be met? *Social Psychiatry & Psychiatric Epidemiology*, 43(5), 410–17.

Expert Group on Mental Health Policy (2006). *A Vision for Change: Report of the Expert Group on Mental Health Policy.* Dublin: The Stationery Office.

Fahey, T., & Murray, P. (1994). *Health and Autonomy Among the Over-65s in Ireland.* Dublin: National Council for the Elderly.

Fisher, J. E., & Noll, J. P. (1996). Anxiety disorders. In Carstensen, L. L., Edelstein, B. A., & Dornbrand, L., eds., *The Practical Handbook of Clinical Gerontology.* Thousand Oaks, CA: Sage, pp. 304–23.

Folstein, M., Folstein, S., & McHugh, P. (1975) "Mini-mental state": A practical method for grading the cognitive state of patients for the clinician. *Journal of Psychiatric Research*, 12, 189–98.

Gallo, J. J., & Lebowitz, B. D. (1999). The epidemiology of common late-life mental disorders in the community: Themes for the new century. *Psychiatric Services*, 50, 1158–66.

Gamliel, T., & Hazan, H. (2006). The meaning of stigma: Identity construction in two old-age institutions. *Ageing & Society*, 26(3), 355–71.

Gannon, M., Ryan, M., & Kinsella, A. (2000). Assessment of need in patients attending an inner city psychiatric service. *Irish Journal of Psychological Medicine*, 17, 25–8.

Gatz, M., Kasl-Godley, J. E., & Karel, M. J. (1997). Aging and mental disorders. In Birren, J. E., & Schaie, K. W., eds., *Handbook of the Psychology of Aging, 4th ed.* San Diego, CA: Academic Press, pp. 365–82.

Gibbons, C., Bédard, M., & Mack, G. (2005). A comparison of client and mental health worker assessment of needs and unmet needs. *Journal of Behavioral Health Services & Research*, 32(1), 95–104.

Goudie, F. (2002). Physical and emotional problems in later life. In Stokes, G., & Goudie, F., eds., *The Essential Dementia Care Handbook*. Milton Keynes: Speechmark, pp. 22–32.

Hadley, C., Brown, S., & Smith, A. (1999). Evaluating interventions for people with severe dementia: Using the Positive Response Schedule. *Aging & Mental Health*, 3(3), 234–40.

Hancock, G. A., Reynolds, T., Woods, B., Thornicroft, G., & Orrell, M. (2003). The needs of older people with mental health problems according to the user, the carer, and the staff. *International Journal of Geriatric Psychiatry*, 18, 803–11.

Harding, K., Baldwin, S., & Baser, C. (1987). Towards multi-level needs assessments. *Behavioural Psychotherapy*, 15, 134–43.

Herrman, H., & Chopra, P. (2009). Quality of life and neurotic disorders in general healthcare. *Current Opinion in Psychiatry*, 22(1), 61–8.

Horwath, J. (2007). The missing assessment domain: Personal, professional and organizational factors influencing professional judgements when identifying and referring child neglect. *British Journal of Social Work*, 37(8), 1285–303.

Horwitz, A., Dubno, J., & Ahlstrom, J. (2002). Recognition of low-pass filtered consonants in noise with normal and impaired high-frequency hearing. *Journal of the Acoustical Society of America*, 111(1, Pt1), 409–16.

Hyer, L. A., & Sohnle, S. J. (2001). *Trauma Among Older People: Issues and Treatment*. Philadelphia, PA: Brunner-Routledge.

Hyer, L., Kramer, D., & Sohnle, S. (2004). CBT with older people: alterations and the value of the therapeutic alliance. *Psychotherapy: Theory, Research, Practice, Training*, 41(3), 276–91.

Jones, E. (2009). Assertive outreach in the context of the care programme approach. *Mental Health Practice*, 12(7), 24–9.

Kaplan, H. I., & Sadock, B. J. (1998). *Synopsis of Psychiatry*. Philadelphia, PA: Lippincott, Williams, Wilkens.

Kelly, B. D. (2004). Mental health policy in Ireland 1984–2004: Theory, overview and future directions. *Irish Journal of Psychological Medicine*, 21, 61–8.

Keogh, F., & Roche, A. (1996). *Mental Disorders in Older Irish People: Incidence, Prevalence and Treatment*. Dublin: National Council for the Elderly.

Law, M., Baptiste, S., McColl, M. A., Opzoomer, A., Polatajko, H., & Pollock, N. (1990). *The Canadian Occupational Performance Measure, 2nd ed.* Toronto: CAOT Publications.

Lebowitz, B. D., & Niederehe, G. (1992). Concepts and issues in mental health and aging. In Birren, J. E., Sloane, R. B., & Cohen, G. D., eds., *Handbook of Mental Health and Aging*, 2nd ed. San Diego, CA: Academic Press, pp. 3–26.

Light, E., & Lebowitz, B. D. (1991). *The Elderly with Chronic Mental Illness*. New York: Springer.

Little, A., & Doherty, B. (2008). Assessing function, behaviour and need. In Woods, R. T., & Clare, L., eds., *Handbook of the Clinical Psychology of Ageing*, 2nd ed. Chichester: Wiley, pp. 385–414.

Maguire, E., Kumaran, D., Hassabis, D., & Kopelman, M. (2010). Autobiographical memory in semantic dementia: A longitudinal fMRI study. *Neuropsychologia*, 48(1), 123–36.

Meeks, S., & Murrell, S. A. (1997). Mental illness in late life: Socioeconomic conditions, psychiatric symptoms, and adjustment of long-term sufferers. *Psychology and Aging*, 12, 296–308.

National Strategy on Domestic, Sexual and Gender-based Violence. (2008). *Summary of Submissions to Cosc.* Dublin: Cosc. (Retrieved 16 March 2009 from http://www.cosc.ie/en/COSC/Submissions%20Summary.pdf/Files/Submissions% 20Summary. pdf)

Nordhus, I. H. (2008). Manifestations of depression and anxiety in older adults. In Woods, R. T., & Clare, L., eds., *Handbook of the Clinical Psychology of Ageing*, 2nd ed. Chichester: Wiley, pp. 97–110.

Nordhus, I. H., Nielsen, G. H., & Kyale, G. (1998). Psychotherapy with older adults. In Nordhus, I. H., Van den Bos, G. R., Berg, S., & Fromholt, P., eds., *Clinical Geropsychology*. Washington, DC: American Psychological Association, pp. 289–312.

Östlund, G., Borg, K., & Wahlin, Å. (2005). Cognitive functioning in post-polio patients with and without general fatigue. *Journal of Rehabilitation Medicine*, 37(3), 147–51.

Otto, R., Slobogin, C., & Greenberg, S. (2007). Legal and ethical issues in accessing and utilizing third-party information. In Goldstein, A. M., ed., *Forensic Psychology: Emerging Topics and Expanding Roles*. Hoboken, NJ: John Wiley & Sons, pp. 190–205.

Pachur, T., Mata, R., & Schooler, L. (2009). Cognitive aging and the adaptive use of recognition in decision making. *Psychology and Aging*, 24(4), 901–15.

Prettyman, R. (2004). 5 ages of mental health old age. *Update*, 69(7), 290–4.

Préville, M., Hébert, R., Boyer, R., Bravo, G., & Seguin, M. (2005). Physical health and mental disorder in elderly suicide: A case-control study. *Aging & Mental Health*, 9(6), 576–84.

Ramsdell, J. W., Swart, J., Jackson, E., & Renvall, M. (1989). The yield of a home visit in the assessment of geriatric patients. *Journal of the American Geriatrics Society*, 13, 17–24.

Reidy, J., & Kirby, M. (2008). A survey of old age psychiatry consultation/liaison services in Ireland. *Irish Journal of Psychological Medicine*, 25(2), 66–8.

Reilly, S., Challis, D., Burns, A., & Hughes, J. (2004). The use of assessment scales in Old Age Psychiatry Services in England and Northern Ireland. *Aging & Mental Health*, 8(3), 249–55.

Reynolds, C. F., & Kupfer, D. J. (1999). Depression and aging: A look to the future. *Psychiatric Services*, 50(9), 1167–72.

Reynolds, C. F., & Charney, D. S. (2002). Unmet needs in the diagnosis and treatment of mood disorders in later life. *Biological Psychiatry*, 52, 145–303.

Rosowsky, E., Abrams, R. C., & Zweig, R. A. (1999). *Personality Disorders in Older Adults: Emerging Issues in Diagnosis and Treatment*. Mahwah, NJ: Lawrence Erlbaum Associates, Inc.

Sanderson, W. (2006). Evaluating adherence and flexibility in the use of a manual in clinical practice. *Pragmatic Case Studies in Psychotherapy*, 2(1), 1–5.

Schön, U., Denhov, A., & Topor, A. (2009). Social relationships as a decisive factor in recovering from severe mental illness. *International Journal of Social Psychiatry*, 55(4), 336–47.

Smith, H. (1998). Needs assessment in mental health services: the DISC framework. *Journal of Public Health*, 20(2), 154–60.

Smyer, M. A., & Qualls, S. H. (1999). *Ageing and Mental Health*. Oxford: Blackwells.

Stanley, M. A. (2001). Mental health issues for older adults in medical settings: Introduction to the special issue. *Journal of Clinical Geropsychology*, 7(2), 91–2.

Stevens, A., & Gabbay, J. (1991). Needs assessment needs assessment . . . *Health Trends*, 23(1), 20–3.

Stuart-Hamilton, I. (2006). *The Psychology of Ageing. An Introduction, 4th ed.* London: Jessica Kingsley.

Tedeschi, R., & Kilmer, R. (2005). Assessing strengths, resilience, and growth to guide clinical interventions. *Professional Psychology: Research and Practice*, 36(3), 230–7.

Tennessee Mental Health Planning Council Older Adult Committee. (2000). *Tennessee Mental Health Planning Council Older Adult Committee Report on Mental Health Issues and Needs of Older Adults*. Nashville, TN: Tennessee Department of Mental Health and Developmental Disabilities.

Teri, L., & Wagner, A. (1991). Assessment of depression in patients with Alzheimer's disease: Concordance between informants. *Psychology and Aging*, 6, 280–5.

University College London. (2009). *Camberwell Assessment of Need for the Elderly (CANE) Summary*. London: UCL. (Retrieved 1 April 2009 from http://www.ucl.ac.uk/cane/#summary)

University College London. (n.d). *Camberwell Assessment of Need for the Elderly (CANE) Summary Sheet*. London: UCL. (Retrieved 21 August 2010 from www.ucl.ac.uk/cane/summarysheet)

Vassilas, C. (2006). Review of 'CANE: Camberwell Assessment of Need for the Elderly'. *British Journal of Psychiatry*, 188, 95.

Verheul, R., Hartgers, C., Van Den Brink, W., & Koeter, M. (1998). The effect of sampling, diagnostic criteria and assessment procedures on the observed prevalence of DSM-III-R personality disorders among treated alcoholics. *Journal of Studies on Alcohol*, 59(2), 227.

Vernon, M. (1989). Assessment of persons with hearing disabilities. In Hunt, T., & Lindley, C. J., eds., *Testing Older Adults: A Reference Guide for Geropsychological Assessments*. Austin, TX: PRO-ED Inc., pp. 150–162.

Walters, K., Iliffe, S., & Orrell, M. (2001). An exploration of help-seeking behaviour in older people with unmet needs. *Family Practice*, 18, 277–82.

Woods, R. T. (2008). Assessing mood, wellbeing and quality of life. In Woods, R.

T., & Clare, L., eds., *Handbook of the Clinical Psychology of Ageing, 2nd ed.* Chichester: Wiley, pp. 415–427.

Wrigley, M., Murphy, B., Farrell, M., Cassidy, B., & Ryan, J. (2006a). Older people with enduring or recurrent severe mental illness (graduates): A literature review. *Irish Journal of Psychiatric Medicine*, 23(4), 151–5.

Wrigley, M., Murphy, B., Farrell, M., Cassidy, B., & Ryan, J. (2006b). Older people with enduring or recurrent severe mental illness in the Eastern Region of Ireland. *Irish Journal of Psychological Medicine*, 23(4), 145–50.

Zarit, S. H., & Zarit, J. M. (1998). *Mental Disorders in Older Adults: Fundamentals of Assessment and Treatment.* New York: Guilford Press.

Zweig, R. A. (2008). Personality disorder in older adults: Assessment challenges and strategies. *Professional Psychology: Research and Practice*, 39(3), 298–305.

Chapter 5

Treatment of mental health issues

Reality versus best practice

Helen Dempsey and Barry J. Coughlan

Introduction

The ageing of populations is one of the greatest achievements of human-kind and Europe is leading this success story (Cruz-Jentoft *et al.*, 2008). This will have serious implications for the provision of health care services for this population. As the world's population grows, and people live longer, preparation is needed for the enormous health changes and challenges that will result (O'Donovan, 2009).[1] The number of older people with mental health problems, like the number of older people in the general population, is growing. Yet, traditional mental health research and treatment has neglected old age issues and excluded older adults in much of the research literature.

Psychological development is considered to continue throughout life, with the unconscious remaining timelessly intact (Crusey, 1985). To grow old gracefully, according to Ardern (2002), implies a pleasing harmony between subjective experience and chronological age. This harmony has proved exquisitely difficult to achieve. Western culture, where youth is celebrated and old age denigrated, does little to foster this harmony (Boduroglu *et al.*, 2006).

As old age approaches, one is confronted with both concrete and conceptual losses i.e. death of loved ones, ill health, loss of the capacities on which our self-esteem is built, loss of status/income, retirement and social isolation. This sense of difference or loss is captured in Jung's reminder: 'We cannot live the afternoon of life according to the programme of life's morning' (Jung, 1930/1933: 266). One way we learn to cope with this imbalance is to always view old age as 'some place else' (Wheelock, 1997: 442), even when we ourselves are truly old.

Erikson's model of personality development conceptualises the major intrapsychic issues faced at the late adulthood stage as the struggle between integrity and despair (Erikson, 1963, 1980; Hughes & Peake, 2002). In the stage preceeding this, Erikson opines that middle-aged adults need to answer how they can provide support to those who have helped create the society they live in (Erikson, 1980). This question scaffolds the discussion that follows on how we currently provide psychological support to older adults and how we can best provide it.

It is now recognised that continued development, growth and change are normative across the lifespan (Sugarman, 2001), therefore psychological therapeutic work with older people is similar to that undertaken with younger people. In reality, the likelihood of receiving psychotherapy for mental health problems declines rapidly for older service users (Lehman & Steinwachs, 1998), indeed Anderson (2007: 8) found that 'with mental health care, older people do not have access to the range of services available to younger adults, despite having the same, and often greater, need'.

Evidence base for psychological treatments[2]

The UK Department of Health (2001a) published evidence-based clinical practice guidelines for treatment choice in psychological therapies, based on systematic reviews. Results indicate that psychological therapy shows benefits over no treatment for a wide range of mental health difficulties, suggesting psychological therapy should be routinely considered when assessing mental health problems for all age groups. In general, no effect on treatment outcome was found by age (Department of Health, 2001a). The two main psychotherapeutic approaches are described here, as they apply to work with older people.

Cognitive-behavioural therapy (CBT)

Cognitive-behavioural therapy has tended to be underused and is not well evaluated by old age psychiatry (Woods, 1995). The CBT trials to date have been conducted in academic institutions by highly skilled therapists and their applicability to other settings is still being determined. This therapy is thought to be particularly appropriate as an intervention with older adults because it is skill enhancing, problem-focused and straightforward (Laidlaw, 2008) and the most extensively researched form of therapy, with good evidence for its efficacy, in depression and anxiety (Butler et al., 2006).

Using CBT with older adults differs from working with a younger group due to the longevity of problems and the likelihood of chronic physical illness. Regarding longevity, a useful modification is to focus on maintenance rather than causal factors.[3] Cognitive-behavioural therapy can be distinguished from other types of psychotherapy as it is explicitly explorative rather than interpretive – the goal is to understand how older adults make sense of their world, while helping them to become their own therapist (Beck, 1995). The challenge for the therapist is to maintain a collaborative stance while adopting a more directive approach. This collaboration encourages a respect for the life experience of the older adult and facilitates a two-way learning process about therapy in later life and the ageing process (Satre *et al.*, 2006).

Psychodynamic psychotherapy

In 2000, a survey of 100 psychotherapy departments in the UK suggested that older people were being short-changed regarding access to psychodynamic psychotherapy (Murphy, 2000). One suggested reason was that older people were viewed as too psychologically rigid to engage. However, as with most groups, large individual differences exist regarding preparedness to engage in psychological work.

The goal of psychodynamic psychotherapy with older people is to make a connection between today's distress and yesterday's experience, thereby enabling energy to be released from regrets and channelled towards a new-found creativity (Limentani, 1995). There are aspects of the work that differentiates it from work with a younger client group. These include a focus on grief and loss; the provision of a safe place to discharge feelings of rage and anger arising from helplessness and lack of control and the provision of opportunities for the older adult to influence the therapist, providing a therapeutic counterpoint to feelings of helplessness and despair (Goldfarb, 1967; Powers & Wisocki, 1992).

Evidence-base for specific disorders

Schizophrenia

The potential role of psychological treatments in the management of psychotic symptoms, associated with schizophrenia in younger clients, is becoming clearer, but older adults with schizophrenia have not been routinely considered for these, which is unfortunate (Aguera-Ortiz & Reneses-Prieto, 1999). The prevalence of schizophrenia, based on Irish data, is up to 40 per 10,000 population. Psychosis with first onset after 60 years of age is estimated to affect 2–4 per cent of older adults, and as many as half will not respond to medication (Giblin *et al.*, 2004).

Regarding interventions, there is a lack of empirically validated psychotherapy interventions for older adults with schizophrenia. In the case of CBT, early evidence of its efficacy in psychosis is promising (Pilling *et al.*, 2002) and applications of CBT with older people have also been described (Laidlaw *et al.*, 2003). The next step is to reduce the gap between research and practice by developing evidence-based interventions designed to help older people with schizophrenia or late-onset psychosis.

In a study exploring the emotional world of people who develop late-onset psychosis, Giblin *et al.* (2004) found life experiences, cognitive schemas and attitudes to ageing to be significant psychosocial correlates of the condition, which suggests that interventions may be improved by attending to these factors. Granholm *et al.* (2005) carried out one of the first randomised controlled trials (RCT) of a psychosocial intervention designed to meet the unique needs of older people with a psychotic disorder. Clients receiving CBT social skills training performed social functioning activities significantly more often than those that did not. The participants also achieved greater insight and improved their coping skills. However, further research is needed to test interventions tailored to meet the needs of specific subgroups within this population.

The adoption of a stress-vulnerability model is a useful framework guiding practice that implies a multiplicity of causal and ameliorating factors[4] (Steinberg *et al.*, 2007). In developing interventions for this group, issues of loneliness, social isolation and depression need to be considered. Many people with psychosis are lonely and in need of support but cannot obtain it through normal peer and family relations through their inability to maintain effective relationships (Sagan, 2008).

Anxiety

Generalised anxiety disorder (GAD)

Until the last decade, anxiety disorders were a relatively unrecognised health problem among older adults (Wetherell *et al.*, 2005). Data since this time have pointed to the high prevalence and significant negative impact of anxiety in later life. Bryant and colleagues (2008) carried out a systematic review of articles from 1980 to 2007 on the prevalence of anxiety in the older adult. They found GAD to be the commonest anxiety disorder of the older adult with prevalence ranging from 1 to 15 per cent in community samples and from 1 to 28 per cent in clinical settings.[5] However, conceptual and methodological inconsistencies are replete in the literature. The authors concluded that issues relating to comorbidity and the nature of anxiety in this group remain unresolved thereby hampering intervention research and the development of evidence-based practice.

Although pharmacological intervention is the most frequently used route of care, older adults seem to have a preference for 'non-medication' interventions in the treatment of mental health problems (Unutzer *et al.*, 2002). Psychological treatments for older adults with anxiety are gradually being empirically tested (Woods & Roth, 1996). Clinical reports have been suggesting since the early 1990s, that CBT is as effective for anxiety in older adults as it is for younger people (King & Barrowclough, 1991). Data suggest the potential value of both CBT and pharmacological interventions for later life anxiety, particularly for GAD (Wetherell *et al.*, 2005). Response rates are lower in older adults and research is needed on the effectiveness of CBT compared with other psychological treatments such as supportive psychotherapy and on the effectiveness of specific forms of psychotherapy for late-life GAD (Flint, 2005), as well as real-world research with heterogeneous groups presenting with complex comorbidity.

Although GAD is one of the most prevalent anxiety disorders among older adults, other common and potentially disabling anxiety conditions, including obsessive–compulsive disorder and specific phobias, have largely been neglected (Wetherell *et al.*, 2005).

Obsessive–compulsive disorder (OCD)

Only one randomised controlled trial has been carried out in this area; this was a retrospective chart review of 11 cases (Abramowitz, 2006). Treatment was multidisciplinary, including exposure to obsessional thoughts combined with prevention of ritualised responses, psychoeducation, anxiety management and group CBT. Self- and staff-reported responses were high; however, there were no objective outcome measures or long-term follow-up. Therefore, definitive conclusions regarding sound evidence-based treatments cannot be drawn.

In a related investigation, Snowdon *et al.* (2007) reviewed over 1000 cases of people living in 'severe domestic squalor' and concluded that over half of those living in this situation are older aged adults. Snowdon and colleagues suggest that severe domestic squalor is as a result of hoarding associated with OCD and conclude that this is a little written about correlate of OCD, affecting older adults, requiring complex management and relying on liaison and cooperation between various services. Although there is a lack of evidence regarding effective intervention, it is thought that CBT and medication is the optimal approach (Saxena & Maidment, 2004).

Panic disorder

Panic disorder is reported to be extremely rare in older people (Flint *et al.*, 1996) but the data on this condition are sparse (Bryant *et al.*, 2008). No controlled randomised psychosocial intervention trials have been conducted exclusively among older adults with panic disorder, therefore definitive conclusions regarding evidence-based treatments cannot be drawn.

Social phobia

Research consistently indicates a low prevalence of this condition among older adults (Bryant *et al.*, 2008). This may be because it is easier for older people to avoid situations that provoke anxiety. An alternate explanation may be that personal maturation leads to lower levels of neuroticism and self-consciousness in older adults (McCrae *et al.*, 2000). No controlled randomised psychosocial intervention trials have been conducted exclusively among older adults with social phobia, therefore definitive conclusions regarding evidence-based treatments cannot be drawn.

Post-traumatic stress disorder (PTSD)

Post-traumatic stress disorder has scarcely been researched in older people, much less the development of evidence-based interventions for this population. People with PTSD of all ages are often not recognised or accurately diagnosed; this is likely to be a greater issue for older adults who under-utilise the mental health services. The 6-month prevalence rate has been estimated at 1 per cent (Van Zelst et al., 2003), with lifetime prevalence of 15 to 20 per cent in those exposed to traumatic events (Hunt & Robbins, 2001). Therefore, PTSD is not a rare condition and has a major negative impact on the lives of those it affects. Van Zelst and colleagues (2006) found that older people with PTSD experience grave impairments in daily life, spend more days in bed, are less satisfied with life and do not receive optimum treatment i.e. from a mental health professional. The researchers concluded that although PTSD is a mental health condition benefitting from treatment with antidepressants and psychotherapy this is not always routine clinical practice.

Exposure treatments[6] are thought to be the most effective, regardless of age. In the UK, the National Institute for Health and Clinical Excellence (NICE) guidelines recommend the use of trauma-focused CBT and eye movement desensitisation and reprocessing (EMDR) (Kitchiner et al., 2006). There is little evidence about the efficacy of particular treatments for older survivors of trauma. Since CBT has been established as an effective treatment for psychological problems of later life (Laidlaw et al., 2003), and for trauma (Follette & Ruzek, 2006), it can be assumed that older people with trauma problems would benefit from exposure-based CBT. Special considerations may include building in more time at the treatment–socialisation stage to overcome the embeddedness of thought suppression often used by older adults as a coping tool (Morse & Lynch, 2004).

Personality disorder

Similar to many mental health issues of later life, personality disorders have received little serious attention. Personality disorders are known to seriously affect the quality of life and to complicate the course and treatment of other mental health disorders (Abrams et al., 2001). Rates of personality disorder appear to be highest in older people with major depression or dysthymia (about 31 per cent), which is about half that of community-dwelling older people. However, the frequency of strictly diagnosable personality disorder shows a slight decline with age (Tracie Shea et al., 2009).

Treatment for personality disorder, particularly those with comorbidity, is an understudied challenge. The applicability of traditional directive psychotherapies such as dialectical behaviour therapy (DBT), interpersonal therapy, CBT or problem-solving therapy have not been well evaluated (Abrams & Bromberg, 2006). In a review of CBTs with older adults with personality disorders, Goismann (1999) recommended targeting symptoms such as impulsiveness, acting out and suicidal behaviour. He also suggested emphasising the 'here and now', agreeing short goal-oriented interventions and including specific adaptations to suit older adults, where appropriate, such as slowing the pace of therapy, using multiple sensory modes to present material, a didactic approach and memory aids.

Dynamic therapies with the older adult in the area of personality disorder are not well reviewed. Abrams (1994) recommended considering dynamic therapy in conjunction with symptomatic medication and reiterated the need to focus on the older adult's present reality rather than childhood events and relationships, which may be the focus of dynamic work with younger adults.

Lynch and colleagues (2007) reviewed two randomised clinical trials using DBT to treat depression and personality disorder in older adults and concluded that applying modified DBT for the treatment of comorbid personality disorder and major depressive disorder is feasible, acceptable and has clinical promise. Modifications address the tendency of older adults with personality disorder to be less open to new experiences and more rigid in behaviours and cognitions than younger adults with personality disorder.

Suicide and deliberate self-harm

Older age suicidology, like many other areas of older age research, is at an early stage of development, with poor risk detection and treatment information available. Older adults worldwide have long had high suicide rates, with older white males in the USA and young males in other countries like the UK and Ireland being particularly at risk (Bertolote, 2001; Woods, 2008). Mental health problems are highly prevalent among older adults who die by suicide (Heisel, 2006), although prevalence rates vary by disorder. Harwood (2002) suggests that as many as 20 per cent of suicides in older people are not associated with any mental health condition. Older adults are more likely than any other age group to die by suicide (Woods, 2008), although rates vary greatly from country to country, and older adults who attempt suicide seem to be different, in important ways, to younger people in this group. Older adults tend to be more lethal and violent in their attempts to take their own lives and hence complete suicide more often than younger people (McIntosh & Santos, 1986). Neulinger and De Leo (2001) found that elderly people who died by suicide were significantly more likely to have had a recent physical illness than those who took their own lives in youth age groups.

Intervention approaches in suicide and deliberate self-harm must necessarily differ from that of other mental health issues in that a conscious personal decision is taken to pursue this act (Chan et al., 2007).[7] Randomised controlled trials on interventions in this area are rare; research supports collaborative models of care linking primary care providers with mental health specialists (Oxman et al., 2003) and interpersonal therapy is thought to alleviate risk (Bruce et al., 2004). Poor interpersonal problem solving and a reduced ability to regulate affect are thought to be implicated as well as difficulties in retrieving autobiographical memories at a specific level and difficulties in anticipating specific positive experiences. These areas have been targeted by some researchers (Unutzer et al., 2006), leading to new therapeutic directions emphasising a problem-solving approach.

Somatoform disorders

Although these disorders cause significant physical and occupational disability and are a major economic burden (Bass et al., 2001), it is suggested that they are usually neglected by mental health services for older people (Wijeratne et al., 2003). This may be as a result of assessment and diagnostic difficulties and the perception that somatoform disorders are infrequent and of little consequence. There is certainly a lack of research examining the rate of these disorders and little evidence of studies investigating the treatment of somatoform disorders in older people, although syndromes such as persistent fatigue can be present in about 25 per cent of older primary care attenders (Agronin, 2007).

Insomnia

Disorders in initiating and maintaining sleep are the most commonly reported and treated of all sleep complaints and the latter are the most frequently reported psychological symptom in primary care (Morgan, 2008). Sleep problems are common in older adults; there is a clear age gradient after 65 years. Prevalence rates in this group range from 20 to 30 per cent, greater in frequency and severity than any other age group (Irwin et al., 2006), while the annual incidence rate is estimated to be about 5 per cent (Foley et al., 1999).

Untreated insomnia is a serious problem in that it severely impacts upon quality of life (Dixon et al., 2006) and increases the risk of major depression (Livingston et al., 1993). Regarding its management, evidence from clinical trials (Buscemi et al., 2005; Glass et al., 2005) has concluded that the benefits of hypnotic medication are inflated and need to be offset against the significant risk posed by these drugs. Meta-analytic studies have also shown that an average of 5 hours psychological treatment produces reliable and lasting improvements in sleep pattern. These methods,[8] have proved effective in treating older adults with and without comorbidity (Morgan *et al.*, 2004; Morin, *et al.*, 1999).

Substance misuse

Although alcohol use and alcohol problems do decline with age, this is still an under-recognised public health problem of moderate proportions.[9] The tendency of symptoms of substance misuse to mimic other medical and behavioural disorders, the reluctance of older adults and their families to disclose problems, faulty recall of level of use and therapeutic pessimism exacerbate underdiagnosis and under-reporting by physicians (Menninger, 2002). However, older people with alcohol problems have tended to fare as well or better than younger people in a variety of treatment settings (Atkinson, 1995).

Older women have specific risks and vulnerabilities to alcohol use, including a swifter progression to alcohol-related illnesses. This subgroup are underscreened and under-recognised (Blow, 2000). There is a lack of research on treatment outcomes for all older adults with substance misuse problems, with the literature focusing almost exclusively on alcohol, and with little if any emphasis on women. The Center for Substance Abuse Treatment (1998) recommended brief intervention, family intervention and age-specific supportive group treatments involving rebuilding social support whereas Gatz and colleagues (1998) recommended reminiscence therapy and age segregation (Katz, 2002).

One recent community intervention clinical trial for older people with comorbid substance misuse (The Geriatric Addictions Program, GAP; D'Agostino *et al.*, 2006), which focused on co-occurring physical and psychological problems of older adults, used a multidimensional approach incorporating geriatric services, motivational counselling, ageing and chemical dependency services. This model provides promising evidence of improved outcomes and stable recovery in addictions of later life.[10] However, further research is needed regarding evidence-based guidelines for psychological therapies for specific groups of older adults with substance misuse problems and other complex needs.

Conclusions on best practice

An emerging evidence base supports the efficacy of mental health interventions for older adults. The most extensive research base exists for psychosocial interventions for depression and dementia in later life, which are dealt with in Chapters 6 and 8. Less is known about effective treatments for the other mental health conditions, although recent advances in research and practice are promising (Bartels *et al.*, 2002; Dallaire *et al.*, 2009).

Practice in reality

Accurate information on population mental health status and prevalence rates is critical in informing mental health care policy and service planning (National Economic and Social Forum, 2006). There is a lack of up-to-date information on prevalence of mental health disorders and use of/access to satisfaction with mental health services for older adults in Ireland. The SLÁN 2007 survey (Barry *et al.*, 2009) gives an estimate of the prevalence of some mental health conditions and their determinants. This survey is optimistic regarding the mental health of older adults in Ireland. Respondents aged 65 and over report less psychological distress, anxiety and depression compared with other age groups. However, 17 per cent of people aged 65 and over reported feeling lonely; this was significantly higher than other age groups in the report. The SLÁN 2007 report reveals a clear social gradient in evidence for mental health, rather than an age gradient, which goes some way towards dispelling the myth that mental health problems are a natural consequence of ageing.

The Irish government's Health Strategy, *Quality and Fairness – A Health System for You* (Department of Health, 2001) makes a commitment to a 'holistic approach' to the planning and delivery of care, and to a coordinated action plan to meet the needs of older people. The evidence suggests that current services are falling far short of these commitments. An example of this is the lack of clarity regarding who provides services for the older adult who has lived with schizophrenia since early adulthood, or for older adults with a learning disability and a mental health problem.

In mental health services, older people pre-65 years of age and with mental health difficulties are routinely discriminated against (National Disability Authority/National Council on Ageing and Older People, 2006). The Inspector of Mental Health Services recently stated that it is 'common practice, in most mental health services for the elderly, to exclude people who have attended the general adult mental health services in a given period prior to referral' (Mental Health Commission, 2005: 118). Concern has been expressed that these exclusions are depriving significant numbers of elderly people from appropriate care.[11]

In 2007, the Quality Framework for Mental Health Services in Ireland was developed and published by the Mental Health Commission. The framework provides a mechanism for continuous quality improvement. Theme 7.1 states that 'service users receive care and treatment from quality staff with appropriate skills' while Theme 8.1 states that 'the mental health service is delivered in accordance with evidence-based codes of practice, policies and protocols' (2007: 17). It can be seen, therefore, that evidence-based practice for older adults in mental health care is underpinned by the national quality framework. The aspirations of the framework document, however, currently serve to highlight the very significant gaps between this goal and the reality.

Service delivery in other countries is also characterised by significant gaps. In the UK, the National Service Framework for Older People (Department of Health, 2001b) was set up to address the inconsistencies and improve the services provided for older people with mental health problems. A survey of over 300 psychiatrists, carried out 3 years after the framework document was published, presents a mixed picture (Tucker *et al.*, 2007). A little more than half of consultant psychiatrists reported an improvement in services available to older people. Considerable differences existed regarding the deployment of core professionals with multidisciplinary teams, with one-third lacking social work, while many respondents particularly highlighted the limited provision of psychologists. This finding echoes previous concerns about the availability of psychological therapies for older adults (Evans, 2004); significant gaps also mirror the situation in other countries (World Health Organization, 2001).

Conclusions on current practice

Older adults with mental health problems are more likely than younger adults to receive inappropriate or inadequate treatment (Bartels, 2002). One of the challenges is the 'expertise gap' between clinical services and research, resulting from inadequate training and resources. There are shortages of health professionals, and in particular, clinical psychologists, on mental health teams delivering care to older adults. There is also a lack of professionals with specific training and expertise in mental health care for the older person. Psychologists with competence in treating adult clients may be able to meet the needs of the young-old (65–74 years), whose physical and psychosocial functioning tends to be similar to that of younger adults. However, the most rapidly growing older population is in the advanced age categories[12] whose physical and psychosocial contexts are significantly different (Qualls *et al.*, 2002). As Pinquart and Sörensen (2001) concluded, theoretical qualifications are not sufficient to guarantee success in psychotherapy with older adults. Additional geropsychological or older adult training is recommended.

The reasons for these significant gaps are unclear but one may speculate that lack of commitment is a symptom of national complacency, by decision makers, regarding provision of older adult mental health services, in general and in clinical psychology services, specifically. This complacency may be an indication of the embeddedness and acceptance of ageism within general society.

Funding

Quite apart from the psychosocial burden on individuals and families, the aggregate financial cost of mental disorders is estimated to be between 2.5 and 4 per cent of global gross national product (World Health Organization, 2003). Despite this, public spending on mental health is disproportionately low, accounting for 7 per cent of the health budget in Ireland (O'Shea & Kennelly, 2008).[13] There is evidence to suggest that mental health problems are risk factors for, or consequences of many other problems, for example depression, anxiety and coronary heart disease; or poor health behaviours such as smoking and reduced activity. These associations between physical and mental health are actually more pronounced in later life and lack of attention to these interactions has serious consequences for the development of appropriate preventive and treatment services.

Discrimination through age and mental illness

Mental illness, like ageing, evokes the connotations that society places on it, whether positive or negative. The stigma attached to mental health problems has long existed, is well documented, is associated with concepts such as shame, loss of face and humiliation (Arboleda-Florez, 2003) and can powerfully erode confidence that mental health problems are valid and treatable conditions (Graham et al., 2003). In a recent large-scale national Irish study (Barry et al., 2009), 52 per cent of respondents reported that they would not want people to know if they were experiencing mental health problems.

Age discrimination is a recognised prejudice, defined as an unjustifiable difference in treatment based solely on age (Centre for Policy on Ageing, 2007). Perceived discrimination can itself have a detrimental effect on the health of older people (Vogt Yuan, 2007), contributing to a downward spiral of ill health and social isolation. It has been suggested that the stigma attached to being old and having a mental illness has a disproportionate impact on those categorised as both (Thomas & Shute, 2006). These researchers argue that the implications of a double stigma may be multiplicative, i.e. having more of an impact on older people with mental health problems than just either being old or having a mental health problem. Lack of policy or lack of implementation of policy is a covert perpetuation of what is already institutionalised discrimination. In turn, lack of attention to this discrimination has had a seriously negative impact on funding, training, employment, service provision, research and development.

Research bias

Older adults are often excluded from treatment studies on the basis of their age, especially longitudinal clinical trials, since researchers are reasonably concerned about natural attrition rates confounding results. This results in a lack of evidence-based research from which to generate best practice interventions. There are also widespread methodological issues in older adult research based on difficulty of recall, cohort effects regarding willingness to discuss psychological issues and lack of consensus internationally regarding measurement and diagnostic categories. Difficulties also exist in assessing mental health disorders in primary care (services the older adult population are frequent users of) and in differentiating physical from psychological problems in the older adult.

Older adults are a diverse group exposed to a wide range of physical, environmental, psychosocial, cultural and historical factors that determine vulnerability to and resilience regarding psychological ill health. Psychosocial factors such as prolonged adversity, life events, early experiences and social relationships have an important influence on the onset and course of psychological disorders in all age groups; however, protective factors and those enhancing recovery have been less extensively studied and in the older adult have been almost entirely overlooked. A recent positive development in Ireland was the establishment of CARDI (Centre for Ageing Research and Development in Ireland) in 2008.[14] Its mission is to advocate for and advance the ageing research agenda by identifying, coordinating and stimulating research on ageing as a means of improving the lives of older people on the island of Ireland.

Current and best practice summary

Limited access to psychological treatments is a problem for health service users of all ages. In the UK and USA, older adults are less likely to receive psychological therapies than younger adults and often medication is the only form of treatment provided (Mental Health Foundation, Mind, Rethink, Sainsbury Centre for Mental Health and Young Minds, 2006).

It was estimated more than 20 years ago that nearly half of older adults with a recognised mental health difficulty have unmet needs for services (George et al., 1988). The evidence presented in this chapter suggests that a high level of unmet need is likely to still exist. It is apparent that the question is not whether there is a gap between best practice and current practice, since it is clear that this is the case, but what is the evidence base for practice in mental health issues in the older adult?

A recent systematic review of prevalence of mental health disorders in old age in the European Union (Riedel-Heller et al., 2006) found all other disorders, outside of depression and dementia, to be under-researched thus making prevalence and comparability conclusions difficult. Interventions cannot be designed without comprehensive epidemiological and clinical trial data. Developing an evidence base for psychological interventions for mental health issues in older adults is one of the most important first steps in promoting the use of psychological interventions with this group. Logsdon and colleagues (2007: 34) stated:

> Psychologists must start with the best available empirical research and individualise it to meet the needs of our clients, and they must continue to develop and test efficacious, cost-effective interventions as the ageing population in need of these treatments continue to increase in coming decades.

Where data have reached a critical mass, and consensus is achieved on best practice, implementation is limited due to ageism and discrimination among service providers and policy makers, organisational barriers, lack of training, inadequate and prejudicial funding for mental health services for the older adult (Bartels *et al.*, 2002) and a lack of coordination between service providers and collaboration with service consumers and their families.

Conclusion

At the start of this chapter, the question arose as to 'How can we help each other? How can society prepare to provide psychological support to those who have built it?' Before we can answer this question, we must decide as a society whether older adults deserve a specifically designated equitable mental health service, and if so, what is required to make this happen? Positive discrimination toward the older adult is needed to redress the current imbalance as well as a deep-seated cultural shift toward acceptance of the third age as a time of integration, consolidation and respectful symbiotic experiences with younger groups in society.[15]

As individuals, we must seek to grow towards a new understanding and as citizens, parents, educators, service providers, policy makers and potential older adults ourselves we must impress these attitudes, similar to the value system based on filial piety found in Eastern cultures, on the very youngest and newest members of our society. According to the National Disability Authority/National Council on Ageing and Older People (2006), a recognition of the universality of interdependence may provide a way to underpin greater connectedness and reciprocity within communities for all people.

Recommendations

- Identify innovative and creative ways to combat the double discrimination of ageing and mental illness, with special emphasis on primary school students, in recognition of the early development of attitudes.
- Generate high-quality information on who provides psychological services to older people and on how well this need is being met, especially with regard to gender, cultural, ethnic and religious factors.

- Improve the methodology of epidemiological research in old age so it is tailored to the special challenges of this age group.
- Increase funding for research and dissemination of evidence-based psychological treatments for the mental health problems of older adults and for the further identification of determinants of successful ageing.
- Improve early identification and treatment through outreach and collaborative primary care services.
- Prioritise the provision of fully resourced multidisciplinary teams for old age mental health services.
- Instigate opportunities for specialist professional training in the psychology of ageing and in all other health and social care professions, including psychiatry and general practice.
- Improve equity by increasing availability and accessibility of mental health services to older adults.
- Improve coordination of mental and physical health care through liaison mental health teams and voluntary organisations.
- Identify innovative ways to apply the recovery approach to the psychiatry of later life.
- Establish effective and responsive advocacy services for older adults.

Notes

1 Many older people have multiple concurrent health problems. Five of the ten leading causes of disability and premature death worldwide are mental health conditions and it is predicted that by 2020, neuropsychiatric problems will constitute the second largest cause of disease burden worldwide (Barry et al., 2009).
2 The main evidence base is in the area of dementia, where reminiscence therapy and life review are widely used. Cognitive therapy, behaviour therapy and brief psychodynamic therapy have also been shown to be useful in depression in older people (Woods & Roth, 2005). However, there has been a lack of research on psychological therapies for other mental health problems, such as the anxiety disorders, schizophrenia and psychotic disorders, personality disorders, suicide, substance misuse and post-traumatic stress disorder.
3 Other modifications may include changing the pace and length of sessions; using multimodal presentation; summarising; allowing time for story telling or existential themes; validating physical factors and holding therapeutic optimism (Wall, 2009).
4 For example: age-related factors may produce conflicts, which threaten an already vulnerable sense of self, causing symptoms to emerge (Fuchs, 1999).
5 The prevalence of anxiety *symptoms*, rather than disorder, was found to be much higher, up to 56 per cent.
6 Since the basic neural process of habituation to a feared stimuli is unlikely to be affected by age trauma work with older adults is similar to that of work with younger adults.
7 Depression is known to be a predominant factor in suicide in older people (Woods, 2008) and hopelessness is widely recognised as linking depression to suicidal intent.

8 Psychological treatment includes CBT, sleep hygiene, stimulus control, sleep restriction, relaxation and cognitive components.

9 It was widely believed that these disorders were seldom seen after the middle years because people with addictions were thought to die prematurely, or recover spontaneously, whereas late-onset addiction was viewed as rare (Atkinson, 2002).

10 Another recent intervention (Primary Care Research in Substance Abuse and Mental Health for the Elderly study (PRISM-E); Lee *et al.*, 2009), incorporating an integrated harm-reduction approach, revealed that at-risk elderly drinkers in the integrated care condition were more likely to access treatment and reduce drinking behaviour than those in the control group.

11 The Inspector of Mental Health Services also cites numerous examples of poor-quality care for long-stay patients in mental health wards, including the absence of care plans, activities or any evidence of therapeutic direction for patients in certain locations (Mental Health Commission, 2005: 144, 154). In addition, elderly long-stay residents of psychiatric wards are being discharged to private nursing home beds and other settings that are unapproved for mental health care (2005: 118).

12 The old-old age category includes 75–84 year olds; the oldest-old comprises those 85 plus.

13 Public spending on mental health lies at about 11 per cent of the national health spend in England and Scotland and 9 per cent in Northern Ireland.

14 This is a not-for-profit organisation set up by leaders from the ageing field across Ireland and hosted by the Institute of Public Health.

15 Common characterisations of the ageing population in terms of 'dependency ratios' and lack of productivity project negative images of ageing and do little to define the diverse needs, gifts and skills of older people (National Council on Ageing and Older People, 2005). Such characterisations serve to hide the valuable contribution older people make to society. For example, grandparents provide a substantial amount of unpaid care to the 54,000 families in Ireland where both parents work (Good & Fitzgerald, 2005).

References

Abramowitz, J. S. (2006). The psychological treatment of Obsessive Compulsive Disorder. *Canadian Journal of Psychiatry*, 51, 407–61.

Abrams, R. C. (1994). Management. In Copeland, J. R. M., Abou-Saleh, M. T., & Blazer, D. G., eds., *Principles and Practice of Geriatric Psychiatry*. Chichester: Wiley, pp. 783–90.

Abrams, R. C., & Bromberg, C. E. (2006). Personality disorders in the elderly: A flagging field of enquiry. *International Journal of Geriatric Psychiatry*, 21, 1013–17.

Abrams, R. C., Alexopoulos, G. S., Speilman, L. A., Klausner, E., & Kakuma, T. (2001). Personality disorder symptoms predict declines in global functioning and quality of life in elderly depressed patients. *American Journal of Geriatric Psychiatry*, 9(1), 49–57.

Agronin, M. (2007). Somatoform disorders. In Blazer, D. G., Steffens, D. C., & Busse, E. W., eds., *Essentials of Geriatric Psychiatry*. Arlington, VA: American Psychiatric Publishing, Inc, pp. 207–18.

Aguera-Ortiz, L., & Reneses-Prieto, B. (1999). The place of non-biological treatments. In Howard, R., Rabins, P. V., & Castle, D. J., eds., *Late-Onset Schizophrenia*. Petersfield: Wrightson Biomedical, pp. 233–60.

Anderson, D. (2007). *The Human Rights of Older Persons in Healthcare. Response from the Faculty of Old Age Psychiatry of the Royal College of Psychiatrists, Eighteenth Report*. London: Royal College of Psychiatrists.

Arboleda-Florez, J. (2003). Considerations on the stigma of mental illness. *The Canadian Journal of Psychiatry*, 48, 645–50.

Ardern, M. (2002). Dynamic psychotherapy with older persons. In Jacoby, R., & Oppenheimer, C., eds., *Psychiatry in the Elderly, 3rd ed*. Oxford: Oxford University Press.

Atkinson, R. (1995). Treatment programs for aging alcoholics. In Beresford, T. P., & Gomberg, E. S. L., eds., *Alcohol and Aging*. New York: Oxford University Press, pp. 186–210.

Atkinson, R. (2002). Substance abuse in the elderly. In Jacoby, R., & Oppenheimer, C., eds., *Psychiatry in the Elderly, 3rd ed*. Oxford: Oxford University Press, pp. 799–834.

Barry, M. M., Lente, E. van, Molcho, M., Morgan, K., McGee, H., Conroy, R. M., et al. (2009). *SLÁN 2007: Survey of Lifestyle, Attitudes and Nutrition in Ireland*. Mental Health and Social Well-Being Report, Department of Health and Children. Dublin: The Stationery Office.

Bartels, S. (2002). Quality, cost and effectiveness of services for older adults with mental disorders: A selective overview of recent advances in geriatric mental health services research. *Current Opinion in Psychiatry*, 15, 411–16.

Bartels, S., Dums, A., Oxman, T., Schneider, L., Areán, P. A., Alexopoulos, G. S., et al. (2002). Evidence-based practices in geriatric mental health care. *Psychiatric Services*, 53(11), 1419–31.

Bass, C., Peveler, R., & House, A. (2001). Somatoform disorders: Severe psychiatric illnesses neglected by psychiatrists. *British Journal of Psychiatry*, 179, 11–14.

Beck, J. (1995). *Cognitive Therapy: Basics and Beyond*. New York: Guilford.

Bertolote, J. M. (2001). Suicide in the world: An epidemiological overview 1959–2000. In Wasserman, D., ed., *Suicide: An Unnecessary Death*. London: Martin Dunitz.

Blow, F. (2000). Treatment of older women with alcohol problems: Meeting the challenge for a special population. *Alcoholism: Clinical and Experimental Research*, 24(8), 1257–66.

Boduroglu, A., Yoon, C., Luo, T., & Park, D. (2006). Age-related stereotypes: A comparison of American and Chinese cultures. *Gerontology*, 52(5), 324–33.

Bruce, M. L., Ten Have, T. R., Reynolds, C. F. III, Katz, Schulberg, H. C. I. I., Mulsant, B. H., et al. (2004). Reducing suicidal ideation and depressive symptoms in depressed older primary care patients: A randomized controlled trial. *Journal of the American Medical Association*, 291, 1081–91.

Bryant, C., Jackson, H., & Ames, D. (2008). The prevalence of anxiety in older adults: Methodological issues and a review of the literature. *Journal of Affective Disorders*, 109(3), 233–50.

Buscemi, N., Vandermeer, B., & Friesen, C. (2005). *Manifestations and Management of Chronic Insomnia in Adults. Evidence Report/Technology Assessment no. 125*. Alberta: University of Alberta Evidence-Based Practice Center.

Butler, A. C., Chapman, J. E., Forman, E. M., & Beck, A. T. (2006). The empirical status of cognitive-behavioral therapy: A review of meta-analyses. *Clinical Psychology Review*, 26, 17–31.

Center for Subtance Abuse Treatment. (1998). *Substance Abuse among Older Adults. Treatment Improvement Protocol, 26.* Rockville, MD: Center for Substance Abuse Treatment.

Centre for Policy on Ageing. (2007). *A Literature Review of the Likely Costs and Benefits of Legislation to Prohibit Age Discrimination in Health and Social Services and Definitions of Age Discrimination that might be Operationalised for Measurement.* London: Department of Health.

Chan, J., Draper, B., & Banerjee, S. (2007). Deliberate self-harm in older adults: A review of the literature from 1995 to 2004. *International Journal of Geriatric Psychiatry*, 22, 720–32.

Crusey, J. E. (1985). Short-term psychodynamic psychotherapy with a sixty-two year old man. In Nemiroff, R. A., & Colarusso, C. A., eds., *The Race Against Time: Psychotherapy and Psychoanalysis in the Second Half of Life.* New York: Plenum Press, pp. 147–66.

Cruz-Jentoft, A. J., Franco, A., Sommer, P., Baeyens, J. P., Jankowska, E., Maggi, A., *et al.* (2008). *European Silver Paper on the Future of Health Promotion and Preventive Actions, Basic Research and Clinical Aspects of Age-Related Disease.* Wroclaw: European Summit on Age-Related Disease.

D'Agostino, C. S., Barry, K. L., Blow, F. C., & Podgorski, C. (2006). Community interventions for older adults with comorbid substance abuse: The Geriatric Addictions Program (GAP). *The Cochrane Central Register of Controlled Trials*, 2(3), 31–45.

Dallaire, B., McCubbin, M., Carpentier, N., & Clément, M. (2009). Representations of elderly with mental health problems held by psychosocial practitioners from community and institutional settings. *Social Work in Mental Health*, 7(1–3), 139–52.

Department of Health (Ireland). (2001). *Quality and Fairness: A Health System for You.* Dublin: The Stationery Office.

Department of Health (UK). (2001a). *Treatment Choice in Psychological Therapies and Counselling: Evidence Based Clinical Practice Guidelines.* London: Department of Health.

Department of Health (UK). (2001b). *National Service Framework for Older People.* London: Department of Health.

Dixon, S., Morgan, K., Mathers, N., Thompson, J., & Tomeny, M. (2006). Impact of cognitive-behavior therapy on health related quality of life among adult hypnotic users with chronic insomnia. *Behavioral Sleep Medicine*, 4, 71–84.

Erikson, E. (1963). *Childhood and Society, 2nd ed.* New York: Norton.

Erikson, E. (1980). *Identity and the Life Cycle.* New York: Norton.

Evans, S. (2004). A survey of the provision of psychological treatments to older adults in the NHS. *Psychiatric Bulletin*, 28, 411–14.

Flint, A., Cook, J., & Rabins, P. (1996). Why is panic disorder less frequent in later life? *American Journal of Geriatric Psychiatry*, 4, 96–109.

Flint, A. (2005). Generalized anxiety disorder in elderly patients: Epidemiology, diagnosis and treatment options. *Drugs & Aging*, 22(2), 101–14.

Foley, D. J., Monjan, A., Simonsick, E. M., Wallace, R. B., & Blazer, D. G. (1999).

Incidence and remission of insomnia among elderly adults: An epidemiologic study of 6,800 persons over three years. *Sleep*, 22, s366–72.

Follette, V., & Ruzek, J. (2006). *Cognitive-Behavioral Therapies for Trauma, 2nd ed.* New York: Guilford.

Fuchs, V. (1999). Health care for the elderly: How much? Who will pay for it? *Health Affairs*, 18, 11–21.

Gatz, M., Fisk, A., Fox, L. S., Kaskie, B., Kasl-Godley, J. E., McCallum, T. J., *et al.* (1998). Empirically validated psychological treatments for older adults. *Journal of Mental Health and Ageing*, 4, 9–46.

George, L. K., Blazer, D. G., Winfield-Laird, I., Leaf, P. J., & Fischback, R. L. (1988). Psychiatric disorders and mental health service use in later life. In Brody, J. A., & Maddox, G. L., eds., *Epidemiology and Aging*. New York: Springer, 147–66.

Giblin, S., Clare, L., Livingston, G., & Howard, R. (2004). Psychosocial correlates of late-onset psychosis: Life experiences, cognitive schemas and attitudes to ageing. *International Journal of Geriatric Psychiatry*, 19, 611–23.

Glass, J., Lanctôt, K. L., Herrmann, N., Sproule, B. A., & Busto, U. E. (2005). Sedative hypnotics in older people with insomnia: Meta-analysis of risks and benefits. *British Medical Journal*, 331, 1169–75.

Goismann, R. M. (1999). Cognitive-behavioral therapy, personality disorders and the elderly: Clinical and theoretical considerations. In Rosowsksy, E., Abrams, R. C., & Zweig, R. A., eds., *Personality Disorders in Older Adults*. Hillsdale, NJ: Lawrence Erlbaum Associates, Inc, pp. 215–28.

Goldfarb, A. I. (1967). The psychodynamics of dependency and the search for aid. In Kalish, B., ed., *Dependencies of Old People. Occasional Papers in Gerontology No. 6, 1–16*. Wayne State Univeristy, MI: Institute of Gerontology, University of Michigan.

Good, A., & Fitzgerald, E. (2005). Understanding dependency: Challenges for planners. In *National Council on Ageing and Older People, Planning for an Ageing Population: Strategic Considerations*. Dublin: National Council on Ageing and Older People.

Graham, N., Lindesay, J., Katona, C., Bertolote, J. M., Camus, V., Copeland, J. R. M., *et al.* (2003). Reducing stigma and discrimination against older people with mental illness: A technical consensus statement. *International Journal of Geriatric Psychiatry*, 18, 670–78.

Granholm, E., McQuaid, J. R., McClure, F. S., Auslander, L. A., Perivoliotis, D., Pedrelli, P., *et al.* (2005). A randomized controlled trial of cognitive behavioral social skills training for middle-aged and older outpatients with chronic schizophrenia. *American Journal of Psychiatry*, 162, 520–9.

Harwood, D. (2002). Suicide in older persons. In Jacoby, R., & Oppenheimer, C., eds., *Psychiatry in the Elderly, 3rd ed.* Oxford: Oxford University Press.

Heisel, M. J. (2006). Review: Suicide and its prevention among older adults. *Canadian Journal of Psychiatry*, 51(3), 143–54.

Hughes, D., & Peake, T. (2002). Investigating the value of spiritual well-being and psychosocial development in mitigating senior adulthood depression. *Activities, Adaptation & Aging*, 26(3), 15–35.

Hunt, N., & Robbins, I. (2001). The long-term consequences of war: The experience of World War II. *Aging & Mental Health*, 5(2), 183–90.

Irwin, M. R., Cole, J. C., & Nicassio, P. M. (2006). Comparative meta-analysis of behavioral interventions for insomnia and their efficacy in middle-aged adults and older adults 55+ years of age. *Health Psychology*, 25(1), 3–14.

Jung, C. G. (1930). *Die Lebenswende.* In *Seelenprobleme der Gegenwart.* Zürich: Rascher. Translated into English (1933) as *The Stages of Life.* In *Modern Man in Search of a Soul.* London: Kegan Paul, Trench, Trübner & Co.

Katz, R. (2002). Older women and addictions. In Straussner, S. L. A., & Brown, S., eds., *The Handbook of Addiction Treatment for Women.* San Francisco, CA: Jossey-Bass, pp. 387–403.

King, P., & Barrowclough, C. (1991). A clinical pilot study of CBT for anxiety disorders in the elderly. *Behavioural Psychotherapy*, 19, 337–45.

Kitchiner, N., Roberts, N., & Bisson, J. (2006). Eye movement desensitisation reprocessing (EMDR). *Mental Health Practice*, 9(7), 40–4.

Laidlaw, K. (2008). Cognitive behaviour therapy with older people. In Woods, R. T., & Clare, L., eds., *The Handbook of Clinical Psychology and Ageing, 2nd ed.* Chichester: Wiley.

Laidlaw, K., Thompson, L. W., Dick-Siskin, L., & Gallagher-Thompson, D. (2003). *Cognitive-Behaviour Therapy with Older People.* Chichester: Wiley.

Lee, H., Mericle, A., Ayalon, L., & Areán, P. (2009). Harm reduction among at-risk elderly drinkers: A site-specific analysis from the multi-site Primary Care Research in Substance Abuse and Mental Health for Elderly (PRISM-E) study. *International Journal of Geriatric Psychiatry*, 24(1), 54–60.

Lehman, A. F., & Steinwachs, D. M. (1998). Patterns of usual care for schizophrenia: Initial results from the Schizophrenia Patient Outcomes Research Team (PORT) Client Survey. *Schizophrenia Bulletin*, 24, 11–20.

Limentani, A. (1995). Creativity and the third age. *International Journal of Psychoanalysis*, 76, 825–33.

Livingston, G., Blizard, B., & Mann, A. (1993). Does sleep disturbance predict depression in elderly people – a study in inner London. *British Journal of General Practice*, 43(376), 445–8.

Logsdon, R. G., McCurry, S. M., & Teri, L. (2007). Evidence-based psychological treatments for disruptive behaviors in individuals with dementia. *Psychology and Aging*, 22, 28–36.

Lynch, T., Cheavens, J., Cukrowicz, K., Thorp, S., Bronner, L., & Beyer, J. (2007). Treatment of older adults with co-morbid personality disorder and depression: a dialectical behavior therapy approach. *International Journal of Geriatric Psychiatry*, 22(2), 131–43.

McCrae, R., Costa, P., Ostendorf, F., Angleitner, A., Hrebickova, M., Avia, M., *et al.* (2000). Nature over nurture: Temperament, personality and lifespan development. *Journal of Personality and Social Psychology*, 78, 173–86.

McIntosh, J., & Santos, J. (1986). Methods of suicide by age: Sex and race differences among the young and old. *The International Journal of Aging & Human Development*, 22(2), 123–39.

Menninger, J. (2002). Assessment and treatment of alcoholism and substance-related disorders in the elderly. *Bulletin of the Menninger Clinic*, 66(2), 166–83.

Mental Health Commission. (2005). *Annual Report on the Mental Health Services.* Dublin: The Stationery Office.

Mental Health Commission. (2007). *Quality Framework for Mental Health Services in Ireland 2007. Annual Report on the Mental Health Services.* Dublin: The Stationery Office.

Mental Health Foundation, Mind, Rethink, Sainsbury Centre for Mental Health and Young Minds. (2006). *We Need To Talk. The Case for Psychological Therapies on the NHS.* (2006). London: Mental Health Foundation, Mind, Rethink, Sainsbury Centre for Mental Health and Young Minds. (Retrieved 29 July 2010 from http://www.mind.org.uk/assets/0000/1929/weneedtotalkreport.pdf)

Morgan, K. (2008). Sleep and insomnia in later life. In Woods, R., & Clare, L., eds., *The Handbook of Clinical Psychology and Ageing, 2nd ed.* Chichester: Wiley.

Morgan, K., Dixon, S., Mathers, N., Thompson, J., & Tomeny, M. (2004). Psychological treatment for insomnia in the regulation of long-term hypnotic drug use. *National Coordinating Centre for Health Technology Assessment*, 8, 8.

Morin, C. M., Colecchi, C. A., Stone, J., Sood, R., & Brink, D. (1999). Behavioral and pharmacological therapies for late-life insomnia. *Journal of the American Medical Association*, 281, 991–9.

Morse, J., & Lynch, T. (2004). A preliminary investigation of self-reported personality disorders in late life: Prevalence, predictors of depressive severity, and clinical correlates. *Aging & Mental Health*, 8(4), 307–15.

Murphy, S. (2000). Provision of psychotherapy services for older people. *Psychiatric Bulletin*, 74, 181–84.

National Disability Authority/National Council on Ageing and Older People. (2006). *Ageing and Disability: A Discussion Paper.* Dublin: National Disability Authority.

National Council on Ageing and Older People (NCAOP). (2005). *An Age Friendly Society: A Position Statement.* Dublin: National Council on Ageing and Older People.

National Economic and Social Forum. (2006). *Mental Health and Routes to Inclusion.* Dublin: National Economic and Social Forum.

Neulinger, K., & De Leo, D. (2001). Suicide in elderly and youth populations – How do they differ? In De Leo, D., ed., *Suicide and Euthanasia in Older Adults: A Transcultural Journey.* Ashland, OH: Hogrefe & Huber Publishers, pp. 137–53.

O'Donovan, J. (2009). Review of 'Practical management of affective disorders in older people'. *International Psychogeriatrics*, 21(2), 420–1.

O' Shea, E., & Kennelly, B. (2008). *The Economics of Mental Health Care in Ireland.* Dublin: Mental Health Commission. (Retrieved 30 July 2010 from http://www.mhcirl.ie/documents/publications/The_Economics_of_Mental_Health_Care_in_Ireland%202008.pdf)

Oxman, T. E., Dietrich, A. J., & Schulberg, H. C. (2003). The depression care manager and mental health specialist as collaborators within primary care. *American Journal of Geriatric Psychiatry*, 11, 507–16.

Pilling, S., Bebbington, P., Kuipers, E., Garety, P., Geddes, J., Orbach, G., et al. (2002). Psychological treatments in schizophrenia: I. Meta-analysis of family intervention and cognitive behaviour therapy. *Psychological Medicine*, 32(5), 763–82.

Pinquart, M., & Sörensen, S. (2001). How effective are psychotherapeutic and other psychosocial interventions with older adults? A meta-analysis. *Journal of Mental Health and Aging*, 7(2), 207–43.

Powers, C., & Wisocki, P. (1992). Age differences and correlates of worrying in young and elderly adults. *The Gerontologist*, 32(1), 82.

Qualls, S. H., Segal, D. L., Norman, S., Niederehe, G., & Gallagher-Thompson, D. (2002). Psychologists in practice with older adults: Current patterns, sources of training and need for continuing education. *Professional Psychology: Research and Practice*, 33(5), 435–42.

Riedel-Heller, S. G., Busse, A., & Angermeyer, M. C. (2006). The state of mental health in old-age across the 'old' European Union – a systematic review. *Acta Psychiatrica Scandinavica*, 113, 388–401.

Sagan, O. (2008). The loneliness of the long-anxious learner: Mental illness, narrative biography and learning to write. *Psychodynamic Practice*, 14(1), 43–58.

Satre, D. D., Knight, B. G., & David, S. (2006). Cognitive-behavioral interventions with older adults: Integrating clinical and gerontological research. *Professional Psychology: Research and Practice*, 37, 489–98.

Saxena, S., & Maidment, K. M. (2004). Treatment of compulsive hoarding. *Journal of Clinical Psychology*, 60, 1143–54.

Snowdon, J., Shah, A., & Halliday, G. (2007). Severe domestic squalor: A review. *International Psychogeriatrics*, 19(1), 37–51.

Steinberg, J., Karpinski, A., & Alloy, L. (2007). The exploration of implicit aspects of self-esteem in vulnerability – stress models of depression. *Self & Identity*, 6(2/3), 101–17.

Sugarman, L. (2001). *Life-Span Development: Frameworks, Accounts and Strategies, 2nd ed.* Hove: Psychology Press.

Thomas, K., & Shute, R. (2006). The old and mentally ill in Australia: Double stigmatised. *Australian Psychologist*, 41(3), 186–92.

Tracie Shea, M., Edelen, M., Pinto, A., Yen, S., Gunderson, J., Skodol, A., *et al.* (2009). Improvement in borderline personality disorder in relationship to age. *Acta Psychiatrica Scandinavica*, 119(2), 143–8.

Tucker, S., Baldwin, R., Hughes, J., Benbow, S., Barker, A., Burns, A., *et al.* (2007). Old age mental health services in England: Implementing the National Service Framework for Older People. *International Journal of Geriatric Psychiatry*, 22, 211–17.

Unutzer, J., Katon, W., Callahan, C. M., Williams Jr, J. W., Hunkeler, E., Harpole, L., *et al.* (2002).Collaborative care management of late life depression in the primary care setting: A randomized controlled trial. *Journal of the American Medical Association*, 288(22), 2836–45.

Unutzer, J., Tang, L., Oishi, S., Katon, W., Williams Jr, J. W., Hunkeler, E., Hendrie, H., *et al.* (2006). Reducing suicidal ideation in depressed older primary care patients. *Journal of the American Geriatrics Society*, 54, 1550–6.

Van Zelst, W. H., de Beurs, E., Beekman, A. T. F., Deeg, D. J. H., & van Dyck, R. (2003). Prevalence and risk factors of posttraumatic stress disorder in older adults. *Psychotherapy and Psychosomatics*, 72, 333–42.

Van Zelst, W. H., de Beurs, E., Beekman, A. T. F., van Dyck, R., & Deeg, D. J. H. (2006). Well-being, physical functioning and use of health services in the elderly with PTSD and subthreshold PTSD. *International Journal of Geriatric Psychiatry*, 21, 180–8.

Vogt Yuan, A. S. (2007). Perceived age discrimination and mental health. *Social Forces*, 86(1), 291–312.

Wall, J. (2009). *Clinical Psychology and Older Adults.* University of Limerick: Presentation, March 2009.

Wetherell, J. L., Lenze, E. J., & Stanley, M. A. (2005). Evidence-based treatments of geriatric anxiety disorders. *Psychiatric Clinics of North America,* 28, 871–96.

Wheelock, I. (1997). Psychodynamic psychotherapy with the older adult: Challenges facing the patient and the therapist. *American Journal of Psychotherapy,* 51, 431–44.

Wijeratne, C., Brodaty, H., & Hickie, I. (2003). The neglect of somatoform disorders by old age psychiatry: Some explanations and suggestions for future research. *International Journal of Geriatric Psychiatry,* 18, 812–19.

Woods, B. (2008). Suicide and attempted suicide in later life. In Woods, R. T., & Clare, L., eds., *The Handbook of Clinical Psychology and Ageing, 2nd ed.* Chichester: Wiley.

Woods, R. (1995). Psychological treatments. I: Behavioural and cognitive approaches. In Lindesay, J., ed., *Neurotic Disorders in the Elderly.* New York: Oxford University Press.

Woods, R. T., & Roth, A. (1996). Effectiveness of psychological interventions with older people. In Roth, A., & Fonagy, P., eds., *What Works for Whom? A Critical Review of Psychotherapy Research.* New York: Guilford, pp. 321–40.

Woods, R. T., & Roth, A. (2005). Effectiveness of psychological interventions with older people. In Roth, A., & Fonagy, P., eds., *What Works for Whom? A Critical Review of Psychotherapy Research, 2nd ed.* New York. Guilford.

World Health Organization. (2001). *Atlas: Mental Health Resources in the World 2001.* Geneva: WHO.

World Health Organization. (2003). *Investing in Mental Health, A report by the Department of Mental Health and Substance Dependence, Non-communicable Diseases and Mental Health.* Geneva: WHO.

Chapter 6

Ageing and dementia
Assessment and intervention

Olive O'Reilly, Deirbhile Lavin and Barry J. Coughlan

Introduction

Dementia is a syndrome characterised by memory impairment associated with deficits in other cognitive abilities and it is usually accompanied by behavioural disorders leading to a progressive loss of the person's autonomy in common daily activities (Caltagirone *et al.*, 2001). As the condition progresses the person can experience some of the following: memory loss, language impairment, disorientation, changes in personality, difficulties with activities of daily living, self-neglect, psychiatric symptoms such as depression and psychosis, aggression, sleep disturbance, wandering or disinherited behaviour (National Institute for Health and Clinical Excellence, 2006).

Dementia is a broad term for over one hundred diseases (www.alzheimers.org.uk). Among the most common are Alzheimer's disease, vascular dementia, dementia with Lewy bodies and frontotemporal dementia (Jacoby & Oppenheimer, 2002). This chapter provides an overview of some broad assessment and intervention issues and also highlights issues in relation to differential diagnosis and specific forms of dementia. Prior to discussing dementia, relevant theoretical models and psychological principles models that have implications for this area of work will be briefly outlined to assist in contextualising the importance of the issues that follow. Pearce (2002) recommends both a person-centred and context-centred approach when working in this field and this approach is reflected in the discussion that follows.

Bronfenbrenner's ecological systems theory

It is proposed here that Bronfenbrenner's (1993) ecological systems theory has clinical applications in the area of assessment and intervention with clients with dementia. This model takes a broad view of the individual in context in terms of influential and interacting systems. Although initially developed with reference to interacting systems in child development, it has become a very useful model for understanding human ecological influences in general.

Table 6.1 Bronfenbrenner's (1993) ecological systems theory, system levels, description, level of influence, and examples of applications when working with clients with dementia

System level	Description	Level of influence	Possible clinical applications for assessment and intervention in the area of dementia
Microsystem	Relationships and interactions in immediate environment, e.g. family, partner, children	Bi-directional and strongest at this level	Family members available to provide history Availability of carers to assist in the home Adjustment of carers to condition
Mesosystem	Community level such as friends, neighbours, church and connections between microsystems	Bi-directional influence	Assistance available in community for both client and carer
Exosystem	Larger social system in which the individual does not function directly but impacts on the individual's microsystem, e.g. partner/carers work schedule and commitments	Indirect influence not interacting directly but impact individual	Appointment times home/medical centre-based assessment Where can care be provided?
Macrosystem	Cultural values, customs, and laws (Berk, 2000)	Cascading influence throughout the interactions of all other layers	Cultural norms regarding care of elderly, property laws
Chronosyst-em	Encompasses the dimension of time as it relates to the individual's environment(s)	Influence can be external or internal, e.g. loss of partner, or internal, e.g. individual's adjustment to ageing	Economy of the time and spending in health care

The interaction of structures within a layer and interactions of structures between layers is key to this theory. Interaction is viewed as bi-directional, that is the individual is being influenced by and is influencing factors at different system levels. This bi-directional influence is particularly strong at the microsystem level, which reflects the individual's immediate environmental relationships and interactions. In relation to assessment and intervention work with those with dementia the influences at the microsystem level are critical. Table 6.1 gives a brief outline of each system level in terms of description, level of influence and possible clinical applications in this field.

Also, due to the high-level needs of people with dementia particularly in the latter stages, factors at the broader system levels frequently become increasingly significant in terms of influence and have implications for practice. For example at the mesosystem level the availability of centres of assessment; and care for dementia suffers that impacts upon the client and carer at the microsystem level in terms of accessing necessary resources. Also issues at the macrosystem level such as driving laws, cultural norms regarding the care of elderly people will have an impact. Pearce (2002) highlights the significance of these system levels and the impact upon the individual stating that progression of the disease is often associated with progression through environments and services. It could also be argued that because of this progression that those experiencing dementia are subjected to a greater degree of influence from these system levels than an individual experiencing normal ageing.

The chronosystem level was added later as a development of the theory. This addresses internal and external influences relating to time. For example at an internal level the individual's adjustments to later life as a stage of development; and at an external level perhaps the loss of a spouse. These factors have a strong influence on what issues will be relevant at the assessment and intervention stages for people with dementia.

Erikson's psychosocial stages of development

There is a large body of literature on the individuals' adjustment to later life that has implications for assessment and intervention with dementia. Erikson's psychosocial stages of development are applicable in this instance (Erikson, 1968). The relevant stages are old age (60–75 years) and very old age (75 years plus). This model views each lifestage as having its own particular dilemma and main process. In old age the dilemma is labelled as integrity versus despair with a mediating process of introspection that can help to resolve the dilemma. In very old age the dilemma is labelled as immortality versus extinction with the mediating process being social support.

The stage of old age is mastered through a sense of personal integrity, accepting and integrating these into a meaningful narrative enabling them to face death without fear. Where this is not achieved the individual develops a sense of despair (Carr, 2006). In terms of dementia, development has implications for comorbid conditions but also as the cognitive decline continues individuals may lose their ability to recall their personal narrative. Both of these issues are relevant in terms of assessment and intervention as will be highlighted. Erikson (1968) argued that in the final stage of life we face the dilemma of immortality versus distinction. A sense of immortality is achieved for example through a belief in an afterlife or the legacy left behind through achievements and family. Adjustment is greatly enhanced by support at this stage. Also how the individual mastered earlier stages including the infancy stage of trust versus mistrust is of significance, as it will affect the client's formation of relationships with carers. Furthermore some theorists use normal developmental stages to illustrate and aid understanding of client regression and their needs at each stage (Mosey, 1981; 1986, as cited in Jacque & Jackson, 2000; Allen, Earhart & Blue, 1992, as cited in Jacque & Jackson, 2000). This approach is somewhat controversial, and has been criticised as demeaning to the client. However, it is argued that used in conjunction with a person-centred approach, and an acknowledgement of client needs, developmental principles have something to offer in terms of meeting client's changing needs through the stages of dementia.

In keeping with the person-centred approach it is argued that the work of Carl Rogers may be useful when working with this client group. Rogers (1961) emphasises the following principles in relation to client work: unconditional positive regard and an empathetic understanding; and congruence to the client needs (Rogers, 2004). It is argued that these principles may have particular benefits for this group as often their sense of identity and integrity are challenged and their needs, particularly at latter stages of dementia, are met by carers as the clients' ability to communicate and/or meet their own needs fail. Pearce (2002) supports this person-centred emphasis.

In summary of these theoretical issues the needs of the individual, his or her personal development through life and the multiplicity of contextual factors have implications for assessment and intervention in this field. Furthermore Kitwood (1997; as cited in Pearce, 2002: 580) describes good care in dementia as 'person centered care' centring on the 'promotion of comfort, meeting the need for attachment and feelings of inclusion, meaningful occupation, and maintenance of personal identity' highlighting the usefulness of the psychological principles outlined.

In keeping with Bronfenbrenner's ecological model, some contextual issues in relation to ageing and dementia will be discussed next. First, the structure of the population is changing internationally and nationally with the elderly population increasing rapidly (Gelder et al., 2006; Jorm, 2002). This will put significant demands upon services and has implications not only for psychological and psychiatric services but also on wider health services as needs tend to be spread across a number of domains. Gelder et al. (2006: 216) highlights the need to assess, plan and intervene on multiple levels with this client group and subsequently the likely need for 'co-operation of several professionals'. In summary, with an increasing elderly population with significant needs in the area of cognitive impairment and also with cognisance of the needs of this group across multiple levels of care a number of questions are raised such as are we equipped to provide such a service as we move to the future? This is a broader social and political issue yet one that needs to be highlighted among management and professionals working within the services at present. In Ireland the document *A Vision for Change* (Expert Group on Mental Health Policy, 2006: 119) outlines that there are 'major gaps in current mental health services for older people (MHSOP) provision'. There is some optimism within the National Council on Ageing and Older People (2005) in terms of time to plan and develop services accordingly; however within the context of the current economic downturn and health service cutbacks it is probable that professionals will need to highlight these issues in arguing for service provision in the context of competing demands on existing resource budgets.

Diagnostic and assessment issues

The diagnosis of dementia is based on clinical data according to guidelines provided by the *Diagnostic and Statistical Manual of Mental Health Disorders* (DSM–IV; American Psychiatric Association, 2000) and *International Classification of Diseases* (ICD–10; World Health Organization, 1992). In both cases, the diagnosis can be made in the presence of prominent memory deficits usually involving learning, retention and recall of new information. To make a diagnosis of dementia one or more deficits in at least one other cognitive ability such as language, visuo-spatial abilities, reasoning and executive functions must be present besides the memory deficit. These deficits must interfere with the person's social and working activities and must represent a decline compared with his/her previous level of functional abilities.

A number of conceptual and methodological issues in relation to dementia need to be highlighted. First, there are conceptual difficulties in defining dementia as distinct from the 'normal' impact of ageing on cognitive functioning, and also from mild cognitive impairment. Also there are conceptual difficulties in defining the differences between the dementias. This is mainly due to the need for further research in the area, the development of more expertise and for advancement in methods of research. However, these issues have implications for the findings of research studies such as in epidemiological studies creating difficulties in getting an accurate picture of prevalence rates. For example, Erkinjuntti *et al.* (1997) examined prevalence rates and found the rates for dementia varied from 3.1 per cent using ICD–10 criteria to 29.1 per cent using DSM–IV criteria in the same population.

In relation to classification systems and diagnostic criteria these are subject to continuous change and in order to overcome some of the conceptual issues highlighted many researchers develop more stringent criteria for research purposes. Also diagnostic criteria, as outlined by the classification systems, do not allow for mixed dementia, which is thought to account for a substantial portion of cases, posing a further challenge (Thomas & O'Brien, 2002). Furthermore there are also issues relating to the reliability and validity of assessment tools in use. Changing concepts, definitions, classification systems, diagnostic criteria, reliability and validity issues with assessment tools, and the associated methodological difficulties in research highlight the need to keep abreast of changes and developments making it both an exciting and challenging field of work.

Thomas and O'Brien (2002) recommend a two-stage process of assessment of individuals with possible dementia, which not only establishes if dementia is present but also the subtype and possible cause. Clarity of diagnosis is critical in order to enable timely intervention where necessary, prevent unnecessary distress in a case where a decline in relation to normal ageing or apparent dementia is misdiagnosed as dementia or the incorrect form of dementia is diagnosed. This last issue is also critical as incorrect treatment with antipsychotic drugs can be 'harmful and even fatal for those with dementia with Lewy bodies', and appropriate treatment can slow the course of vascular dementia and assist in the treatment of Alzheimer's disease (Thomas & O'Brien, 2002: 508). Therefore clarity of diagnosis is vital for assessment to ensure best care and practice. This involves a thorough assessment; which we consider next with specific emphasis on assessment in dementia.

General principles of assessment of an elderly client include assessment of medical, psychiatric, social and developmental history, history of the presenting concerns (onset, course, descriptions, severity, disruption to daily functioning, impact upon carers/family/others), risk assessment, support available, current medical factors and living, financial and social circumstances, psychological assessment, e.g. clinical interview/mini-mental state examination, the use of screening measures and other services involved.

A thorough physical examination is required and subsequent physical investigations where necessary. A more focused assessment in specific areas is necessary where dementia is concerned. It should be noted also that clients can often present following an illness or change in social/living circumstances when decline in abilities becomes more apparent (Gelder et al., 2006). Factors to consider in the clinical assessment for dementia include presentation (appearance, behaviour, mood, psychosis/paranoia, attention, orientation, language, insight), history of the problems experienced (sudden, progressive, stepped), symptoms (cognitive, behavioural, emotional, social/ occupational functioning), other physical complaints and extensive physical examinations (both routine and investigative regarding reported complaints), personal history (educational, occupational and possible exposure to environmental hazards, alcohol, cigarette and substance misuse) and individual and family medical and psychiatric history (Edgeworth, 2008).

One controversial area at the assessment stage is the involvement of carers/family members, which raises some legal and ethical issues such as confidentiality, e.g. when seeking a collaborative history or consent issues such as capacity to consent to treatment. There may also be legal issues such as the capacity to drive and management of financial affairs that have ethical implications.

When assessing someone with possible dementia first it is critical to clarify what cognitive functioning changes can occur in normal ageing as distinct from the patterns of impairment observed in dementia. This is a controversial issue within the field and the lines that demarcate normal ageing from dementia are somewhat blurred. Some theorists propose a continuum hypothesis; which asserts that dementia is on a continuum with these changes in normal ageing and dementia is represented at 'the most extreme form of the cognitive ageing process' (Milwain & Iversen, 2002: 63). Variances between clinicians on the validity of this theory will impact upon practice. We dispute this hypothesis, however, it does highlight that the onset of dementia can be missed and interpreted as 'normal' ageing and that a diagnosis of dementia does not demarcate 'the boundary between benign and pathological decline' (Milwain & Iversen, 2002: 69).

Overall it is concluded that ageing has some negative implications for cognition particularly in the areas of memory, language and visuo-spatial functions. It is hypothesised that this is because of a decline in the efficiency of the attentional network, which affects functioning throughout the cognitive system but 'does not cause fundamental damage to the cognitive components' thought to underpin the associated functions (Milwain & Iversen, 2002: 62). What differentiates ageing from dementia is the funda-mental damage to these cognitive components and the subsequent pattern of impairment and pathology. Also there are a multitude of reasons for people presenting with decline in cognitive functioning that can look like dementia. Particularly with the elderly population we need to remain cognisant of the possibility that it is as a result of remote causes such as sensory decline or health deterioration (Schaie, 1996, as cited in Milwain & Iversen, 2002). 'Apparent dementia' and 'pseudodementia' are terms used within the field to encompass this area. Some of these issues will be high-lighted further in the discussion that follows that outlines the clinical presentations of dementia and similar conditions from which dementia needs to be differentiated.

Clinical features of dementia

The most common presentation, where dementia may be the cause, usually involves memory difficulties and one or more changes in terms of cognition, behaviour, mood, thinking, perception and insight. Cognitive features are central; and memory loss and forgetfulness are key aspects. Memory loss is more obvious for recent than distant events. Forgetfulness is usually an early symptom and clients typically have difficulty in learning new infor-mation. Impairment of attention and concentration is evident and disorien-tation becomes more prominent in the latter stages. Behavioural changes also occur and again may become more apparent in the latter stages and may be overlooked in the early stages. Disorganised behaviour, restlessness, wandering, inappropriateness, disinhibition and self-neglect are some of the main features. Mood changes in the early stages include increased anxiety, depression and variability of mood. In the latter stages affect is more likely to be blunted, however more extreme variability may also be evident in the latter stages. Thinking abilities deteriorate in terms of speed, judgement and content. Abstract reasoning and flexibility of thinking can be affected in the early stages and in the latter stages thinking becomes incoherent as reflected in speech. Delusions may become apparent. At advanced stages client's utterances can become incomprehensible, meaningless or the client may become mute. Perceptual disturbances in the form of illusions and hallucinations (usually visual) are common as dementia progresses. Individuals usually have a lack of insight into impairments particular in the mid to late stages.

Dementia as a result of degenerative and vascular causes develops gradually, is progressive and irreversible; and reduces life expectancy (Schoenberg et al., 1981). The course of the dementias varies to some degree. Clients are estimated to live on average 8.5 years and approximately two-thirds die in a debilitated state (Keane et al., 2000, as cited in Pearce, 2002). Ritchie and Kildea (1995) found prevalence rates for dementia with a range of 1.5 per cent at age 65 years up to 44.8 per cent at age 95 years. More recent studies show similar rates (e.g. Fratiglioni et al., 1999).

Most dementias are caused by degenerative and vascular causes and are irreversible however it is essential to be cognisant of the range of causes so as not to overlook possible treatable forms (Gelder et al., 2006). Some treatable causes of 'apparent dementia' include depression, delirium, cerebral tumour, hypothyroidism, vitamin B_{12} or folic acid deficiency and renal failure. It is estimated that up to 10 per cent of clients first thought to have dementia will have a treatable form of 'apparent dementia' (Gelder et al., 2006). In relation to the area of differential diagnosis two areas warrant particular mentioning: delirium and depression. The clinical features of both of these presentations share similarities and therefore there is a need for a thorough assessment.

Other case-management factors to consider where the individual does not meet the criteria for a dementia is whether there is evidence of mild cognitive impairment. Mild cognitive impairment is a term used to describe the 'transitional state between cognition associated with normal ageing and mild dementia' where the client is experiencing some cognitive impairment but impairment is not sufficient to interfere with activities of daily living and warrant diagnosis (Zaudig, 2002: 387). The presence of mild cognitive impairment highlights the need for case monitoring and continuous case review to enable the client to avail of timely interventions if or when necessary.

We will now provide the reader with a flavour of some of the complex issues involved in assessment and intervention in relation to specific forms of dementia. There are a number of issues that need to be highlighted in relation to Alzheimer's disease. Epidemiological studies have shown that Alzheimer's is the most prevalent form of dementia (Fratiglioni et al., 1999). First, in relation to the issue of diagnostic differentials it is possible that some cases are diagnosed by default due to these high prevalence rates, which in turn leads to an increase in prevalence rates in studies where case registers are used as the source of data. Second, Alzheimer's disease can only be given as a definite diagnosis following examination of brain tissue. Although this procedure can be performed while patients are living it poses high risks and is unnecessarily invasive. Therefore a probable diagnosis is usually given.

Vascular dementia is a controversial area and the usefulness of the diagnostic category has been called into question by the findings of numerous research studies (Stewart, 2002). Vascular dementia can be defined as dementia due to vascular causes. Its main clinical features include: a stepwise progression, patchy impairment of cognitive functioning, seizures, episodes of confusion and personality change (Gelder et al., 2006). Stewart (2002: 534) argues that the 'diagnostic categories underestimate the contribution of vascular pathology to dementia, does not accurately represent mixed pathology and makes assumptions about causality that may not be biologically valid'. A useful suggestion made is to use the traditional diagnostic formulation, diagnosing dementia as the principal diagnosis and including vascular disease as a factor predisposing, precipitating and/or maintaining the experienced difficulties. This broad approach allows for the acknowledgement of case-specific factors rather than assuming a broad term that is not clearly defined. Taking this approach a number of established risk factors are of significance. Stroke is an established risk factor in that it predicts cognitive impairment (Ferrucci et al., 1996) and dementia following stroke predicts further stroke episodes (Moroney et al., 1997). In identification of further risk factors clinicians look towards risk factors for cerebrovascular disease, which include hypertension, cholesterol levels and diabetes. Although treatments are limited, Stewart (2002) argues for preventative measures such as targeting these population risk factors while also acknowledging the dearth of research in this area. Some evidence such as the positive effect of cholesterol-lowering agents in preventing dementia raises hope for future preventative interventions in this area (Jick et al., 2000; Wolozin et al., 2000).

Lewy bodies are neuronal inclusion bodies found in the cerebral cortex and substantia nigra of the brain. These bodies can be present in the brain without impinging upon functioning to a degree to warrant diagnosis, however where a large number are present dementia results (McShane, 2002) Lewy body disease may be distinguished from Alzheimer's by its fluctuating course, the occurrence of hallucinations (especially visual), delusions and signs of parkinsonism. These are four broadly recognised patterns of dementia pathology where there is the significant presence of Lewy bodies:

1   dementia with Parkinson's disease;
2   dementia with Lewy bodies;
3   diffuse Lewy bodies disease or 'pure dementia with Lewy bodies';
4   Lewy bodies with Alzheimer's disease.

Although we need to be cognisant of the different forms yet again there is a lack of clarity between these categories. Diffuse Lewy bodies disease or 'pure dementia with Lewy bodies' is very rare. Of those that develop Parkinson's disease it is estimated that approximately 15 per cent develop dementia characterised by poor attention and memory, impaired reasoning, visuo-spatial deficits and executive function deficits (Edgeworth, 2008).

Frontotemporal dementia (FTD) is caused by a degenerative disease predominately affecting the frontal and temporal lobes. It is estimated to account for approximately 10 per cent of all dementias and 20 per cent of presenile dementia (Edgeworth, 2008). Its main clinical features include: concentration and attention difficulties; poor abstraction; minor IQ change; distractible; disinhibition; motor impairment; dietary changes; stereotyped/ utilisation behaviours; compulsive behaviours; anxiety; depression; emotional bluntness and lack of insight. The mean age of onset being 56 (±7.6) years and mean duration 8 (±3.4) years (Gustafson, 1993, cited in Gustafson, 2002). Early FTD is characterised by behavioural, speech (expressive) and personality deterioration rather than cognitive impairment, although memory and cognitive impairment are almost always affected but become more apparent in later stages.

The issues for assessment in relation to FTD are cognisance of presenile onset and the importance of early and specific diagnosis. Also there are difficulties in tracking its course due to subclassification and patient variation in stage progression adding to the difficulties in relation to diagnostics and planning for intervention (Gustafson, 2002). There is a need for physical activity to assist with restlessness and impulsivity, also preserved memory, spatial and practical abilities, particularly in the early stages, need to be channelled in a meaningful ways for the client (Gustafson, 2002). Family intervention issues include assistance to support the family in addressing hereditary factors and also long-term care. These factors highlight the need for regular review and both a person-centred and context-centred approach in this area.

In summary of the issues of importance in relation to assessment and intervention with specific forms of dementia those that stand out from the literature are: the need for thorough and early assessment, the need for an in-depth knowledge of the differentiating features and the importance of clarity of diagnosis to guide appropriate intervention.

Psychological intervention

There is no means of curing dementia or preventing its ultimate progression. Current pharmacological treatment can modify symptoms but not the disease (e.g. cholinesterase inhibitors have been found to improve cognitive and functioning scales; Brayne *et al.*, 2007). However, there is a great deal from a psychosocial perspective that can be achieved and current treatments have concentrated on ameliorating the impact of dementia on patient's behavioural and cognitive resources and improving quality of life.

Impact of diagnosis

The current question of disclosure of the diagnosis of dementia to the patient has become of greater significance in recent years due to an emphasis on early detection of the disorder. National Institute for Health and Clinical Excellence guidelines (2006) state that the patient and family should be given full information and education about its nature and the progression of the disease unless the person with dementia specifically requests not to receive it. Clare (2003) points out that a diagnosis of dementia is a devastating experience that strikes at the core of the self and close relationships. Robinson and colleagues (2005), who conducted a qualitative analysis of couples' reactions to the diagnosis of dementia, highlight a cyclical process of denial, minimisation and gradual realisation where the couples gradually begin to accept the permanent changes in the individual with dementia. After a period of time couples then can focus on what remains and where to go from there. Husband (1999) highlighted that disclosing a diagnosis of dementia in a single session does not adequately meet the psychological needs of the person. Therapeutic counselling at this point is important in dealing with anxiety and depression, challenging cognitions such as catastrophising, self-stigmatisation (e.g. I am stupid/ mad) and social withdrawal.

Cognitive rehabilitation

There are specific types of memory impairment apparent in those with early-stage dementia. There is a marked change in episodic memory (Brandt & Rich, 1995) that allows people to remember events that have happened in their life and link these with the context in which they were experienced. Semantic memory (the person's stored knowledge about the world) is much more resistant and this can be used to help combat the effects of episodic memory loss. For example, people with dementia can be directly taught new semantic information that supports everyday functioning such as the names of the people they need to interact with frequently or a set of directions to somewhere they need to visit regularly. Learning can be facilitated by specific techniques that maximise encoding and retrieval (Bäckman, 1992). At the point of learning a person with dementia may require more learning trials and more guidance in encoding the material as well as more retrieval cues (Woods, 1999). A training technique such as 'spaced retrieval' where material is recalled after gradually increasing the interval can be helpful.

Compensatory strategies or behavioural strategies can also be used. Prompting and fading (giving cues and reminders, decreasing in frequency as the idea becomes more familiar) may be effective or the use of a memory board or a calendar can reduce the need to repeatedly question the caregiver. Implicit skills (memory for skills and routines), despite of dementia, are also maintained. This can be used to help people re-learn certain skills or manage them better (e.g. washing, dressing, making a cup to tea).

Research evaluating cognitive rehabilitation strategies shows some support for their effectiveness. Orrell and colleagues (2007) found that three out of four randomised controlled trials showed some positive results where there were early behavioural improvements in clients. However after 9 months there were no significant differences between intervention and control groups.

Reality orientation therapy

The aim of this therapy is to orient patients in their environment with continuous stimulation. In sessions clients concentrate on learning each other's names and information about the day, date and weather is included. Symbols are used more often than words and a weatherboard is used to focus the attention of the clients. Reality orientation can be implemented on a 24-hour or a classroom basis and ideally these approaches are used in combination. One of the criticisms of this therapy is that it lacks a person-centred approach and is over-reliant on cognitive aspects (Woods, 1996). There are also different ideas about who benefits the most from reality orientation. Scott and Clare (2003) report on conflicting studies that find evidence for and against the use of reality orientation in those with advanced stages of dementia. Overall evidence from meta-analyses (Orrell et al., 2007; Bates et al., 2004) suggest that changes in cognitive functioning may be observed with reality orientation. However, these were limited to the information given in the sessions, with changes in behaviour and general functioning harder to detect (Scott & Clare, 2003).

Reminiscence therapy

Reminiscence therapy encourages patients to share memories stimulated by newspaper files, photographs and other resources. In this sense it gives the person with dementia an opportunity for social interaction and enjoyment.

It allows the individual to make use of remote memories that are more accessible than newer memories and hence strengthens the sense of self. There is limited evidence to suggest the efficacy of this approach (Orrell *et al.*, 2007, report only five studies). In general studies have failed to find significant changes in cognition or functioning following reminiscence therapy. However, one study by Goldwasser and colleagues (1987) did find an initial decrease in depression but this rose again following completion of the intervention.

Validation therapy

Validation therapy (Feil, 1992) addresses the patient's need to maintain contact with the environment by confirming the patient's internal emotional state rather than focusing on an external environmental orientation. It is based around the idea that events in the past influence present feelings and behaviour so it is important to acknowledge the feelings people are experiencing even though their factual statements may be incorrect. Topics covered may include anger, separation and loss with the aim of allowing members to verbalise unresolved feelings and conflicts. Meta-analyses report a paucity of studies on validation therapy; Orrell *et al.* (2007) found three studies. Results did not find any significant improvements in individuals who engaged in validation therapy

Sensory integration therapy

Approaches such as music therapy, art therapy and snoezelan therapy (multisensory stimulation) have been implemented with people with dementia. Results of their effectiveness have demonstrated that these therapies can be effective in ameliorating disruptive behaviour during and after the intervention and decrease levels of agitation (Orrell *et al.*, 2007). However, the effects are apparent only for a very short time after the session (Midence & Cunliffe, 1996).

Behavioural interventions

Behavioural difficulties in people with dementia may include incontinence, aggression, eating difficulties, personal hygiene and wandering. Responding appropriately to behavioural problems has a significant impact on the person suffering with dementia and it is important to take an individualised approach to intervention. Two people for example may show aggression in different ways or in different circumstances (Woods, 1999) and a thorough assessment of the individual situation should be conducted.

Assessment of the situation should take on board the following factors.

- Physical health: is the person in pain? What are the effects of the medication?
- Neuropsychological problems: does the person recognise the toilet, have a dressing dyspraxia?
- Environmental factors: e.g. does the person find the room too noisy, is the layout confusing?
- Emotional factors: is the person feeling anxious and insecure?
- Abnormal factors: is the person experiencing hallucinations/delusions?
- Interpersonal factors: does the person respond differently to different staff or approaches?

Intervention can then be tailored specifically for the individual and will draw on aspects of behavioural theory such as classical conditioning, operant conditioning or intermittent reinforcement. Specific interventions may include changing the environment, establishing consistent routines, reinforcement programmes such as tokens, scheduling pleasant activities, addressing interpersonal interactions and relaxation strategies.

Meta-analysis studies of behavioural interventions have shown strong support. Orrell *et al.* (2007) identified 25 studies and found encouraging results. Findings from the larger randomised controlled trials were consistent and positive and significant improvements were found in individuals' behaviour and there were reductions in caregiver distress and this effect was found to last for several months.

Working with families and caregivers

Caregiving for people with dementia places people under considerable risk with regard to their own health and emotional well-being. Livingston and colleagues (1996) reported that 47 per cent of those caring for people with dementia were depressed compared with only 3 per cent caring for someone with physical health problems. Caregiver distress can be associated with the breakdown of care and institutionalisation for the care recipient.

Edwards and colleagues (2002) advocate that any intervention with caregivers must assess the unique stressors, resources and values of the caregiver and tailor interventions to specific problems and concerns. For example, caregivers may find problems stressful to varying degrees (e.g. some people may find incontinence difficult whereas other people may not be bothered by it). Secondary stressors may also be different in different contexts where for example holding down a job may add to one person's stress but could also be an outlet for another person.

Education is an important treatment strategy with caregivers and highlights what information they already know about their relative's illness, the implications of the illness and the long-term care options. Often caregivers may misinterpret symptoms of the illness (e.g. see the person they are looking after repeatedly asking them questions as that person deliberately trying to aggravate them). Caregivers may also need to understand that their relative can no longer manage independently and they need to take charge of the situation. Selwood and colleagues (2007) reported that studies evaluating generic education programmes (often in a group setting) have not found significant improvements in caregiver well-being. However, Orrell *et al.* (2007) report that when specific kinds of education are given, that is tailored to the individual, significant benefits are found.

Teaching caregivers behavioural strategies that help them respond appropriately to difficult behaviours can help bring a variety of everyday problems under control and thus reduce caregiver stress. There is strong evidence to show the effectiveness of this approach (Selwood *et al.*, 2007; Orrell *et al.*, 2007). For example, Selwood *et al.* (2007) found that six sessions or more of individual behavioural management therapy is an effective intervention in improving caregiver depression for up to 32 months. Of note, group behavioural management therapy was not found to be effective. It is thought that teaching general principles of managing behaviour rather than how to manage specific behaviour is not efficacious.

Counselling for caregivers (both group and individual) has also been found to be effective in alleviating caregiver distress and depression immediately and for some months after the intervention (Selwood *et al.*, 2007). Caregivers often need support in relation to a relative moving into residential care, as evidence shows that family members still experience significant distress although the nature and focus of the stress changes (Zarit & Whitlatch, 1993). Families are often keen to still be involved in care and Clare (2003) highlights the development of training materials to allow staff and families to come together and understand each other's perspective. Support groups that involve a discussion format to offer a combination of education, emotional support and practical assistance (Yale, 1995) are also available for caregivers and have gained in popularity. There are, however, no formal studies evaluating its effectiveness.

Table 6.2 provides an overview of possible carer and individual interventions in this area. It shows that carers' needs are a significant issue and indicates the extent of services needed across a number of system levels.

The importance of carer/family involvement is reflected in the extent of the literature in the area. There are a number of issues to be highlighted beyond the ethical and legal issues outlined earlier. These include the barriers to involvement such as denial, lack of insight, capacity and the cultural meaning for the individual carers, families and cultural groups. Clinicians need to be aware of these issues when working with carers and families. Many interventions are also needed at the family level; these include practical strategies to assist/reduce carer and family stress, and aid

Table 6.2 An overview of some interventions for use with carers and
sufferers of dementia

Systemic and social intervention measure	Examples
Psychosocial treatments	Self-care, e.g. nutrition
	Social contact
	Programme of activities including pleasurable activities
	Informing of diagnosis, available services, support, principles of care, psychoeducation
	Behavioural programmes
Functional interventions	Early advice and monitoring, structure to daily routine, memory aids, reduction in complexity of tasks and optimising communication
Legal and financial	Financial planning assistance/advice
	Driving
	Capacity
Social Services	Domiciliary and palliative care, counselling
	Day care
	Residential and nursing care, respite care
Voluntary services	Alzheimer's Association Carers Groups
Medical Team	Regular reviews
	Pharmacological interventions
Family	Interventions such as counselling to assist in supporting families in dealing with the impact upon family relationships and wider social relationships
	Problem-focused interventions to address abuse and/or neglect issues

their adjustment to the reduced ability of the client in many areas of functioning including communication and also adjustment to the impact of dementia on the relationship (Jacoby & Oppenheimer, 2002).

One important issue beyond diagnosis is the need for continuous assessment, incorporating many of the principles outlined earlier and revision of interventions as appropriate. In this context it is vital that the outcomes of plans and interventions are identified, monitored and adjusted as necessary. This requires a commitment and coordination of staff. Pearce (2002) highlights that it is often necessary to draw upon a full range of local and specialist services when planning interventions in order to assist both carers and the cared for, and addresses the importance of liaison between the care settings, a range of services, family, carers and staff. Frequently there is also a need to reconcile the best interests of the patient with those of carers, raising a further ethical issue. Overall in terms of the range of possible interventions the issue to be highlighted here for clinicians working in the field is that the ability of a mental health team to implement these measures depends upon multiple factors at each of the system levels from immediate environmental factors at the microsystem level to the macrosystem level, taking into account chronosystem influences.

Conclusion

In conclusion this chapter argues for both a person-centred and context-centred approach to assessment and intervention within the area of dementia. A number of psychological models and theories were drawn upon to illuminate these issues. As stated this field of study is broad and under continuous development; expertise will continue to develop, theories will continue to be generated and expanded, classification systems and diagnostic criteria be refined, studies will continue to contradict, clinical practice will change and methods of research and assessment will advance. However, it is argued that a context- and person-centred approach is the key to advancement and best practice. It is hoped that this chapter has provided an overview of some of the current issues for assessment and intervention when practising within the field of dementia.

References

American Psychiatric Association. (2000). *Diagnostic and Statistical Manual of Mental Health Disorders, 4th edn, Text Revision*. Washington, DC: American Psychiatric Association.

Bäckman, L. (1992). *Memory Functioning in Dementia*. Oxford: North-Holland.

Bates, J., Boote, J., & Beverley, C. (2004). Integrative literature reviews and meta-analyses. Psychosocial interventions for people with a milder dementing illness: a systematic review. *Journal of Advanced Nursing*, 45(6), 644–58.

Berk, L. (2000) *Child Development, 5th ed*. Boston: Allyn & Bacon.

Brandt, J., & Rich, J. (1995). Memory disorders in the dementias. In Baddeley, A. D., Wilson, B. A., & Watts, F. N., eds., *Handbook of Memory Disorders*. Chichester: John Wiley & Sons, pp. 243–70.

Brayne, C., Fox, C., & Boustani, M. (2007). Dementia screening in primary care. *Journal of the American Medical Association*, 298(20), 2409–11.

Bronfenbrenner, U. (1993). The ecology of cognitive development. In Wozniak, R. H., & Fischer, K. W., eds., *Development in Context: Acting and Thinking in Specific Environments*. Hillsdale, NJ: Lawrence Erlbaum Associates, Inc.

Caltagirone, C., Perri, R., Carlesimo, G., & Fadda, L. (2001). Early detection and diagnosis of dementia. *Archives of Gerontology and Geriatrics Suppl.*, 33, 67–75.

Carr, A. (2006). *The Handbook of Child and Adolescent Clinical Psychology, 2nd ed*. London: Routledge.

Clare, L. (2003). Cognitive training and cognitive rehabilitation for people with early-stage dementia. *Reviews in Clinical Gerontology*, 13(1), 75–83.

Edgeworth, J. (2008). *Neuropsychology and Older Adults*. University of Limerick: Department of Education and Professional Studies & Beaumont Hospital, Dublin, Ireland.

Edwards, A., Zarit, S., Stephens, M., & Townsend, A. (2002). Employed family caregivers of cognitively impaired elderly: An examination of role strain and depressive symptoms. *Aging & Mental Health*, 6(1), 55–61.

Erikson, E. (1968). *Identity: Youth and Crisis*. Oxford: Norton & Co.

Erkinjuntti, T., Ostbye, T., Steenhuis, R., & Hachinski, V. (1997). The effect of different diagnostic criteria on the prevalence of dementia. *New England Journal of Medicine*, 337(23), 1667–74.

Expert Group on Mental Health Policy. (2006). *A Vision for Change: Report of the Expert Group on Mental Health Policy.* Dublin: Department of Health and Children. (Retrieved 30 July 2010 from http://www.dohc.ie/publications/pdf/ vision_for_change.pdf)

Feil, N. (1992). Validation therapy with late-onset dementia populations. In Jones, G., & Miesen, B. M. L., eds., *Care-giving in Dementia: Research and Applications.* New York: Routledge, pp. 199–218.

Ferrucci, L., Guralnik, J., Salive, M., Pahor, M., Corti, M. C., Baroni, A., *et al.* (1996). Cognitive impairment and risk of stroke in the older population. *Journal of the American Geriatrics Society*, 44(3), 237–41.

Fratiglioni, L., de Ronchi, D., & Agüero Torres, H. (1999). Worldwide prevalence and incidence of dementia. *Drugs & Aging*, 15, 365–75.

Gelder, M., Mayou, R., & Geddes, J. (2006). *Psychiatry, 3rd ed.* Oxford: Oxford University Press.

Goldwasser, A., Auerbach, S., & Harkins, S. (1987). Cognitive, affective, and behavioral effects of reminiscence group therapy on demented elderly. *The International Journal of Aging & Human Development*, 25(3), 209–22.

Gustafson, L. (2002). Frontotemporal dementia. In Jacoby, R., & Oppenheimer, C., eds., *Psychiatry in the Elderly, 3rd ed.* Oxford: Oxford University Press.

Husband, H. (1999). The psychological consequences of learning a diagnosis of dementia: three case examples. *Aging & Mental Health*, 3(2), 179–83.

Jacoby, R., & Oppenheimer, C. (2002). *Psychiatry in the Elderly, 3rd ed.* Oxford: Oxford University Press.

Jacque, A., & Jackson, G. A. (2000). *Understanding Dementia, 3rd ed.* Edinburgh: Churchill Livingston.

Jick, H., Zornberg, G., Jick, S., Seshadri, S., & Drachman, D. (2000). Statins and the risk of dementia. *Lancet*, 356(9242), 1627–31.

Jorm, A. (2002). Epidemiology of the dementias of late life. In Jacoby, R., & Oppenheimer, C., eds., *Psychiatry in the Elderly, 3rd ed.* Oxford: Oxford University Press.

Kitwood, T. (1997). The experience of dementia. *Aging & Mental Health*, 1(1), 13–22.

Livingston, G., Manela, M., & Katona, C. (1996). Cost of community care for older people. *British Journal of Psychiatry*, 171, 56–9.

McShane, R. (2002). Dementia with Parkinson's disease and dementia with Lewy bodies. In Jacoby, R., & Oppenheimer, C., eds., *Psychiatry in the Elderly, 3rd ed.* Oxford: Oxford University Press.

Midence, K., & Cunliffe, L. (1996). The impact of dementia on the sufferer and available treatment interventions: An overview. *Journal of Psychology*, 130(6), 589.

Milwain, E., & Iversen, S. (2002). Cognitive change in old age. In Jacoby, R., & Oppenheimer, C., eds., *Psychiatry in the Elderly, 3rd ed.* Oxford: Oxford University Press.

Moroney, J., Bagiella, E., Desmond, D., Hachinski, V., Mölsä, P., Gustafson, L., *et al.* (1997). Meta-analysis of the Hachinski Ischemic Score in pathologically verified dementias. *Neurology*, 49(4), 1096–105.

National Council on Ageing and Older People. (2005). *An Age Friendly Society – A Position Statement.* Dublin, National Council on Ageing and Older People. (Retrieved 19 April 2008 from http://www.ncaop.ie/newsevents/88_AFS_Statement.pdf)

National Institute for Health and Clinical Excellence. (2006). *Dementia: Supporting People with Dementia and their Carers in Health and Social Care. NICE Clinical Guideline 42.* London: National Institute for Health and Clinical Excellence.

Orrell, M., Hancock, G., Hoe, J., Woods, B., Livingston, G., & Challis, D. (2007). A cluster randomised controlled trial to reduce the unmet needs of people with dementia living in residential care. *International Journal of Geriatric Psychiatry,* 22(11), 1127–34.

Pearce, J. (2002). The management of dementia. In Jacoby, R., & Oppenheimer, C., eds., *Psychiatry in the Elderly, 3rd ed.* Oxford: Oxford University Press.

Ritchie, K., & Kildea, D. (1995). Is senile dementia 'age-related' or 'ageing-related'? – evidence from meta-analysis of dementia. *Lancet,* 346(8980), 931–4.

Robinson, L., Clare, L., & Evans, K. (2005). Making sense of dementia and adjusting to loss: Psychological reactions to a diagnosis of dementia in couples. *Aging & Mental Health,* 9(4), 337–47.

Rogers, C. (1961). The process equation of psychotherapy. *American Journal of Psychotherapy,* 15, 27–45.

Rogers, C. (2004). *On Becoming a Person: A Therapist's View of Psychotherapy.* London: Constable & Company.

Schoenberg, B. S., Okazaki, H., & Kokmen, E. (1981). Reduced survival in patients with dementia: a population study. *Transactions of the American Neurological Association,* 106, 306–8.

Scott, J., & Clare, L. (2003). Do people with dementia benefit from psychological interventions offered on a group basis? *Clinical Psychology & Psychotherapy,* 10(3), 186–96.

Selwood, A., Johnston, K., Katona, C., Lyketsos, C., & Livingston, G. (2007). Systematic review of the effect of psychological interventions on family caregivers of people with dementia. *Journal of Affective Disorders,* 101(1–3), 75–89.

Stewart, R. (2002). Vascular dementia. In Jacoby, R., & Oppenheimer, C., eds., *Psychiatry in the Elderly, 3rd ed.* Oxford: Oxford University Press.

Thomas, A. J., & O'Brien, J. T. (2002). Alzheimer's disease. In Jacoby, R., & Oppenheimer, C., eds., *Psychiatry in the Elderly, 3rd ed.* Oxford: Oxford University Press.

Wolozin, B., Kellman, W., Ruosseau, P., Celesia, G. G., & Siegal, G. (2000). Decreased prevalence of Alzheimer disease associated with 3-hydroxy-3-methyglutaryl coenzyme A reductase inhibitors. *Archives of Neurology,* 57, 1439–43.

Woods, R. (1996). Psychological 'therapies' in dementia. In Woods, R., & Clare, L., eds., *Handbook of the Clinical Psychology of Ageing.* Chichester: John Wiley & Sons, pp. 575–600.

Woods, R. (1999). The person in dementia care. *Generations,* 23(3), 35.

World Health Organization. (1992). *The ICD-10 Classification of Mental and Behavioural Disorders. Clinical Descriptions and Diagnostic Guidelines.* Geneva: WHO.

Yale, R. (1995). *Developing Support Groups for Individuals with Early-stage*

Alzheimer's Disease: Planning Implementation and Evaluation. Baltimore, MD: Health Professions Press.

Zarit, S., & Whitlatch, C. (1993). The effects of placement in nursing homes on family caregivers: Short and long term consequences. *Irish Journal of Psychology*, 14(1), 25–37.

Zaudig, M. (2002). Mild cognitive impairment in the elderly. *Current Opinion in Psychiatry*, 15(4), 387–93.

Chapter 7

Older adults' experience of loss, bereavement and grief

Patrick Ryan, Barry J. Coughlan, Zarqa Shahid and Cian Aherne

Introduction

Ageing involves the potential experience of psychological, physiological and sociocultural declines, which may render older people more vulnerable and more exposed to risk factors for developing mental health problems. Older adults are also more likely to suffer losses and bereavement (Osgood, 1992). As individuals, however, they are likely to take the same amount of time as other age groups to return to baseline personal functioning following bereavement. Normal ageing is not necessarily associated with psychopathology and may, in fact, be associated with resilience (Greve & Staudinger, 2006). Theories about successful ageing, including the selective optimisation with compensation theory (Baltes & Dickson, 2001), lifespan theory (Takahashi, 2005) and dual-process model/theory of accommodation and assimilation (Caserta & Lund, 2007), elaborate goal changes with age due to loss of resources, highlighting goal selectivity where people move away from developmental goals of growth towards goals of maintenance and regulation of loss.

Taking these into consideration, it could be argued that older individuals may adapt to increasingly salient resource limitations in late age by employing available resources more effectively in the interest of their goals. This explains how older adults cope and manage even though they live with objectively more pronounced resource limitations (Preyde *et al.*, 2009). The different theories and perspectives that have been suggested in order to understand ageing and experience of loss propose that although expectations about gains and losses co-exist throughout life, there is an age-related shift in expected developmental change from a predominance of gains in early adulthood to increasing losses in old age. Finally, when a developmental phenomenon, such as age-related loss, is addressed, a theoretical framework of coping and adaptation that incorporates a developmental component is important. The conceptual framework that attempts to explain resilience in old age in terms of the dual process of accommodative and assimilative coping (e.g. Heckhausen, 1997; Brandtstädter & Rothermund, 2002) focuses on the interplay between active interventions and adjustment of personal goals and standards to changing action resources.

Loss and grief: definitions

Bereavement is the state of having suffered a loss. It is defined as a fundamentally biological, behavioural, cognitive and emotional process. It is a response of individuals in situations of crisis, trauma, and stress. Bereavement is caused by detachment from the deceased person (Paletti, 2008). Grief can be defined as the experience of one who has lost a loved one to death and mourning is the process of adapting to loss (Enright & Marwit, 2002).

Bereavement may be thought of as a continuum from 'uncomplicated' to 'pathological' (Rosenzweig et al., 1997). The *Diagnostic and Statistical Manual of Mental Disorders* (DSM–IV) labels a complicated reaction to the perception of loss as complicated bereavement rather than as complicated grief (American Psychiatric Association, 1994). Studies on loss brought new terminology to explain the phenomena; for example, anticipatory grief (Schoenberg et al., 1970), grief work (Worden, 2009), cultural variations in bereavement (Rosenblatt et al., 1972), complicated mourning (Rando, 1992, 1993), disenfranchised grief (Doka, 1986) and transcendence of loss (Weenolsen, 1988). The ultimate goal in contending with any major loss is for the individual experiencing it to be able to recognise it and to make necessary internal (psychological) and external (behavioural and social) changes to incorporate that loss into his/her ongoing life. Accommodation or adaptation to loss refers to re-adjustment to the absence of what has been lost. Lehmann, Jimerson, and Gaasch (2001) suggest that there are a range of tasks involved in healthy grieving including establishing facts, identifying related changes and finding help.

Bereavement is an increasingly frequent experience as people grow older, which makes it important to the psychology of ageing (Osgood, 1992). Death is truly an old age issue and is associated with a pre-existing period of disability. In a Canadian survey of seniors, 19 per cent of individuals, aged 70 years and over, reported experiencing the death of a close relative during the previous six months (Dalby et al., 1999). The World Health Organization (WHO) indicates that healthy life expectancy in developing countries lags by 7–10 years behind actual life expectancy for men and women (WHO, 2006). The most common causes of death in those aged 65 years or over in the European Union (Niederlander, 2006), USA (WHO, 2006) and Australia (Australian Bureau of Statistics, 2006) are circulatory disease, cancer, and respiratory diseases.

Loss – more than just the experience of death

Loss is an inevitable consequence of ageing. Losses for older people can be cumulative and may include loss of health and functioning (including hearing, vision and other communication abilities), financial difficulties, loss of autonomy, loss of social networks, loss of relationships and loss of independence. In addition, significant life events; for example, retirement and relocation of homes etc, are also commonly experienced by older adults. Examples of biological events are developmental changes in the endocrine system or in the nervous system. Among other losses, dementia is one of the serious disorders of later life, affecting 5 per cent of people over 65 years of age (Pendlebury & Rothwell, 2009).

Multiple losses can represent a substantial threat to the individuals' identity and may result in profoundly increasing their disorientation and distress. Compensatory activities are important in maintaining a positive balance of gains and losses in later life (Baltes & Lang, 1997; Marsiske *et al.*, 1995), however, with fading resources it becomes increasingly difficult to maintain a desired level of functioning and the cost–benefit ratio of compensatory efforts may become increasingly unfavourable when such efforts approach the limits of resources or exhaust reserve capacities (Baltes & Lindenberger, 1988; Brandtstädter & Rothermund, 2002; Brandtstädter & Wentura, 1995). This makes it more difficult to preserve a positive outlook about the self and personal development (Brandtstädter & Rothermund, 2002; Brandtstädter *et al.*, 1999; Brandtstädter *et al.*, 1993; Heckhausen, 1997).

Age-graded and ontogenetic changes tend to curtail the physical, temporal, and psychological resources that can be deployed or preventive, compensatory and optimising efforts (Baltes & Lang, 1997; Brandtstädter *et al.*, 2003; Hobfoll & Wells, 1998); for example, memory training procedures have been found to produce decreasing gains in performance with advancing age (Kliegl *et al.*, 1989). Furthermore, the efficient use of compensatory aids may be hampered by age-related losses in cognitive and sensory functioning (Li *et al.*, 2001; Lindenberger *et al.*, 2000). They all affect the direction life takes and life events play a role in regulating the nature of developmental change (Brim *et al.*, 2004; Hultsch *et al.*, 1976).

Although the management of loss is envisioned as the most private and personal of life transitions, the psychological and social consequences of loss are inextricably linked to prevailing macro social conditions and experiences of loss can affect individuals in a variety of ways. For instance, ageing can entail losing family and friends to death thus affecting social resources and cumulative losses can put individuals at risk for social isolation (Meis, 2005). Butcher and McGonigal-Kenney (2005: 54) summarised the risk factors for depression in older adults. These are: 'living alone, having little or no social support, being unmarried/widowed, going through recent bereavement, enduring chronic pain, being a care giver, having a history of depression/ chronic illness, fearing death, abusing substances, having a history of suicide attempts or having a functional disability such as loss of mobility/vision (especially a recent loss)'. Difficulty in later life, in identifying losses when a person is still alive (i.e. in the case of psychosocial, cognitive functioning or other physical impairments) makes the psychology of ageing further complicated.

All humans grieve a loss to one degree or another; there is no 'right' or 'wrong' way to grieve. Attempts to describe the stages of grief have resulted in numerous theories that do not adequately capture the grief process in a given individual. The phases are often presented as static, sequential steps of grief, when in fact the process appears to be more fluid and non-linear (Hayes et al., 2007).

Three stages, however, have been outlined consistently by several researchers (Zisook & Shuchter, 1992). Despite a wide variety of individual grief experience and regardless of age, there is some consensus as to these typical experiences/symptoms among the bereaved.

1   Initial shock and disbelief.
2   An acute mourning phase, involving emotional, somatic discomfort and social withdrawal.
3   A restitution phase where the individual establishes new roles and is able to go on living (Zisook & Shuchter, 1992).

It is when these experiences are not part of the grief process or when they are present but prolonged that individuals can be described as having difficulties in the management of their grief.

Management of loss in older adults

Grieving is a normal process but nonetheless can be associated with considerable psychiatric morbidity. The experience of loss and grief has been identified as a risk factor for the development of mental health problems (Jacobs, 1993; Zisook et al., 1997). It is widely accepted that experience of irreversible loss in old age has a negative impact on subjective life quality. Research findings in this area are quite inconclusive suggesting that ageing plays a mixed role in coping with loss (i.e. bereavement/experience of loss can play an important role for increased coping skills, personal growth and resilience, e.g. psycho-spiritual transformation) or can put individual's mental and physical well-being at risk (Murrell et al., 1988). Hansson and Strobe (2007) reviewed evidence with respect to losses in late life and found that ageing both facilitates and hinders adjustment to bereavement.

There is evidence that older people can manage the experience of loss well after going through the normal reactions/processes of grieving.

Meta-analytic and longitudinal studies reveal a considerable degree of stability in measures of life satisfaction, self-esteem and depression during middle and later adulthood (e.g. Bengtson *et al.*, 1985; Diener & Suh, 1998; Rothermund & Brandtstädter, 2003; Okun *et al.*, 1984). Shuchter and Zisook (1993) found that, 13 months post loss, over 75 per cent of their sample reported feeling self-efficient and good about themselves and about life in general. Large-scale longitudinal research indicates that the majority of bereaved people cope effectively with acute symptoms of distress (e.g. digestive disturbance, dry mouth, etc.). However as many as 40 per cent display prolonged signs of neuroendocrine disturbance and sleep disruption as well as diagnosable anxiety/panic syndromes during the first year of bereavement (Jacobs, 1993).

Although there are individual differences in duration of grieving, most of the empirical studies demonstrate that grief usually lasts for 1 year (Norris & Murrell, 1990). Bereaved individuals typically report sadness, poor appetite, reduced concentration and insomnia. Commonly, those who grieve describe longing and yearning for their deceased loved one (Butcher, 2002). Some bereaved individuals consciously and unconsciously assume mannerisms and characteristics of their deceased loved ones. Frequent and regular visits to a loved one's grave can be comforting for some but others may choose to avoid going to the cemetery entirely. It is assumed that as people age, the length of time they have been in a relationship may make it harder to accept the loss and several studies have revealed that older adults have stronger reactions to bereavement and may take longer to adapt to loss (Bowling, 1989; Sable, 1991). Aspects of a continuing relationship with the deceased spouse have also been reported in the study by Shuchter and Zisook (1993). They found that emotional pain and disbelief affected the majority of the sample at 2 and 7 months post loss, with a decline to about 50 per cent by 13 months. The loss of an intimate relationship through death poses profound challenges to individuals' adaptation as living beings. Beem and Schut (2000), in their older widows' sample, found that 4 months post loss, the majority had a decrease in psychological functioning with a range of psychiatric symptoms including depression, agoraphobia, anxiety, hostility and somatisation.

Older people may find somatic complaints a more acceptable way of showing their emotional pain; for example, Laditka and Laditka (2003) found that recently bereaved women in their longitudinal study had a 40 per cent higher risk of hospitalisation than married women. A British study (Charlton *et al.*, 2001) found increased visits to doctors in 100 bereaved spouses following bereavement and prescriptions for both mental and physical health showed that there was a perceived rather than actual health need.

One can assume that the frequent experience of loss in old age can make individual's anxious about his or her own death. On the contrary, Field

(2000) in his qualitative study of 65–80 year old people found that most did not have a strong fear of their own death *per se* but were more concerned about the possible nature of their death. So the process that leads to death seems to be more worrying than the actual event of death itself.

Among the bereaved, psychiatric morbidity is also prevalent. At some point during the first year of bereavement, 45 to 50 per cent of widows and widowers will experience a major depression, whereas 15 to 30 per cent will experience depression for the first entire year (Zisook & Shuchter, 1991). Widowed, older adults are also vulnerable to anxiety symptoms (Schut *et al.*, 1991). Symptoms of anxiety and depression early in the course of bereavement predict subsequent medical and psychiatric morbidity (Chen *et al.*, 1999). Loss and grief have been identified as the most serious risk factors for suicidal behaviours in adults (De Leo *et al.*, 2002). A Danish whole population study (Erlangsen *et al.*, 2004), found that there is a significant suicide risk for men over 80 years of age in the year after death of their spouse (five times higher than the suicide risk in middle-aged married men).

Rates for attempted suicide in later life are less reliable due to a lack of robust research in this area. There is a particular lack of both quantitative and qualitative studies examining the motivations and the interaction of biological, psychological and social factors within the 'suicidal process' (Chan *et al.*, 2007). However, it is estimated that there are four attempts for every completed suicide in older adults in the UK. In the USA, in the year 2000, the rate of completed suicides among those aged 65–74 years old was 12.5 per 100,000, and 18.2 per 100,000 for those aged 75 and over (WHO, 2005) and males aged 75 and older the rate was 42.4 per 100,000. In the UK, the suicide rate for males aged 65 and older is over 13.5 per 100,000 (Department of Health, 2002). The rate for women in the age range 45–74 in 2008, was 6.1 per 100,000 (Office for National Statistics, 2010). Men have higher suicide rates than women in every country (WHO, 2005). The current rate of suicide among older people in Ireland is in the region of 15 per 100,000 (Chambers & Callanan, 2005).

It is difficult to generalise the research findings of the management of loss in the older adult as people may react differently to different losses of which there is a wide range, e.g. loss of siblings (Hays *et al.*, 1997), spousal bereavement and loss of child in old age (which has been explored by very few studies; Moss *et al.*, 2001; Moss & Moss, 1986). Evidence indicates that mental and physical health deteriorates the most following the bereavement of an adult child (De Vries & Lana, 1994). In a study of 102 families, where a family member was dying of cancer, Kissane *et al.* (1994) found that distress levels reached clinical significance in 50 per cent of patients. Studies show that the grief response to the loss of a pet is similar to that after the loss of a person with over one-fifth of people still reporting at least one symptom of grief on 1 year post loss (Wrobel & Dye, 2003).

Factors/mediators affecting coping with experience of loss in older adults

There are many factors that appear to be related to differences in the nature and intensity of grief in older adults (Byrne & Raphael, 1997). The nature of the loss is an important factor. For example, losses that are unexpected do not allow the opportunity to engage in anticipatory grieving and losses that are long anticipated result in depleted resources including wearing out potential networks of social support. This may make grieved individuals more vulnerable (Lamb, 1988).

The relationship with the deceased in terms of its quality and nature, the process of grieving and the individual's personality factors (such as insecure attachment style or tendency to ruminate) may make some people particularly vulnerable to loss. It is important to acknowledge that the ongoing needs for attachment and intimacy across the lifespan are affected by the experience of loss. This includes the need for sexual expression at a time where sexual needs are usually overlooked, particularly where there are issues of sexual orientation (Hansen et al., 2009).

An individual's spiritual belief system and how that influences the view of the loss can complicate or simultaneously facilitate the grieving process. A belief system based on the notion of life as part of a transition to an 'afterworld' should generate qualitatively different reactions than one based on the premise of 'one life, one chance'. Equally the expression of normal bereavement/grieving may differ considerably among different cultural groups. Differences in adjustment, often attributed to gender, may actually be related to other intertwined cultural factors (Wisocki & Skowron, 2000). Or as is often the experience of mental health practitioners, the presentation, in fact, may mimic a major depressive episode.

Pre-loss functioning and well-being are important predictors of post-loss levels of functioning (Boerner et al., 2004). In a prospective study, Carnelley et al. (1999) investigated the impact of widowhood on depression and how resources and contextual factors, that define the meaning of loss, modified this effect. They concluded that the spouse's death and not experiencing depression during this period are risk factors for developing depression after the spousal loss through death.

Protective factors have been explored by different researchers. For example, Nilsson et al. (2000) identified factors that influenced life satisfaction and subjective quality of life in older people as being:

1   functional capacity;
2   perceived health;
3   good housing conditions;
4   an active lifestyle and;
5   good social relationships.

Exercise is probably one of the most identified, protective factors in mental well-being and is particularly validated for the prevention of depression (Llewellyn-Jones & Baikie, 1999; Singh *et al.*, 2001). Recent cross-sectional studies and controlled trials have indicated positive benefits from exercise. These include greater life satisfaction, positive mood states and mental well-being, reductions in psychological distress and depressive symptoms, lower blood pressure and reduction in the brain pathology typically associated with dementia (Lautenschlager & Almeida, 2006).

Viewpoints and theories

Different theories have been suggested over a number of years to explain grief work. Freud in 1917 proposed that a person whose loved one died needed to work through the loss with the final outcome being to detach emotionally from the deceased. Proponents of psychoanalytic theory focused on reactions to loss and separation as tied to psychic conflicts in childhood (Schoenberg *et al.*, 1970). Proponents of attachment theory (Bowlby, 1980a, 1980b) perceived grief as an adaptive response that takes account of present as well as past meanings of loss and environmental as well as intra-psychic influences. Attachment theory holds that when a close emotional bond is severed, whether through death or separation, the grief process follows (Bowlby, 1980a). Both perspectives provided the bases for subsequent studies on loss and bereavement in children and adolescents.

Knowledge of bereavement in adult life was stimulated by Parkes and Brown's (1972) studies, which included identification of predictor variables for estimating bereavement outcomes after the loss of a spouse (Glick *et al.*, 1974). It was also suggested that the grief process may involve feelings of sorrow/sadness and anxiety, as well as yearning for the deceased (Parkes, 1985).

Theories of lifespan development name acceptance of one's own mortality as one of the two main tasks of older adult life (Röcke & Cherry, 2002). Erikson (1950) suggested that the major developmental task of old age is being able to achieve integrity, through accepting one's death. In his classical developmental model, Erik Erikson characterised the final stage of human development as a tension between ego integrity and despair (ibid).

Theories developed by Erikson (1959) and Butler (1963, 1974) have suggested that older adults benefit from making internal, cognitive adjustments to how they view their regrets and losses and older age compels people to review and accept their mortality. Only a successful review contributes to personal well-being and growth (Cappeliez & O'Rourke, 2006; Erikson *et al.*, 1986). Previous research has suggested that those who come to terms with regrets about losses of opportunities adapt to those losses better than those who cannot resolve such regrets (Landman *et al.*, 1995). Older adults are most likely to resolve their regrets than younger adults and that resolution of regrets should facilitate the adaptation and adjustment to loss. Additionally older adults are more likely to resolve their regrets using internal resources to resolve their experience of loss (Torges *et al.*, 2005) thus adding to the sense of mastery and influence that further buffers against future losses. Findings also indicate that those older adults, who are more prone to ruminate, tend to generate more negative appraisals of events and more negative memories from the past (Tkach & Lyubomirsky, 2006) but those who resolve their regrets 6 months post loss adjust better to their overall experience of loss.

Neimeyer (2000, 2005) argues that at the core of adaptation, particularly in the case of traumatic loss, is the human need to find meaning. He takes a social constructionist approach to meaning-making where continuation of meaning-making in the survivor's lives, his or her world view and social, cultural, familial and personal context can all be considered as dynamic processes that take place over a period of time and are likely to combine aspects of reality and subjectivity. Tomer (2000) and McCoy and colleagues (2000), based on previous findings, proposed the ways in which older people may learn to accommodate the knowledge of their mortality. Tomer suggested that life/review/reminiscence with one's own culture/worldview is protective. Finally, aspects of self-transcendence including self-detachment and identification with the wider universe may also reduce anxiety. This process of transcendence according to McCoy *et al.* (2000), gives people a sense of a type of immortality.

McCoy *et al.* (2000) have proposed that older people can no longer deny death through the use of defences used earlier in life. This provokes a push to reorganise that truth thus enabling one's continued sense of well-being. Tomer (2000) suggested that future and past related regrets and the meaningfulness of death have a direct influence on death anxiety. In a systematic review of 49 studies of the relationship between death anxiety and age in older samples, Fortner and Neimeyer (1999) concluded that there was no further general decrease across the later decades of life and greater death anxiety was associated with high levels of psychological and physical health problems.

Dual-process model of accommodative and assimilative coping

The dual-process model of assimilative and accommodative coping (Brandtstädter, 1999; Brandtstädter & Rothermund, 2002) provides a more comprehensive account of adjustment of personal goals and active interventions contributing to adaptation in old age. In terms of this model, it attempts to avoid or diminish actual/anticipated losses by instrumental, self-corrective and compensatory activities to constitute an assimilative mode of coping. Through assimilative strategies, the individual tries to transform a negatively evaluated situation in such a way that it conforms to his or her goal. These accommodative processes involve a devaluation of/disengagement from blocked goals and lowering of personal performance standards. Assimilative efforts should dominate as long as people feel able to actively change the situation or enact efficient self-regulatory interventions. By contrast, accommodative processes should become dominant when action-outcome expectancies have been eroded through repeated unsuccessful attempts to change the situation (Brandtstädter & Rothermund, 2002; Brandtstädter et al., 1999). Assimilative and accommodative modes of coping are not seen as mutually exclusive but as sometimes operating simultaneously. Personal coping tendencies could be reflected in an individual reporting one mode more than the other, reporting high levels of both or reporting little usage of both. Apart from the idea of personal coping tendencies, the model also predicts that assimilative processes tend to dominate as long as the situation appears changeable and that accommodative process should be activated when assimilative efforts become ineffective (Brandtstädter & Rothermund, 2002).

When this dual-process model is applied to understand age-related dynamics of management of loss, the accommodative shift (i.e. individual's adaptation to more lenient standards of performance with decline in performance levels due to advancing age) is of key importance in maintaining a sense of control in life and in buffering the emotional strain that may arise from the experience of irreversible losses (Brandtstädter & Rothermund, 1994; Brandtstädter et al., 1993; Heckhausen, 1997). Similarly, Rothermund and Brandtstädter (2003) demonstrated that as people age and experience losses they shift from using assimilative means to using accommodative means to cope with the losses. He concluded that as people age and decrease in ability to effect instrumental changes, they change their goals and perception of the situation instead. Similarily, Wrosch and Heckhausen (2002) suggested that ageing decreases the opportunity to address regret behaviours; older adults effectively deactivate their regrets by making low internal control attributions about the regrettable.

Specifically, in the face of increasing decline, accommodative processes are thought to help prevent or reduce severity and duration of mental health problems. Thus, older adults with functional impairments may show more flexibility in terms of readjusting their priorities and goals than middle-aged adults because of greater life experience and the 'on-time' character of limitation and losses in old age (Brandtstädter & Rothermund, 1994; Krueger & Heckhausen, 1993).

Conclusion

Loss is a common human experience. Understanding the complex influence of loss on human life has come about in the twentieth century through scientific approaches to the development of the knowledge base that has been empirically tested, modelled and refined to bring us to our current understanding. Experience of loss varies across different developmental stages and different theories have been proposed with respect to the basic features and these often only partially converge. It is suggested, however, that ageing and its loss-related concepts and theories provide useful constructs and measures that can be used to assess adaptation at different levels.

Throughout the different phases of life, developmental tasks refer to the domains of friends and acquaintances, leisure and politics and world issues. As long as people have had the necessary resources at their different developmental milestones, it can be concluded that older adults can focus on growth, psychological health maintenance and the prevention of maladaptive loss-coping strategies. For older adults, grieving the loss of a loved one, receiving information about local bereavement services and involvement in any religious or social activity are beneficial.

Life experience, associated with age, offers resources for the resolution of the experience of loss and older adults may be better able to resolve/manage bereavement-related loss. Death can generate cognitive processes and opportunities for reviews of life for which there is little opportunity to use assimilative or external coping; this suggests that internal coping mechanisms in older adults are helpful in healthy coping with the experience of loss. Furthermore, older people who successfully deal with change and challenges by using their personal resources, restructuring the meaning of the changes, utilising social supports and maintaining a sense of control over their lives, will be less likely to develop mental health problems as they age.

Age-related challenges are characterised by increasing and ultimately inescapable constraints in functioning and losses in the potential for attaining growth. This process is particularly pronounced in advanced old age (Baltes & Smith, 2003). The experience of the overall pattern of adjustment, including the overall load of recent (and subsequent) bereavement, physical and emotional resources for adaptation and quality of social network cannot be ignored when exploring the issues related with the management of loss in old age. People who have unresolved grief experience lower levels of well-being. The acceptance of death and view of the loss appears to be a major factor in loss management and mental and physical well-being are inextricably connected. The flexibility in adjusting to one's goal orientation appears to be necessary for goal attainment. Age-related changes versus developmental gains with respect to resources vary between different life domains (Baltes, 1987, 1997; Baltes & Smith, 2003). In the domains in which gains outweigh losses across life, people may possess the necessary resources to attain their goals and therefore select goals accordingly (toward growth) even in old age.

Coping with loss is a complex experience, it takes place on multiple levels and is influenced by multiple factors (i.e. the nature of the loss, personal and social factors and recovery or adaptation seem to have a range of markers). Many factors such as gender, ethnicity/race, relationship with the deceased and type of death (expected/unexpected) influence the reaction to loss and well-being of the grieving individuals. Consequently, loss/bereavement is a highly variable experience with a few typical symptoms. Older adults cope with the experience of loss in a variety of ways and several aspects of the individual, environment and/or circumstances surrounding the death have an impact on the course of bereavement. Factors such as personal and social competence, family coherence, social support and personal structure can be considered important in contributing to resilience and healthy coping with difficult life experiences. A major factor in successful ageing is adjustment of personal goals to the constraints and irreversible losses that cumulate in later life. Tenaciously clinging to goals may become a source of hopelessness/depression in later life.

The dearth of knowledge into older adults' experiences of loss and their needs is not well recognised; there is a the lack of research in this area. Bereavement is an increasingly frequent experience as people grow older, which makes it important to the psychology of ageing. Clinical evaluation of grieving older patients should be comprehensive with a complete bio–psycho–social evaluation. Although normal grief is not pathological and requires no treatment, ongoing monitoring with assessment of mood, suicidality, health and functional status is recommended. Increased awareness of the features of normal grieving, management of loss, understanding age-related performance decrements, older adults' developmental needs and the complications of bereavement in older adults is important not only to understand what is age-normative and to understand coping processes that are adaptive, but is critical to the design and optimisation of intervention programmes and in helping improve quality of life.

References

American Psychiatric Association. (1994). *Diagnostic and Statistical Manual of Mental Disorders, 4th ed.* Washington, DC: American Psychiatric Association.
Australian Bureau of Statistics. (2006). *National Health Survey: Summary of Results, 2004–05*. Canberra: Australian Bureau of Statistics.
Baltes, B., & Dickson, M. (2001). Using life-span models in industrial-organizational psychology: the theory of selective optimization with compensation. *Applied Developmental Science*, 5(1), 51–62.
Baltes, M., & Lang, F. (1997). Everyday functioning and successful aging: The impact of resources. *Psychology and Aging*, 12(3), 433–43.
Baltes, P. (1987). Theoretical propositions of life-span developmental psychology: On the dynamics between growth and decline. *Developmental Psychology*, 23(5), 611–26.
Baltes, P. (1997). On the incomplete architecture of human ontogeny: Selection,

optimization, and compensation as foundation of developmental theory. *American Psychologist*, 52(4), 366–80.

Baltes, P., & Lindenberger, U. (1988). On the range of cognitive plasticity in old age as a function of experience: 15 years of intervention research. *Behavior Therapy*, 19(3), 283–300.

Baltes, P., & Smith, J. (2003). New frontiers in the future of aging: from successful aging of the young old to the dilemmas of the fourth age. *Gerontology*, 49(2), 123–35.

Beem, E., & Schut, H. (2000). Psychological functioning of recently bereaved middle-aged women: The first 13 months. *Psychological Reports*, 87(1), 243.

Bengtson, V., Reedy, M., & Gordon, C. (1985). Aging and self-conceptions: Personality processes and social contexts. In Birren, J. E., & Schaie, K. W., eds., *Handbook of the Psychology of Aging, 2nd ed.* New York: Van Nostrand Reinhold, pp. 544–93.

Boerner, K., Schulz, R., & Horowitz, A. (2004). Positive aspects of caregiving and adaptation to bereavement. *Psychology and Aging*, 19(4), 668–75.

Bowlby, J. (1980a). *Loss*. New York: Basic.

Bowlby, J. (1980b). *Attachment and Loss: Vol. III: Loss, Sadness and Depression.* New York: Basic.

Bowling, A. (1989). Who dies after widow(er)hood? A discriminant analysis. *Omega: Journal of Death and Dying*, 19(2), 135–53.

Brandtstädter, J. (1999). Sources of resilience in the aging self. In Hess, T. M., & Blanchard-Fields, F., eds., *Social Cognition and Aging*. San Diego, CA: Academic Press, pp. 123–41.

Brandtstädter, J., & Rothermund, K. (1994). Self-percepts of control in middle and later adulthood: Buffering losses by rescaling goals. *Psychology and Aging*, 9(2), 265–73.

Brandtstädter, J., & Rothermund, K. (2002). The life-course dynamics of goal pursuit and goal adjustment: a two-process framework. *Developmental Review*, 22(1), 117.

Brandtstädter, J., & Wentura, D. (1995). Adjustment to shifting possibility frontiers in later life: Complementary adaptive modes. In Bäckman, L., & Dixon, R. A., eds., *Compensating for Psychological Deficits and Declines: Managing Losses and Promoting Gains*. Hillsdale, NJ: Lawrence Erlbaum Associates, Inc, pp. 83–106.

Brandtstädter, J., Wentura, D., & Greve, W. (1993). Adaptive resources of the aging self: Outlines of an emergent perspective. *International Journal of Behavioral Development*, 16(2), 323–49.

Brandtstädter, J., Wentura, D., & Rothermund, K. (1999). Intentional self-development through adulthood and later life: Tenacious pursuit and flexible adjustment of goals. In Brandtstädter, J., & Lerner, R. M., eds., *Action & Self-Development: Theory and Research through the Life Span*. Thousand Oaks, CA: Sage Publications, Inc, pp. 373–400.

Brandtstädter, J., Meiniger, C., & Gräser, H. (2003). Handlungs- und Sinnressourcen: Entwicklungsmuster und protektive Effekte. *Zeitschrift für Entwicklungspsychologie und Pädagogische Psychologie*, 35(1), 49–58.

Brim, O., Ryff, C., & Kessler, R. (2004). *How Healthy are We? A National Study of Well-Being at Midlife*. Chicago, IL: University of Chicago Press.

Butcher, A. (2002). A grief observed: Grief experiences of East Asian international students returning to their countries of origin. *Journal of Studies in International Education*, 6(4), 354–68.

Butcher, H., & McGonigal-Kenney, M. (2005). Depression and dispiritedness in later life: a 'gray drizzle of horror' isn't inevitable. *American Journal of Nursing*, 105(12), 52–61.

Butler, R. (1963). Psychiatric evaluation of the aged. *Geriatrics*, 18(3), 220–32.

Butler, R. N. (1974). Successful aging and the role of the life review. *Journal of the American Geriatrics Society*, 22, 529–35.

Byrne, G., & Raphael, B. (1997). The psychological symptoms of conjugal bereavement in elderly men over the first 13 months. *International Journal of Geriatric Psychiatry*, 12(2), 241–51.

Cappeliez, P., & O'Rourke, N. (2006). Empirical validation of a model of reminiscence and health in later life. *Journals of Gerontology Series B: Psychological Sciences and Social Sciences*, 61B(4), 237–44.

Carnelley, K., Wortman, C., & Kessler, R. (1999). The impact of widowhood on depression: Findings from a prospective survey. *Psychological Medicine: A Journal of Research in Psychiatry and the Allied Sciences*, 29(5), 1111–23.

Caserta, M., & Lund, D. (2007). Toward the development of an Inventory of Daily Widowed Life (IDWL): guided by the dual process model of coping with bereavement. *Death Studies*, 31(6), 505–35.

Chambers, D., & Callanan, A. (2005). *National Office for Suicide Prevention: Annual Report 2005*. Dublin: National Office for Suicide Prevention.

Chan, J., Draper, B., & Banerjee, S. (2007). Deliberate self-harm in older adults: a review of the literature from 1995 to 2004. *International Journal of Geriatric Psychiatry*, 22, 720–32.

Charlton, R., Sheahan, K., Smith, G., & Campbell, I. (2001). Spousal bereavement – implications for health. *Family Practice*, 18, 614–18.

Chen, J., Bierhals, A., Prigerson, H., Kasl, S., Mazure, C., & Jacobs, S. (1999). Gender differences in the effects of bereavement-related psychological distress in health outcomes. *Psychological Medicine*, 29, 367–380.

Dalby, D., Sellors, J., Fraser, F., Fraser, C., Van Inveld, C., Pickard, L., *et al.* (1999). Screening seniors for risk of functional decline: results of a survey in family practice. *Canadian Journal of Public Health*, 90, 133–7.

De Leo, D., Buono, M., & Dwyer, J. (2002). Suicide among the elderly: the long-term impact of a telephone support and assessment intervention in northern Italy. *British Journal of Psychiatry*, 181, 226–9.

Department of Health. (2002). *National Suicide Prevention Strategy for England: Consultation Document*. London: Department of Health.

De Vries, B., & Lana, R. (1994). Parental bereavement over the life course: A theoretical intersection and empirical review. *Omega: Journal of Death and Dying*, 29(1), 47.

Diener, E., & Suh, M. (1998). Subjective well-being and age: An international analysis. In Warner Schaie, K., & Powell Lawton, M., eds., *Annual Review of Gerontology and Geriatrics, Vol. 17: Focus on Emotion and Adult Development*. New York: Springer Publishing Co, pp. 304–24.

Doka, K. J. (1986). Loss upon loss: The impact of death after divorce. *Death Studies*, 10, 441–9.

Enright, B., & Marwit, S. (2002). Diagnosing complicated grief: a closer look. *Journal of Clinical Psychology*, 58(7), 747–57.

Erikson, E. (1950). Growth and crises of the 'healthy personality'. In Senn, M., ed., *Symposium on the Healthy Personality*. New York: Josiah Macy, Jr. Foundation, pp. 91–146.

Erikson, E. (1959). Identity and the life cycle: Selected papers. *Psychological Issues*, 1, 1–171.

Erikson, E. H., Erikson, J. M., & Kivinick, H. Q. (1986). *Vital Involvements in Old Age*. New York: Norton.

Erlangsen, A., Jeune, B., Bille-Brahe, U., & Vaupel, J. (2004). Loss of partner and suicide risks among oldest old: a population-based register study. *Age and Ageing*, 33(4), 378–83.

Field, D. (2000). Older people's attitudes towards death in England. *Mortality*, 5(3), 277–97.

Fortner, B., & Neimeyer, R. (1999). Death anxiety in older adults: A quantitative review. *Death Studies*, 23(5), 387–411.

Glick, I., Weiss, R., & Parkes, C. (1974). *The First Year of Bereavement*. Oxford: John Wiley & Sons.

Greve, W., & Staudinger, U. (2006). Resilience in later adulthood and old age: Resources and potentials for successful aging. In Cicchetti, D., & Cohen, D. J., *Developmental Psychopathology, Vol 3: Risk, Disorder, and Adaptation, 2nd ed*. Hoboken, NJ: John Wiley & Sons, Inc, pp. 796–840.

Hansen, N., Vaughan, E., Cavanaugh, C., Connell, C., & Sikkema, K. (2009). Health-related quality of life in bereaved HIV-positive adults: Relationships between HIV symptoms, grief, social support, and Axis II indication. *Health Psychology*, 28(2), 249–57.

Hansson, R. O., & Strobe, M. S. (2007). *Bereavement in Late Life: Coping, Adaptation, and Development Influences*. Washington, DC: American Psychological Association.

Hayes, J., Yeh, Y., & Eisenberg, A. (2007). Good grief and not-so-good grief: Countertransference in bereavement therapy. *Journal of Clinical Psychology*, 63(4), 345–55.

Hays, J., Gold, D., & Pieper, C. (1997). Sibling bereavement in late life. *Omega: Journal of Death and Dying*, 35(1), 25–42.

Heckhausen, J. (1997). Developmental regulation across adulthood: Primary and secondary control of age-related challenges. *Developmental Psychology*, 33(1), 176–87.

Hobfoll, S., & Wells, J. (1998). Conservation of resources, stress, and aging: Why do some slide and some spring? In Lomranz, J., ed., *Handbook of Aging and Mental Health: An Integrative Approach*. New York: Plenum Press, pp. 121–34.

Hultsch, D., Nesselroade, J., & Plemons, J. (1976). Learning-ability relations in adulthood. *Human Development*, 19(4), 234–47.

Jacobs, S. (1993). *Pathologic Grief: Maladaption to Loss*. Washington, DC: American Psychiatric Press.

Kissane, D., Bloch, S., Burns, W., & Posterino, M. (1994). Psychological morbidity in the families of patients with cancer. *Psycho-Oncology*, 3(1), 47–56.

Kliegl, R., Smith, J., & Baltes, P. (1989). Testing-the-limits and the study of adult age differences in cognitive plasticity of a mnemonic skill. *Developmental Psychology*, 25(2), 247–56.

Krueger, J., & Heckhausen, J. (1993). Personality development across the adult life span: Subjective conceptions vs cross-sectional contrasts. *Journals of Gerontology*, 48(3), 100–8.

Laditka, J., & Laditka, S. (2003). Increased hospitalization risk for recently widowed older women and protective effects of social contacts. *Journal of Women & Aging*, 15(2–3), 7–28.

Lamb, D. (1988). Loss and grief: Psychotherapy strategies and interventions. *Psychotherapy: Theory, Research, Practice, Training*, 25(4), 561–9.

Landman, J., Vandewater, E., Stewart, A., & Malley, J. (1995). Missed opportunities: Psychological ramifications of counterfactual thought in midlife women. *Journal of Adult Development*, 2(2), 87–97.

Lautenschlager, N., & Almeida, O. (2006). Physical activity and cognition in old age. *Current Opinion in Psychiatry*, 19(2), 190–3.

Lehmann, L., Jimerson, S., & Gaasch, A. (2001). *Grief Support Group Curriculum: Facilitator's Handbook*. New York: Brunner-Routledge.

Li, K., Lindenberger, U., Freund, A., & Baltes, P. (2001). Walking while memorizing: Age-related differences in compensatory behavior. *Psychological Science*, 12(3), 230–7.

Lindenberger, U., Marsiske, M., & Baltes, P. (2000). Memorizing while walking: Increase in dual-task costs from young adulthood to old age. *Psychology and Aging*, 15(3), 417–36.

Llewellyn-Jones, R., & Baikie, K. (1999). Multifaceted shared care intervention for late life depression in residential care. *British Medical Journal*, 319(7211), 676.

McCoy, S., Pyszczynski, T., Solomon, S., & Greenberg, J. (2000). Transcending the self: A terror management perspective on successful aging. In Tomer, A., ed., *Death Attitudes and the Older Adult: Theories, Concepts, and Applications*. New York: Brunner-Routledge, pp. 37–63.

Marsiske, M., Lang, F., Baltes, P., & Baltes, M. (1995). Selective optimization with compensation: Life-span perspectives on successful human development. In Bäckman, L., & Dixon, R. A., eds., *Compensating for Psychological Deficits and Declines: Managing Losses and Promoting Gains*. Hillsdale, NJ: Lawrence Erlbaum Associates, Inc, pp. 35–79.

Meis, M. (2005). Geriatric orphans: A study of severe isolation in an elderly population. *Dissertation Abstracts International Section A*, 65.

Moss, M., & Moss, S. (1986). Death of an adult sibling. *International Journal of Family Psychiatry*, 7(4), 397–418.

Moss, M., Moss, S., & Hansson, R. (2001). Bereavement and old age. In Stroebe, M., Hansson, R., Stroebe, W., & Schut, H., eds., *Handbook of Bereavement Research: Consequences, Coping, and Care*. Washington, DC: American Psychological Association, pp. 241–60.

Murrell, S., Himmelfarb, S., & Phifer, J. (1988). Effects of bereavement/loss and pre-event status on subsequent physical health in older adults. *International Journal of Aging & Human Development*, 27(2), 89–107.

Neimeyer, R. (2000). Searching for the meaning of meaning: Grief therapy and the process of reconstruction. *Death Studies*, 24(6), 541.

Neimeyer, R. (2005). From death anxiety to meaning making at the end of life:

recommendations for psychological assessment. *Clinical Psychology: Science and Practice*, 12(3), 354–7.

Niederlander, E. (2006). *Causes of Death in the EU. Statistics in Focus – Population and Social Conditions 10/2006*. Luxembourg: Eurostat.

Nilsson, M., Sarvimäki, A., & Ekman, S. (2000). Feeling old: being in a phase of transition in later life. *Nursing Inquiry*, 7(1), 41–9.

Norris, F., & Murrell, S. (1990). Social support, life events, and stress as modifiers of adjustment to bereavement by older adults. *Psychology and Aging*, 5(3), 429–36.

Office for National Statistics. (2010). *Suicides*. London: Office for National Statistics.

Okun, M., Stock, W., Haring, M., & Witter, R. (1984). The social activity/subjective well-being relation: A quantitative synthesis. *Research on Aging*, 6(1), 45–65.

Osgood, N. (1992). Suicide in the elderly: Etiology and assessment. *International Review of Psychiatry*, 4(2), 217–23.

Paletti, R. (2008). Recovery in context: bereavement, culture, and the transformation of the therapeutic self. *Death Studies*, 32(1), 17–26.

Parkes, C. (1985). Bereavement. *British Journal of Psychiatry*, 146, 11–17.

Parkes, C., & Brown, R. (1972). Health after bereavement: A controlled study of young Boston widows and widowers. *Psychosomatic Medicine*, 34(5), 449–61.

Pendlebury, S., & Rothwell, P. (2009). Prevalence, incidence, and factors associated with pre-stroke and post-stroke dementia: a systematic review and meta-analysis. *Lancet Neurology*, 8(11), 1006–18.

Preyde, M., Macaulay, C., & Dingwall, T. (2009). Discharge planning from hospital to home for elderly patients: A meta-analysis. *Journal of Evidence-Based Social Work*, 6(2), 198–216.

Rando, T. (1992). The increasing prevalence of complicated mourning: The onslaught is just beginning. *Omega: Journal of Death and Dying*, 26(1), 43–59.

Rando, T. (1993). *Treatment of Complicated Mourning*. Champaign, IL: Research Press.

Röcke, C., & Cherry, K. (2002). Death at the end of the 20th century: Individual processes and developmental tasks in old age. *International Journal of Aging & Human Development*, 54(4), 315–33.

Rosenblatt, P., Jackson, D., & Walsh, R. (1972). Coping with anger and aggression in mourning. *Omega: Journal of Death and Dying*, 3(4), 271–84.

Rosenzweig, M., Prigerson, P., Miller, M., & Reynolds III, M. (1997). Bereavement and late-life depression: Grief and its complications in the elderly. *Annual Review of Medicine*, 48(1), 421.

Rothermund, K., & Brandtstädter, J. (2003). Coping with deficits and losses in later life: From compensatory action to accommodation. *Psychology and Aging*, 18(4), 896–905.

Sable, P. (1991). Attachment, loss of spouse, and grief in elderly adults. *Omega: Journal of Death and Dying*, 23(2), 129–42.

Schoenberg, B., Carr, A., Peretz, D., & Kutscher, A. (1970). *Loss and Grief: Psychological Management in Medical Practice*. New York: Columbia University Press.

Schut, H., de Keijser, J., Van den Bout, J., & Dijkhuis, J. (1991). Post-traumatic stress symptoms in the first years of conjugal bereavement. *Anxiety Research*, 4(3), 225–34.

Shuchter, S., & Zisook, S. (1993). The course of normal grief. In Stroebe, M., Hansson, R., & Stroebe, W., eds., *Handbook of Bereavement: Theory, Research, and Intervention*. New York: Cambridge University Press, pp. 23–43.

Singh, N., Clements, K., & Fiatarone Singh, M. (2001). The efficacy of exercise as a long-term antidepressant in elderly subjects: a randomized, controlled trial. *Journals of Gerontology Series A: Biological Sciences and Medical Sciences*, 56A(8), M497–504.

Takahashi, K. (2005). Toward a life span theory of close relationships: the affective relationships model. *Human Development*, 48(1/2), 48–66.

Tkach, C., & Lyubomirsky, S. (2006). How do people pursue happiness? Relating personality, happiness-increasing strategies, and well-being. *Journal of Happiness Studies*, 7(2), 183–225.

Tomer, A. (2000). Death-related attitudes: Conceptual distinctions. In *Death Attitudes and the Older Adult: Theories, Concepts, and Applications*. New York: Brunner-Routledge, pp. 87–94.

Torges, C., Stewart, A., & Miner-Rubino, K. (2005). Personality after the prime of life: Men and women coming to terms with regrets. *Journal of Research in Personality*, 39(1), 148–65.

Weenolsen, P. (1988). *Transcendence of Loss over the Life Span*. Washington, DC: Hemisphere Publishing Corp.

Wisocki, P., & Skowron, J. (2000). The effects of gender and culture on adjustment to widowhood. In Eisler, R. M., ed., *Handbook of Gender, Culture, and Health*. Mahwah, NJ: Lawrence Erlbaum Associates, Inc, pp. 429–47.

Worden, J. (2009). *Grief Counseling and Grief Therapy: A Handbook for the Mental Health Practitioner*, 4th ed. New York: Springer Publishing Co.

World Health Organization. (2005). *International Suicide Statistics*. Geneva: WHO.

World Health Organization. (2006). *World Health Organization: Weekly Epidemiological Record*, 31(81), 297–308.

Wrobel, T., & Dye, A. (2003). Grieving pet death: Normative, gender, and attachment issues. *Omega: Journal of Death and Dying*, 47(4), 385–93.

Wrosch, C., & Heckhausen, J. (2002). Perceived control of life regrets: Good for young and bad for old adults. *Psychology and Aging*, 17, 340–50.

Zisook, S., & Shuchter, S. R. (1991). Depression through the first year after the death of a spouse. *American Journal of Psychiatry*, 148, 1346–52.

Zisook, S., & Shuchter, S. (1992). Depression after the death of a spouse: Reply. *American Journal of Psychiatry*, 149(4), 580.

Zisook, S., Paulus, M., Shuchter, S. R., & Judd, L. L. (1997). The many faces of depression following spousal bereavement. *Journal of Affective Disorders*, 45, 85–95.

Chapter 8

Depression and ageing
Assessment and intervention

Mary O'Donoghue and Patrick Ryan

Introduction

Depression has a powerful negative impact on an individual's ability to function, resulting in high rates of disability. However, becoming old does not necessarily lead to the development of depressive disorders. First, this chapter will focus on the 'demographic transition' that is evident throughout the world where most nations today have many more elders and many fewer children than 50 years ago. Second, the focus will shift to 'successful ageing' as a positive process where the body slows down but the mental and spiritual capacities mature. Third, the focus will turn to 'depression and ageing' where the different categories of depression will be explored, specifically major depression, minor depression, dysthymia and the concept of subsyndromal depression, as well as some theories. Fourth, the area of vascular depression among elderly people will be considered; this occurs in approximately one-third of all ischemic stroke patients. Fifth, the focus will shift to the area of assessing depression in elderly people. A three-stage assessment is discussed: screening, interview-based assessment and individual goal setting. Finally, three effective treatments for depression in late life (psychotherapy, pharmacotherapy and electroconvulsive therapy) will be discussed.

Societies have divided the lifespan in various ways. Life is seen as progressing through the stages of infancy, childhood, adolescence and adulthood. Old age can be arbitrarily divided into young-old age (65–80 years) and oldest-old age (>80 years). *Primary ageing* is universal and believed to be inevitable; it begins early in life and affects all systems. As it progresses, the body's adaptability diminishes. *Secondary ageing* happens to most people but it is neither universal nor inevitable, secondary ageing is the result of disease, abuse or disuse but it can be modified by changes in lifestyle. *Tertiary ageing* is a final, rapid deterioration that heralds the end of life (Perlmutter & Hall, 1992; Jean *et al.*, 2008). Worldwide life expectancy is increasing. For mental health, changing shifts in the profile of our population structure will mean an increase in conditions such as

Alzheimer's disease and dementia but also in depressive disorders. Depression affects about one in ten people over 65 years of age, making it the most common mental health disorder in later life (Anderson, 2000).

Successful ageing

Old age, like other dimensions of the human condition, is a social construct. Some functions and capacities do insidiously but persistently decline although certain other faculties may actually increase (Johnson *et al.*, 2005). Ageing has been defined as a progressive deterioration of physiological function, an intrinsic age-related process of loss of viability and an increase in vulnerability (Buffum & Buffum, 2005). However, it seems that our bodies may age but our mental and spiritual capacities mature.

Gerontology studies suggest that typically older people maintain life satisfaction and well-being, in the face of losses and life events and difficult life circumstances (Windle & Woods, 2004). The most common adversities in later life relate to health problems and severe illness is one of the life events shown by Kraaij and de Wilde (2001) to be related to depressive symptoms in late life. Depression and physical health have a complex relationship; older adults often suffer from multiple comorbid medical conditions or age-related declines in functional reserve, which can compromise their level of independence (Callahan *et al.*, 2005).

Contrary to the stereotypical belief that ageing is essentially an unavoidable process of retreat, of withdrawal into passivity and dependence, the truth is that, for most people, late life is a time of active challenge (Jopp *et al.*, 2008). Old age can be a time of releasing the many false burdens humans carry with them for years (O'Donohue, 1997).

Depression and ageing

Depression is a spectrum of chronic disorders ranging from major depression, bipolar mood disorder, minor depression, dysthymia, cyclothymiacs and the concept of subsyndromal depression (Lyness *et al.*, 2006). Several categories of depression have been defined in both the *Diagnostic and Statistical Manual for Mental Disorders* (DSM–IV; American Psychiatric Association, 1994) and the *International Classification of Disease* (ICD–10; World Health Organization [WHO], 1993) including major depressive disorder and dysthymia. Major depressive disorder (MDD) is a psychiatric disorder of at least 2 weeks' duration during which the patient experiences dysphoria (feeling down, sad, helpless, hopeless, irritable or angry, agitated or anxious or any combination of the preceding group) and/or anhedonia (loss of interest or pleasure in previously enjoyed activities such as hobbies and social or sexual interactions; Belmaker & Agam, 2008). Furthermore, the symptoms must not be exclusively the physiological effect of substance use (i.e. drugs, alcohol or medication) and these symptoms must be severe (associated with clinically significant distress and/or impairment in social, occupational or other types of functioning; McClintock *et al.*, 2010).

Dysthymia is characterised by depressive symptoms that may be less severe than major depression but endure for at least 2 years. Major depression and dysthymia may co-occur as 'double depression'. Subsyndromal depression is defined as having symptoms that do not meet the DSM–IV's criteria for major depression but are recognised as common and important among elderly people (Unutzer *et al.*, 1999). A related set of disorders including bipolar disorder and cyclothymia involve alternating episodes of depression and mania; these disorders differ from unipolar depression and are rare in later life. It is evident that an exclusively categorical approach to depression among elderly people does not provide adequate means for classification of mood disorders in old age. Perhaps a multidimensional approach would allow the clinician to evaluate the overall severity of the clinical presentation (Angst & Merikangas, 2001).

Minor depression is most commonly defined as persistent dysphoria or anhedonia plus one to three depressive symptoms that are present nearly every day for at least 2 weeks (Stones *et al.*, 2006). It is a heterogeneous group of syndromes that may either represent a prodromal or residual form of major depression or dysthymia or constitute a response to an identifiable stressor. Risk factors for developing depression after 65 years of age are similar to those in younger individuals and include: past history and/or a family history of depression, bereavement, onset of medical illness, socially isolated, brain changes (e.g. stroke), living in an institution and care giving (Block, 2000). If depression is not treated it can subside completely or persist.

Depression has been described as a continuum of disorders that evolve and remit over time (Lavretsky, 2002). Untreated episodes typically last 6 months or longer. Eventually, the episode ends with complete remission of symptoms in about 70 per cent of patients. The remaining patients experience persistent symptoms that interfere significantly with their ability to function normally. The risk of recurrence of MDD for people with or without residual symptoms is 50 per cent after one episode, 70 per cent after a second episode and 90 per cent after a third episode of depression (Pasternak *et al.*, 2007). Risk factors for recurrent episodes include, female gender, not married, an initial onset of depression after 60 years of age, substance misuse and family discord (Mueller *et al.*, 1999).

Most elderly people who have clinically significant depressive symptoms do not meet the DSM–IV criteria for depression and this is particularly common in medical settings (Debruyne *et al.*, 2009). Health care professions may interpret persistent depressive symptoms as an acceptable response to other serious illnesses and the social and financial hardships that often accompany ageing. This view is sometimes shared by the older adults themselves (Johnson *et al.*, 2005). This can contribute to low rates of diagnosis and treatment of depression in older adults. Although depression is a highly treatable mood disorder, only one-third of depressed individuals receive appropriate intervention (Lavretsky & Kumar, 2002). It seems that when old people get physically ill, we accept that they will be depressed and this influences the assessment and intervention they receive.

The most common reasons for underdiagnosis of depression are lack of screening and active denial by the patients. The patient, however, often seeks help from the general practitioner (GP) for somatic symptoms that may be masking the underlying depression. It is estimated that 10 per cent of the elderly population living independently in the community have been diagnosed with clinically significant depression, compared to 25 per cent for those with chronic illness, especially people with ischemic heart disease, stroke, cancer, chronic lung disease, arthritis, Alzheimer's disease and Parkinson's disease (Reynolds *et al.*, 1999). It is important to emphasise that the rates of depressive disorder in older people in the community are no greater than those of younger age groups (Gutmann, 1987). According to Chen and colleagues (2000), a family history of depression is most commonly associated with major depression whereas stressful life events more often predict minor depression.

In addition, life events that threaten the person's social roles and social identity are especially difficult as they reduce the potential for the person to exert control in areas of life of particular salience and importance (Gillies & Johnston, 2004). Kuypers and Bengtson (1973) suggest, in their social breakdown theory, that older people have a poorly defined role in society and that the lack of a positive reference group can potentially decrease their abilities to cope in a constructive manner. For example, if work was fundamental to a person's sense of worth they could find retirement very difficult. The developmental diathesis-stress model was proposed by Gatz and colleagues (1996) and proposed that the way individuals react to stressful life events is influenced by psychological attributes, genetic suscep-tibility and biological vulnerability. Therefore, individuals with a strong sense of control, mastery and resilience are best equipped to deal with problems in later life. This can be true of some older people because of the wisdom they have acquired throughout their lives, whereas others can be more susceptible to depression due to genetic and environmental factors (Schindler & Staudinger, 2008).

The risk of developing depression is between 5 and 9 per cent for women and between 5 and 12 per cent for men (Kessler *et al.*, 1994). Studies of monozygotic and dizygotic twins have shown that the propensity to develop MDD is 40 per cent genetic and 60 per cent environmental (Kendler & Prescott, 1999). It is also suggested that an inborn genetic susceptibility to depression may be triggered by the challenges of ageing, such as the loss of a spouse and close friends, co-existing medical problems and increasing disability, cognitive impairment and social isolation (Callahan et al., 2005). It is important, however, that the clinician assesses the physical health and medication history of each individual to determine if he or she is contributing to his or her depressive symptoms (Wiesmann et al., 2009). In some people, treating the underlying medical problem and dealing with the side-effects or contraindications of medications in the elderly population will alleviate the depression but others may require medication, psychotherapy or both to address their mood disorder (Williamson et al., 2000). It is therefore important that every person (young and old) has a thorough assessment and receives the appropriate treatment in order to enhance the quality of their lives.

Late-life depression

Becoming old does not necessarily lead to the development of a depressive disorder, however, major depression affects 1–2 per cent of adults over 65 years of age, minor depression is said to be present in 3–13 per cent of older people and dysthymia affects 2 per cent of the older adult population (Johnson et al., 2005). Major depressive disorder is currently ranked by the WHO as the fourth most common cause of disability and premature death in the world and is the most common cause of emotional disorder in individuals over 65 years of age (Murray & Lopez, 1996). The number of old people suffering from depression in Ireland in 2001 was 47,300 and it is predicted that this number will rise to 69,000 by 2016. Older depressed patients tend to report more somatic and cognitive symptoms than affective ones (Alexopoulos, 2005).

Furthermore, major depression occurs in 10–30 per cent of older medical in-patients and, when depression is comorbid with general medical illness, dysfunction and pain are exacerbated, motivation is compromised, compliance is reduced and recovery is slow (Cole et al., 2006). Major depression is a frequent outcome of stroke, occurring in approximately one-third of all ischaemic stroke patients (Blazer & Hybels, 2005). Boosted by new tools of inquiry, especially magnetic resonance imaging (MRI), investigators have proposed a vascular-based depression among elderly people (Blazer & Hybels, 2005). Currently vascular depression is conceptualised as a major depression occurring in patients with ischaemic vascular changes typically in the small blood vessels in the brain (Naarding et al., 2009). Compared with early-onset depression, patients with vascular depression have a greater overall cognitive impairment, psychomotor retardation, apathy and less agitation, as well as less guilt, less insightfulness, no family history of depression, anhedonia, risk factors for cerebrovascular disease and/or MRI evidence of structural change within fronto-subcortical paths (Alexopoulos, 2005).

In addition, it is suggested that depression not only predisposes people to vascular disease but also worsen outcomes (Thomas *et al.*, 2004). According to the 'vascular depression hypothesis', blood vessel pathology disrupts the neural circuits in the brain contributing to symptoms of depression (Blazer & Hybels, 2005). There is a bi-directional pattern association between physical morbidities, functional disabilities and late-onset depression (Williamson *et al.*, 2000). The impact of late-life challenges such as physical illness and disability are thought to influence depression through two pathways. The first is the psychosocial pathway and it focuses on the loss of independence and control over one's life as well as the psychological and behavioural coping strategies individuals have effectively used to deal with these stressors. The second pathway focuses on how organic disease may compromise brain function that may directly lead to depression and/or reduce the individual's cognitive–behavioural coping strategies (Guelfi *et al.*, 2004). Older adults who demonstrate physical or emotional distress should be screened for depression (Trief *et al.*, 2003).

Assessment

A comprehensive assessment of functioning, comorbid physical disorders and medications is important to help clinicians and patients select the most effective treatment. A three-stage assessment to evaluate the severity and symptom profile of depression has been recommended by Gotlib and Hammen (2000). These three stages are screening, interview-based assessment and individual goal setting. According to Nezu *et al.* (2000) there are 52 different and empirically based measures of depression. Examples of these are The Beck Depression Inventory (BDI; Beck *et al.*, 1961) and the Centre for Epidemiological Studies Depression Scale (CES–D; Radloff, 1977); which are valid and reliable instruments used to assess the levels of depression in both the adult and the older adult population. The Geriatric Depression Scale (GDS; Yesavage *et al.*, 1983) seems to be the most widely used instrument by health care professionals because it excludes somatic symptoms and it only contains items that are pertinent to the older adult. Some somatic symptoms, such as sleep disturbance and lack of energy, however, are prognostic (Cohen-Cole & Stoudemire, 1987). Furthermore, older adults may endorse these symptoms more readily than specific symptoms of depression because of the stigma attached to depression for that age group (Tweed *et al.*, 1992).

Before commencing any type of formal assessment, a rapport must be established with the client; it is the fundamental bases for all therapeutic work. To offer an individual any type of intervention, be it individual therapy, family therapy, memory training or counselling, the clinician needs to have assessed the nature of the needs and issues experienced by the client and associated support systems (Carr & McNulty, 2006). Due to the complex interplay of physical, psychological and social factors in older people, a multidisciplinary assessment will be needed in order to ensure a comprehensive and holistic intervention is provided (Carr & McNulty, 2006).

Positive screening should be followed by interview-based assessment. According to Powers and colleagues (2002) other instruments that appear to be effective in assessing the level of depression in the elderly are the in-depth structured interview such as the Structured Clinical Interview for the DSM–IV Axis I disorders (SCID; Spitzer *et al.*, 1988) and the Schedule for Affective Disorder and Schizophrenia, geared towards the DSM–III criteria (SADS; Spitzer & Endicott, 1978). These have been used extensively in both research and clinical practice to diagnose late-life depression according to the DSM–III criteria. Because individuals who exhibit psychopathology, particularly those who meet the criteria for major depressive disorder are at elevated risk for suicide attempts and death by suicide, explicit questions about morbid thoughts, suicidal thoughts, hopelessness and suicide behaviour should be included in any assessment interview (Gotlib & Hammen, 2000). It is important to fully explore the patient's range and depth of suicidal thoughts and behaviour at assessment because, by doing so, the clinician elicits examples of current symptoms and alerts the client to the idea that the interviewer will continue to be interested in hearing about any morbid/suicidal thoughts if they continue or recur (Lynch *et al.*, 1999).

Regardless of the particular screening and interview measures used to make a diagnosis, a third stage of assessment is also necessary (Crooks *et al.*, 2008). This stage focuses on establishing specific treatment goals and baselines for individual patients involving systematic assessment of particular medical, psychological and social problems that the client may have. The aim is to ensure that the treatment fits the client's needs and to outline the specific target problems and set goals for treatment accordingly (Powers *et al.*, 2002).

Following a comprehensive assessment, the clinician decides on a formulation, which may be altered at any stage if new information becomes available to the clinician. It is considered to be a client's right to be informed regarding investigations and findings (Hopkins University, 1998). There appears to be a different attitude, however, towards older people (Cherniack, 2002). Sometimes the assumption is made that sharing a diagnosis with a client might distress the patient and exacerbate or even trigger an episode of depression or anxiety (Keightley & Mitchell, 2004). There is also the assumption that if the client is suspected of having some cognitive impairment that he or she will not understand or remember the impact of the assessment or diagnosis (Rimmer, 1993). Research has shown, however, that clients want to be informed of their diagnosis (Maguire *et al.*, 1996). It has been found useful for both the client and the therapist to monitor change in mood and there are a host of geropsychiatric measures for use in monitoring treatment progress.

Intervention

A range of effective treatments are available for treating depression in late life, including psychotherapy, pharmacotherapy and electroconvulsive therapy (Johnson *et al.*, 2005). As depression in older people is often associated with poor health, social conditions and economics, any measures that can be put in place to improve general welfare and living standards may help to prevent the occurrence of depression. The myths shared by many older people, professionals and policy makers are that ageing and mortality are synonymous (Lang *et al.*, 2009). Consequently, depression in later life is seen as being justified and understandable as all older people descend into dependency and disability (Espinosa-Aguilar *et al.*, 2007). They ignore the individual experience of ageing and this leads to stereotyped generalisations about older people. Old age can be a time of freedom, opportunity, new social roles such as grand parenting, part-time or voluntary working and travel (Rosenberg & Letrero, 2006). Just as becoming depressed in later life is usually the result of a combination of complex medical and psychosocial factors, so the pathway out of depression is also complex. Despite numerous pathways to late-life depression, it can be effectively diagnosed and treated (Alexopoulos, 2005). The question is not what intervention is effective for a particular group of clients but what will be effective for a specific patient (Helgason, 2004). Interventions need to be individually tailored by a multidisciplinary team and based on careful assessment and formulation (Vedel *et al.*, 2009).

Treatment for older adult depression is typically grouped into two modalities: psychosocial and somatic (Espinosa-Aguilar *et al.*, 2007). A variety of forms of psychotherapy have been used to treat depressive disorder and depression symptoms in older people. They include psychodynamic psychotherapy, life review or reminiscence approaches, and various cognitive–behavioural therapies (Scogin *et al.*, 2005). According to Carr and McNulty (2006), most psychological and therapeutic interventions are generally as effective in treating older people as in other groups. However, reminiscence and life review therapy are geared specifically towards the developmental stages of elderly people. This intervention may be based on Erikson's lifespan development model where the task of late life is seen as involving a process of life review. The successful resolution of this stage involves a sense of integrity that comes from acceptance of life's achievements and regrets (Erikson, 1963).

According to Chambless and colleagues (1996), cognitive–behavioural therapies are well established and empirically validated treatments for depression in older adults and in the general adult population. Behavioural/

problem-solving therapy was also found to be effective in the treatment of depression for older adults (Lamers *et al.*, 2006). Psychodynamic therapies are thought to be probably efficacious for treatment of depression in older adults, although some variants such as interpersonal therapy (IPT) have been demonstrated to be well established in treating depression in the general adult population (Gatz *et al.*, 1998). Life review and reminiscence therapies are categorised as probably efficacious in treating depression in the older adult, however, Gatz *et al.* (1998) noted that studies comparing life review therapy with other treatments generally favoured the other treatments and gains may not be maintained. There is a clear need for further research on psychotherapy for geriatric depression in order to further validate the effectiveness of the treatments studied so far.

A large number of older adults present with depression associated with multiple health problems or concurrent psychiatric diagnoses such as dementia (Bowirrat *et al.*, 2006). According to Gotlib and Hammen (2000), studies are just beginning to report on the effectiveness of psychotherapeutic treatment of depression in demented older adults. Teri and Gallagher-Thompson (1991) reported that older adults, who are diagnosed with depression, could be treated more effectively when their carers were trained to implement a behavioural treatment for the patients. This observation should be given consideration when developing an intervention as it will help to decrease caregivers' level of distress. A modified version of cognitive–behavioural therapy (CBT) has been suggested to be an effective treatment of depression in the chronically ill elderly (Williamson *et al.*, 2000), post-stroke depression patients (Hibbard *et al.*, 1990) and patients with dementia (Teri & Gallagher-Thompson, 1991). Brief psychodynamic therapies have been shown to be effective with patients in the acute phase of depression whereas maintenance with IPT reduces rates of relapse (Gatz *et al.*, 1998). Furthermore, problem-solving therapy and modified dialectical behavioural therapy both show promise but require further research (Johnson *et al.*, 2005). Medication has also been proposed as the first-line treatment for depression in the elderly (Dhondt *et al.*, 1999).

Despite the large number of antidepressant medications available for elderly people, the most studied ones are the tricyclics (TCAs, e.g. nortriptyline) and selective serotonin reuptake inhibitors (SSRIs; e.g. paroxetine, fluoxetine, sertraline). The different response rates obtained from pharmacotherapy, for old age depression trials, reflect the way medication is administered, monitored, the duration of treatment and the variability in efficacy of different drugs (Dhondt *et al.*, 1999). Selective serotonin reuptake inhibitors are the first-line treatment for depression in the older adult. The key issues in the use of medication in older adults are effectiveness, side-effects profile and considerations in special populations. In a meta-analysis of 102 randomised controlled trials, SSRIs were found to be similar to TCAs in overall effectiveness in treating depression in the general population (Anderson, 2000). Even though older adults were more likely than younger adults to discontinue treatment (21 per cent versus 14–8 per cent) there was a minimal, non-significant difference in drop-out rates between SSRIs and TCAs within the adult population (21.3 per cent versus 22.4 per cent, $p > .05$; Gotlib & Hammen, 2000). Furthermore, TCAs and SSRIs appear to be equally effective for treating depression in older adults (Gotlib & Hammen, 2000; Mukai & Tampi, 2009). The risk of relapse is high in the elderly population when antidepressants are discontinued, and studies have shown that maintenance treatment demonstrates the importance of continuing antidepressant medication at the same dosages as the acute phase (Buffum & Buffum, 2005). Interpersonal therapy has been shown to be as effective as medication for depression (de Mello et al., 2005). Sloane and colleagues (1985) compared the effect of IPT with pharmacological treatment for older-adult depression. Results revealed that IPT was as effective as medication (e.g. nortriptyline) at 6 and 12 weeks in obtaining initial remission of depression symptoms and was also associated with lower drop-out rates. Williamson and colleagues (2000) compared the effectiveness of medication (paroxetine), placebo and a psychosocial treatment called problem-solving treatment – primary care (PST–PC) for treating dysthymia and minor depression in older adults. The study was over an 11-week period where the clients received six therapeutic sessions. Paroxetine was deemed to be significantly more effective in treating depression as measured on the Hamilton Rating Scale for Depression (HRSD) compared with the placebo and PST–PC. It has to be stated, however, that six sessions of psychosocial intervention would be considered to be brief and improvement seen in later weeks of treatment may have been the beginning of a therapeutic dose effect (Gotlib & Hammen, 2000). Other studies have compared CBT (both in individual and group format) with pharmacotherapy (e.g. Beutler et al., 1989) and it has been shown that CBT is at least as effective as pharmacological treatment of late-life depression and more effective than a waiting-list control condition. Few studies examining the efficacy of combining pharmacotherapy and psychotherapy in both acute and maintenance phases of treatment of older adult depression have been documented but psychotherapy and pharmacotherapy do appear to be equivalent (Johnson et al., 2005). Thompson and Gallagher-Thompson (1991) reported no difference between combined treatment and CBT alone. Recognising that side-effects and drug interaction are a major problem for the elderly patient, it would be worth considering psychotherapy as the first line of treatment when research has shown it to be equally as effective as medication in treating depression in the older adult.

Electroconvulsive therapy (ECT) is considered to be an effective and rapidly acting treatment for late-life depression (Kelly & Zisselman, 2000). It has been recommended specifically for treatment-resistant depression, for patients who cannot tolerate medication and for those at risk of dying imminently because of a refusal to eat or due to severe suicidal impulses (Friedlander & Mahler, 2001). Electroconvulsive therapy should be used extremely cautiously because of the risk of cardiac complications; delirium and the fact that the individual is actually receiving so many volts of electricity into his/her body (Tielkes *et al.*, 2008).

Conclusion

In conclusion, old-age depression is widespread, has serious health consequences and entails increased health costs and increased mortality related to suicide and medical illness. Nonetheless, old-age depression can be effectively diagnosed and treated. This in turn would lead to decreased emotional suffering, improved physical health and lessened disability; and ensure a better quality of life for the older adult and their families. An intervention should consist of a multidisciplinary consultation and collaboration with GPs and other health care professionals in detection and management of depression. In reviewing the literature, it appears that following diagnoses of old-age depression, the appropriate treatment is often not provided and there seems to be a reluctance to refer the patient for specialist mental health treatment (Mellor *et al.*, 2008). Psychoeducation for family members and carers, and all those involved in the care of elderly people is important. Currently when older adults are referred to mental health services, medication seems to be the first line of treatment even though the literature suggests that psychotherapy is equally as effective as medication and is free from side-effects and drug interaction. Research shows that the quality of our social supports has direct positive effects on our health and can buffer or reduce some of the health-related effects of ageing (Chan *et al.*, 2009). Further research is required in the area of vascular depression and the DSM–IV criteria for diagnosing geriatric depression needs to be reviewed. Finally, we should try and detach ourselves from the stereotypical view that old age is a time of withdrawal into passivity and dependence. Instead, old age can be seen as a time of clearance where people can step back with a sense of wonder, critique and appreciation of all they have achieved and develop new capabilities and seek new challenges.

References

Alexopoulos, G. (2005). Depression in the elderly. *Lancet*, 365, 1961–70.

American Psychiatric Association. (1994). *Diagnostic and Statistical Manual of Mental Disorders, 4th ed.* Arlington, VA: American Psychiatric Association.

Anderson, I. (2000). Selective serotonin reuptake inhibitors verses tricyclic antidepressants: A meta-analysis of efficacy and tolerability. *Journal of Affective Disorders*, 58, 19–36.

Angst, J., & Merikangas, K. (2001). Multi-dimensional criteria for the diagnosis of depression. *Journal of Affective Disorders*, 62(1–2), 7–15.

Beck, A., Ward, C., Mendelson, M., Mock, J., & Erbaugh, J. (1961). An inventory for measuring depression. *Archives of General Psychiatry*, 4, 561–71.

Belmaker, R., & Agam, G. (2008). Mechanisms of disease: Major depressive disorder. *New England Journal of Medicine*, 358(1), 55–68.

Beutler, L., Scogin, F., Kirkish, P., Schretten, D., Corbishley, A., Hamblin, D., et al.(1987). Group cognitive therapy and alprazolam in the treatment of depression in older adults. *Journal of Consulting and Clinical Psychology*, 55, 550–6.

Blazer, D., & Hybels, C. (2005). Origins of depression in later life. *Psychological Medicine*, 35, 1241–52.

Block, S. (2000). Assessing and measuring depression in the terminally ill patient. *Annals of Internal Medicine*, 132, 209–18.

Bowirrat, A., Oscar-Berman, M., & Logroscino, G. (2006). Association of depression with Alzheimer's disease and vascular dementia in an elderly Arab population of Wadi-Ara, Israel. *International Journal of Geriatric Psychiatry*, 21(3), 246–51.

Buffum, M., & Buffum, J. (2005). Treating depression in the elderly: an update on antidepressants. *Geriatric Nursing*, 26, 138–42.

Callahan, C., Kroenke, K., Counsell, S., Hendrie, H., Perkino, A. J., Katon, W., et al. (2005). Treatment of depression improves physical functioning in older adults. *Journal of the American Geriatrics Society*, 53, 367–73.

Carr, A., & McNulty, M. (2006). *The Handbook of Adult Clinical Psychology*. London: Routledge.

Chambless, D., Sanderson, W., Shoham, V., Johnson, S., Pope, K., Crits-Christoph, P., et al. (1996). An update on empirically validated therapies. *Clinical Psychologist*, 49, 5–18.

Chan, S., Jia, S., Chiu, H., Chien, W.-T., Thompson, D., Hu, Y., et al. (2009). Subjective health-related quality of life of Chinese older persons with depression in Shanghai and Hong Kong: relationship to clinical factors, level of functioning and social support. *International Journal of Geriatric Psychiatry*, 24(4), 355–62.

Chen, L., Eaton, W., Gallo, J., Nestadt, G., & Crum, R. (2000). Empirical examination of current depression categories in a population-based study: symptoms, course, and risk factors. *American Journal of Psychiatry*, 157, 573–80.

Cherniack, E. (2002). Informed consent for medical research by the elderly. *Experimental Aging Research*, 28(2), 183–98.

Cohen-Cole, S., & Stoudemire, A. (1987). Major depression and physical illness: Special considerations in diagnosis and biological treatment. *Psychiatric Clinics of North America*, 10, 1–17.

Cole, M., McCusker, J., Elie, M., Dendukuri, N., Latimer, E., & Belzile, E. (2006). Systematic detection and multidisciplinary care of depression in older medical patients. *Canadian Medical Association Journal*, 174, 38–44.

Crooks, V., Lubben, J., Petitti, D., Little, D., & Chiu, V. (2008). Social network, cognitive function, and dementia incidence among elderly women. *American Journal of Public Health*, 98(7), 1221–7.

Debruyne, H., Van Buggenhout, M., Le Bastard, N., Aries, M., Audenaert, K., De Deyn, P., et al. (2009). Is the geriatric depression scale a reliable screening tool for depressive symptoms in elderly patients with cognitive impairment? *International Journal of Geriatric Psychiatry*, 24(6), 556–62.

de Mello, M., de Jesus Mari, J., Bacaltchuk, J., Verdeli, H., & Neugebauer, R. (2005). A systematic review of research findings on the efficacy of interpersonal therapy for depressive disorders. *European Archives of Psychiatry and Clinical Neuroscience*, 255(2), 75–82.

Dhondt, T., Derksen, P., Hooijer, C., Van Heycop Ten Ham, B., Van Gent, P., & Heeren, T. (1999). Depressogenic medication as an aetiological factor in major depression: an analysis in a clinical population of depressed elderly people. *International Journal of Geriatric Psychiatry*, 14(10), 875–81.

Erikson, E. (1963). *Childhood and Society, 2nd ed.* New York: W. W. Norton.

Espinosa-Aguilar, A., Caraveo-Anduaga, J., Zamora-Olvera, M., Arronte-Rosales, A., Krug-Llamas, E., Olivares-Santos, R. (2007). Guía de práctica clínica para el diagnóstico y tratamiento de depresión en los adultos mayores. *Salud Mental*, 30(6), 69–80.

Friedlander, A., & Mahler, M. (2001). Major depression disorder: Psychopathology, medical management and dental implications. *Journal of the American Dental Association*, 132, 629–38.

Gatz, M., Kasl-Godley, J., & Karel, M. (1996). Aging and mental disorder. In Birren, J. E., & Schaie, K. W., eds., *Handbook of the Psychology of Aging, Vol. 4.* San Diego, CA: Academic Press, pp. 365–82.

Gatz, M., Fiske, A., Fox, L., Kaskie, B., Kasl-Godley, J., McCallum, T., & Wetherell, J. (1998). Empirically validated psychological treatment for older adults. *Journal of Mental Health and Aging*, 4, 9–46.

Gillies, B., & Johnston, G. (2004). Identity loss and maintenance: commonality of experience in cancer and dementia. *European Journal of Cancer Care*, 13(5), 436–42.

Gotlib, I., & Hammen, C. (2000). *Handbook of Depression*. New York: Guilford Press.

Guelfi, J., Rousseau, C., & Lancrenon, S. (2004). Depression and associated organic diseases: are there any specific depressive symptoms? Results from the dialogue-2 survey. *European Psychiatry*, 19(7), 446–9.

Gutmann, D. (1987). *Reclaimed Powers*. New York: Basic Books.

Helgason, C. (2004). The application of fuzzy logic to the prescription of anti-thrombotic agents in the elderly. *Drugs & Aging*, 21(11), 731–6.

Hibbard, M., Grober, S., Gordon, W. A., & Aletta, E. (1990). Modification of cognitive psychotherapy for the treatment of post-stroke depression. *Behavior Therapist*, 1, 15–17.

Hopkins University. (1998). Informed choices – every client's right. *Population Reports*, 26(4), 15.

Jean, W., Ng, S. H., Chong, A., Kwan, A., Lai, S., & Sham, A. (2008). Contribution of lifestyle to positive ageing in Hong Kong. *Ageing International*, 32(4), 269–78.

Johnson, M., Bengtson, V., Coleman, P., & Kirkwood, B. (2005).*The Cambridge Handbook of Age and Ageing*. Cambridge: Cambridge University Press.

Jopp, D., Rott, C., & Oswald, F. (2008). Valuation of life in old and very old age: the role of sociodemographic, social, and health resources for positive adaptation. *Gerontologist*, 48(5), 646–58.

Keightley, J., & Mitchell, A. (2004). What factors influence mental health professionals when deciding whether or not to share a diagnosis of dementia with the person? *Aging & Mental Health*, 8(1), 13–20.

Kelly, K., & Zisselman, M. (2000). Update on electroconvulsive therapy (ECT) in older adults. *Journal of the American Geriatrics Society*, 48, 560–6.

Kendler, K., & Prescott, C. (1999). A population-based twin study of lifetime major depression in men and women. *Archives of General Psychiatry*, 56(1), 39–44.

Kessler, R., McGonagle, K., Zhao, S., Nelson, C. B., Hughes, M., Eshleman, S., *et al.* (1994). Lifetime and 12-month prevalence of DSM-III psychiatric disorders in the United States: results from the National Comorbidity Survey. *Archives of General Psychiatry*, 51(1), 8–19.

Kraaij, V., & de Wilde, E. (2001). Negative life events and depressive symptoms in the elderly: A life span perspective. *Aging & Mental Health*, 5(1), 84–91.

Kuypers, J., & Bengtson, V. (1973). Social breakdown and competence. A model of normal ageing. *Human Development*, 16, 181–201.

Lamers, F., Jonkers, C., Bosma, H., Diederiks, J., & van Eijk, J. (2006). Effectiveness and cost-effectiveness of a minimal psychological intervention to reduce non-severe depression in chronically ill elderly patients: the design of a randomised controlled trial [ISRCTN92331982]. *BMC Public Health*, 6, 161–9.

Lang, P., Michel, J., & Zekry, D. (2009). Frailty syndrome: A transitional state in a dynamic process. *Gerontology*, 55(5), 539–49.

Lavretsky, H. (2002). Late-life depressive spectrum disorders: implications for clinical practice/research. *Program and Abstracts of the American Association for Geriatric Psychiatry, 15th Annual Meeting; Orlando, Florida.*

Lavretsky, H., & Kumar, A. (2002). Clinically significant non-major depression: old concepts, new insights. *American Journal of Geriatric Psychiatry*, 10, 239–55.

Lynch, T., Johnson, C., Mendelson, T., Robins, C., Krishnan, K., & Blazer, D. (1999). Correlates of suicidal ideation among an elderly depressed sample. *Journal of Affective Disorders*, 56(1), 9–15.

Lyness, J., Heo, M., Datto, C., Ten Have, T., Katz, I. R., Drayer, R., *et al.* (2006). Outcomes of minor and subsyndromal depression among elderly patients in primary care setting. *Annals of Internal Medicine*, 144(7), 496–504.

Maguire, C., Kirby, J., Coen, R., Coakley, D., Lawlor, B., & O'Neill, D. (1996). Family members' attitudes towards telling the patient with Alzheimer's disease their diagnosis. *British Medical Journal*, 313, 529–30.

McClintock, S., Husain, M., Greer, T., & Cullum, C. (2010). Association between depression severity and neurocognitive function in major depressive disorder: A review and synthesis. *Neuropsychology*, 24(1), 9–34.

Mellor, D., Davison, T., McCabe, M., & George, K. (2008). Professional carers' knowledge and response to depression among their aged-care clients: The care recipients' perspective. *Aging & Mental Health*, 12(3), 389–99.

Mueller, T., Leon, A., Keller, M., Solomon, D. A., Endicott, J., Coryell, W., *et al.* (1999). Recurrence after recovery from major depression disorder during 15 years of observational follow-up. *American Journal of Psychiatry*, 156, 1000–6.

Mukai, Y., & Tampi, R. (2009). Treatment of depression in the elderly: A review of the recent literature on the efficacy of single- versus dual-action antidepressants. *Clinical Therapeutics*, 31(5), 945–61.

Murray, C., & Lopez, A. (1996). *The Global Burden of Disease*. Cambridge, MA: Harvard University Press, p. 21.

Naarding, P., Veereschild, M., Bremmer, M., Deeg, D., & Beekman, A. (2009). The symptom profile of vascular depression. *International Journal of Geriatric Psychiatry*, 24(9), 965–9.

Nezu, A., Ronan, G., Meadows, E., & McClure, K. (2000). *Practitioner's Guide to Empirically Based Measures of Depression*. New York: Kluwer Academic Press.

O'Donohue, J. (1997). *Anam Cara Spiritual Wisdom from the Celtic World*. New York: Bantam Press.

Pasternak, R., Prigerson, H., Hall, M., Miller, M., Fasiczka, A., Mazumdar, S., *et al.* (1997). The posttreatment illness course of depression in bereaved elders high relapse/recurrence rates. *American Journal of Geriatric Psychiatry*, 5(1), 54–9.

Perlmutter, M., & Hall, E. (1992). *Adult Development and Aging*. New York: John Wiley & Sons.

Powers, D., Thompson, L., Futterman, A., & Gallagher-Thompson, D. (2002). Depression in later life: epidemiology, assessment, impact and treatment. In Gotlib, L. H., & Hammen, C. L., eds., *Handbook of Depression*. New York: Guilford Press.

Radloff, L. (1977). The CES-D scale; a self report depression scale for research in the general population. *Applied Psychology Measurement*, 1, 385–401.

Reynolds, C., Perel, J., Frank, E., Cornes, C., Miller, M., Houck, P., *et al.* (1999). Three-year outcomes of maintenance nortriptylene treatment in late-life depression: A study of two fixed plasma levels. *American Journal of Psychiatry*, 156, 1177–81.

Rimmer, T. (1993). Bad news – who should be informed first? *Journal of Cancer Care*, 2, 6–10.

Rosenberg, E., & Letrero, I. (2006). Using age, cohort, and period to study elderly volunteerism. *Educational Gerontology*, 32(5), 313–34.

Schindler, I., & Staudinger, U. (2008). Obligatory and optional personal life investments in old and very old age: Validation and functional relations. *Motivation & Emotion*, 32(1), 23–36.

Scogin, F., Welsh, D., Hanson, A., Stump, J., & Coates, A. (2005). Evidence-based psychotherapies for depression in older adults. *Clinical Psychology: Science and Practice*, 12(3), 222–37.

Sloane, R., Staples, F., & Schneider, L. (1985). Interpersonal therapy versus nortriptyline for depression in the elderly. In Burrows, G. D., Norman, T. R., & Dennerstein, L., eds., *Clinical and Pharmacological Studies in Psychiatric Disorders*. London: Libby, pp. 344–6.

Spitzer, R., & Endicott, J. (1978). *NIMH Clinical Research Branch Collaborative Program on the Psychobiology of Depression: Schedule for Affective Disorders and Schizophrenia (SADS)*. New York: Biometrics Research Department, New York State Psychiatric Institute.

Spitzer, R., Williams, J., Gibbon, M., & First, M. (1988). *Structured Clinical Interview for DSM-III: patient version (SCID)*. New York: Biometrics Research Department, New York State Psychiatric Institute.

Stones, M., Clyburn, L., Gibson, M., & Woodbury, M. (2006). Predicting diagnosed depression and anti-depressant treatment in institutionalized older adults by symptom profiles: a closer look at anhedonia and dysphoria. *Canadian Journal on Aging*, 25(2), 153–9.

Teri, L., & Gallagher-Thompson, D. (1991). Cognitive-behavioral interventions for the treatment of depression in Alzheimer's patients. *The Gerontologist*, 31, 413–16.

Thomas, A., Kalaria, R., & O'Brien, J. (2004). Depression and vascular disease: what is the relationship? *Journal of Affective Disorders*, 79(1–3), 81–95.

Thompson, L., & Gallagher-Thompson, D. (1991). *Comparison of Desimpramine and Cognitive/Behavioral Therapy in the Treatment of Late-life Depression. A Progress Report.* Paper presented at the annual meeting of the Gerontological Society of America, San Francisco.

Tielkes, C., Comijs, H., Verwijk, E., & Stek, M. (2008). The effects of ECT on cognitive functioning in the elderly: a review. *International Journal of Geriatric Psychiatry*, 23(8), 789–95.

Trief, P., Wade, M., Pine, D., & Weinstock, R. (2003). A comparison of health-related quality of life of elderly and younger insulin-treated adults with diabetes. *Age and Ageing*, 32(6), 613–18.

Tweed, D., Blazer, D., & Ciarlo, J. (1992). Psychiatric epidemiology in elderly populations. In Wallace, R. B., & Woolson, R. F., eds., *The Epidemiologic Study of the Elderly*. New York: Oxford University Press, pp. 213–33.

Unutzer, J., Katon, W., Sullivan, M., & Miranda, J. (1999). Treating depressed older adults in primary care: narrowing the gap between efficacy and effectiveness. *The Millbank Quarterly*, 77, 225–6.

Vedel, I., De Stampa, M., Bergman, H., Ankri, J., Cassou, B., Blanchard, F., *et al.* (2009). Healthcare professionals and managers' participation in developing an intervention: A pre-intervention study in the elderly care context. *Implementation Science*, 4, 21.

Wiesmann, U., Niehörster, G., & Hannich, H. (2009). Subjective health in old age from a salutogenic perspective. *British Journal of Health Psychology*, 14(4), 767–87.

Williamson, G., Shaffer, D., & Parmelee, P. (2000). *Physical Illness and Depression in Older Adults. The Handbook of Theory and Practice.* New York: Kluwer Academic/Plenum Publishers.

Windle, G., & Woods, R. (2004). Variations in subjective wellbeing: The mediating role of a psychological resource. *Ageing & Society*, 24, 583–602.

World Health Organization. (1993). *The ICD-10 Classification of Mental and Behavioural Disorders: Diagnostic Criteria for Research.* Geneva: WHO.

Yesavage, J., Brink, T., Rose, T., Lum, O., Huang, V., Adey, M., *et al.* (1983). Development and validation of a geriatric depression screening scale: a preliminary report. *Journal of Psychiatric Research*, 17, 37–49.

Chapter 9

Elder abuse
Understanding pathways and processes

Lucy Smith

Introduction

Improved nutrition, medicine and sanitation over the generations mean that humans now live far longer than evolution demands. With retirement age generally set at age 65, there are some positive benefits that most people look forward to, be they looking after grandchildren, indulging more frequently in hobbies, visiting friends, travelling, or simply waking up later in the morning. What many people do not expect is to be treated as redundant or superfluous to society. Although more frequent illness and accidents are part of the ageing process, we certainly do not expect deliberate physical harm against us. However, neglect, abuse and exploitation of the elderly does occur, and with more people expected to live longer in the future, the prevalence of such problems will increase.

This chapter aims to identify some facts, figures and definitions of elderly abuse generated by research. Three case studies will be outlined in the attempt to look closely at some specific forms of abuse. Each will consider how the abuse developed and what has, could, or might have been done about it.

Who are 'the elderly'?

A review of clinical, epidemiological and pathological studies conducted by Orimo *et al.* (2006) indicates that people over the age of 65 are generally referred to as 'elderly'. More specifically, those between the ages of 65 and 74 are the 'early elderly' and those over 75 are the 'late elderly'. The World Health Organization (WHO, 2009) also uses the age of 65 to define the 'elderly person' but admits this to be an arbitrary choice and one that is generally associated with retirement, pensionable pay and benefits. In Ireland according to the Health Service Executive (HSE), those people aged 60 or older may apply for housing aid for older people (which covers grants for repair work needed in a home), whereas those aged 65 years or older may apply for home care packages (which includes services from health care providers such as physiotherapists, occupational therapists, public health nurses and health care attendants). With specific reference to abuse, the HSE refers to the age of 65 as '. . . the point beyond which abuse may be considered to be elder abuse' (HSE, 2010: para. 3). As far back as 1875, in Britain, the Friendly Societies Act, enacted the definition of old age as, 'any age after 50', yet pension schemes mostly used age 60 or 65 years for eligibility (Roebuck, 1979).

What is elder abuse?

The HSE takes its definition of elder abuse from *Protecting Our Future: A Report of the Working Group on Elder Abuse* (Department of Health and Children, 2002: 25). This reports defines elder abuse as 'A single or repeated act, or lack of appropriate action, occurring within any relationship where there is an expectation of trust which causes harm or distress to an older person or violates their human and civil rights'.

Such a definition very closely resembles that produced by the World Health Organization in 2002 (WHO, 2002: 3) which also states abuse '. . . can be of various forms: physical, psychological/emotional, sexual, financial or simply reflect intentional or unintentional neglect'. The HSE also identifies similar subtypes of abuse and supplies examples of each category. These include physical abuse and restraint (including hitting, slapping, pushing, poor administration of medication); financial or material abuse (including deliberate or deceived taking or misuse of finances, land, property, inheritance, possessions or benefits); sexual abuse (including sexual assault or sexual acts to which the older adult has not or could not consent or was compelled to consent); psychological abuse (including emotional abuse, threats, deprivation of contact, humiliation, coercion or intimidation); neglect and acts of omission (including ignoring medical or physical care needs, failure to provide access to appropriate health, social care or educational services, the withholding of medication, adequate nutrition or heating) and discriminatory abuse (of age, race, sex or disability). The UK components of the definition are the same (House of Commons Health Committee, 2004).

The prevalence of elder abuse

Abuse of elderly people is considered to affect between 3 and 5 per cent of the elderly population (Hunter, 2007), which in Irish terms accounts for about 14–23,000 people (HSE, 2009), in the UK accounts for about 227,000 (National Centre for Research, 2007) and in the USA accounts for about 1–2 million people (National Center on Elder Abuse, 2005). Unfortunately, abuse is often a secretive or hidden problem that can remain undetected and unreported (Swagerty *et al.*, 1999), thus it is unlikely that all cases of maltreatment will ever be fully identified. The issue of elderly abuse is, nevertheless, one that is gaining more and more recognition within the medical, academic and statutory literature with reference to it originating from the mid-1970s (Burston, 1975) and research snow-balling since then. According to the National Center on Elder Abuse (1994), neglect accounts for over half of the abuse cases reported (58.5 per cent). This is followed by physical abuse (15.7 per cent) and financial exploitation (12.3 per cent). Emotional abuse is reported to account for 7.3 per cent of reports whereas sexual abuse accounts for 0.04 per cent. The reporting of abuse is more likely to be made initially by health care professionals (21.3 per cent) than family members (14.9 per cent) or service providers (9.4 per cent); these statistics are likely to vary from one form of abuse to another. It has also been suggested that *self-neglect* accounts for at least half, if not more, of the elder abuse cases (Payne & Gainey, 2005) although it is less likely to be included within the research and literature on elderly abuse.

Risk factors for abuse

The factors that make elderly people as a group susceptible to abuse are similar to those risk factors identified as increasing the likelihood of an individual experiencing such abuse. These factors include cognitive and physical impairments such as poor vision and hearing, reduced mobility and decreased coordination (Polisky, 1995), poor access to resources, low income, social isolation and minority status (Swagerty *et al.*, 1999).

Why does abuse occur?

There is no simple answer to why abuse occurs. In many instances the circumstances leading to an abusive situation are likely to be multifactorial. Furthermore, individual factors may vary in nature. These can often be related in some way to caregiver stress and the personal/psychological difficulties of the caregiver.

Caregiver stress

Caregivers are people who help to look after the day-to-day welfare of an elderly person. These may be family, friends, staff at a nursing home or home help. Carers may be more likely to hurt, neglect or exploit an elderly person should their levels of stress be stretched beyond their limits. Stress develops when there are insufficient resources to meet demand. A carer without adequate supports, i.e. insufficient energy, knowledge, skill, training, money and social support may well experience high levels of stress from the day-to-day pressure of looking after another person. This, in turn, may increase their risk for hurting that person. Research suggests that mood disturbances, particularly anger, act as the intermediate step between stress and abuse (Bendik, 1992; Garcia & Kosberg, 1992). For some, looking after an elderly person may be juggled with work, studies and/or a family; which may act to further reduce their capacity to deal with difficult, or even minor, situations.

Personal/psychological difficulties

The personal or psychological difficulties of the carer can affect, guide or alter the experience of looking after an elderly person. The long-term quality of the relationship between a carer and elderly person will affect care. A man who perceives his elderly mother as a burden, for example, might feel greater resentment and be more neglectful of her needs than a son who feels a sense of reward and warmth towards his mother. Furthermore, parents who employed violent and neglectful behaviours towards their children when young may experience similar treatment from those children when the role of carer and care-receiver reverse as they age. Psychological difficulties such as anxiety and depression are commonly reported by caregivers (Tennstedt, 1999) and mental health status has been found to affect risk of abuse (Coyne et al., 1993; Pavesa et al., 1992). Depression, high anxiety and addictions, for example, may affect judgement and motivation of care not just of the elderly person but of the carer themselves. Without adequate personal self-care and coping skills, a carer is more likely to experience personal burnout thus leaving themselves *and* the elderly person in a vulnerable position.

Case studies

As outlined above, there are many forms of elderly abuse and the course, causes and consequences of each type of abuse could potentially be quite different. Three examples of elderly abuse follow that highlight how different cases can be.

Case 1: the financial abuse of Brooke Astor

Action on Elder Abuse (AEA) is a charity in the United Kingdom and Ireland that focuses on the protection and prevention of elderly abuse. This charity has identified financial abuse to include the direct theft of money and/or possessions; the taking or withholding of benefits belonging to the elderly; and forcing the elderly person to sell his or her home to provide finance (AEA, 2007). In Ireland, as in many countries worldwide, any person in a good mental state can appoint another person (an 'attorney') to take actions on their behalf should they become incapacitated in the future (Citizens Information Board, 2008). In the USA, the latest reports indicate a recent upsurge of financial exploitation cases involving individuals holding power of attorney (Block, 2008). In many cases, the current weak economic climate predisposes financial abuse as some people elect to employ disparate strategies to supplement their own income.

However, financial abuse is not confined to those in desperate need of money. One of the most recent and famous cases of financial abuse is that of Brooke Astor, a wealthy New York philanthropist who died in 2007, aged 105.

Brooke Astor married her first husband, a rich man by the name of Dryden Kuser, at the age of 16. Brooke and Kuser had one child, Anthony. Anthony is reported to have experienced little love or attention from his father (Liesl, 2007). When Brooke and Kuser later divorced, Anthony was not accepted by his mother's second husband, Charles Marshall. Furthermore, it is suggested that Brooke had little affection left over for her son; so in love was she with Marshall. She sent Anthony away to boarding school. In return, it seems that Anthony became jealous and rude towards his mother. Marshall died suddenly in 1952 when Brooke was 49 years old. She quickly found a third husband, Vincent Astor, another rich alcoholic with a strong dislike of her son. Among his other interests, Vincent funded various charities that provided a vocation for Brooke both during her third husband's life (which lasted another 6 years) and after it. Although Brooke had inherited over $120 million dollars, she donated much money to charities for the homeless, the youth, the elderly, the church, New York theatre, museums and libraries.

Meanwhile, Brooke's son, Anthony, had twin boys, Philip and Alec. Vincent Astor had taken a great liking to these boys despite his feelings towards Anthony. Anthony himself joined and left both the armed and diplomatic services as part of his early career, positions sourced and secured for him by his mother. He later controlled his mother's portfolio and, using his power of attorney, gave himself a huge financial bonus of several million dollars. Anthony's main concern appears to have been his potential inheritance of his mother's fortune.

As she aged, Brooke was diagnosed with Alzheimer's dementia. Anthony used this to his advantage in order to amend her will on three separate occasions. Further abuse of his power saw Anthony sell his mother's treasured paintings; pass her summer holiday home and millions of dollars as 'gifts' to himself and his wife; fire Brooke's staff and see that his own were paid from her accounts. Furthermore, half of the Vincent Astor Foundation assets (worth $50,000,000) were passed to a new organisation, the Anthony Marshall Fund, against Brooke's wishes. To add insult to injury, Anthony allowed his mother very little cash, leading her to believe that she was now broke. He also sent her beloved dogs to an animal medical centre, reduced her medical treatments and prevented many of her friends from visiting her. Following her death, Anthony's family had her buried on the left hand side of her third husband not the right hand side as she had wished and left her grave untended and uncared for.

Why did this case occur?

Brooke Astor had Alzheimer's, which given the nature of the disease, meant that she was not always aware of what was happening. Although she reportedly had moments of clarity when she knew that she was being manipulated, her mental state meant that she was not sufficiently able to defend herself legally or emotionally. Brooke Astor was luckier than many people who suffer financial and emotional abuse in that she had a great many friends who were concerned for her and had their own financial means to support her. A further source of light for Brooke, whether she was aware of it or not, came from her grandson, Philip. Following his realisation in 2006 of his father's actions, Philip began to seek justice for Brooke. With the help of Brooke's closest (and perhaps richest friends), Philip filed a petition for guardianship of Brooke, reinstated her medical treatments, re-hired her personal staff and most importantly, helped to reignite her spirit throughout the final year of her life. Although not everyone will have the wealthy associates and notoriety that Brooke had, the importance of friendship and external supports cannot be overemphasised as a means to overcoming abusive situations.

Psychologically, Anthony may have been exacting his revenge on his mother by rejecting and neglecting her in her time of need as she did him throughout his childhood by choosing husbands who disliked him and sending him away to school. In return, he stripped her of her identity by taking over her trust, removing her from her homes, banishing her pets and limiting her finances and visits from friends. Perhaps through his stolen power as an adult, Anthony could throw his childhood self a lifeline at his mother's expense. Alternatively, the act of identifying and chasing easy sources of money may have been a lifestyle modelled to him by Brooke throughout her days of selecting wealthy husbands.

Case 2: residential abuse at Leas Cross Nursing Home

Residential abuse may be considered either a form of abuse or a setting in which abuse takes place (Buzgova & Ivanova, 2009). A recent phenomenological study conducted by Buzgova and Ivanova (2009) identified the forms and causes of abuse in residential settings through interviews with employees and residents. The forms of abuse reflected the types discussed above, such as financial, psychological, physical abuse and neglect. Perhaps one additional concept highlighted by this piece of research was that of 'Rights Violation' that described the violation of free choice and decision making, the disregard for privacy and the disregard for dignity. The causes of the abuse within the residential setting fall into three main categories according to this piece of research: institutional characteristics, employee characteristics and residents' characteristics. The problems identified with institutional characteristics included: the poor organisation of work, the daily schedule as dictated by staff/managers and staff shortages. Employee characteristics included: burnout, personal problems and inadequate education for dealing with elderly people. Residents' characteristics included: personalities and difficulties such as dementia, hostility and aggressiveness as well as their level of isolation. Those residents with fewer visitors were likely to experience greater levels of abuse.

The following residential abuse case description fits with the institutional form of abuse identified in the study of Buzgova and Ivanova.

Leas Cross nursing home was situated in Swords, north County Dublin, Ireland. This residential home was closed down in 2005 following revelations by an RTE television programme of substandard care that resulted in a public outcry (Hogan, 2006). A later report commissioned by the Health Service Executive (HSE) and written by gerontologist, Des O'Neill, referred to the management at Leas Cross as 'consistent with a finding of institutional abuse' (2006: 5). So, what did happen at Leas Cross?

One hundred and five deaths were registered at Leas Cross from 2002 to 2004. Although it is understood that death rates are higher in nursing homes than in the community at large (Raines & Wight, 2002), low or high rates of death at nursing homes should trigger a review of practice to ensure that the reasons for this are understood. The death register at Leas Cross was poorly completed. In some cases the cause of death was not even mentioned. A number of unreported deaths were identified.

Case notes of the patients at Leas Cross were criticised by the commission for being inconsistent, incomplete and often unsigned, proposals for care needs were few, limited and rarely achieved. Basic information such as diagnosis of illness, medical history, weight, continence, eating and mobility needs were often missed from assessment forms. Similar problems were identified in the reports following complaints made by the families of elderly patients. The reports of two patients, one in July 2004 and one in March 2005 made reference to the poor skill mix, lack of senior staff and care standards. A further report in January of 2005 identified the lack of consistency in the files and expressed concern for patient welfare as a result. In January of 2005, a designated nursing home inspection team was set up to monitor the standards of care in private nursing homes. The first visit was to be pre-arranged with follow-up visits unannounced. The Nursing Home Inspection Team visited Leas Cross on at least three occasions throughout the first half of 2005. On each occasion they noted and reported on the substandard care. O'Neill (2006) suggests that insufficient action or communication of findings was implemented on the back of these reports.

One-third of the elderly patients at the nursing home were identified at one stage as having pressure sores and only a small number of these were recorded as having been seen by a doctor (O'Neill, 2006). Pressure sores are considered an indicator of quality of care in residential settings (Spector, 1994) given that they are preventable and treatable. One 73-year-old woman who stayed at Leas Cross for a period of 9 weeks developed 8 sores on her body over that period of time. These sores were identified by the woman's daughter who had to insist on having her mother transferred to hospital. The sores were reported to have been as large as 9 × 8 cms and one in particular, on the woman's hip, extended as deep as the bone (Hogan, 2005). Unfortunately the bedsores were so infected that the woman developed septicaemia and eventually died as a result.

The review conducted by O'Neill (2006) indicated that, in 2005, the majority of patients at Leas Cross nursing home were highly dependent. The 111 bed facility was far bigger than the mean capacity of 45 beds provided by most nursing homes. Despite this, no senior staff with specialist training in older adult health care were recruited, nor did the HSE demand it. Care staff at the nursing home were not adequately trained nor were they offered training of any kind. Furthermore, physiotherapy and occupational therapy treatment was sparse and older age medical and psychiatric care was insufficient.

In summary, patients at Leas Cross suffered from an insufficient amount of care as well as a lack of expertise within the available care. According to the review any complaints made about these problems by inspectors and family members of the patients were not appropriately responded to by the HSE, which served to prolong the suffering of these elderly patients.

Why did this case occur?

Although at the centre of the scandal, Leas Cross was not considered to be an isolated incident (O'Neill, 2006). Why? The social, economic and political climate in which Leas Cross functioned suggested that this nursing home could not be the only one lacking sufficient resources for care. What had happened? Throughout the first half of this decade, the Minister for Health identified a strategy for dealing with the shortage of beds in public acute hospitals. This bed shortage was a very real issue at the time that required necessary attention. In its wisdom, the HSE decided that long-stay patients in public hospitals should be moved out of the hospital setting into long-term care. This plan affected many elderly patients. At the time there was no investment or provision into extra numbers of public long-term beds, which meant that such beds had to be found in private nursing homes (Burke, 2006). Private nursing homes are primarily businesses meaning their focus is on profit, not the health or the needs of the client. They do not have as much access to multidisciplinary care as do public homes and, as has been documented above, they can lack the expertise necessary for dealing with very vulnerable patients. According to the O'Neill review (2006) the HSE did not sufficiently finance its plan, nor did it comprehensively put into action its inspection protocols. Furthermore, it dealt inadequately with complaints. Leas Cross represented the tip of the iceberg; as a result of an undercover television programme, it became the example.

Case 3: Michael Scott Simons – sexual abuse of elderly people

One form of abuse not identified and discussed as part of the study conducted by Buzgova and Ivanova was sexual abuse. Sexual abuse is not as well researched in the elderly population as physical or emotional abuse (Ramsey-Klawsnik, 1991; Payne, 2009) nor is it as well researched as sexual abuse of younger people (Payne, 2009). Superficially, reports suggest sexual abuse of elderly people to be quite rare (0 per cent to 0.03 per cent) which might account for the limited research in the area (Payne, 2009). The likelihood is that this crime is severely under-reported (Payne & Gainey, 2005) be it due to fear, denial, stigma, cognitive impairment of the victim (Payne & Gainey, 2005) or poor detection, protocol and knowledge by clinicians (Burgess, 2006).

Limited research does not mean that no research has been conducted. A preliminary community survey on 28 elderly female sexual abuse victims was conducted by Ramsey-Klawsnik (1991). This indicated that most of the women were unable to care for themselves due to personal difficulties such as dementia, physical illness or mobility problems. Further findings revealed that this population are subject to a full range of sexual assault, almost all of which are completed by men. This has been substantiated in later research (Burgess & Phillips, 2006; Roberto & Teaster, 2005). Payne's (2009) most recent research compared the characteristics of elderly sexual abuse with the characteristics of elderly physical abuse. Whereas the offenders of sexual abuse were usually male (78 per cent), the offenders of physical abuse were usually female (73 per cent). Furthermore, females were more likely to be sexually abused than men (67 per cent versus 33 per cent) although males and female were equally likely to be physically abused.

At home, perpetrators are usually caregivers and often the husband or son (Ramsey-Klawsnik, 1991). Within the nursing home setting, the profile of perpetrators of elderly sexual abuse is generally that of staff member. Payne's 2009 study identified care aides to be responsible for 70 per cent of sexual abuse; nurses responsible for about 10 per cent and directors responsible for less than 5 per cent of such abuse.

The case of Michael Scott Simons exemplifies elderly sexual abuse as it matches many of the characteristics highlighted in the research. Simons worked in a nursing home as an aide to elderly people with Alzheimer's disease. Aged 23, he worked nights alone at the facility in Oregan State where some of his tasks included washing and dressing the residents (John, 2004). In 2004, Simons confessed to having abused four of the women in his care. His crimes included rape, sodomy, sexual penetration, sexual assault and private indecency. Legally, this case was fraught with difficulty because of the inability of the victims to corroborate the confession or testify in court. The case was built around the circumstantial evidence supporting the confession. Simons had previously admitted to one colleague that he was sexually attracted to elderly women and told another of one patient's sexual reaction during a shower. Furthermore, he had been fired from his job following a sexual assault against a female colleague while at work.

Why did this case occur?

This case, as in any sexual abuse case, can be argued to have occurred and to have continued to occur because of the combination of a number of factors. These include Simons' psychological make-up, poor institutional care procedures and insufficient clinical knowledge of the signs of elderly sexual abuse.

PSYCHOLOGICAL MAKE-UP

Simons had admitted that he was attracted to elderly women. The cause of his personal attraction is not clear in any of the available literature on his case. Research suggests that sexual offenders of elderly people experienced difficulties in early adolescent adjustment, unstable family backgrounds, showed a lack of respect for their mothers and perceived their mothers as overprotective, domineering or provocative (Groth, 1978). Furthermore, Pollack (1988) found personality differences between control and offender groups using the Minnesota Multiphasic Personality Inventory (MMPI). Offenders scored highly on the Psychasthenia and Schizophrenia scales of the MMPI. These measure anxiety/ruminative disposition and unusual thinking patterns/poor social adjustment respectively. Of six offender case studies presented by Ball and colleagues (1992), three were psychotic, one had a personality disorder and two were sexually attracted to elderly people. A more recent Irish study by Collins and O'Connor (2000) reported schizophrenia and alcohol dependence to be the most common diagnoses among their sample of ten offenders. Delusions and cognitive distortions are common to those with schizophrenia and psychosis (American Psychiatric Association, 2000) and it is possible that such problems may have contributed to the sexual offences committed by these men. In the case of Simons, we know that he told others of a patient's sexual response while he showered her. It seems plausible that Simons' telling of the occurrence may have been an example of his general inability to inhibit himself around elderly people, particularly where sexual stimuli were involved. Such inhibition may well be indicative of deeper cognitive distortions in his case.

Two conceptual models for explaining sexual abuse of elderly people have been identified by Ball (2005). These include sexual orientation towards the elderly (gerontophilia) and 'anger rape'. The former suggests genuine sexual attraction towards elderly people. Whereas the second suggests that it is the emotions, not the act, which is dominant; the act is a form of control whereby the perpetrator vents emotions of anger and rage against the victim who represents, for them, an authority figure. Simons did not express forms of anger or rage against the women he abused. Combined with his admission of sexual attraction towards older women, it would seem that it is the former model that better accounts for Simons' actions.

POOR INSTITUTIONAL CARE PROCEDURES

Simons' report of the sexual response of a patient while in the shower and his disclosure of being sexually attracted to elderly women should have reached management without delay in order to prevent further abuse from occurring. This did not happen, which suggests that staff were neither alert to the dangers and/or had no protocol to follow regarding potential dangers. In fact, judging from the newspaper reports of the case, it seems that the abuse only came to light after Simons had sexually assaulted another member of the care staff, i.e. a woman who was able to defend herself and able to make a statement. Should this event not have taken place it seems conceivable that Simons could have carried on abusing the elderly women within the home without interruption.

The ethics and protocol of the nursing home facilitated Simons' activity. According to newspaper reports, Simons worked alone, at night, supplying very personal care to the patients (John, 2004). This provided opportunity, time, space and reason to be alone with the patients in vulnerable situations. Strategies to prevent the abuse might have been to employ extra staff or ensure males were never alone with female patients.

The ideal scenario in this case, as in any case of abuse, would have been the prevention of the problem. Any employment agency needs to take responsibility for their employees. This responsibility can be better facilitated by a comprehensive applicant screening system that guides the selection of staff (Burgess, 2006). Given that past behaviour is predictive of future behaviour, an applicant with a history of sexual offending should not be considered for a job working with vulnerable people. Whether or not an employer uses an agency or completes their own checks, the following should be verified: identity, previous employment, education standards, professional licenses, whether they are on the sex offender registry including any registries for child or elder sexual abuse, lists of excluded individuals and present or previous drug abuse (Edwards, 2005). Of course, background checks are subject to human error or might not be regularly updated which make a thorough interview process equally important. This can identify how well an employee might handle stress. Furthermore, staff training in identifying and anonymously reporting abuse might help to halt abuse in development (Burgess, 2006).

INSUFFICIENT CLINICAL KNOWLEDGE OF ELDER ABUSE

It has already been mentioned that elder abuse is under-reported, particularly sexual abuse of the elderly (Payne & Gainey, 2005). One reason for this is that the signs of such abuse have been missed, or miss-perceived, by the very people who have the opportunity to identify it and do something about it. Only half of junior doctors in a recent Irish study had even heard of the term 'elder abuse', only one-third had read any literature on it and none had received any formal training in the area (O'Regan, 2007). Knowledge of the risk factors for abuse can facilitate detection of the problem (Burgess, 2006) and these have been documented earlier in this report. Knowing the physical and emotional signs will also promote detection. Physical signs include: bruising on the inner thighs, genital or anal bleeding, sexually transmitted diseases, difficulty walking or standing, pain or itching in the genital area and the exacerbation of existing illnesses (Dugan, 2004). Emotional signs include: fear or timidity, depression/ withdrawal, sudden changes in personality, misplaced comments regarding sex or sexual behaviour and fear of certain people (Dugan, 2004).

In order to help clinicians identify and assess elder sexual abuse, Burgess and a working group of experts joined forces to design an appropriate assessment tool. They took the existing Comprehensive Sexual Assault Assessment Tool (CSAAT) (Burgess & Fawcett, 1996) and tailored it to include questions relevant to elder sexual abuse victims and their offenders (CSAAT–E). Various elder-specific difficulties were taken into consideration when designing this tool, some of which included the tendency for such victims to delay reporting abuse, their impaired mental and physical functioning, the differential diagnosis between accidental bruising and bruising from deliberate harm, the psychological response of elder people and their relationship with the abuser. The use of such a tool increases understanding of the nature, extent and impact of elder sexual abuse. Uniform employment of the tool would permit the collection of data within a database as a resource for clinicians, researchers and the justice system (Burgess, 2006).

Conclusion

The three cases discussed are very different yet all contain the common elements of victim and offender. Cases one and three involved one individual offender but differed in the number of victims affected by the abuse. The offender in case two, reviewed in the report by O'Neill (2006), however, is harder to pin down but in my opinion can be attributed to failings in government and policy.

Elderly abuse, like any other form of abuse is not something that happens 'out there some where'. In all cases of abuse, the bystander, the witness and the oblivious are played by all of us as we busy ourselves with our own affairs and permit abuse to develop, occur and continue under our noses. It could be argued that society has learned what it knows from our elders. If we have been taught to leave well enough alone, it is little wonder that we do. However, do any of us expect to live a long, productive life to find socially acceptable abuse, neglect and exploitation at the end of it? Will any of us then continue to think that others should mind their own business? Unlikely.

More than 30 years after Burston's 1975 article on 'Granny Battering' in the *British Medical Journal*, Ireland took on the problem in 2008 by developing a specialist service to help prevent and deal with the problem of elder abuse (HSE, 2009). Specialist staff are now employed to raise awareness of elderly abuse, a National Centre for the Protection of Older People has been established in University College, Dublin and the reports of abuse are being properly collected and collated in order to inform service delivery (HSE, 2009). Of course, ideally no one would have to benefit from this service. Unfortunately some of us will.

References

Action on Elder Abuse. (2007). *Position Paper on Financial Abuse*. London: AEB. (Retrieved 3 August 2010 from http://www.elderabuse.org.uk/About%20Abuse/What_is_abuse_signs%20financial.htm)

American Psychiatric Association. (2000). *Diagnostic and Statistical Manual of Mental Disorders, 4th ed., Text Revision*. Arlington, VA: American Psychiatric Association.

Ball, H. N. (2005). Sexual offending on elderly women: A review. *Journal of Forensic Psychiatry & Psychology*, 16(1), 127–38.

Ball, H. N., Snowdon, P. R., & Strickland, I. (1992). Sexual offences on older women: Psychopathology of the perpetrator. *Journal of Forensic Psychiatry & Psychology*, 3, 160–6.

Bendik, M. F. (1992). Reaching the breaking point: Dangers of mistreatment in elder caregiving situation. *Journal of Elder Abuse & Neglect*, 4(3), 39–60.

Block, S. (2008). Power of attorney can victimise elderly. *USA Today* 04/12/2008.

Burgess, A. (2006). *Elderly Victims of Sexual Abuse and their Offenders*. Rockville, MD: US Department of Justice.

Burgess, A., & Fawcett, J. (1996). The comprehensive sexual assault assessment tool. *Nursing Practice*, 21(4), 66, 71–6, 78.

Burgess, A., & Phillips, S. (2006). Sexual abuse, trauma, and dementia in the elderly: A retrospective study of 284 cases. *Victims & Offenders*, 1, 193–204.

Burke, S. (2006). Neglect came from our choices on private for-profit care for the elderly. *Irish Independent*, 11 November 2006. (Retrieved 3 August 2010 from http://www.independent.ie/opinion/analysis/neglect-came-from-our-choices-on-private-forprofit-care-for-the-elderly-68195.html)

Burston, G. R. (1975). Granny-battering. *British Medical Journal*, 3, 592.

Buzgova, R., & Ivanova, K. (2009). Elder abuse and mistreatment in residential settings. *Nursing Ethics*, 16(1), 110–26.

Citizens Information Board. (2008). *Power of Attorney*. Dublin: Citizens Information Board. (Retrieved 3 August 2010 from http://www.citizensinformation.ie/categories/death/before-a-death/power_of_attorney)

Collins, P. G., & O'Connor, A. (2000). Rape and sexual assault of the elderly: An exploratory study of 10 cases referred to the Irish forensic psychiatry service. *Irish Journal of Psychological Medicine*, 17(4), 128–31.

Coyne, A., Reichman, W., & Berbig, L. (1993). The relationship between dementia and elder abuse. *American Journal of Psychiatry*, 150(4), 643–6.

Department of Health and Children. (2002). *Protecting Our Future: A Report of the Working Group on Elder Abuse*. Dublin: The Stationery Office. (Retrieved 2 August 2010 from http://www.dohc.ie/publications/pdf/pof.pdf?direct=1)

Dugan, K. (2004). Elderly often unrecognised victims of sexual abuse. *Senior Journal.com*. (Retrieved 3 August 2010 from http://seniorjournal.com/NEWS/Eldercare/4-11-09SexualAbuse.htm)

Edwards, D. J. (2005). Thinking about the unthinkable: Staff sexual abuse of residents. *Nursing Homes/Long Term Care Management*, 54 (6), 44–7. (Retrieved 12 March 2009 from https://www.guideone.com/SafetyResources/SLC/Docs/sm0605.pdf)

Garcia, J. L., & Kosberg, J. I. (1992). Understanding anger: Implications for formal and informal caregivers. *Journal of Elder Abuse & Neglect*, 4(4), 87–99.

Groth, A. N. (1978). The older rape victim and her assailant. *Journal of Geriatric Psychiatry*, 11(2), 203–15.

Health Service Executive (HSE). (2009). *HSE Elder Abuse Service Developments: Open your Eyes. Dublin: Health Service Executive*. (Retrieved 2 August 2010 from http://www.hse.ie/eng/services/Publications/services/Older/OpenYourEyesServiceDevelopments2008.pdf)

Health Service Executive (HSE). (2010). *What is Elder Abuse?* Dublin: Health Service Executive. (Retrieved 3 August 2010 from http://www.hse.ie/eng/services/Find_ a_Service/Older_People_Services/Elder_Abuse/)

Hogan, L. (2005). Bed sores left gaping holes down to the bone. *Irish Examiner*, 1 June 2005. (Retrieved 3 August 2010 from http://archives.tcm.ie/irishexaminer/2005/06/01/story348306775.asp)

Hogan, S. (2006). New laws 'will stop repeat of scandal'. *Irish Independent*, 11 November 2006. (Retrieved 3 August 2010 from http://www.independent.ie/national-news/new-laws-will-stop-repeat-of-scandal-68264.html)

House of Commons Health Committee. (2004). *Elder Abuse, Second Report of Session 2003-2004, Vol. 1*. London: The Stationery Office.

Hunter, N. (2007). Elder abuse figure could be 20,000. *IrishHealth.com*, 19

November 2007. (Retrieved 3 August 2010 from http://www.irishhealth.com/ article.html?id=12571)

John, F. H. (2004). Former nursing home aide convicted. *Albany Democrat Herald*, 9 June 2004. (Retrieved 3 August 2010 from http://www.democratherald.com/ news/local/article_bd82e54f-a264-5356-b169-c34a4519c9b2.html)

Liesl, S. (2007). Astor's Place (Book Review). *New York Times*, 17 June 2007.

National Center on Elder Abuse. (1994). *The National Elder Abuse Incidence Study: Final Report*. Washington, DC: Administration for Children & Families and Administration on Aging, US Department of Health and Human Services.

National Center on Elder Abuse. (2005). *Fact Sheet: Elder Abuse, Prevalence and Incidence*. Washington, DC: National Association of State Units on Aging.

National Centre for Research. (2007). *UK Study of Abuse and Neglect of Older People*. London: National Centre for Research, Kings College London.

O'Neill, D. (2006). *Leas Cross Review*. Dublin: HSE. (Retrieved 3 August 2010 from http://www.hse.ie/eng/services/Publications/services/Older/Leas_Cross_Report_ .pdf)

O'Regan, E. (2007). Doctors lack 'elder abuse' knowledge. *Irish Independent*, 9 February 2007. (Retrieved 3 August 2010 from http://www.independent.ie/health/ doctors-lack-elder-abuse-knowledge-54021.html)

Orimo, H., Ito, H., Suzuki, T., Araki, A., Hosoi, T., & Sawabe, M. (2006). Reviewing the definition of 'elderly'. *Geriatrics & Gerontology International*, 6(3): 149–58.

Pavesa, G., Cohen, D., Eisdorfer, C., Freels, S., Semla, T., Ashford, J. W., *et al.* (1992). Severe family violence and Alzheimer's disease: Prevalence and risk factors. *The Gerontologist*, 32(4), 493–97.

Payne, B. K. (2009). Understanding elder sexual abuse and the criminal justice system's response: Comparisons to elder physical abuse. *Justice Quarterly*, 26(1), 1–19.

Payne, B. K., & Gainey, R. R. (2005). Differentiating self-neglect as a type of elder mistreatment: How do these cases compare to traditional types of elder mistreatment? *Journal of Elder Abuse & Neglect*, 17(1), 21–36.

Polisky, R. A. (1995). Criminalizing physical and emotional elder abuse. *Elder Law Journal*, 3(2), 379.

Pollack, N. (1988). Sexual assault of older women. *Annals of Sex Research*, 1, 523–32.

Raines, J. E., & Wight, J. (2002). The mortality experience of people admitted to nursing homes. *Journal of Public Health Medicine*, 24(3), 184–9.

Ramsey-Klawsnik, H. (1991). Elder sexual abuse: Preliminary findings. *Journal of Elder Abuse & Neglect*, 3(3), 73–90.

Roberto, K., & Teaster, P. B. (2005). Sexual abuse of vulnerable young and old women. *Violence Against Women*, 11, 473–504.

Roebuck J. (1979). When does old age begin? The evolution of the English definition. *Journal of Social History*, 12(3), 416–28.

Spector, W. D. (1994). Correlates of pressure sores in nursing homes: Evidence from the National Medical Expenditure Survey. *Journal of Investigative Dermatology*, 102(6), 42–5.

Swagerty, D. L., Takahashi, P. Y., & Evans, J. M. (1999). Elder mistreatment. *American Family Physician*, 59, 2804–08.

Tennstedt, S. (1999). *Family Caregiving in an Aging Society*. Washington, DC: Administration on Aging.

Working Group on Elder Abuse. (2002). *Protecting Our Future: A Report of the Working Group on Elder Abuse*. Dublin: The Stationery Office. (Retrieved 2 August 2010 from http://www.dohc.ie/publications/pdf/pof.pdf?direct=1)

World Health Organization. (2002). *World Health Organization/International Network for the Prevention of Elder Abuse. The Toronto Declaration on the Global Prevention of Elder Abuse*. Geneva: WHO. (Retrieved 2 August 2010 from http://www.inpea.net/images/TorontoDeclaration_English.pdf)

World Health Organization. (2009). *Definition of an Old or Elderly Person*. Geneva: WHO. (Retrieved 2 August 2010 from http://www.who.int/healthinfo/survey/ageingdefnolder/en/index.html)

Chapter 10

Elder abuse

What works and does not work to prevent it?

Elaine Smith and Niamh Maria Long

Introduction

Under the guise of 'Granny Battering' the issue of elder abuse was first introduced to the literature in 1975 (Burston, 1975). Since then, it has been slow to gain public concern as it is often a secretive or hidden problem that can remain undetected and unreported (Swagerty *et al.*, 1999), thus it is unlikely that all cases of maltreatment will ever be fully identified. Although it is acknowledged that across cultures the term may be defined differently, the definitions common to the Western World are employed here. The National Academy of Sciences in the USA formed a panel in 2002 to assess the research in the area of elderly abuse and the (Irish) National Council on Ageing and Older People (NCAOP) commissioned a study into elder abuse, published in 1998 (O'Loughlin & Duggan). Two definitions of elder abuse are detailed in Box 10.1.

Box 10.1 Definitions of elder abuse

National Academy of Sciences, USA (2003: 1)
(a) Intentional actions that cause harm or create a serious risk of harm (whether or not harm is intended), to a vulnerable elder by a care-giver or other person who stands in a trust relationship to the elder.
(b) Failure by a care-giver to satisfy the elder's basic needs or to protect the elder from harm.

Action on Elder Abuse (2007: 2)
A single or repeated act or lack of appropriate action occurring within any relationship where there is an expectation of trust which causes harm or distress to an older person.

The NCAOP also declared that such abuse is not limited to any particular setting, type of older person or type of perpetrator. In most cases, there are multiple forms of abuse with multiple causes (O'Loughlin & Duggan,

1998). The above definitions focus on the importance of trust between the elderly person and the caregiver and the consequences of actions, whether intentional or not.

Of the kinds of abuse found within the elder abuse literature, many are typical of abuse more generally. These include physical abuse, psychological abuse, sexual abuse, as well as intentional and unintentional neglect. In the case of the elderly, the Working Group on Elder Abuse whose report *Protecting the Future* was commissioned by the Irish Department of Health and Children (2002) notes that physical abuse is not limited to hitting but may include the inappropriate use of drugs, restraints or confinement. Intentional neglect refers to refusal on the part of the caregiver to provide basic needs (e.g. nutrition, hygiene and medical care) whereas unintentional neglect refers to ignorance on the part of the caregiver or denial of the needs of the elderly person (Pang, 2000). Material and financial abuse of elderly people is more common compared with other populations, and are defined as the illegal or improper exploitation, and or use of funds or resources. In addition, there is the wider issue of civil rights violation (O'Loughlin & Duggan, 1998). A surprise finding by an Austrian study (Hörl, 2002) was the elderly respondents' focus on the failure of society to treat them as 'adult citizens' with equal rights, to such an extent that they felt disregarded, insulted and ignored by government or social security agencies. A similar definition, entitled 'violation of rights' includes denial of privacy or participation in decision making about health, marriage and other personal issues (Kleinschmidt, 1997).

Prevalence

International studies suggest that the prevalence of elder-abuse ranges from 2 to 10 per cent (Thomas, 2000). The number of people over the age of 60 worldwide, is currently 721 million,[1] and this number is expected to rise to 1.2 billion by 2025 (Randal & German, 1999). Giurani and Hasan (2000) expect the number of abused elders to increase over this time, possibly because of decreasing respect shown to traditional age roles and the ability of current technology to prolong the time lived with chronic disease (Council on Scientific Affairs, 1987).

Little definitive research has been done in the Republic of Ireland although experts in geriatric medicine claim there is no reason to expect it to be any different from international studies (O'Neill, 2001). This would correspond to between 14,000 and 23,000 victims although this estimate does not include those in nursing homes (Mulholland, 2008; Greene, 2002). A study in Northern Ireland showed that where dementia is present the probability of elder abuse increases to 37 per cent (Compton *et al.*, 1997) of which 10 per cent involve physical abuse and 34 per cent verbal abuse, with overlap in some cases.

Prevention

Definition

The World Report on Violence and Health (World Health Organization [WHO], 2002a) recommends that the prevention of violence be targeted in an ecological way, at multiple levels including individual, relationship/family, community and societal levels. As is common in public health issues, the WHO also distinguishes between primary, secondary and tertiary prevention. Primary prevention is prevention that attempts to avoid (i.e. prevent) abuse before it occurs; this is often the top priority in abuse prevention and largely targets the societal level. It may consist of research initiatives, education programmes and public safety initiatives/announcements. Secondary prevention focuses mainly on the individual and aims to limit the impact of abuse by providing screening programmes and immediate responses such as emergency services. Tertiary prevention also focuses on the individual but in a long-term and rehabilitative way (e.g. mental health services, mentoring programmes). In reality there may be overlap and bi-directional relationships between all three levels.

What follows is a brief review of some of the international work that has addressed the issue of elder abuse. Although conceptualised as primary, secondary and tertiary sections, it is acknowledged that real-world work does not always fit into such discrete categories.

Review of the literature

Scott (2008) lists a number of challenges faced by effective programme delivery and research in the world of violence prevention. They include the need for increased overall training, sustained funding of long-term interventions, translation of small but effective programmes to the population level supported by community-based workers, the addressing of societal factors affecting families and communities as well as political issues, and the funding of impact evaluation of interventions with continued replication of these findings to help understand what affects change. This reflects views in Australia,[2] warning against a narrow person-centred framework around elder abuse. Elder abuse, they concluded, results not just from individual carers but at community and government levels, such as community attitudes toward elderly people, a lack of community education against elder abuse and a scarcity of support, education and training for carers.

Primary prevention

Ireland has been slow to get elder abuse research and other initiatives off the ground. The Department of Health and Children did establish a working group in 1999, the recommendations of which (*Protecting our Future*) became health policy in November 2002. They included the formulation of a national policy on elder abuse, strategy implementation of each health board to implement this policy complete with a steering group and dedicated officer, recruitment of a senior case worker in all community areas to respond to referrals, a National Centre for Research and Training, financial abuse campaigns, public awareness programmes and law reform. Since then an implementation group has been formed to oversee these recommendations and a couple of health boards have appointed policy developers. However, ongoing Health Service Executive recruitment bans have not helped in the fruition of these recommendations (see Penhale, 2006, for a fuller review) and as such evaluation of their impact has not been possible. Given the promising intention of this policy, it is disappointing that the experiences of elderly people, 8 years after the publication of the recommendations, are indicative of elder abuse on a wider scale. According to Hörl (2002) and Kleinschmidt (1997) the failure of society to serve its elderly population appropriately also constitutes elder abuse. A recent study conducted by the Social Policy and Ageing Research Centre in Trinity College, Dublin, has found a lack of independence-maintaining services and supports available to those over the age of 60 in north Dublin (see *Nursing in the Community*, 2008: 4), with a significant number of their elderly sample feeling isolated, 25 per cent having transport difficulties, many suffering as a result of long waiting-lists for respite care, home care and access to day care centres and such a high demand for services that there is a frequent mismatch between a client's need for a service and the availability of that service.

The United Nations International Plan of Action on the global prevention of elder abuse was adopted by all countries in Madrid in April, 2002 and the Toronto Declaration on the Global Prevention of Elder Abuse (WHO, 2002b) asked nations to consider points that can be summarised as follows:

- that legal frameworks for elder abuse prevention are missing;
- multiple sectors of society need to be involved in elder abuse prevention;
- the importance of primary health care workers in identification of abuse;
- the importance the education and dissemination of information, both professionally and through the media;
- the universality of the problem.

Thus, identification of elder abuse is not enough. Health, social, legal protection, police referral and any other relevant services, the declaration suggests, should be developed to respond to the problem.[3] This is a reasonable set of suggestions although Lithwick *et al.* (1999) have previously cautioned against the automatic involvement of law enforcement procedures. They promote a 'value-neutral',[4] rather than a criminalised, approach to elder abuse. The criminalised approach in the USA, where mandatory reporting exists in many states, has been widely criticised on the basis of insufficient funds or staff to handle the number of referrals resulting from this law and also on the basis that it interferes with confidentiality between clients and professionals (Pillemer *et al.*, 2007). In addition, Pillemer *et al.* conclude that, to date, no evidence exists to support or refute the efficacy of such a law.

The use of academia and training (which address the third and fourth points above) was highlighted recently in Ireland by 'Age Action' that called for a review of doctors' training in prescribing to elderly patients, given the recent finding in Cork university accident and emergency department that 16 per cent of elderly patients had sustained adverse effects after inappropriate medication was prescribed to them (i.e. often antipsychotic drugs, especially in nursing homes) (*Nursing in the Community*, 2008: 4). Hirsch and Vollhardt (2002) recommend structural and cultural interventions for the prevention of elder abuse, as well as personal interventions. Structural interventions include educational programmes for professional service providers and media attention of the problem. The Victorian Community Council Against Violence (2005) suggests ensuring attendance at training for those in the health care system by building elder abuse modules into accreditation systems. Lachs and Pillemer (2004) also suggest that improved general detection of elder abuse among relevant professionals be achieved by incorporating education at training or professional level, rather than relying on screening tools. Training programmes have been devised for physicians, nurses, social workers and other professions (see Pillemer *et al.*, 2007, for a review). Research thus far suggests that knowledge about elder abuse among such groups does increase, unfortunately, there is no evidence as of yet to indicate whether they actually prevent elder abuse (Pillemer *et al.*, 2007). This must be viewed as a long-term goal.

In terms of awareness at the general population level, Hirsch and Vollhardt (2002) recommend that victims avoid colluding with the abuser, by blowing the whistle to the media about their abuse in order to focus more attention to the problem. Cultural interventions include educating the public about violence in general particular with regard to apathetic responses to violence as well as providing education about ageing and fighting ageist attitudes. This has been successful in Ireland recently in the case of the Leas Cross Nursing Home scandal that resulted in both the closure of the home in 2005 and the establishment of a commission of investigation into the management, operation and supervision of the home (Department of Health and Children, 2007).

Table 10.1 Elder abuse risk factors by relationship role

Relationship role	Risk characteristics	Author
Caregiver	Responsibilities related to caregiving: Stress Emotional/physical exhaustion	Levine, 2003
	Dependence upon victim for: Accommodation Funding	Levine, 2003
	Dependence usually related to: Alcoholism Legal difficulties Deviant behaviours Mental illness: depression, anxiety, confusion	Kleinschmidt, 1997
Victim	Poor health Inability to self-care Cognitive impairment (e.g. dementia) Living alone (financial abuse)	Levine, 2003; Lachs and Pillemer, 2004

Research has a preventative role in that it can help to identify predictors of abuse in order to identify those at risk, and also, prevent abuse occurring (Scott, 2008). Risk factors can relate either to the caregiver or to the victim (summarised in Table 10.1).

Studies have also attempted to distinguish between types of abusers (e.g. physical abuse and neglect) based on a detailed history of risk factors and psychological inventories. For example, Reay and Browne (2001) found in a retrospective study that those who engaged in physical abuse were significantly more likely to show conflict, depression scores and heavy alcohol consumption on psychological measures as well as having experienced past childhood abuse than were those who neglected elderly dependents. The neglect group showed significantly higher anxiety scores than those who engaged in physical abuse. Elderly persons who live alone are more likely to be the victims of financial abuse (Levine, 2003; Lachs & Pillemer, 2004). The identification of such problems can lead to their incorporation into the risk assessment of potential future abuse, although Fulmer *et al.* (2004) argue that identifying potential elder abuse on the basis of relationship-based predictor variables is a difficult matter due to the conceptual disagreement amongst experts on what constitutes 'normal', 'adequate' and 'appropriate' relationships between one person and another. They also question how the concept of 'minimal care' can be determined unless these constructs are also defined.

The importance of efficacy research has also been mentioned by Scott (2008: 53) who points out that part of violence prevention rests on demonstrating whether or not violence prevention programmes work. The importance of this was highlighted by an evaluation of a law enforcement intervention programme, inspired by domestic abuse programmes (Davis & Medina-Ariza, 2001). They found that a programme involving home visits by police officers and domestic violence counsellors resulted in *increased* physical violence for victims, compared with a control group. They speculated that the programme may have angered abusers thereby putting the victims at increased risk. This demonstrates two points: first, the importance of efficacy research and second, the difficulty of translating family violence models directly to the elder abuse domain (Glendenning, 1999). However, efficacy research is thin on the ground, not least because Europe in general is still in the stages of identification and development of responses to the problem (Penhale, 2006).

Secondary prevention

The signs and symptoms of physical abuse and neglect are often less evident in elderly people than in other vulnerable sectors because of the difficulty in distinguishing them from the normal consequences of ageing and disease (Fulmer *et al.*, 2004). Thus, it is extremely important that medical staff combine physical examination with adequate screening for abuse. Although there are protocols available for such screening, Lachs and Pillemer (2004) report that few of these are effective and where they are implemented there is no evidence to support that the subsequent intervention actually improves outcome. A review of elder abuse screening techniques, conducted by Fulmer *et al.* (2004) determined that, although there are several screening tests available, they are often used indiscriminately, may be subject to overinterpretation (due to biased ratings, lack of sensitivity and inappropriate assignment of scores) and are often not of any practical value because of the length it takes to administer them. For example, the caregiver, dyadic relationship and environment all contribute to abuse, and thus, intervention (and screening) should target not just the victim but the context of abuse, as this increases the likelihood of ending the abusive cycle. Yet, the limited time available in practice makes such an ecological approach to screening difficult. In addition, some worry that screening tools put users at risk of liability if they fail to stop the abusive problem after having documented its occurrence (Nerenberg, 2008: 105). Wolf (2000) concluded that risk assessment essentially remains a clinical judgement, rather than an objective process, despite the attempts made to standardise the process.

Lachs and Pillemer (2004) illustrate the difficulty in constructing a methodologically sound screening protocol by comparing the process to a medical example, a cervical smear, in which the patient is interested in her own health, presents without symptoms for a negligibly invasive test and seeks early detection for a problem where a definitive test is in place. In contrast, screening methods for elder abuse involve patients who are often unable to be involved in their own health, for cognitive or physical reasons, who are often accompanied by their abuser, who, due to shame or fear, may wish to hide the fact that they are being abused and where the screening method is not agreed.

'Independent living', in which the victim is separated from the perpetrator, is considered a distinct goal compared with that of 'maximising clients' independence' in which the client may remain within their abusive environment (Nerenberg, 2008). In this situation, the provision of home-delivered meals, transportation, home modification, day programmes and telephone or home-visit support allows for a degree of independent living in situations where the victim may be unwilling to take action against his or her abusers. Although such measures may act as a first step in gaining the trust of the victim before further action is taken, or may help alleviate caregiver stress, Pillemer et al. (2007) suggest that they have a limited preventative potential, however, given the large number of other risk factors that predispose elder abuse (e.g. mental illness, substance abuse). Further goals include the resolution of crises/emergencies, ensuring victim safety, supporting victims, protecting assets and ensuring justice. Although some emergency services such as emergency funds and in-home attendant care sound ideal, forced psychiatric hospitalisations and 'protective custody' provisions, in use in parts of the USA, may raise questions about autonomy and elderly rights. Victim safety plans include rehearsal of what to do in an emergency situation (e.g. identifying safe contacts, having a packed bag ready, knowing where to go, using a safety 'code word', etc), shelters and protective orders. However, shelters largely prioritise younger women and the issue of admitting elderly people on an emergency basis can raise issues with licensing or monitoring agencies. Protective orders (e.g. personal conduct orders, stay away orders, residence exclusions) can be invoked by elderly people as they can by other victims of abuse, although Nerenberg reports that their effectiveness is uncertain given the physical disabilities that might prevent elderly people from attending court or even using the phone appropriately.

Where elder abuse has been identified, the principle 'help before punishment' has been suggested as a guideline for response. Only when social support or other intervention fails to stop abuse should legal services be engaged (Hirsch & Vollhardt, 2002: 911). The importance of identifying risk factors, in carers as well as victims, allows for corrective arrangements to be tried. Carer dependency on the elderly person is a known risk factor for abuse, therefore an adequate distance between the two can be arranged to reduce the impact of this dependency. Simple measures such as the carer having his or her own room, having respite and sharing the task with other family members can be effective measures in this regard (Hirsch & Vollhardt, 2002).

Financial abuse is the most recent of elder abuse crimes to receive preventative attention although several responses are emerging to tackle it.

'Daily Money Management' services[5] are often provided by banks or other businesses for victims, or potential victims, of abuse. Research (Wilber, 1995) has found support for enhanced financial security and reduced financial exploitation of elderly people by using this method. The 'FAST' (Financial Abuse Specialist Team) is another example of a financial abuse service and involves an immediate response team to urgently examine potential abuse. It is a successful example of both primary and secondary prevention in that it has acted both as a deterrent to financial elder abuse and as a fast response to reported financial abuse through the use of a 'seamless service delivery system' (Malks et al., 2003). The Financial Abuse Specialist Team, based in Santa Clara Country, California, consists of a team representing the Department of Aging and Adult Services, Adult Protective Services and Public Administrator/Guardian/Conservator, the District Attorney's Office and the County Council. It also incorporates law enforcement and financial institutions. Their tasks are to urgently screen for, and if necessary implement, a freezing of assets, referral to law enforcement, continuing of further investigations and evaluation of the need for power of attorney or guardianship. Although no formal qualitative evaluation of services was reported by Malks and colleagues (2003) the programme has returned hundreds of millions of dollars to its rightful owners.

Tertiary prevention

Response programmes to elder abuse can focus either on the victim or on the perpetrator of that abuse. A common response has been, and remains still, a physical removal of the victim to alternative accommodation; one study found that abuse ceased in 37 per cent of cases for this reason (Kurrle et al., 1997) and another that long-term care resulted in case-closure for 29 per cent of cases (Neale et al., 1996). However, the removal of elderly victims to long-term care institutions can cause problems of its own. Although much of the abuse that takes place among elderly people does so within the home environment, much of it also occurs within institutional environments.

The UK-based organisation 'Action on Elder Abuse' reported that although only 4.9 per cent of the elderly reside in residential homes, phone-calls to their charity concerning this sector accounted for 23 per cent of all calls (Thurlow, 2008). Thus, there is a disproportionate amount of abuse-related concerns involving residential homes for elderly people. Past inquiries into serious examples of institutional abuse have identified ignorance, denial, poor management, low morale, staff shortages/turnover and inadequate training as contributing factors related to the institution (e.g. the Beech House inquiry; Tonks & Bennett, 1999; Levine, 2003). Studies of institutional abuse have found the incidence of carer abuse to be high. In one German study, 79 per cent of staff admitted to having abused or neglected a resident at some point during the previous 2 months and 66 per cent witnessed a colleague victimising a resident (Goergen, 2001). An American study found that 10 per cent of staff admitted physically abusing a resident and 40 per cent admitted to psychological abuse (Pillemer & Moore, 1989). Examples of abuse are varied, including infantilisation (e.g. Salari, 2005), derogation, uncleanliness, improper medication, vermin infestation, inadequate diet, passive neglect, lack of time to walk, talk to and help residents, etc (see Glendenning, 1999, for a review). Thus, complete removal may not be an ideal response.

Glendenning (1999) also points out that the family violence model has become the dominant approach to elder abuse in the literature despite the widely documented accounts of institutional abuse in the last 20 years and that there is an urgent need for better training, better working conditions and a recognition of burnout among staff by managers, issues which are not accounted for by the family model. Salari's (2005) review of infantilisation in care homes demonstrates the poor quality of life that can be offered to elderly people. Lessons learned from this study suggest that privacy, means for physical escape, adult décor and autonomy/choice in sleep, movement and conversation are important in the continuity of adult status which affords better quality of life.

Psychological interventions are also beginning to surface. In the UK, Reay and Browne (2002) have shown that an intervention for perpetrators, based on education and anger management, was successful in reducing the cost of care,[6] strain, depression and anxiety for those who had engaged in physical abuse and those who had engaged in neglect, both at post-programme delivery and at 6-month follow-up. The physical abuse group also showed a significant reduction in conflict tactics (i.e. hostility, threats, aggression) in response to conflict situations. However, this study is one of very few such evaluations that have been done, and failed to include a control group. It also does not indicate whether or not it was successful in reducing repeat offences. An older study of training for abusive caregivers also found evidence of reduced 'costs' (i.e. of care) although did not show any change in feelings of anger or self-esteem (Scogin et al., 1989). Group facilitators can face ethical dilemmas where support groups for carers might reveal tendencies towards abuse, especially in states of the USA where mandatory reporting of suspected elder abuse is in place. Support groups for carers provide an array of positive functions, including respite, reduction in feelings of isolation, sharing of feelings, affirmation of carer roles, education about ageing and techniques for coping (Bergeron & Gray, 2003), and the benefits of these may be compromised where facilitators feel obliged to report their concerns. In comparison with removal to a nursing home, where the benefit for the older person may be questionable, 24-hour care (even from a stressed carer) may be more beneficial than the limited resources, and possible neglect, of a busy nursing home.

Vladescu and colleagues (1999) reviewed a Canadian-based client-centred case-management programme for elder abuse victims. The strategies of the programme were:

- explanation/discussion of options to the victim;
- involvement of other people or services in the plan of action;
- building trust and confidence of the client;
- supporting the client's decisions;
- helping to set short- and long-term goals;
- advocating on their behalf.

They found that it resulted in abuse elimination as a result of relocation in 27.3 per cent of cases where duration of abuse was less than 2 years and in 40 per cent of cases where abuse duration was more than 2 years, of which the majority (9 out of 10 cases) were relocated to independent settings rather than care settings. The client could also opt for harm reduction (i.e. accept services, attend community programmes, leave the premises of the abuse, Vladescu et al. 1999: 11) and a competent client was as likely to choose one as the other. In total, 65.4 per cent of clients experienced either partial or total reduction in their abuse following this intervention. The study concluded that empowering clients to make decisions is more important than trying to 'rescue' them away from their abusive situation.

There has been little research on the role of support groups for elder abuse victims, despite findings that elderly people view support groups favourably, particularly the mutual support of peers (Podnieks, 1999). One study by Brownell and Heiser (2006) did evaluate a psychoeducational support group for victims of elder abuse, in which they measured risk, depression, guilt, anxiety, health, self-esteem and sense of social support as outcome variables but they did not find changes in any of these measures.

Conclusion

Determining what 'works' or 'does not work' in the case of elder abuse is not an easy task and depends upon the outcome in question (Figure 10.1). With regards to secondary prevention, elderly abuse cannot be detected if staff knowledge of abuse is poor, whether due to personal (i.e. disinterest) or environmental reasons (i.e. lack of professional development opportunities, poor management and a busy department). However, staff awareness may be of little use anyway where access to screening tools is limited (e.g. because of cost). Indeed, even where screening tools are available they must be psychometrically sound to be of any use and research suggests that this is not the case. Therefore, initial detection, and thus, secondary prevention, may fail early on. Even where definitions and screening tools are employed, there is evidence that practitioners continue to bring their own values of

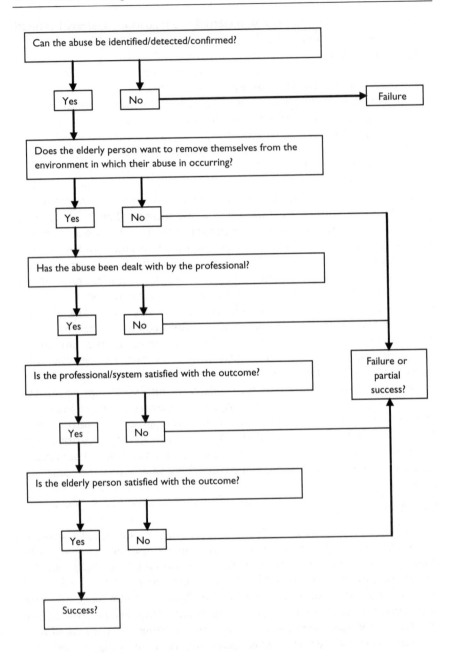

Figure 10.1 Diagram illustrating the difficulty in determining whether or not a preventative approach has been successful.

elder abuse to screening and evaluation (e.g. by focusing more on intent than consequences in defining their notion of abuse, where consequences are generally the defining concept) (Lithwick *et al.*, 1999).

Abuse may be identified either with or without the assistance of the victim, and even where the victim is willing to disclose information, it may not be that he or she wishes to remove him/herself from the environment. According to Neale and colleagues (1996) 20 per cent of cases refuse services. This results in two, less than ideal, possibilities: respecting the victim's wishes or forcing an intervention. Human rights charters would advocate both the right to self-determination and the right to safety and a mistreatment-free life, yet the two could conflict in the case of abuse intervention (Lithwick *et al.*, 1999: 108). Where the victim consents to the implementation of intervention, outcome may nevertheless be inadequate due to insufficient resources, lack of clear procedures and further practical/ ethical barriers. Often, the professional discovers that all available options are unsatisfactory or that the intervention may place the victim at further risk of abuse. The removal, for example, of an elderly person from his or her abusive home to a nursing home, was deemed in a discourse analysis of social workers by Wilson (2002) to place the victim at risk of institutional abuse (see Goergen, 2001; Pillemer & Moore, 1989; Salari, 2005). Thus, the system may allow for prevention of abuse, but be stalled at any subsequent stage. Even where a case may initially be viewed as successfully resolved, one wonders whether it is ever adequately reviewed. Is 'outcome' determined by the resolution of a single case of abuse or by the sustained monitoring of the victim? Wolf and Pillemer (1988) reviewed three intervention models in response to 328 cases of elder abuse, where 74.5 per cent were deemed to have been resolved. 'Resolved' meant 'the reduction or elimination' of circumstances that had resulted in the abuse or neglect (1988: 264). This demonstrates that the efficacy of a programme is often judged by its ability to do *anything*, rather than its ability to solve the problem. There is a dearth of intervention studies guiding abuse prevention programmes anyway (Pillemer *et al.*, 2007: 241; Nerenberg, 2008: 142) and Vladescu *et al.* (1999: 7) point out that even in those studies that do exist, the details of their interventions are often lacking.

In their list of criteria for the development of elder abuse interventions, Lithwick *et al.* (1999: 97) warn that there will always be limits to the intervention implemented, that success in resolving mistreatment is often measured by small steps and that complete resolution to the problem is often not possible or realistic.

In summary, this is by no means an exhaustive review of the preventative measures that have arisen globally in response to elder abuse, however, it has given a flavour of the different levels of prevention (i.e. primary, secondary and tertiary) that exist and of the ecological way in which prevention can take place (i.e. individual, relationship, community and societal). The findings often seem ambiguous, with limitations and counter-arguments arising from most of the studies and reviews for preventing such abuse. It would appear that government funding is necessary in order to promote all levels of prevention, given Penhale's (2006) review of elder abuse prevention across Europe; which suggests that those countries with government backing (e.g. France) are ahead of countries without it. The importance of well-controlled efficacy studies, as well as research more generally, which looks in particular at elder abuse as distinct from other forms of abuse, such as child and domestic abuse, is also apparent. However, research is still in its relative infancy compared with that for other forms of abuse and there is hope that continued interest and funding will improve the services and responses available to older people.

Notes

1 US Census Bureau, International database (http://www.census.gov/).
2 As represented by the Victorian Community Council Against Violence (2005) report.
3 These refer primarily to the first two recommendations of *The Toronto Declaration on the Global Prevention of Elder Abuse*.
4 Value-neutral approach: this recognises that some degree of conflict and difficulty is normal in relationships, is less emotionally charged and is more likely to elicit the cooperation of the perpetrator than a criminalised approach (Lithwick *et al.*, 1999: 98).
5 Daily Money Management services assist those who have problems managing their financial affairs (Nerenberg, 2003). They are deputy services, often via banks or other financial services, and are often provided for vulnerable adults who have no suitable relatives or friends that can undertake such management on their behalf. The role of Daily Money Management may include information provision, benefit application assistance, debt management, power of attorney appointment (for those with mental capacity) and guardianship (for those without mental capacity).
6 Cost of care: a case management tool designed to identify problem areas in the care of elderly relatives, as defined by measures of (1) physical and emotional health, (2) personal and social restrictions, (3) value.

References

Action on Elder Abuse. (2007). *Trustees' Report*. London: Action on Elder Abuse (Retrieved 3 August 2010 from http://www.elderabuse.org.uk/documents/Constitution%20and%20Governance/Annual%20Reports/Annual%20Report%202006.pdf)
Bergeron, L., & Gray, B. (2003). Ethical dilemmas in reporting suspected elder-abuse. *Social Work*, 48(1), 96–105.
Brownell, P., & Heiser, D. (2006). Psycho-educational support groups for older women victims of family mistreatment: A pilot study. *Journal of Gerontological Social Work*, 46(3/4), 145–60.
Burston, G. R. (1975). Granny battering. *British Medical Journal*, 3, 592.

Compton, S. A., Flanagan, P., & Gregg, W. (1997). Elder-abuse in people with dementia in northern Ireland: Prevalence and predictors in cases referred to a psychiatry of old age service. *International Journal of Geriatric Psychiatry*, 12(6), 632–35.

Council on Scientific Affairs. (1987). Elder-abuse and neglect. *Journal of the American Medical Association*, 257(7), 966–71.

Davis, R. C., & Medina-Ariza, J. (2001) *Results from an Elder Abuse Prevention Experiment in New York City. Research in Brief*. Washington, DC: National Institute of Justice.

Department of Health and Children. (2002). *Protecting Our Future: A Report of the Working Group on Elder Abuse*. Dublin: The Stationery Office. (Retrieved 2 August 2010 from http://www.dohc.ie/publications/pdf/pof.pdf?direct=1)

Department of Health and Children. (2007). *Establishment of Commission of Investigation into the Management, Operation and Supervision of Leas Cross Nursing Home*. Dublin: The Stationery Office. (Retrieved 4 April 2008 from http://www.dohc.ie/press/releases/2007/20070424.html)

Fulmer, T., Guadagno, L., Dyer, C., & Connolly, M. T. (2004). Progress in elder abuse screening assessment instruments. *Journal of the American Geriatrics Society*, 52, 297–304.

Giurani, F., & Hasan, M. (2000). Abuse in elderly people: The Granny Battering revisited. *Archives of Gerontology and Geriatrics*, 31(3), 215–20.

Glendenning, F. (1999). Elder abuse and neglect in residential settings: The need for inclusiveness in elder abuse research. *Journal of Elder Abuse & Neglect*, 10(1/2), 1–11.

Goergen, T. (2001). Stress, conflict, elder abuse and neglect in German nursing homes: A pilot study among professional caregivers. *Journal of Elder Abuse & Neglect*, 13(1), 1–26.

Greene, K. (2002). Study finds many nursing homes fail to promptly report abuse allegations. *Wall Street Journal - Eastern Edition*, 4 March, B2.

Hirsch, R., & Vollhardt, B. (2002). Elder maltreatment. In Jacoby, R., & Oppenheimer, C., eds., *Psychiatry in the Elderly*. Oxford: Oxford University Press.

Hörl, J. (2002). National Report on Elder Abuse in Austria (from *Missing Voices: Views of Older Persons on Elder-abuse*). Vienna: Institute of Sociology, University of Vienna. (Retrieved 30 March 2008 from http://www.who.int/ageing/projects/elder_abuse/alc_ea_aut.pdf)

Kleinschmidt, K. (1997). Elder abuse: A review. *Annals of Emergency Medicine*, 30, 463–72.

Kurrle, S., Sadler, P., Lockwood, K., & Cameron, I. (1997). Elder abuse: Prevalence, intervention and outcomes in patients referred to four Aged Care Assessment Teams. *Medical Journal of Australia*, 166, 119–22.

Lachs, M. S., & Pillemer, K. (2004). Elder abuse. *The Lancet*, 364, 1263–72.

Levine, J. M. (2003). Elder neglect and abuse: A primer for primary care physicians. *Geriatrics*, 58(10), 37–44.

Lithwick, M., Beaulieu, M., Gravel, S., & Straka, S. (1999). The mistreatment of older adults: Perpetrator–victim relationships and interventions. *Journal of Elder Abuse & Neglect*, 11(4), 95–112.

Malks, B., Buckmaster, J., & Cunningham, L. (2003). Combating elder financial abuse: A multi-disciplinary approach to a growing problem. *Journal of Elder Abuse & Neglect*, 15(3/4), 55–70.

Mulholland, P. (2008). Elder abuse widespread. *Irish Medical News*, 11 February. (Retrieved 30 April 2008 from http://www.imn.ie)

National Academy of Sciences (2003). *Elder Mistreatment: Abuse, Neglect, and Exploitation in an Aging America*. Washington, DC: National Academy of Sciences.

Neale, A., Hwalek, M. Goodrich, C., & Quinn, K. (1996). The Illinois elder abuse system: Program description and administrative findings. *The Gerontologist*, 36(4), 502–11.

Nerenberg, L. (2003). *Daily Money Management Programs: A Protection Against Elder Abuse*. Washington, DC: National Center on Elder Abuse.

Nerenberg, L. (2008). *Elder Abuse Prevention*. New York: Springer.

Nursing in the Community. (2008). Key services for elderly found lacking. *Nursing in the Community*, 9(2), 4.

O'Loughlin, A., & Duggan, J. (1998). *Abuse, Neglect and Mistreatment of Older People: An Exploratory Study. Report no. 52*. Dublin: National Council on Ageing and Older People.

O'Neill, D. (2001). *Respect for Older People. Irishhealth.com*, 21 March 2001. (Retrieved 3 April 2008 from http://www.irishhealth.com/index.html?level=4& section=&5&id=1903)

Pang, W. S. (2000). Elder abuse: Under-recognised and under-reported. *Singapore Medical Journal*, 41(12), 567–70.

Penhale, B. (2006). Elder abuse in Europe: An overview of recent developments. *Journal of Elder Abuse & Neglect*, 18(1), 107–16.

Pillemer, K., & Moore, D. W. (1989). Abuse of patients in nursing homes: Findings from a survey of staff. *The Gerontologist*, 29, 314–20.

Pillemer, K., Mueller-Johnson, K., Mock, S., Suitor, J., & Lachs, M. (2007). Interventions to prevent elder mistreatment. In Doll, L. S., Bonzo, S. E., Sleet, D. A., Mercy, J. A., & Haas, E. N., eds., *Handbook of Injury and Violence Prevention*. New York: Springer, pp. 241–56.

Podnieks, E. (1999). Support groups: A chance at human connection for abused older adults. In Pritchard, J., ed., *Elder Abuse Work: Best Practice in Britain and Canada*. London: Jessica Kingsley Publishers, pp. 457–83.

Randal, J., & German, T. (1999). *The Ageing and Development Report: Poverty, Independence and the World's People*. London: HelpAge International.

Reay, A. M., & Browne, K. D. (2001). Risk factor characteristics in carers who physically abuse or neglect their elderly dependants. *Aging & Mental Health*, 5(1), 56–62.

Reay, A. M., & Browne, K. D. (2002). The effectiveness of psychological interventions with individuals who physically abuse or neglect their elderly dependents. *Journal of Interpersonal Violence*, 17(4), 416–31.

Salari, S. M. (2005). Infantilization as elder mistreatment: Evidence from five adult day centers. *Journal of Elder Abuse and Neglect*, 17(4), 53–91.

Scogin, F., Beall, C., Bynum, J., Stephens, G., Grote, N., Baumhover, L. A., *et al.* (1989). Training for abusive caregivers: An unconventional approach to an intervention dilemma. *Journal of Elder Abuse & Neglect*, 1(4), 73–86.

Scott, K. A. (2008). *Violence Prevention in Low and Middle Income Countries:*

Finding a Place on the Global Agenda. Workshop Summary. Washington, DC: The National Academies Press.

Swagerty, D. L., Takahashi, P. Y., & Evans, J. M. (1999). Elder mistreatment. *American Family Physician*, 59, 2804–8.

Thurlow, R. (2008). *Safeguarding Vulnerable Adults: National Developments and Best Practice.* London: Action on Elder Abuse. (Retrieved 30 August 2010 from http://www.newham.gov.uk/NR/rdonlyres/74D1744E-E9E9-49C4-AD5E-C8AC22EA265F/0/SafeguardingVulnerableAdultsActionOnElderAbuse08.pdf)

Thomas, C. (2000). The first National Study of Elder Abuse and Neglect: contrast with results from other studies. *Journal of Elder Abuse & Neglect*, 12, 1–14.

Tonks, A., & Bennett, G. (1999). Elder abuse: Doctors must acknowledge it, look for it, and learn how to prevent it. *British Medical Journal*, 318(7179), 278–80.

US Census Bureau.`(2008). *International Database.* Washington DC: US Census Bureau. (Retrieved 30 March 2010 from http://www.census.gov/)

Victorian Community Council Against Violence. (2005). *Preventing Elder Abuse Through the Health Sector: A Background Paper by the Victorian Community Council Against Violence.* Melbourne: Victorian Community Council Against Violence. (Retrieved 30 March 2008 from http://www.seniorscard.vic.gov.au/Web19/osv/rwpgslib.nsf/GraphicFiles/Victorian+Community+Council+Against+Violonce+Report+November+2005.doc/$file/Victorian+Community+Council+Against+Violonce+Report++November+2005.doc, March, 2008)

Vladescu, D., Eveleigh, K., Ploeg, J., & Patterson, C. (1999). An evaluation of a client-centered case management program for elder abuse. *Journal of Elder Abuse & Neglect*, 11(4), 5–22.

Wilber, K. (1995). The search for effective alternatives to conservatorship: Lessons from a daily money management diversion study. *Journal of Aging & Social Policy*, 7(1), 39–56.

Wilson, G. (2002). Dilemmas and ethics: Social work practice in the detection and management of abused older women and men. *Journal of Elder Abuse & Neglect*, 14(1), 79–94.

Wolf, R. (2000). Risk assessment instruments. *National Center on Elder Abuse Newsletter*, 3(1).

Wolf, R., & Pillemer, K. (1988). Intervention, outcome, and elder abuse. In Hotaling, G. T., Finkelhor, D., Kirkpatrick, J. T., & Straus, M. A., eds., *Coping with Family Violence: Research and Policy Perspectives.* Thousand Oaks, CA: Sage, pp. 257–74.

World Health Organization (WHO). (2002a). *World Report on Violence and Health: Summary.* WHO, Geneva.

World Health Organization (WHO). (2002b). *The Toronto Declaration on the Global Prevention of Elder Abuse.* WHO, Geneva. (Retrieved 2 August 2010 from http://www.inpea.net/images/TorontoDeclaration_English.pdf)

Chapter 11

Ageing and attachment

Maja Barker

Introduction

Despite Bowlby's early assertion that attachment representations are likely to exert influence 'from the cradle to the grave' (Bowlby, 1969/1982: 208), relatively little attention has been paid to the importance of attachment in later life in comparison with other stages of the lifespan (Bradley & Cafferty, 2001). This chapter considers the relationship between attachment and ageing with a particular focus on later life. First, the broader context of attachment and later life is introduced by highlighting issues relating to population and individual ageing. Against this backdrop the attachment framework is explored and its utility in fostering developmental insights into later life is considered.

Population ageing

A key factor creating impetus for investigating developmental experiences in later life is population ageing. After remaining fairly constant for most of human history, life expectancy at birth in the industrialised ('developed') world has approximately doubled in the past two centuries, reaching 79 years for women, and 72 years for men (United Nations, 2002). This shift in the distribution of a country's population towards older ages is termed population ageing. It is a highly generalised process but is most advanced in more developed countries.

Worldwide, the proportion of people aged 65 years and over is growing faster than any other age group. In 2004, the global population aged 65 and over was estimated at 461 million, an increase of 10.3 million since 2003. Global projections suggest that the annual net gain will continue to exceed 10 million over the next decade – more than 850,000 each month. Developed nations have the highest percentages of older people in the world today; before the middle of the twenty-first century, some of these countries may have more grandparents than children under age 18 (see Kinsella & Phillips, 2005).

Although population ageing represents, in one sense, a success story for humankind, it also poses profound challenges to societies that must adapt to a changing age structure. In particular, population ageing poses a significant challenge for health care systems. A primary challenge is the dramatic increase in the prevalence of chronic diseases (Strong *et al.*, 2005). Strategies are required to prevent and decrease ill health and disability and maximise well-being in what will be an increasing proportion of the population in society (Brenner & Shelley, 1998). Policies and health promotion programmes that prevent poor health outcomes among older people can reduce the impact of an population ageing on health care costs. In order to plan and deliver these policies and programmes, more detailed consideration of development in later life is a research and clinical priority.

Individual ageing

As part of the broader developmental continuum of the life cycle, ageing is a dynamic process that challenges an individual to make continuing behavioural adaptations (Diehl *et al.*, 1996). Although the processes of ageing are by no means uniform (Rowe & Kahn, 1987), there are challenges that occur with greater frequency in later life. These include changes in family structure and roles, object loss and bereavement and the experience of illness or health threat (Heckhausen *et al.*, 1989). In later life, these challenges are often multiple, they occur across a number of domains of functioning, and their effects can be cumulative.

In considering developmental challenges in later life, the experience of health threat or illness is one that is particularly significant from the perspective of health promotion. The increased frequency and severity of chronic health strains in later life has been well documented (e.g. Smith *et al.*, 2002) with studies showing that the majority of older adults have a diagnosis of at least one mild to severe internal, neurological or orthopaedic disease (Steinhagen-Thiessen & Borchelt, 1999).

Although individuals can experience a variety of challenges in later life that may lead to decrements in performance and physical and psychological functioning, the magnitude of these decrements can also be partially prevented (Baltes & Lang, 1997; Ryff, 1989). As a group, older people are more diverse than younger people and display great variation in how they adapt to challenges (O'Reilly *et al.*, 2003).

Questions such as how people adapt to late-life challenges, why some people age more optimally or successfully, and why some older people cope better with adversity need to be addressed. Given that older adults are representing an increasing proportion of the population worldwide the need to address such questions is increasing (Duke *et al.*, 2002). Several factors have been posited as playing a role in explaining how people adapt to late-life challenges. These factors can be conceptualised as falling into two broad domains: inter- and intra-personal factors. In relation to interpersonal factors, later-life family relations, intimacy, friendship and other social relations and intergenerational issues (Bengtson, 2001) have been identified as playing an important role in the ageing process. In relation to intrapersonal factors, empirical evidence suggests that factors such as perceptions of control (Baltes *et al.*, 1999), a disposition of accommodative flexibility (Rothermund & Brandtstädter, 2003), and situation-specific self-referent beliefs of personal competence (Slangen-de Kort *et al.*, 2001) feature as critical components of adaptability and psychological resilience. Several influential theoretical perspectives also highlight the role of intrapersonal factors in psychological resilience. Erikson's theory of the life cycle (Erikson, 1959, cited in Carr, 2006: 32) is one such theory. This theory has been ground-breaking as it was among the first theories to consider later life as a developmental period in the life cycle.

Although attempts to increase insight into late-life development are apparent, the complexity of the ageing experience and its differentiation from other life periods (Ryff, 1991) highlights the need for more detailed investigation. Such investigation can contribute to the broader scientific understanding of the ageing process, while simultaneously supporting efforts to foster optimal outcomes in later life.

Attachment

In considering factors that can account for adaptation to challenges, i.e. adaptive outcomes, in later life, one that has received limited attention is attachment. Later life, however, is a stage that shares similarities with all other stages of life (e.g. Laidlaw *et al.*, 2004) and as such, warrants consideration from a developmental perspective. Some theorists have begun to recognise the unique significance that attachment phenomena might hold for older adults, as the potential for distressing separation and loss experiences increases.

Attachment can be conceptualised as an intrapersonal factor embedded in an interpersonal context (Feeney, 2006). Attachment theory (e.g. Bowlby, 1969/1982) has profoundly influenced theoretical and empirical formulations about the nature of human development. The theory states that attachment is a developmental process based on the evolved adaptive tendency for young children to maintain proximity to a familiar person, called the attachment figure (Bowlby, 1980). The primary assumption of attachment theory is that humans form close emotional bonds in the interest of survival (Pietromonaco & Feldman Barrett, 2000).

According to attachment theory, emotional bonds with attachment figures facilitate the development and maintenance of mental representations, or 'internal working models' (Bowlby, 1973). Factors such as the availability of the attachment figure and his or her ability and willingness to provide care, particularly during episodes of distress, are likely to determine the quality of an individual's internal working models (Ainsworth *et al.*, 1978). These internal working models of attachment are theorised to consist of beliefs about the self, others and the self in relation to others (Bowlby, 1980; Carlson *et al.*, 2004). Internal working models are the hypothesised mechanism through which attachment-related experience influences human development throughout the lifespan (Bretherton & Munholland, 1999; Caspers *et al.*, 2006). As such, they form the cornerstone of attachment theory.

Working models may be expressed through patterns of relating to others. These patterns of relating are often operationalised as attachment *styles*. Attachment style classifications were initially based on Ainsworth et al.'s (1978) typology of attachment styles in infancy – secure, anxious and avoidant. Later theorists extended conceptualisations to other life stages. Main and colleagues (1985) used the terms 'dismissing of attachment' and 'preoccupied with attachment' to describe insecure patterns among adults. Crittenden (1997, cited in Ingebretsen & Solem, 1998: 150) has extended this with a number of subpatterns in four groups: dismissing, integrated, preoccupied and anti-integrated. More recent studies (e.g. Brennan *et al.*, 1998), however, show that attachment in adults is best conceptualised as regions in a two-dimensional space. The dimensions defining this space are attachment anxiety and attachment avoidance. Although attachment styles have been shown to reflect differences in internal working models (Ross *et al.*, 2006) conclusions about attachment differences in working models are tempered by research limitations. First, investigation relating to beliefs about others has been limited (Pietromonaco & Feldman Barrett, 2000). Given that beliefs about others represent one domain of the internal working model of attachment these beliefs need to be investigated with greater complexity. With respect to beliefs about the self, research on internal working models of the self has typically measured these in terms of global positive and negative feelings about the self and therefore provides only limited information about the content of self-models. Social cognitive research on the self, however, suggests that the self includes not only positive and negative feelings but also a broader range of content (Markus & Kitayama, 1991). As such, views of the self in the context of attachment relationships need to be investigated with greater specificity, including examining elaborated knowledge about different aspects of the self.

In considering the structure of working models, several theorists have proposed that working models are organised in a hierarchical fashion, ranging from general to specific models (see Pietromonaco & Feldman Barrett, 2000). From this perspective, people do not hold a single working model of the self and others; rather, they hold a family of models. This implies that working models are not a single entity but are multifaceted representations in which information at one level need not be consistent with information at another level.

Some consideration has been given to the processes by which working models may exert their effect. In the first instance, working models may influence developmental outcomes through cognitive processes; specifically they may function to direct attention to representation-consistent information and to produce interpretations of interpersonal events that are consistent with their working models (Ainsworth, 1989; Fraley & Shaver, 1997). Working models may also exert an effect on outcomes through affective processes. This might occur directly or indirectly by means of their effect on cognition. Pietromonaco and Feldman Barrett (2000) have proposed that two similar affect-related processes are implicated in the operation of working models for adults, emotional reactivity, defined as the frequency with which the need for felt-security is activated, and emotional regulation strategies, defined as the pattern of relationship behaviour that individuals enact in an attempt to maintain or restore felt-security.

Another fundamental way in which internal working models may influence outcomes is through 'attachment behaviour'. According to Bowlby, attachment behaviour is any behaviour that results in a person attaining or retaining proximity to some other differentiated and preferred individual (Bowlby, 1969/1982). Attachment behaviour is activated when safety needs are threatened. Its purpose is to meet the primary goal of survival. Three broad types of attachment behaviour have been recognised (Belsky & Cassidy, 1994). First, signalling behaviours are those that indicate an interest in social interaction. Such behaviours include smiling, vocalising and laughter. These behaviours bring the attachment figure to the person so that they can both enjoy the interaction. A second type of attachment behaviour is aversive behaviour, for example, crying. In childhood attachment, this type of behaviour serves in bringing the mother to the child. Finally, active behaviours are behaviours that take the child to the mother or primary caregiver. These broad types of attachment behaviour can be recognised throughout the lifespan. When people want emotional closeness or experience distress, they will either behave in a socially appealing manner; send out distress signals designed to invite attention and concern, or actively approach and seek out others for the things that they believe close relationships should have or could provide. These attachment behaviours are pivotal in describing interpersonal behavioural patterns that reflect specific attachment styles.

The literature on attachment suggests that there a number of key concepts that can be considered in formulating late-life development within an attachment framework. These concepts or attachment-related experiences primarily relate to attachment figures, internal working models, attachment styles and attachment behaviours.

Significance of attachment in later life

The significance of attachment in later life has been considered within the context of two broad areas of investigation; namely, the profile of attachment in later life and the role of attachment in adaptive outcomes.

Profile of attachment in later life

Hypothesised changes in attachment-related experiences gain credence from suggestions that new life events and new relationship experiences can cause changes in attachment style (Bowlby, 1969/1982). Given the increased frequency of life events and challenges in later life it is possible that attachment changes will become increasingly evident during this developmental period.

One possible attachment-related change pertains to the importance of the attachment system relative to other systems. Throughout the lifespan other systems operate in parallel with the attachment system to influence functioning and development. For example, it has been proposed that in adulthood, individuals are motivated not only by the attachment system but also by the caregiving and reproductive systems (Pietromonaco & Feldman Barrett, 2000). Most theorists have conceptualised these as separate, evolved systems that can have independent effects on developmental outcomes (Simpson & Rholes, 2000). This suggests that the relative role of these systems may vary as a function of lifestage such that attachment might play a more prominent role at different times.

Another possible change relates to the figure to which individuals become attached. It has been proposed that with development individuals develop an increased propensity to forge attachments not only to people, but also to places, pets, cherished possessions, and even symbolic representations of these such as memories (Cookman, 2005). Although these proposals have received scant empirical attention it has been reported that attachment to place, in particular, gains particular significance in later life (Hidalgo & Hernández, 2001; Swenson, 1998). Moreover, it has been suggested that attachment to place or home may act as a mediator between the quality of an individual's housing and psychological outcomes such as positive affect (Evans et al., 2002).

Pivotal to an investigation of changes in attachment-related experiences is a consideration of changes in internal working models. It has been proposed that the structure of working models, in all its complexity, will evolve substantially across the lifespan (Bowlby, 1969/1982). In keeping with this it is plausible that later life may foster increased specificity in different aspects of working models. For example, given that age and ageing are inherent components of the self for most people in later life (e.g. Ryff, 1991) it may be the case that as people get older they develop working models of self that are increasingly specific to ageing. Related to this, it has also been suggested that as people get older they develop more health-related self-concepts and tend to monitor age-related changes in their most salient physical and psychological functions (Gomez & Madey, 2001; Whitbourne & Collins, 1998). This in turn suggests that as people get older internal working models that reflect health-related issues may become increasingly salient. It is possible that this increasing specificity will be seen across all internal working models, namely, of self, others, and self in relation to others. Related to changes in the specificity of working models, are changes in their overall complexity. It has been proposed that models become more complex and sophisticated as individuals develop more abstract and cognitive skills (Bowlby, 1969/1982). As such, any loss of cognitive skills in later life, as in dementia, may have the effect of reducing the complexity of internal working models.

Related to changes in internal working models are changes in attachment style. According to Bowlby, attachment styles are not immutable as development 'turns at each and every stage of the journey on an interaction between the organism as it has developed up to that moment and the environment in which it then finds itself' (Bowlby, 1973: 364). Despite this conjecture, attachment styles are often postulated as tending more toward assimilating, rather than accommodating to later experiences (Zhang & Labouvie-Vief, 2004). Pre-existing attachment styles tend to be carried over to new relationships by guiding and influencing an individual's perception, evaluations and behaviour (Bretherton & Munholland, 1999). Data on stability of attachment styles, however, portrays a mixed picture. A number of studies have shown that individuals show shifts in attachment styles over time (see Zhang & Labouvie-Vief, 2004). In light of propositions that working models may be modified in later life, it is reasonable to deduce that attachment styles will also reflect these changes. The literature on attachment styles in later life suggests that attachment patterns in older adults may not conform to the distributions found in younger adults (Diehl et al., 1998; Magai et al., 2001). Specifically, scores on dismissing attachment tend to be higher among older adults whereas security scores are lower. A possible explanation for this is that attachment styles change over time and that older adults are undergoing a voluntary disengagement process. From this standpoint, higher rates of dismissing attachment styles may reflect a process of accommodation, in that older adults who have lost or fear the loss of an attachment figure may attempt to minimise the emotional significance of the attachment. By the same token, however, it is also possible that generational differences in attachment style may reflect cohort effects. Until longitudinal studies have been conducted the extent to which attachment differences reflect developmental phenomena or cohort effects cannot be determined.

In conclusion, the literature on the profile of attachment in later life suggests that there are likely to be fluctuations in aspects of attachment-related experience. In order to further advance our conceptualisation of attachment across the lifespan there is a need to empirically explore the specific nature of these fluctuations. As such, the challenge of qualifying the structure and processes of late-life attachment remain.

Role of attachment in late-life outcomes

Attachment-related experience is likely to be significant in influencing adaptive outcomes in later life. This conjecture gains support from theories that conceptualise development in later life. One of these theories is Erikson's psychosocial stage model (Erikson, 1959, cited in Carr, 2006: 32). According to Erikson's model individuals experience specific dilemmas or crises across the lifespan. In later life, the main crisis is that of integrity versus despair. During this stage individuals need to direct energy into accepting the events that make up their life. This crisis manifests itself as a review of the individual's life career. Ego integrity results from positive resolution of this life crisis. Conversely, despair is the result of negative resolution or lack of resolution of this life crisis. In this stage of development, the capacity to trust others is brought to the fore (Martindale, 1998). This suggests that attachment-related experience may be relevant in determining how this stage of development is resolved. As such, attachment-related experience will also have direct implications for adaptive outcomes.

In considering specific adaptive outcomes in later life, one area that warrants consideration is the relationship between attachment and quality of life. In recent years, quality of life has become a predominant issue for older adults (Hamill & Connors, 2004). Shifts in health care philosophy in the past 50 years have placed the issue firmly in the centre of health care delivery and the development of the health care environment. Quality of life is a global concept that has been assessed by various measures including happiness, life satisfaction, depressions, anxiety, and loneliness (Webster, 1998). A growing body of evidence provides preliminary support for an association between attachment style and quality of life in the general population of older adults. Secure attachment styles have been linked with higher levels of social integration (Wensauer & Grossman, 1995), life satisfaction (Park & Vandenberg, 1994; Wensauer & Grossman, 1995), happiness (Webster, 1997), optimism (Wensauer & Grossman, 1995) and health-related quality of life (Zhang & Labouvie-Vief, 2004). Conversely, insecure attachment styles have been linked with defensive coping (Zhang & Labouvie-Vief, 2004), anxiety (Andersson & Stevens, 1993), depressive symptoms (Zhang & Labouvie-Vief, 2004) and loneliness (Andersson & Stevens, 1993). These findings suggest that attachment-related experiences may act as risk factors or resources for adaptive outcomes in later life.

Given the significance of illness or health threat in later life, it is important to consider the role that attachment-related experiences might play in influencing adaptive outcomes within this context. The literature to date suggests that attachment-related experience may influence reactions to illness in theoretically and practically meaningful ways. According to Unutzer *et al.* (1997) medical illness constitutes the most important factor distinguishing older adults from those aged 65 years or less. Moreover, the experience of illness may be particularly challenging in later life as it is often associated with a growing sense of fear, vulnerability and insecurity (Wright *et al.*, 1995). Such challenges may also be accompanied by separation anxiety and fears of abandonment that prompt the older person to engage in behaviours aimed at maintaining attachment figure proximity.

Related to this, attachment-related experiences may have behavioural implications that directly affect the course of the illness or health threat. For instance, attachment theory can be used to make hypotheses about orientations towards professional medical intervention. Theoretical and empirical evidence suggests that the experience of supportive and sensitive parenting characteristic of individuals with secure attachment is thought to promote a belief that others are available during episodes of distress. This in turn increases the likelihood of seeking support during challenging encounters (Caspers *et al.*, 2006; Ciechanowski *et al.*, 2004). Conversely, experiences of rejection or neglect typically associated with dismissing attachment may promote feelings of self-reliance and a view that others are unavailable when distressed. Consequently, individuals classified as dismissing may be less likely to turn to others for assistance. Finally, inconsistent parenting, which is characteristic of preoccupied attachment, is thought to produce a hyper-vigilance towards others coupled with a continued dissatisfaction with support received. As such, individuals classified as preoccupied may report higher rates of seeking professional support due to the unsuccessful impact of intervention.

Although attachment is likely to play a significant role across illnesses the magnitude of its role may vary as a function of the illness. For instance, there may be an initial division between acute, cyclical and chronic illnesses. Many acute conditions are caused by external pathogens and are time limited. Chronic illnesses, by contrast, are permanent and as such are embedded in the very fabric of the self (Leventhal *et al.*, 2003). Thus, it is plausible that attachment-related experience may have more prominent implications for the experience of chronic illnesses.

In considering specific chronic illnesses, one that has been considered within an attachment framework is dementia. Primarily a disease of older adults (Vernooij-Dassen & Downs, 2005), dementia is a generic term most often applied to geropsychological problems, reflecting progressive, persistent losses of cognitive and intellectual functions, such as memory, language, visuo-spatial skills, emotion and personality without impairment of perception or consciousness. The nature of dementia makes it likely that attachment-related issues will become salient. Specifically, the process of dementia is characterised by experiences of loss, separation from attachment figures and feelings of insecurity, each of which reflect the central themes of attachment theory (Browne & Schlosberg, 2006). Moreover, people with dementia continually find themselves in situations that they experience as 'strange', and this is deemed to activate the need for attachment or security and reassurance (Kitwood, 1997).

Several studies have investigated attachment-related experiences in dementia care-recipients. Miesen (1993) was one of the first researchers to report that patients with dementia could be classified as having secure, avoidant or ambivalent styles of attachment. The occurrence of attachment behaviours in people with dementia has also been documented (Browne & Shlosberg, 2005; Miesen, 1993; Wright *et al.*, 1995). Commonly occurring behaviours include shadowing caregivers when they are present and calling out or searching for caregivers when they are absent. These behaviours reflect the behaviours of infants faced with separation from their caregivers (e.g. Ainsworth *et al.*, 1978). Related to this is evidence of 'parent fixation' in individuals with dementia (e.g. Miesen, 1993). This is the belief that one or both parents are still alive, when in fact they have been deceased for some years. Parent fixation may be exhibited by people referring to their parents in conversation as if they are still alive, asking how their parents are, calling out and searching for parents and begging to be allowed to return to the parental home (Browne & Schlosberg, 2005). According to Miesen this behaviour reflects an individual's reliance on internal sources of security, specifically, it reciprocates the need for safety from within the person him or herself. In addition to descriptive findings documenting the presence of attachment behaviours and parent fixation in older adults with dementia, research has also considered the extent to which attachment behaviours and parent fixation can vary as a function of attachment style (Browne & Schlosberg, 2005). Findings show that overt attachment behaviours but not parent fixation can vary as a function of attachment style such that participants with avoidant attachment styles exhibit more overt attachment behaviour than participants with secure attachment styles.

Other studies have extended descriptive findings by examining the implications that attachment style might have for adaptive outcomes in dementia. Magai *et al.* (1997) found that secure attachment in older adults with dementia was related to greater expression of positive emotions. Conversely, avoidant attachment was related to negative emotional expression. In keeping with this, Magai and Cohen (1998) showed that premorbid attachment was related to physician-rated symptomatology. Specifically, dementia patients with an avoidant attachment style were reported to have higher levels of paranoid delusions, whereas those with an ambivalent attachment style were reported to have high levels of anxiety. As such, preliminary evidence suggests that the attachment styles of chronically ill older adults with dementia are related to patterns of emotional expression and symptom manifestation.

Attachment may also provide a relevant framework for considering the experiences of those who care for people with dementia. The relationship between attachment and caregiving has its roots in early formulations of attachment theory and warrants more detailed consideration particularly in the context of an illness as challenging as dementia. Although attachment theory emphasises that attachment and caregiving are two separate systems, there is a general consensus that caregiving behaviour is influenced by attachment. Related to this, there is an assumption that internal working models of attachment are closely related to internal working models of caregiving (Pietromonaco & Feldman Barrett, 2000).

Within the context of caregiving, caring for someone with dementia has been found to be one of the most demanding and stressful experiences for both formal and informal carers. Moreover, the experience is often more demanding and stressful than caring for people who are physically impaired (Brodaty et al., 2005). Loss is a primary challenge that caregivers have to face. The content of the losses may differ, but feelings of loss seem to be a common challenge for family caregivers (Ingebretsen & Solem, 1998). For spousal caregivers the loss may represent the loss of a secure attachment figure. For some the loss of a responsible problem-solver is most prominent, whereas others may be most disturbed by losing a discussion partner or a sexual partner. The process of regulating the relationship by reducing expectations, accepting role changes and maintaining the balance of proximity–distance is a primary task that caregivers face. Attachment is likely to be prominent in completing this task with preliminary evidence suggesting that the attachment style of the caregiver and the attachment style of the care-recipient have important effects on how the relationship is regulated (Ingebretsen & Solem, 1998).

In conclusion, the literature to date highlights the role of attachment in late-life adaptive outcomes. More detailed consideration of attachment-related experience is important both for understanding variation in late-life outcomes and for fostering efforts to promote adaptive outcomes in the older-adult population.

Summary and conclusions

This chapter has considered the relationship between attachment and ageing with a particular focus on later life. Within the context of population and individual ageing it is apparent that the rapid growth of the world's older population has stimulated the need to understand individual variation in late-life outcomes. Against this backdrop attachment theory has significant theoretical and practical relevance. Key attachment-related experiences or concepts that are relevant to later life include attachment figures, internal working models, attachment styles and attachment behaviours. The significance of these concepts for later life has been considered within the context of two broad areas of investigation; namely, the profile of attachment in later life and the role of attachment in adaptive outcomes. The literature on the profile of attachment in later life suggests that there are fluctuations in aspects of attachment-related experience. Furthermore, a consideration of the role of attachment-related experience in adaptive outcomes in later life suggests that it may have important implications, particularly in the context of illnesses or health threats such as dementia.

This review has several implications. First, from a theoretical and empirical perspective, it is apparent that the field of late-life attachment is in its infancy. As such, there is a need for more detailed conceptualisations and investigations of attachment in older adults. Future research should examine trajectories in attachment-related phenomena in later life while elucidating the adaptive or maladaptive value that attachment profiles can have in different individual and environmental contexts. In practical terms, the present review suggests that investigating variation in attachment-related experience may enable identification of subgroups at risk for poorer outcomes in later life. In keeping with this, attachment theory could be useful as a framework for promoting recovery and adaptation in older-adult populations. Health care professionals can play a role by implementing attachment-related concepts as a systematic orientation and perspective in daily activities and professional clinical practice. Within this context, knowledge about attachment could be routinely used to elucidate clients' attachment experience. This could help to identify patterns that might be incongruent with the goals of the health care alliance. Such information could in turn create conditions for conceptual change by facilitating health care professionals to deliver interventions that are specific, individualised, meaningful to the client and consistent with the goals of the professional relationship.

In conclusion, attachment theory is highly relevant for understanding developmental experience in later life. Systematic efforts need to be made to incorporate attachment as a framework in ageing research and practice. Such efforts can serve to reduce the impact of population ageing both at a national and an international level.

References

Ainsworth, M. D. S. (1989). Attachments beyond infancy. *American Psychologist*, 44, 709–16.
Ainsworth, M. D. S., Blehar, M., Waters, E., & Wall, S. (1978). *Patterns of Attachment: A Psychological Study of the Strange Situation*. Hillsdale, NJ: Lawrence Erlbaum Associates, Inc.

Andersson, L., & Stevens, N. (1993). Associations between early experiences with parents and well-being in old age. *Journal of Gerontology*, 48, 109–16.

Baltes, M. M., & Lang, F. R. (1997). Everyday functioning and successful aging: The impact of resources. *Psychology and Aging*, 12, 433–43.

Baltes, P. B., Staudinger, U. M., & Lindenberger, U. (1999). Lifespan psychology: Theory and application to intellectual functioning. *Annual Review of Psychology*, 50, 471–507.

Belsky, J., & Cassidy, J. (1994). Attachment: Theory and evidence. In Rutter, M. L., Hay, D. F., & Baron-Cohen, S., eds., *Development through Life: A Handbook for Clinicians*. Oxford: Blackwell, pp. 373–402.

Bengtson, V. L. (2001). Beyond the nuclear family: The increasing importance of multigenerational bonds. 1998 Burgess Award Lecture. *Journal of Marriage and Family*, 63, 1–16.

Bowlby, J. (1973). *Attachment and Loss: Vol. 2. Separation*. New York: Basic Books.

Bowlby, J. (1980). *Attachment and Loss: Vol. 3. Loss*. New York: Basic Books.

Bowlby, J. (1982). *Attachment and Loss: Vol. 1. Attachment*. New York: Basic Books. (Original work published 1969.)

Bradley, J. M., & Cafferty, T. P. (2001). Attachment among older adults: Current issues and directions for future research. *Attachment & Human Development*, 3, 200–21.

Brennan, K. A., Clark, C. L., & Shaver, P. R. (1998). Self-report measurement of adult attachment: An integrative overview. In Simpson, J. A., & Rholes, W. S., eds., *Attachment Theory and Close Relationships*. New York: Guilford Press, pp. 46–76.

Brenner, H., & Shelley, E. (1998). *Adding Years to Life and Life to Years: A Health Promotion Strategy for Older People*. Dublin: National Council on Ageing and Older People.

Bretherton, I., & Munholland, K. A. (1999). Internal working models in attachment relationships: A construct revisited. In Cassidy, J., & Shaver, P. R., eds., *Handbook of Attachment: Theory, Research, and Clinical Applications*. New York: Guilford Press, pp. 89–111.

Brodaty, H., Thomson, C., Thompson, C., & Fine, M. (2005). Why caregivers of people with dementia and memory loss don't use services. *International Journal of Geriatric Psychiatry*, 20(6), 537–46.

Browne, C. J., & Shlosberg, E. (2005). Attachment behaviours and parent fixation in people with dementia: the role of cognitive functioning and pre-morbid attachment style. *Aging & Mental Health*, 9(2), 153–61.

Browne, C. J., & Shlosberg, E. (2006). Attachment theory, ageing and dementia: A review of the literature. *Aging & Mental Health*, 10(2), 134–42.

Carlson, E. A., Sroufe, L. A., & Egeland, B. (2004). The construction of experience: A longitudinal study of representation and behavior. *Child Development*, 75(1), 66–83.

Carr, A. (2006). *The Handbook of Adult Clinical Psychology: An Evidence-Based Practice Approach*. London: Routledge.

Caspers, K. M., Yucuis, R., Troutman, B., & Spinks, R. (2006). Attachment as an organizer of behavior: implications for substance abuse problems and willingness to seek treatment. *Substance Abuse Treatment, Prevention, and Policy*, 1, 32.

Ciechanowski, P., Russo, J., Katon, W., Von Korff, M., Ludman, E., Lin, E., *et al.* (2004). Influence of patient attachment styles on self-care and outcomes in diabetes. *Psychosomatic Medicine*, 66, 720–8.

Cookman, C. (2005). Attachment in older adulthood: concept clarification. *Journal of Advanced Nursing*, 50, 528–35.

Diehl, M., Coyle, N., & Labouvie-Vief, G. (1996). Age and sex differences in strategies of coping and defense across the life span. *Psychology and Aging*, 11, 127–39.

Diehl, M., Elnick, A., Bourbeau, L., & Labouvie-Vief, G. (1998). Adult attachment styles: their relations to family context and personality. *Journal of Personality and Social Psychology*, 74(6), 1656–69.

Duke, J., Leventhal, H., Brownlee, S., & Leventhal, E. A. (2002). Giving up and replacing activities in response to illness. *Journals of Gerontology Series B: Psychological Sciences and Social Sciences*, 57, 367–76.

Evans, G., Kantrowitz, E., & Eshelman, P. (2002). Housing quality and psychological well-being among the elderly population. *Journals of Gerontology Series B: Psychological Sciences and Social Sciences*, 57(4), 381–3.

Feeney, B. C. (2006). An attachment theory perspective on the interplay between intrapersonal and interpersonal processes. In Vohs, K. D., & Finkel, E. J., eds., *Self and Relationships: Connecting Intrapersonal and Interpersonal Processes*. New York: Guilford Press, pp. 133–59.

Fraley, R. C., & Shaver, P. R. (1997). Adult attachment and the suppression of unwanted thoughts. *Journal of Personality and Social Psychology*, 73, 1080–91.

Gomez, R. G., & Madey, S. F. (2001). Coping-with-hearing-loss model for older adults. *Journals of Gerontology Series B: Psychological Sciences and Social Sciences*, 56, 223–5.

Hamill, R., & Connors, T. (2004). Sonas aPC: Activating the potential for communication through multisensory stimulation. In Jones, G., & Meisen, B. M. L., eds., *Care-Giving in Dementia, Vol. 3*. London: Routledge, pp. 119–37.

Heckhausen, J., Dixon, R. A., & Baltes, P. B. (1989). Gains and losses in development throughout adulthood as perceived by different adult age groups. *Developmental Psychology*, 25, 109–21.

Hidalgo, M. C., & Hernández, B. (2001). Place attachment: conceptual and empirical questions. *Journal of Environmental Psychology*, 21(3), 273–81.

Ingebretsen, R., & Solem, P. E. (1998). Spouses of persons with dementia: Attachment, loss and coping. *Norwegian Journal of Epidemiology*, 8, 149–56.

Kinsella, K., & Phillips, D. R. (2005). Global aging: The challenge of success. *Population Bulletin*, 60(1), 1–44.

Kitwood, T. (1997). *Dementia Reconsidered. The Person Comes First*. Buckingham: Open University Press.

Laidlaw, K., Thompson, L., & Gallagher-Thompson, D. (2004). Comprehensive conceptualization of cognitive behaviour therapy for late life depression. *Behavioural and Cognitive Psychotherapy*, 32, 389–99.

Leventhal, H., Brissette, I., & Leventhal, E. (2003). The common-sense model of self-regulation of health and illness. In Cameron, L., & Leventhal, H., eds., *The Self-Regulation of Health and Illness Behaviour*. New York: Routledge, pp. 42–65.

Magai, C., & Cohen, C. I. (1998). Attachment style and emotion regulation in dementia patients and their relation to caregiver burden. *Journal of Gerontology: Psychological Sciences*, 53B(3), 147–54.

Magai, C., Cohen, C. I., Culver, C., Gomberg, D., & Malatesta, C. (1997). Relation between pre-morbid personality and patterns of emotion expression in mid- to late-stage dementia. *International Journal of Geriatric Psychiatry*, 12, 1092–7.

Magai, C., Cohen, C., Milburn, N., Thorpe, B., McPherson, R., & Peralta, D. (2001). Attachment styles in older European American and African American adults. *Journals of Gerontology, Social Sciences*, 46B, S28–35.

Main, M., Kaplan, N., & Cassidy, J. (1985). Security in infancy, childhood, and adulthood: A move to the level of representation. In Bretherton, I., & Waters, E., eds., *Growing Points of Attachment Theory and Research. Monographs of the Society for Research in Child Development, 50 (1–2, Serial No. 209)*. Chicago, IL: Chicago University Press, pp. 66–104.

Markus, H., & Kitayama, S. (1991). Culture and the self: Implications for cognition, emotion, and motivation. *Psychological Review*, 98, 224–253.

Martindale, B. (1998). On ageing, dying, death and eternal life. *Psychoanalytic Psychotherapy*, 12, 259–70.

Miesen, B. M. L. (1993). Alzheimer's disease, the phenomenon of parent fixation and Bowlby's attachment theory. *International Journal of Geriatric Psychiatry*, 8, 147–53.

O'Reilly, N. D., Thomlinson, R. P., & Castrey, M. U. (2003). Women's aging benchmarks in relation to their health habits and concerns. *American Journal of Health Behavior*, 27, 268–77.

Park, D., & Vandenberg, B. (1994). The influence of separation orientation on life satisfaction in the elderly. *International Journal of Aging & Human Development*, 39, 177–87.

Pietromonaco, P. R., & Feldman Barrett, L. (2000). The internal working models concept: What do we know about the self in relation to others? *Review of General Psychology*, 4, 155–75.

Ross, L. R., McKim, M. K., & DiTommaso, E. (2006). How do underlying "self" and "other" dimensions define adult attachment styles? *Canadian Journal of Behavioural Science*, 38(4), 294–310.

Rothermund, K., & Brandtstädter, J. (2003). Depression in later life: Cross-sequential patterns and possible determinants. *Psychology and Aging*, 18, 80–90.

Rowe, J. W., & Kahn, R. L. (1987). Human aging: Usual and successful. *Science*, 237, 143–9.

Ryff, C. D. (1989). Happiness is everything, or is it? Explorations on the meaning of psychological well-being. *Journal of Personality and Social Psychology*, 57, 1069–81.

Ryff, C. D. (1991). Possible selves in adulthood and old age: A tale of shifting horizons. *Psychology and Aging*, 6, 286–95.

Simpson, J. A., & Rholes, W. S. (2000). Care giving, attachment theory, and the connection theoretical orientation. *Psychological Inquiry*, 11, 114–17.

Smith, J., Borchelt, M., Maier, H., & Jopp, D. (2002). Health and well-being in the young old and oldest old. *Journal of Social Issues*, 58, 715–32.

Slangen-de Kort, Y. A., Midden, C. J., Aarts, H., & van Wagenberg, F. (2001). Determinants of adaptive behavior among older persons: Self-efficacy, importance, and personal dispositions as directive mechanisms. *International Journal of Aging & Human Development*, 53, 253–74.

Steinhagen-Thiessen, E., & Borchelt, M. (1999). Morbidity, medication, and functional limitations in very old age. In Baltes, P. B., & Mayer, K. U., eds., *The Berlin Aging Study: Aging from 70 to 100*. Cambridge: Cambridge University Press, 131–66.

Strong, K., Mathers, C., Leeder, S., & Beaglehole, R. (2005). Preventing chronic diseases: how many lives can we save? *Lancet*, 366, 1578–82.

Swenson, M. M. (1998). The meaning of home to five elderly women. *Health Care for Women International*, 19(5), 381–93.

United Nations. (2002). *World Population Ageing: 1950–2050*. New York: UN.

Unutzer, J., Patrick, D., Simon, G., Grembowski, D., Walker, E., Rutter, C., *et al.* (1997). Depressive symptoms and the cost of health services in HMO patients aged 65 years and older: a 4-year prospective study. *Journal of the American Medical Association*, 277(20), 1618–23.

Vernooij-Dassen, M., & Downs, M. (2005). Cognitive and behavioural interventions for carers of people with dementia. (Protocol). *Cochrane Database of Systematic Reviews*, 2. Art. No.: CD005318. DOI: 10.1002/14651858.

Webster, J. D. (1997). Attachment style and well-being in elderly adults: A preliminary investigation. *Canadian Journal on Aging*, 16, 101–11.

Webster, J. D. (1998). Attachment styles, reminiscence functions and happiness in young and elderly adults. *Journal of Aging Studies*, 12, 315–30.

Wensauer, M., & Grossman, K. E. (1995). Quality of attachment representation, social integration, and use of social network resources in advanced age. *Zeitschrift für Gerontologie und Geriatrie*, 28, 444–56.

Whitbourne, S. K., & Collins, K. J. (1998). Identity and physical changes in later adulthood: Theoretical and clinical implications. *Psychotherapy*, 35, 519–30.

Wright, L. K., Hickey, J. V., Buckwalter, K. C., & Clipp, E. C. (1995). Human development in the context of aging and chronic illness: The role of attachment in Alzheimer's disease and stroke. *International Journal of Aging & Human Development*, 41, 133–50.

Zhang, F., & Labouvie-Vief, G. (2004). Stability and fluctuation in adult attachment style over a 6-year period. *Attachment & Human Development*, 6, 419–37.

Chapter 12

Ageing, relationships and sexuality

Patrick Ryan, Jessica Dudley, Colum MacMahon,
Lorraine Feeney and Alison Bonham

Introduction

Remarkably little research has been carried out regarding relationships and
sexuality in later life, despite researchers' reported findings that 'sex
matters', and that related personal characteristics are critical variables
regarding health and illness throughout the lifespan (Institute of Medicine,
2001). More pointedly, despite a handful of papers on change and decline in
ageing, little attention has been dedicated to the role of sexuality and
relationships in the context of the individual, rather then the collective
'elderly'. Limited attention has been dedicated to specific critical value
concepts, i.e. key determinants that make-up personal value systems, for
understanding sexuality and relationships in the context of human development across the lifespan. Perhaps it is our love (or ease and simplicity) of
collective nouns (toddlers, teenagers, geriatrics and so forth) and global
concepts ('quality of life', 'life satisfaction', 'mental health' and 'well-being')
that simply make it easier for younger generations to group information
about 'the elderly' into collective spheres.

In order to redress the dearth in the knowledge base, this chapter will
examine a number of key areas that should underlie any discussion
regarding the role of relationships and how the experience of sexuality for
older adults is embedded in these. These areas include the following:

1　understanding the role of relationships for older adults;
2　having a comprehensive understanding of what sexuality is;
3　addressing societal attitudes towards older adults; and consequently
4　determining older adults' attitudes towards their sexuality and
　　relationships;
5　acknowledging how health professionals engage with older adults'
　　sexuality;
6　the health and psychological benefits of sexual relationships;
7　barriers to sexual relationships such as dementia or societal attitudes
　　towards homosexuality.

Ultimately this chapter aims to highlight that although we inevitably age, feelings and the need for closeness, intimacy and relationships with others does not disappear and that despite ageing, we remain valuable and relevant to others.

Relationships and older adults

Of course sexuality and its expression are embedded in the experience of relationships. Whereas adults across the lifespan enjoy similar numbers of close relationships, Antonucci (2001) suggests that the underlying motivation for social contact may change as one gets older. Older adults may actively choose to reduce the quantity of their relationships, while concentrating their energies on more beneficial relationships. Samter (2003) proposed that elderly people tend to choose relationships with others with whom they can exchange confidences, particularly regarding ageing and life-course experiences (Nussbaum et al., 2005). In some cases older people choose to invest their time in relationships with friends ahead of some relatives.

The likelihood that older adults will experience the death of a partner only increases the possibility that elderly people would seek more rewarding relationships. After losing a spouse older adults tend to look to friends to assist them in dealing with the loss and may select friends that will provide similar support to what was previously offered by their deceased loved one. Litwin (1999) proposed that older adults' morale is bolstered more by interactions with friends rather than interactions with their adult children. Since older adults would tend to regard themselves as equals, they 'seldom patronize or play up to each other, respecting the integrity and validity of their individual experiences and situations' (Rawlins, 1995: 245). Consequently, friendships might offer elderly people more opportunity for empowering language and communication patterns than familial relationships.

This would suggest that rather than being forced into social isolation as suggested by cultural assumptions, older adults make a conscious decision to reduce their number of friends. Feldman (2003) suggests that the importance of friendship in old age is linked to the element of control. Whereas no choice exists in family relations, individuals have the option of choosing which friends they like or dislike. As old age can be associated with the gradual loss of control in other aspects of one's life, the ability to form and maintain relationships assumes greater significance. Similarly, as friendships are voluntary, Crohan and Antonucci (1989) suggest that friendships in old age are not bound by familial commitments. Larson et al. (1986) proposed that relationships with friends do not focus on mundane matters of daily issues such as monies or administrative issues, managing a household and caregiving. Since they tend to be more equitable in nature,

Field (1999) suggests it offers a chance for older adults to make personal choices that in turn can improve self-perception and independence (Nussbaum *et al.*, 2005). Because interactions with friends tend to be more socially supportive, reciprocal and identity-affirming interactions, such relationships are often viewed as more rewarding than family. Such findings are in keeping with qualitative studies undertaken by Johnson and Barer (1997) in which they discovered that adults over the age of 80 years reported few problems with social partners.

The sexual world of older adults

The area of sexual activity and relationships with older adults has remained under-researched in the UK and Ireland. There has been discussion of wider critical concepts for understanding sexuality and relationships in relation to age-related transitions, such as the numerous declines, inabilities, shortcomings and inadequacies of the older person, physical functioning, safety, medical and economic issues. However despite this, or perhaps because of this, the twenty-first century era, crucially, has neglected the development of value concepts. What has ensued is a collection of papers replete with global concepts i.e. broad, generic, umbrella terms understood at a global level, on the loss and decline of sexual activity (Evans & Garner, 2004; Jagus & Benbow, 2002), the impact of biological changes in the form of the menopause (Trudel *et al.*, 2000; Bancroft, 2007) and the subsequent related issues of intimacy (Birnbaum *et al.*, 2007), desire (Kingsberg, 2000; DeLamater & Moorman, 2007), mental health (Yang *et al.*, 2000; Jagus & Benbow 2002) and psychological well-being (Story *et al.*, 2007). Although research has been carried out in the USA in relation to older adults and sexuality, this research also has focused on sexual behaviours and sexual intercourse rather than intimacy and relationships in later life. Several explanations are suggested here for this.

It is possible that this lack of literature is due to assumptions that sexuality and intimacy are not relevant to this age group (Hinchliff & Gott, 2004). Some authors have suggested that older people are perceived as 'sexless' or 'de-sexed' (Ford, 1998; Ward *et al.*, 2005). In addition, there is widespread belief that older people are reluctant to discuss the sexual aspect of their lives (Pointon, 1997) or because the cultural norms of their upbringing were one where sex was not openly discussed (Drench & Losee, 1996). Drench and Losee (1996: 118) noted that an 'elderly person who deviates from the stereotype and wants an active sexual life may be derided as foolish (a "dirty old man")'. Estes and Binney (1991) argue that old age has been equated with illness and that it is taken for granted that ageing is a negative process of decline and decay. As Victor (1991: 1) posits 'To be old is to be unhealthy'. We conclude that to be old is also to be asexual and in order to understand the sexual world of the older adult, it is necessary to investigate how the concepts of sexual activity and sexuality are seen generally.

What is sexuality?

Hogan (1980: 3) argues that sexuality comprises 'Much more than the sex act . . . the quality of being human, all that we are as men and women . . . encompassing the most intimate feelings and deepest longings of the heart to find meaningful relationships'. Hinchliff and Gott (2004) emphasise that older people may not automatically equate sex with intercourse but that this is not recognised in the literature, where it is still assumed that if you ask someone how often they have sex, what you are really asking them is how often do they have sexual intercourse. Lemieux and colleagues (2004) found that for patients in palliative care, sexuality encompassed many things but was centred on emotional connectedness. This study found that sexuality was an important aspect of participants' lives, even in the last weeks and days of life. Their experience of sexuality changed over time, from expression that tended to include sexual intercourse, to one of intimacy through close body contact, hugging, touching of hands, kissing, 'meaningful' eye contact and other non-physical expressions of closeness and companionship. These expressions of sexuality were an essential part of their quality of life.

And it seems that although society is unwilling to discuss this issue, older adults are having relationships that include a wide range of sexual experiences. Normal age-related changes in sexual functioning such as slowed sexual response time, decrease in orgasmic intensity and longer refractory periods, do not explain older adults' ceasing sexual activity or loss of sexual desire (Skultety, 2007). Early longitudinal studies on ageing and sexuality found that the majority of older adults maintain a steady interest in sexual activity throughout the lifespan (Bretschneider & McCoy, 1988). Bretschneider and McCoy (1988) studied healthy residents of retirement homes in California and found that 62 per cent of men and 30 per cent of women over 80 had had recent sexual intercourse, whereas 87 per cent of men and 68 per cent of women had had physical intimacy of some sort. Unfortunately, no recent longitudinal studies have been carried out, making conclusions about the relationship between sexual activity and age difficult to make (Skultety, 2007). A more recent study carried out in the USA with a racially and ethnically diverse sample of adults found no differences between middle-aged and older adults who had partners, in engaging in kissing, hugging, sexual touching or caressing. Over 60 per cent of those over age 70 with partners reported engaging in sexual touching or caressing at least once a week and reported a high level of satisfaction with their sex lives. Older adult couples did engage less often in sexual intercourse, self-stimulation and oral sex than middle-aged adults did; however, more than 30 per cent of those over age 70 reported having intercourse at least once a week (AARP, 2005).

Biological mediators of sexual activity

Of course, sexual behaviour cannot be divorced from its biological mediators at this stage of life, no more than it can be so at any other stage. Sexual drive is the biological component of sexual desire; it is produced by neuroendocrine mechanisms within the body and is experienced as spontaneous, endogenous sexual interest (Kingsberg, 2000). Drive produces genital tingling, sexual thoughts, erotic attraction towards others and ultimately sexual activity.

Drive is highly influenced by testosterone in both sexes. In the older male, testosterone reduction occurs in varying degrees and neuron loss occurs in brain mechanisms associated with testosterone-dependent arousal, e.g. the locus ceruleus (Marr & Kershaw, 1998). This in addition to age-related changes in smooth muscle and vascular tissues have a direct influence on erectile function and sexual interest (Bancroft, 2007; Marr & Kershaw, 1998). Ageing men need more time and more direct stimulation of the penis in order to achieve an erection and there is a prolonged plateau phase with reduced urge to pass to orgasm or ejaculation. Orgasm is generally weaker and semen volume is reduced (Jung & Schill, 2004). Contractions of the penis, rectum and prostate are also weaker at the time of ejaculation (Trudel et al., 2000). Although the erection is not as hard and is more difficult to obtain, there is usually enough pressure for penetration until late life for most men. The refractory period between ejaculations also increases from a few minutes for young men in their twenties to over 24 hours for men in their seventies (Trudel et al., 2000).

Chronic pulmonary diseases associated with ageing such as myocardial infarction and hypertension, are associated with erectile dysfunction and sexual response problems in older adults (Pope et al., 2007). Prostate cancer is the second most prevalent cancer and the treatment involved is adversely associated with sexual dysfunction (Pope et al., 2007). Several types of medication exist, which mainly act on the arousal phase in the treatment of ejaculation and erectile dysfunction problems. This has allowed ageing couples to improve aspects of their sexual functioning; however these treatments are best used as part of a multimodal strategy in combination with marital and sexological therapy (Trudel et al., 2008).

Diabetes is frequently cited as a disorder associated with sexual dysfunction in older adults (Pope et al., 2007; DeLamater & Sill, 2005), due to its vascular effects on the blood vessels and also its deleterious effect on the nerve supply to the pelvis, resulting in reduced sexual desire in women. Arthritis has also been quoted as a cause of major discomfort during sex and is associated with reduced sexual desire in both sexes.

The use of medication also influences the level of sexual desire in older people, especially females. Alpha blockers used to treat hypertension are reported to have the greatest effect on sexual desire and selective serotonin reuptake inhibitors also have a strong association with reduced sexual desire. The accumulation of long-term usage of this drug in older people appears to be even more consequential to their sexual health (DeLamater & Sill, 2005). It is noteworthy that the majority of studies that have researched the effects of disease on sexual functioning have failed to take account of the individual's level of sexual functioning before the onset of illness; therefore they are methodologically flawed (DeLamater & Sill, 2005).

Older women are at increased risk of pelvic floor disorders such as vaginal and uterine prolapse, due to muscular and vascular changes associated with age and childbirth. Fatigue, insomnia, hot flushes and sensorial problems are also associated with the onset of menopause. Older women who have undergone hysterectomy have reported painful sexual relations, poorer quality orgasms and reduced sexual desire. However, hysterectomy can also provide positive outcomes, and increased sexual desire due to dispelling fear of becoming pregnant (Trudel et al., 2000), this is also the case for menopausal women (Marr & Kershaw, 1998). Hormonal medications that attempt to manage sexual dysfunction in women improve vaginal sensitivity and increases libido, while reducing levels of vaginal dryness and pain during intercourse. Testosterone supplementation for women has been shown to improve mood and well-being leading to increased sexual desire in post-menopausal women (Walsh & Bermen, 2004). Although it takes longer for older women to reach orgasm and they are less intense, women are still able to achieve multiple orgasms and the refractory period between orgasms does not change (Trudel et al., 2000).

In females the onset of menopause is associated with decreased oestrogen levels. This hormone is strongly related to sexual functioning and both the neurological and vascular systems are affected (Walsh & Berman, 2004). Reduced oestrogen levels are also associated with decreased vaginal lubrication, which in turn may cause pain during sex (DeLamater & Sill, 2005). There is less acidity in the vaginal canal due to changes in the vaginal mucus membrane, which can lead to vaginal infections, urinary incontinence, urinary tract infections and sexual dysfunction (Walsh & Berman, 2004). There is a thinning of the vaginal wall, shrinkage of the length and width of the vagina and the vagina also loses some elasticity with the onset of age (Trudel et al., 2000). Reduced testosterone levels in females are associated with decreased arousal, libido, sexual responsiveness, genital sensation and orgasm. Testosterone is the most potent androgen in women; levels in 20-year-old women are twice that of 40-year-old women (Walsh & Berman, 2004). Other changes in females include a shorter orgasmic phase and a decrease in the size of the clitoris and uterus (Marr & Kershaw, 1998).

DeLamater and Moorman (2007) found that frequency of all sexual behaviours was undermined by age, which precipitated onset of various age-related health problems. Naturally, greater physical satisfaction with the partner and a healthy partner was found to be associated with higher frequencies of intercourse for men and women. However, DeLamater and Moorman (2007) did find that diagnosed illness and associated medications had very little influence on frequency of sexual behaviour when protected by positive attitudes about desire for sex and a physically satisfying relationship with the partner. Although there is a strong relationship between increased age and decreased level of sexual desire, this association occurs at a much later stage then one might anticipate. Research indicates that low levels of sexual desire are not reported until after age 75 (DeLamater & Sill, 2005).

What our understanding of the biological bases of sexual experience suggests is that there are changes to how the expression of sex and sexuality is experienced. This is entirely different from the notion that older adults are or should be 'sexless'. Age does not take away the capacity for initiating and enjoying a sexual world as part of continuing identity development. It simply presents new challenges and opportunities for learning how to maintain sexual identity as an integral part of overall identity. If it is one thing that older adults are generally adept at, it is using their resilience and knowledge collected over the years to respond to learning opportunities.

Images of ageing and sexual attractiveness

The particular view that Western society holds of older people centres around an image of wrinkles, grey hair or hair loss, weight gain, the loss of bodily control, sexual dysfunction and the assumption that older adults are less competent and may incur loss in physical and cognitive function (Hockey & James, 1993; Featherstone & Hepworth, 1990). As late as 1970, the American doctor David Reuben wrote that: 'without oestrogen, the quality of being female gradually disappears. . .[and] a woman becomes as close as she can to being a man. . . . decline of breasts and female genitalia all contribute to a masculine appearance. . .Having outlived their ovaries, they may have outlived their usefulness as human beings' (1970: 288–9). How an individual is viewed or perceived ties in with his or her sexual attractiveness. What it means to be sexually active in a society where beauty is associated with youth, and for women, where sexuality is often linked to reproduction are important issues for the experience of sexuality in later life. This is an area which is under-researched.

Societal attitudes and beliefs

Attention has been drawn to societies' attitudes and expectations and the role and influence of tradition and culture (Guan, 2004; Howard et al.,

2006; Wang *et al.*, 2008). For example, some of the more interesting findings include research indicating that sexual activity among older persons was found to be lower in countries such as Vietnam and Thailand than the USA (Knodel *et al.*, 2005), with suggestions that lower levels of education may play a role in this, as has been found in countries such as Taiwan (Wang *et al.*, 2008). Different traditions have also contributed to different interpretations of sexuality in different countries. For example, Chinese culture has traditionally placed an emphasis on sexuality primarily for procreation, as opposed to the satisfaction of sexual needs (Guan, 2004).

Our perceptions of sexual attractiveness and images of older people are often compared with Eastern culture. In contrast to Western culture, Eastern societies are perceived to adopt a more positive view of ageing. In countries such as Japan, South Korea and China, ageing is associated with increased respect and a greater status within society (Chang *et al.*, 1984; Levy & Langer, 1994; Sung, 1994). These beliefs tend to come from the strong influence of Confucian principles that emphasise concepts of respect for elderly people and give these older members a more esteemed role in both familial and social contexts (Ingersoll-Dayton & Saengtienchai, 1999; Levy & Langer, 1994; Sung, 1994). However, other studies have suggested differently. Harwood and colleagues (1996) investigated traits associated with old age in Hong Kong, South Korea, Philippines, Australia, New Zealand and the USA. Findings indicated that participants from the Asian cultures did not necessarily hold more positive images of old age than their Western counterparts. The research found that participants from Hong Kong demonstrated the most negative attitudes towards ageing overall. South Koreans also held views of ageing similar to those participants from the USA. Young adults were viewed as more attractive, active, healthy, strong and liberal than older adults.

Of interest, and encouraging in that it represents at least some dissemination of whole universal terms into composite strands, is discussion in the form of gender differentiation. Some recent research into how women versus men view sexuality and relationships has provided interesting findings such as the suggestion that women may value relationship factors such as the quality of their relationships, and mental health issues more than the physiological factors of sexuality in later life (Bancroft, 2007; Umidi *et al.*, 2007). Research by DeLamater and Moorman (2007) also found that for older individuals with a partner, sexual desire was based on physical and emotional satisfaction as well as the duration of relationships. Their research also provided evidence that grief and the loss of a partner, especially after a long-term relationship, were a primary reason why older persons did not re-engage in sexual activity.

Bouman *et al.* (2006) outlined three categories of attitudes that society holds towards later life sexuality. The first is 'discrete silence', i.e. it is nicer not to speak of such things outside the bedroom. In this way privacy within the relationship is respected and people choose what is right for them, without questions or interference outside that relationship. In this category though, when problems arise there is a sense that there is no one to confide in, and embarrassment and often misery ensue. The second category is one of 'distaste'. This mindset entails that older people should not be having sex, it is unacceptable and grotesque. It is the attitude that underlies the most common reaction in general discourse when the issue of sexual intercourse in older adults is mooted. The third attitude is one of 'tunnel vision' whereby sexuality is classified only in physiological terms describing functioning only in terms of sexual organs and in relation to heterosexual relationships. It is the attitude that pervades the visual media presentation of sexual experiences – performance of a sexual act over the more subtle but in the long term more important, dynamics of sexual experience. And if sexual behaviour in older adults is rarely seen on screen, then less so is the sexual interaction between homosexual couples. This area will be addressed later in this chapter.

The arena of advertising and, in particular, cosmetics, highlights the issue of sexual image where the older body is rarely to be seen. We may conclude this is because for this industry the visible signs of ageing are unattractive and unwanted. Of note recently, is the targeting of older people as consumers of particular products and services, i.e. Dove and Mueller Yoghurts that have created some positive representations. However, as Laws (1997: 97) points out, these images are 'geared to a very particular embodied identity – an active, affluent, senior population'. In advertising, the older person as consumer is depicted as white, middle class and healthy and attention is diverted from the needs of low-income elderly people (Minkler, 1991). In 2001, cosmetics giant L'Oréal recruited Catherine Deneuve, the 61-year-old film star, to be the face of a hair-treatment product while Danone, the 'French food and beverage multi-national is currently targeting seniors with its "immunity boosting" yogurt drink, Actimel' (Boyer King, 2004: para 16). A recent article by Boyer King (2004) on brandchannel stated that advertisers rarely target older adults. 'Unless they are in the business of selling retirement homes or hearing aids, companies have turned a blind eye to this graying market' (2004: para. 4). Boyer King states that 86 per cent of older adults surveyed felt that advertising is not aimed at them and a report in the Economist magazine in 2002 stated that companies still spend over 95 per cent of their marketing and advertising budgets on the under-50 age categories (cited in Boyer King, 2004).

On a more positive note, society's impressions of older adults continues to shift and change. The release of the medication Viagra (sildenafil) highlighted older adults' interest in sexual intercourse; which was received favourably by some and less favourably by others. More recently, in 2006, the film *Away From Her* brought issues of sexuality in couples dealing with dementia into more sympathetic attention, with Julie Christie acting as an older woman with Alzheimer's disease whose sexuality remains alive.

So it appears that in general, older adults are seen as less attractive and possibly less important than our young, vibrant population and that a consequence of this is the creation of a distorted belief system denying the existence of a vibrant sexual dimension to the personality of older adults.

Health and psychological benefits of sexual behaviour

However, despite this negative image of older adults and society's denial of their continued sexuality, it appears that engaging in sexual relationships is good for our health. Hinchliff and Gott (2004) examined sexual health and quality of life with 28 participants who were aged 50 or older and had been married 20 years or longer. It was found that sharing intimate sexual relations with a loved one allowed older people to feel needed and valued by their partner (Hinchliff & Gott, 2004; Riley, 1999). In Sweden, a study of 70-year-olds found that sexually active men woke less frequently during the night and sexually active women experienced less anxiety (Persson, 1980). It was also found that the participants who were sexually active had better mental health ratings, as determined by a global evaluation, than those who were not. Kaluger and Kaluger (1979) found that people with active sex lives were more likely to continue to remain active in later life. But the literature seems to indicate that it is not just engagement with sexual relations. Relationships of a long-term nature have been recognised as important sources of sexual fulfilment (Jerrome, 1993). The benefits of engaging in sex with a partner of many years appears to consider more than the interpersonal, encompassing the accumulation of past shared experiences. Neugebauer-Visano (1995: 21) found that the sexual side of relationships for couples in long-term relationships 'improved with time' and that the love and affection partners held for one another became stronger.

Attitudes towards sexuality held by older adults

The perceptions and opinions of society about older adults and their sexuality is one side of the story. However, it is necessary to also examine older adults' own attitudes towards sexuality and relationships. How aware is the ordinary man and woman in the street of their own feelings about themselves as they get older? What is it that defines sexuality and relationships to self-experience? Within these two fundamental questions lies the essence of the 'self-culture' of ageing, i.e. how aspects of ageing such as sexuality and relationships are defined by the self. This is what lies at the crux of what ageing actually means. It is not just the sexual act and the decline of physical sexual prowess that defines sexuality. Rather it encompasses the self-system of the individual as a whole entity, one's sexual role and one's relational role, and the associated awareness of what one feels about oneself as one gets older – the possibilities, self-discovery and the fullness of individual potential of what makes us human. So rather than viewing sexuality within the confines of 'being elderly', and 'being cared for', it is about defining potential by oneself rather than being defined, and discovering personal potential rather than being told how limited potential has become. Two of the most important aspects of this that need to come to the forefront of current discussion and care practice, are first the right to be a sexual being and second a 'human' approach. In this context, our notion of relationships raises awareness of the multifaceted nature of this term, in relation to four composite strands:

- the relationship with oneself (and one's inner dialogue);
- the relationship with past others (and the dynamics of attachment patterns);
- the relationship with present others (and one's individual context of experience);
- the relationship with the inevitability of death (the fact).

When these have been accounted for by an individual, then openness to the possibility of continuing to experience and develop the sexual side of identity as a resilience and protective factor into later life can be a normal and normative behaviour. Research consistently finds that older adults maintain an overall positive attitude about sex (Zeiss & Kasl-Godley, 2001). The AARP survey (2005) found that the majority of older adults with a sexual partner agreed on the importance of sexual activity for their quality of life and over 90 per cent of adults age 70 or older disagreed that 'sex is only for younger people'. The study found some differences in attitudes towards sexuality among ethnic groups. Caucasian and Asian Americans were more likely than African Americans or Hispanics to agree that 'sex becomes less important to people as they age' and Caucasians were more likely than all other groups to indicate that people should not have sexual relationships if they are not married. Gott and Hinchliff (2003) contributed valuable information about attitudes by adding qualitative information from the older adults in their study. The researchers found that all of the older adults with a current sexual partner valued sex as an important part of their relationship.

> It adds to the quality of your life and your relationship, besides living and working together and doing leisure activities together but that [sex] complements it. Perhaps it's just a way of sealing that relationship . . .

an extension of communication really in a lot of respects, instead of communicating orally, you're communicating with your bodies.

(Male participant, aged 55: cited in Hinchliff & Gott, 2004: 602)

Some of the participants reported sex as having become more pleasurable with age or with a new partner they had met in later life. Those without a partner expressed less interest in sex, and many of those whose partner had passed away stated that they would not pursue another sexual relationship.

Lemieux and colleagues (2004) carried out face-to-face interviews with patients receiving palliative care and found that emotional connection to others was an integral component of sexuality and an important source of validation during their illness experience. This took priority over the physical expression of sexuality. Participants' descriptions included the following: 'Sexuality means more than sexual intercourse. It's a broad, broad spectrum of feelings . . . closeness' (2004: 632). Another participant stated that, for him sexuality was 'an eye across the room; it's a holding of hands' (2004: 632). Lemieux and colleagues (2004: 632) also found that sexuality continues to be important at the end of life, especially for those who experience it as a way of connecting with their partner. '[Intimacy] . . . it's more important to me than basically anything in life'. The need to connect, to discuss important issues in comfort and privacy were important elements of maintaining togetherness and quality of life.

Health professionals' attitudes to sexuality

According to the literature, sexual relationships are beneficial to our health. However, this knowledge does not seem to be applied by health professionals. Stead and colleagues (2001) stated that given the impact on quality of life, sexuality is just as relevant and important to enquire about as it is to enquire about bowel action and sleep. However, despite its importance, sexuality and relationships receive little attention in later life. Health professionals find it difficult to discuss sexuality as an aspect of quality of life with their patients (Lemieux et al., 2004). MacElveen and McCorkle (1985: 60) have commented that 'being treated as an asexual being because of age or illness by health-care providers can be a powerful experience for someone whose sexuality is already traumatised and vulnerable'. For example, older adults are often called by their first names by health professionals in a similar manner as is done with children, which may reflect a tendency to view the older adult as less competent. Given the health promoting aspects of an active relationship and sexual life, then surely it is a matter of disquiet that routine enquiry as to the state of key relationships does not happen. It is a sign of the narrow view of the sexual world of older adults that sees sexual activity as being divorced from its social and emotional contexts and reduces it to an appraisal of the presence of absence of sexual intercourse.

Barriers to sexual relationships in older couples

Despite our understanding that intimacy and sexual relations are important in old age and are beneficial both physically and psychologically, much of research focuses on the barriers to sexual relationships in older adults. As indicated, the most common reason for lack of sexual activity is the loss of a partner through death, divorce or illness (Gott & Hinchliff, 2003). Sexual dysfunction in either partner can also be a barrier within older adult relationships. Research has documented the prevalence of sexual dysfunction within this age group, including erectile dysfunction (Prins et al., 2002; Laumann et al., 2005; Nicolosi et al., 2004) and early ejaculation and lack of sexual interest, inability to reach orgasm, lubrication difficulties and health problems and related medical side-effects (Morley & Tariq, 2003). Cardiovascular disease, diabetes, prostate cancer and lower urinary tract symptoms may all greatly affect sexual functioning (Skultety, 2007).

Where you live, as well as with whom you live in later life, are also likely to be crucial to the opportunities available to you to express your sexuality. The UK 2001 census revealed that 4 per cent of people aged 65 and over were living in communal institutions, increasing to 20 per cent of those aged 85 years and older. In addition, 1 per cent of men and 4 per cent of women lived with their adult children and 10 per cent of men and 5 per cent of women lived with a spouse and others (Office for National Statistics, 2001). Many long-term residential units do not provide rooms for couples and do not provide facilities where individuals can have privacy to be intimate with a partner. Lemieux and colleagues (2004) found that lack of privacy, shared rooms with other patients, uninviting physical space, intrusion by staff and the size of beds were considered barriers to expressing sexuality within hospital and hospice settings.

Gierveld and Peeters (2003) also note that many older couples reside with an adult child which creates difficulties in terms of privacy as well as coping with negative attitudes their family may have about the older couple expressing their sexuality, particularly if they are not married too or living with their sexual partner. In addition, research has found that many staff members in residential facilities have a negative attitude toward sexual activity in older adults and discouraged the expression of sexuality in these environments (Eddy, 1986). Kaas (1978: 376) reported that 'the aged in nursing homes must frequently live in celibacy'. Ehrenfeld and colleagues (1997) found that many staff in geriatric institutions reported feelings of confusion, embarrassment, helplessness and negative responses and rejection when confronted with sexual situations. Ehrenfeld and colleagues (1999) studied specific incidents in geriatric institutions and how they were dealt with by staff. Results indicated that staff accepted and supported incidents perceived as 'loving and caring', whereas more 'romantic or erotic' incidents were perceived as humorous or caused staff anger and disgust. In addition, there was a concern relating to sexual abuse, particularly if one member of the couple was in poor health. So, much work remains to educate those who engage professionally with older adults in order to dilute the denial of what is a natural expression of a normal human function and need.

Homosexual, bisexual and transgendered couples

It seems that many factors can interact to make sexual relationships in older life more difficult, with medical problems, accommodation restrictions, societal perceptions and negative attitudes. In addition to these factors, being categorised as an 'older adult' and preferring same-sex relations adds an additional burden that is rarely examined in the literature. Neither in policy nor practice does the older lesbian or gay man exist as a category of client (Lee, 2002; Heaphy et al., 2003). A common stereotype of older people is that they are all heterosexual. They are clearly not; as gay, lesbian and bisexual people get older too (Age UK, 2010). Very little has been written about how sexuality is understood and expressed in later life among gay, lesbian and bisexual older people. This is despite estimates that approximately 10 per cent of the general population is non-heterosexual (Reinish & Beasley, 1990), indicating that there are potentially 1.9 million non-heterosexual individuals in the UK aged over 50 years (Office of Populations, Censuses and Surveys, 2001).

Heaphy and colleagues (2003) explored the social implications of non-heterosexual ageing. They reported that, although the 266 study participants aged 50 to over 80 valued couple relationships greatly, 41 per cent of women and 65 per cent of men lived alone. Participants reported that it became more difficult to meet a partner in later life and younger participants were more likely than older participants to be in a current relationship. In relation to the relationship itself, many participants stressed that same-sex relationships were very emotionally fulfilling and allowed more scope for role negotiation than opposite-sex relationships. The authors reported that whereas female participants felt that having a non-heterosexual orientation can make oneself less conscious of ageing, many male participants reported the reverse, pointing to 'excessively youth-orientated non-heterosexual media and commercial scenes (i.e. bars and clubs)' (2003: 8). It is reported that older gay men face more pressure to maintain a youthful physical appearance than their same-age heterosexual counterparts. However, lesbian women seem, to some degree, to escape this pressure (Gott, 2005).

Marr and Kershaw (1998) also reported that older gay men not only must contend with the stigma associated with ageing, but also continue to bear stigma associated with their sexuality. Other findings indicate that homosexuals can tolerate the stigma associated with getting old very well as they have experience managing the stigma of 'coming out' and accepting their sexuality, rejecting stereotyped negative images and negotiating marginalisation (Sharp, 1997). According to Boxer (1997), age influences the social organisations of gay, lesbian and bisexual communities both at the level of individual's social experience and at an institutional level within these communities. Lee (2002) found further evidence of this in a qualitative study on gay men, reporting that older gay men felt out of place in gay bars and clubs and were insulted when 'cruising' for other gay men because of their age. Few homosexual groups have demonstrated interest in targeting their services or programmes towards older adults (Boxer, 1997). Generally within society gay men place great value on their own physical attractiveness and level of sexual activity. The onset of ageing threatens these values and may influence self-esteem and anxiety levels in this group (Marr & Kershaw, 1998; Boxer, 1997). Lee (2002) found little evidence to suggest that gay men have a sense of accelerated ageing in comparison to heterosexual men, due to obsession with body image, but alternatively they feel marginalised and not accepted because of their age. Also, a fear of living alone and having nobody to care for them is frequently reported in the gay community (Boxer, 1997). However, the experiences of older gay men do vary greatly. On the one hand many gay men achieve more satisfying sex lives later in life as they have reached a level of self-acceptance not attainable in their youth. Alternatively the level of rejection experienced by family and within society may result in withdrawal and reluctance to trust others resulting in isolation in later years (Marr & Kershaw, 1998).

Although they may not have the support of their family, Sharp (1997) reported that most lesbians rely on 'peer-group' families and therefore enjoy integrating with a family that is ageing together. On a positive note, older lesbian women have more flexible gender roles and may not become burdened with expectation-laden roles such as wife, mother and grandmother (Sharp, 1997). There is evidence that sexual activity declines with the onset of menopause in Irish lesbians, however a diminished interest in sex does not appear to cause a great deal of relationship conflict (The Women's Health Council, 2008). The length and quality of the relationship was found to negate worries about libido reduction for these women.

The spread of sexually transmitted diseases (STDs) such as AIDS has affected the lifestyle choices and stigma associated with being homosexual. Irrational denial of the risk can lead to promiscuous sexual activity without using suitable protection. Those who react with fear may obsess about the risks involved and abstain from all sexual contact. Anger, survivor guilt and depression may result from loss of partners or gay friends due to the

AIDS pandemic (Marr & Kershaw, 1998). Literature has highlighted the importance of availability of accurate information about STDs for those who are 'coming out' later in life (Pope *et al.*, 2007). Increasing numbers of people with HIV are living longer and have better quality lives while strictly adhering to new drug combinations.

Sexuality and dementia

Despite reforms to care practice in the UK proposed under the Care Standards Act 2000 (Office of Public Sector Information, 2000) there remains a silence regarding sexuality in policy and legislation in relation to care for older people. Harris and Wier (1998) illustrate that assessments by professionals rarely include attention to sexual functioning or seek to elicit information from a partner regarding the sexual dimension of a relationship. Little is known about the perspectives or experiences of individuals with dementia in relation to the effects of the condition upon their sexuality. It appears that existing literature largely omits reflection of the sexual identity of people with dementia (Arber & Ginn, 1995; Bernard *et al.*, 2000). Sexuality is often understood as, and reduced to, acts of sexual expression. And the main focus of attention is on the challenges for care staff in managing and intervening when sexual expression is deemed inappropriate (Barnes, 2001; Ehrenfeld *et al.*, 1997; Wallace, 1992). Rarely is such expression viewed as positive or beneficial to the individual. Rather, it is largely discussed in terms of the disruption to the dynamics of care settings (Ward *et al.*, 2005). Studies suggest that sexuality is a particularly neglected issue in older adults with mental health problems, as providers often fail to address sexuality and focus solely on symptom management (Jagus & Benbow, 2002; Benbow & Jagus, 2002). Sociocultural factors include cultural messages regarding sex, ageing and also beliefs regarding gender, gender role, attractiveness, relationships in older age and the possibility of new relationships after a partner has passed away (Skultety, 2007).

Conclusion

In conclusion, the area of sexuality and relationships in later life requires considerably more research of a sensitive nature in order to examine the needs, views, opinions and sexual behaviour of older adults as well as some attempts at societal attitudinal change in how older adults are perceived. There is a growing older population worldwide. Life expectancy for women now exceeds 80 years in at least 35 countries (World Health Organization, 2009). Quality of life includes sexuality and sexual relationships and this will become even more of an important issue given this ageing population. Perhaps it is useful to consider that older adults are in fact quite similar to younger people with different obstacles to overcome. We are all entitled to interpersonal relationships and we know that they are important for quality of life, health and well-being. From the evidence presented above, it appears that for older adults at present it is difficult to maintain a sense of sexual attractiveness with the denial and/or negative attitudes from both advertising and society and the apparent lack of interest from health professionals. Barriers do exist for older adults in terms of sexual relationships and further research is required into these areas and the fields of homosexuality and dementia in older life in order to understand how it has an impact on older people and how best to support them.

References

AARP. (2005). *Sexuality at Midlife and Beyond.* Washington, DC: AARP.

Age UK. (2010). *Being an Older Lesbian, Gay or Bisexual Person.* London: Age UK. (Retrieved 31 August 2010 from http://www.ageuk.org.uk/health-wellbeing/relationships-and-family/older-lesbian-gay-and-bisexual/?paging=false)

Antonucci, T. C. (2001). Social relations. In Birren, J. E., & Schaie, K. W., eds., *Handbook of the Psychology of Aging.* San Diego, CA: Academic Press, pp. 427–53.

Arber, S. & Ginn, J. (1995). *Connecting Gender and Ageing: A Sociological Approach.* Buckingham: Open University Press.

Bancroft, J. (2007). Sex and aging. *New England Journal of Medicine*, 357(8), 820–2.

Barnes, I. (2001). Sexuality and cognitive impairment in long-term care. *Canadian Nursing Home*, 12(3), 5–15.

Benbow, S. M., & Jagus, C. E. (2002). Sexuality in older women with mental health problems. *Sexual and Relationship Therapy*, 17(3), 261–270.

Bernard, M., Phillips, J., Machin, L., & Davies, V. H. (2000). *Women Ageing: Changing Identities, Challenging Myths.* London: Routledge.

Birnbaum, G. E., Cohen, O., & Wertheimer, V. (2007). Is it all about intimacy? Age, menopausal status, and women's sexuality. *Personal Relationships*, 14, 167–85.

Bouman, W., Arcelus, J., & Benbow, S. (2006). Nottingham study of sexuality and ageing. Attitudes regarding sexuality and older people: a review of the literature. *Sexual and Relationship Therapy*, 21(2), 149–61.

Boxer, A. (1997). Gay, Lesbian, and Bisexual aging into the twenty first century: An overview and introduction. *Journal of Gay, Lesbian and Bisexual Identity*, 2(3), 187–98.

Boyer King, E. (2004). *Engaging the Aging: Marketing to Europe's Seniors.* New York: Brandchannel.com. (Retrieved 4 August 2010 from http://www.brandchannel.com/features_effect.asp?pf_id=228)

Bretschneider, J. G., & McCoy, N. L. (1988). Sexual interest and behavior in healthy 80- to 102-year-olds. *Archives of Sexual Behavior*, 17(2), 109–29.

Bytheway, B. (1995). *Ageism.* Buckingham: Open University Press.

Chang, B. L., Chang, A. F., & Shen, Y. (1984). Attitudes toward aging in the United States and Taiwan. *Journal of Comparative Family Studies*, 15(1), 109–30.

Crohan, S. E., & Antonucci, T. C. (1989). Friends as a source of social support in old age. In Adams, R. G., & Blieszner, R., eds., *Older Adult Friendship Structure and Process*. Newbury Park, NJ: Sage, 129–46.

DeLamater, J., & Sill., M. (2005). Sexual desire in later life. *The Journal of Sex Research*, 42(2), 138–49.

DeLamater, J., & Moorman, S. M. (2007). Sexual behavior in later life. *Journal of Aging and Health*, 19(6), 921–45.

Drench, M., & Losee, R. (1996). Sexuality and sexual capacities of elderly people. *Rehabilitative Nursing*, 21, 118–23.

Eddy, D. M. (1986). Before and after attitudes toward aging in a BSN program. *Journal of Gerontological Nursing*, 12(5), 30–4.

Ehrenfeld, M., Bronner, G., Tabak, N., & Bergman, R. (1997). Ethical dilemmas concerning sexuality of elderly patients suffering from dementia. *International Journal of Nursing Practice*, 3, 255–9.

Ehrenfeld, M., Bronner, G., Tabak, N., Alpert, R., & Bergman, R. (1999). Sexuality among institutionalized elderly patients with dementia. *Nursing Ethics*, 6, 144–9.

Estes, C. L., & Binney, E. A. (1991). The biomedicalization of aging: dangers and dilemmas. In Minkler, M., & Estes, C., eds., *Critical Perspectives on Aging: The Political and Moral Economy of Growing Old*. Amityville, NY: Baywood Publishing Company Inc.

Evans, S., & Garner, J. (2004). *Talking over the Years: A Handbook of Dynamic Psychotherapy with Older Adults*. New York: Brunner-Routledge.

Featherstone, M., & Hepworth, M. (1990). Images of ageing. In Bond, J., & Coleman, P., eds., *Ageing in Society: An Introduction to Social Gerontology*. London: Sage.

Feldman, R. (2003). *Development Across the Lifespan, 3rd ed.* Upper Saddle River, NJ: Prentice Hall.

Field, D. (1999). Continuity and change in friendships in advanced old age: Findings from the Berkeley older generation study. *International Journal of Aging & Human Development*, 48, 325–46.

Ford, P. (1998). Sexuality and sexual health. In Marr, J., & Kershaw, B., eds., *Caring for Older People: Developing Specialist Practice*. London: Arnold, pp. 132–48.

Gierveld, J. D. J., & Peeters, A. (2003). The interweaving of repartnered older adults' lives with their children and siblings. *Ageing & Society*, 23(2), 187–205.

Gott, M. (2005). *Sexuality, Sexual Health and Ageing*. Buckingham: Open University Press.

Gott, M., & Hinchliff, S. (2003). How important is sex in later life? The views of older people. *Social Science & Medicine*, 56(8), 1617–28.

Guan J. (2004). Correlates of spouse relationship with sexual attitude, interest, and activity among Chinese elderly. *Sexuality & Culture*, 8, 104–31.

Harris, L., & Wier, M. (1998). Inappropriate sexual behavior in dementia: A review of the treatment literature. *Sexuality and Disability*, 16(3), 205–17.

Harwood, J., Giles, H., Ota, H., Pierson, H. D., Gallois, C., Ng, S. H., et al. (1996). College students' trait ratings of three age groups around the Pacific Rim. *Journal of Cross-Cultural Gerontology*, 11(4), 307–17.

Heaphy, B., Yip, A., & Thompson, D. (2003). *Lesbian, Gay and Bisexual Lives Over 50*. Nottingham: York House Publications.

Hinchliff, S., & Gott, M. (2004). Intimacy, commitment, and adaptation: Sexual relationships within long-term marriages. *Journal of Social and Personal Relationships*, 29(5), 595–609.

Hockey, J., & James, A. (1993). *Growing Up and Growing Old: Ageing and Dependency in the Life Course*. London: Sage.

Hogan, R. (1980). *Human Sexuality: A Nursing Perspective*. New York: Appleton-Century-Crofts.

Howard, J. R., O'Neill, S., & Travers, C. (2006). Factors affecting sexuality in older Australian women: sexual interest, sexual arousal, relationships and sexual distress in older Australian women. *Climacteric*, 9, 355–67.

Ingersoll-Dayton, B., & Saengtienchai, C. (1999). Respect for the elderly in Asia: Stability and change. *International Journal of Aging & Human Development*, 48(2), 103–13.

Institute of Medicine. (2001). *Exploring the Biological Contributions to Human Health: Does Sex Matter?* Washington, DC: IOM. (Retrieved 4 August 2010 from http://www.iom.edu/Reports/2001/Exploring-the-Biological-Contributions-to-Human-Health-Does-Sex-Matter.aspx)

Jagus, C. E., & Benbow, S. M. (2002). Sexuality in older men with mental health problems. *Sexual and Relationship Therapy*, 17(3), 271–9.

Jerrome, D. (1993). Intimate relationships. In Bond, J., Coleman, P., & Peace, S., eds. *Ageing and Society: An Introduction to Social Gerontology, 2nd ed*. London: Sage, pp. 226–54.

Johnson, C., & Barer, B. (1997). *Life Beyond 85 Years: The Aura of Survivorship*. New York: Springer.

Jung, A., & Schill, W. (2004). Male sexuality with advancing age. *European Journal of Obstetrics and Gynaecology and Reproductive Biology*, 113, 123–5.

Kaas, M. (1978). Sexual expression of the elderly in nursing homes. *Gerontologist*, 18, 372–8.

Kaluger, G., & Kaluger, M. F. (1979). *Human Development: The Span of Life, 2nd ed*. St Louis, MO: Mosby.

Kingsberg, S. A. (2000). The psychological impact of aging on sexuality and relationships. *Journal of Women's Health & Gender-Based Medicine*, 9 (suppl 1), 33–8.

Knodel, J., Huy, V. T., Loi, V. M., & Ghuman, S. (2005). *Marital Sexual Behavior and Aging in Vietnam in Comparative Perspective. Report 05-583*. Ann Abor, MI: University of Michigan Population Studies Center.

Larson, R., Mannell, R., & Zuzanek, J. (1986). Daily well-being of older adults with friends and family. *Psychology and Aging*, 1, 117–26.

Laumann, E. O., Nicolosi, A., Glasser, D. B., Paik, A., Gingell, C., Moreira, E., & Wang, T. for the GSSAB Investigators' Group. (2005). Sexual problems among women and men aged 40 – 80: prevalence and correlates identified in the Global Study of Sexual Attitudes and Behaviors. *International Journal of Impotence Research*, 17(1), 39–57.

Laws, G. (1997). Spatiality and age relations. In Victor, C., Harper, S., & Jamieson, A., eds., *Critical Approaches to Ageing and Later Life*. Buckingham: Open University Press, pp. 90–101.

Lee, A. (2002). *Older Gay Men: A Call for Inclusion in Welfare Services.* Paper presented at the 31st Annual Conference of the British Society of Gerontology, Birmingham, UK.

Lemieux, L., Kaiser, S., Pereira, J., & Meadows, L. M. (2004). Sexuality in palliative care: patient perspectives. *Palliative Medicine,* 18, 630–7.

Levy, B., & Langer, E. (1994). Aging free from negative stereotypes: Successful memory in China among the American deaf. *Journal of Personality and Social Psychology,* 66(6), 989–97.

Litwin, H. (1999). Formal and informal network factors as sources of morale in a senior center population. *International Journal of Aging & Human Development,* 48, 241–56.

MacElveen, H., & McCorkle, R. (1985). Understanding sexuality in progressive cancer. *Seminars in Oncology Nursing,* 1, 56–62.

Marr, J., & Kershaw, J. (1998). *Caring for Older People: Developing Specialist Practice.* London: Arnold.

Minkler, M. (1991). Gold in gray: reflections on business' discovery of the elderly market. In Minkler, M., & Estes, C., eds., *Critical Perspectives on Aging: The Political and Moral Economy of Growing Old.* Amityville, NY: Baywood Publishing Company.

Morley, J. E., & Tariq, S. H. (2003). Sexuality and disease. *Clinical Geriatric Medicine,* 19(3), 563–73.

Neugebauer-Visano, R. (1995). *Seniors and Sexuality: Experiencing Intimacy in Later Life.* Toronto: Canadian Scholars' Press, pp. 17–34.

Nicolosi, A., Laumann, E. O., Glasser, D. B., Moreira, E. D. Jr, Paik, A., Gingell, C., Global Study of Sexual Attitudes and Behaviors Investigators' Group (2004). Sexual behavior and sexual dysfunctions after age 40: the global study of sexual attitudes and behaviors. *Urology,* 64(5), 991–7.

Nussbaum, J., Pitts, M., Huber, F. N., Raup Krieger, J., & Ohs, J. (2005). Ageism and ageist language across the life span: intimate relationships and non-intimate interactions. *Journal of Social Issues,* 61(2), 287–305.

Office for National Statistics. (2001). *Census 2001.* London: Office for National Statistics. (Retrieved 31 August 2010 from http://www.statistics.gov.uk/census2001/access_results.asp).

Office of Populations, Censuses and Surveys. (1991). *Census Statistics Information Obtained from 1990–1994.* London: Office of Populations, Censuses and Surveys.

Office of Public Sector Information. (2000). *Care Standards Act 2000.* London: OPSI. (Retrieved 4 August 2010 from http://www.opsi.gov.uk/acts/acts2000/ukpga_20000014_en_1)

Persson, G. (1980). Sexuality in a 70-year-old urban population. *Journal of Psychosomatic Research,* 24, 335–42.

Pointon, S. (1997). Myths and negative attitudes about sexuality in older people. *Generations Review,* 7(4), 6–8.

Pope, M., Wierzalis, E., Barret, B., & Rankins, M. (2007). Sexual and intimacy issues for aging gay men. *Adultspan Journal,* 6(2), 68–82.

Prins, J,. Blanker, M. H., Bohnen, A. M., Thomas. S., & Bosch, J. L. (2002). Prevalence of erectile dysfunction: a systematic review of population-based studies. *International Journal of Impotence Research,* 14(6), 422–32.

Rawlins, W. K. (1995). Friendships in later life. In Nussbaum, J. F., & Coupland, J., eds., *Handbook of Communication and Aging Research*. Mahwah, NJ: Lawrence Erlbaum Associates, Inc, pp. 227–58.

Reinish, J., & Beasley, R. (1990). *The Kinsey Institute New Report on Sex: What You Must Know to be Sexually Literate*. London: Penguin.

Reuben, D. R. (1970). *Everything You Ever Wanted to Know About Sex*. London: W. H. Allen.

Riley, A. (1999). Sex in old age: Continuing pleasure or inevitable decline? *Geriatric Medicine*, 29, 25–8.

Samter, W. (2003). Friendship interaction skills across the life span. In Greene, J. O., & Burleson, B. R., eds., *Handbook of Communication and Social Interaction Skills*. Mahwah, NJ: Lawrence Erlbaum Associates, Inc., pp. 637–84.

Sharp, C. (1997). Lesbianism and later life in an Australian sample: how does development of one affect anticipation of another? *Journal of Gay, Lesbian and Bisexual Identity*, 2(3), 247–63.

Skultety, K. M. (2007). Addressing issues of sexuality with older couples. *Couples in Later Life*, 31, 31–7.

Stead, M. L., Fallowfield, L., Brown, J. M., & Selby, P. (2001). Communication about sexual problems and sexual concerns in ovarian cancer: qualitative study. *British Medical Journal*, 323, 836–7.

Story, T. N., Berg, C. A., Smith, T. W., Beveridge, R., Henry, N. J. M., & Pearce, G. (2007). Age, marital satisfaction, and optimism as predictors of positive sentiment override in middle-aged and older married couples. *Psychology and Aging*, 22(4), 719–27.

Sung, K. T. (1994). A cross-cultural comparison of motivations for parent care: The case of Americans and Koreans. *Journal of Aging Studies*, 8(2), 195–209.

Trudel, G., Turgeon, L., & Piché, L. (2000). Marital and sexual aspects of old age. *Sexual and Relationship Therapy*, 15(4), 381–406.

Trudel, G., Villeneuve, V., Anderson, A., & Pilon, G. (2008). Sexual and marital aspects of old age: an update. *Sexual and Relationship Therapy*, 23(2), 161–69.

Umidi, S., Pini, M., Ferretti, M., Vergani, C., & Annoni, G. (2007). Affectivity and sexuality in the elderly: often neglected aspects. *Archives of Gerontology Geriatrics Suppl.*, 1, 413–17.

Victor, C. (1991). *Health and Health Care in Later Life*. Buckingham: Open University Press.

Wallace, M. (1992). Management of sexual relationships among elderly residents of long-term care facilities. *Geriatric Nursing*, 13(6), 308–11.

Walsh, K., & Berman, J. (2004). Sexual dysfunction in the older woman. *Drugs & Aging*, 21(10), 655–75.

Wang, T.-F., Lu, C.-H., Chen, I.-J., & Yu, S. (2008). Sexual knowledge, attitudes and activity of older people in Taipei, Taiwan. *Journal of Clinical Nursing*, 17, 443–50.

Ward, R., Vass, A. A., Aggarwal, N., Garfield, C., & Cybyk, B. (2005). A kiss is still a kiss? The construction of sexuality in dementia care. *Dementia*, 4(1), 49–72.

Women's Health Council. (2008). *Women's Experiences and Understandings of Menopause*. Dublin: Department of Health & Children.

World Health Organization. (2009). *Women's Health*. (Retrieved 31 August 2010 from http://www.who.int/mediacentre/factsheets/fs334/en/index.html)

Yang, H., Toy, E., & Baker, B. (2000). Sexual dysfunction in the elderly patient. *Primary Care Update Obestrics/Gynaecology*, 7(6), 269–74.

Zeiss, A. M., & Kasl-Godley, J. (2001). Sexuality in older adults' relationships. *Generations*, 25(2), 18–25.

Chapter 13

Caring for older adults
Who cares and who does not?

Patrick Ryan and Anna Wroblewska

Introduction

Among one of the demographic changes of the twentieth century has been the increasing survival of people to old age. Once a rare event achieved by a very small proportion of each generation, now reaching an age of 75 and 85 is commonplace and increasingly expected. The growth in the proportion of older people in the population includes many who are healthy and independent, but also an unprecedented number who need assistance. No matter how healthy or autonomous older people appear to be, the fact remains that age brings heightened risks of a variety of diseases and psychosocial concerns. Common health problems elderly people can suffer from are cardiovascular diseases, diabetes, osteoporosis and difficulties with hearing and vision, not to mention Parkinson's disease and dementia. Although many of these illnesses are treatable, they cannot be cured. Instead, they are becoming the chronic diseases of modern society, often difficult to manage socially and even more costly to manage medically. Apart from physical illnesses some individuals develop psychological problems such as depression and others continue to cope with mental health problems acquired earlier in life. Because of developments in modern medicine there is also a growing population of elderly people with intellectual disability. Today, many people spend their final years unable to care for themselves. As they enter their seventies and eighties, many can expect years marked by frequent trips to doctors and emergency rooms and, when the time comes, when for various reasons home care is no longer an option, years spent in assisted living and long-term care facilities.

The definition of care

In order to set the scene for this discussion it is essential to define the term 'care'. According to the Cambridge International Dictionary of English (online) care is synonymous with protection and constitutes 'the process of protecting and looking after someone or something'.

Who cares

Help for disabled elderly people is provided first, and for the longest period of time, by family members. Even in the Scandinavian countries, where public policies encouraged the development of formal service systems to free younger generations to participate fully in the workforce, family care continues to have a predominant and, as the population ages, an even more important role in assisting elders. It seems that for some ethnic groups or societies, care of the person at home takes priority over everything else, whereas other groups are more likely to view professional help in a positive light (Thorslund, 1991).

In order to establish what a typical view of caring for the elderly might be, one of the authors interviewed[1] staff in one of 20 nursing homes for elderly people. Staff were asked what their clients and their families would prefer: continue living at home or care in a nursing home. Respondents were in agreement that the majority of families and, most importantly, the clients would opt for care in the comfort of their own home and known surroundings. The professionals approached also revealed that most families needed a long time to cope with the guilt associated with placing their loved one in an institution – a predicament contributing to their emotional distress. Even in modern times, placing a loved one under the care of strangers creates an underlying sense of letting the elderly person down.

Adult children and elderly parents

Where there is consistent contact between children and parents support is more likely to be given and received (Hogan *et al.*, 1993). In addition the more children the elderly person has, the more likely they are to receive support (Eggebeen, 1992). When elderly parents are asked who they would receive support from, children are chosen more often than any other family member (Hogan *et al.*, 1993).

Socioeconomic status (SES)

It could be hypothesised that people with lower SES would have fewer economic resources and therefore have more difficulty achieving a happy and healthy retirement. However, it seems that elders on a low income and their caregivers often enjoy greater access to publicly supported programmes. They may also be more likely to be able to obtain help from extended family and friends because of more available free time as a result of part-time or no employment opportunities.

Family caregiving

As the number of people providing care to an older relative has increased, attention has focused on the often challenging, demanding circumstances involved in caregiving and identifying approaches that can help families manage care of their elderly relatives more effectively while experiencing less strain. According to The Carers Association there are 161,000 family carers in Ireland (Carers Association, 2008). In the UK the figure is just under 6 million (Carers UK, 2009). A 2005 study by the National Alliance for Caregiving in the USA estimated that 33.9 million people there were providing care to at least one person over the age of 50 years. A large proportion of family carers look after an elderly member of the family while the peak age for caring in the UK is between the ages of 50 and 59 years.

Carers' predicament

Caring for a family member is a challenge for the main caregiver, who can report considerable psychological and physical morbidity (anxiety, sadness, depression) leading to a greater use of psychotropic drugs (Baumgarten, 1989). There is also evidence for a higher number, and greater severity of chronic physical conditions, use of medications and medical visits and a poorer self-rated physical health compared with non-caregivers (Brodaty *et al.*, 2003). Caregivers reduce their social activities and are at a higher risk of mortality than non-caregiving controls (Haley *et al.*, 1987).

Many studies (Burns & Rabins, 2000; Farcnik & Persyko, 2002) have been focused on identifying factors that can predict caregiver's distress. The factors mentioned include patient's characteristics, such as decline or loss of functional activities or severity of clinical symptoms. Schulz *et al.* (1997) found a low economic status, scarce social support, low levels of self-esteem and mastery and poor prior relationship with the person the individual was caring for were associated with caregiver's health problems.

Developing a thorough understanding of the factors that determine carer's stress is a major priority as high levels of stress have been linked to increased use of primary care and respite services and earlier admittance to institutional care (Brown *et al.*, 1990). Stemming from that finding it would appear advisable to invest in providing carers with support. Apart from financial, there are many factors affecting the manner of how caregiving is carried out and a review of cultural perspectives usefully highlights this.

Cultural perspective

Ethnic groups differ in values and beliefs regarding the importance of caring for older people. Literature regarding care delivery shows that children tend to live at an increasing distance from their parents; a trend noted both in the USA (Soldo, 1980) and in the European Union (Hermanova, 1995). This being the case, the adult children may find it difficult to first identify the type and intensity of help needed and second objectively monitor quality of service delivered. However, in many countries physical distance does not play a significant role. The following examples from Uganda, Kenya, Brazil, India and Vietnam of care for older adults provide an insight into the challenges being experienced in these countries.

African caregivers have been found to show less distress while providing a more intense level of care than their white or Latin counterparts (Navaie-Waliser *et al.*, 2001). For example, in Uganda, faith groups have set up homes where older adults, requiring a lot of daily care, can move to when their families are unable to continue providing the care they need. According to the Global Health through Education Training and Service (GHETS, 2005) in Kenya, community-based care for elderly people is uneven due to poor socioeconomic conditions. Kenya lacks services for taking care of, or helping, people to remain at home whereas such services do exist for the richer Kenyans. African culture frowns on separation of elderly people from their families and African socialisation promotes keeping older relatives in the community (Mattelaer, 2005). For example, older adults take care of the domestic animals and look after grandchildren.

The GHETS (2005) Position Paper reports that, in Brazil, community-based care for elderly people is important due to the pressures of modernisation, urbanisation and changes in social values. Women's role as the traditional caregiver for elderly people in many countries changed with increasing female employment and transformations in cultural values causing a change in living arrangements (Frankel & McCarty, 1993). For example, seniors have moved from extended families and multigenerational households to living alone (Kramarow, 1995). Technological and urban change has resulted in older people losing their role as leaders in families. Decline in health of the older person leads to discrimination and fuels the false idea that they cannot contribute to society (Tataru & Dicker, 2009).

The GHETS (2005) Position Paper reports that almost 50 per cent of the world's elderly live in Asia, of which 23 per cent live in India. In Indian society, the cultural values and the traditional practices emphasise that the elderly members of the family be treated with honour and respect. Studies conducted in India and other countries of this region show that a majority of the elderly population are not in a position to afford an economically independent life after their retirement (Balagopal, 2009). In the absence of pension benefits, many old people have to work for their livelihood until they are physically exhausted. The breakdown of the joint family system, inflationary trends and growth of individualism further aggravate the problems of elderly people. A substantial number of elderly people in villages live in a state of poverty, malnutrition, illiteracy, lack of sanitation and chronic diseases (Prasad, 2007).

In Vietnam, the government promotes home care insurance that families can buy for their elderly parents. Also, courses are offered in the evening so that family members can learn about nursing care for their elders who typically live with them (Evans & Harkness, 2008).

Some understanding in relation to why Asian cultures value elderly people may be found in their belief systems. The concept of care functions as one of the fundamental elements of Confucianism. The notion of care is based on two main premises: first, that every child receives love from parents, and second, that the society and state, to which a person belongs, are extensions of the family. Filial duty forms a large part of the notion of care in Confucianism. The reason that a person should fulfil filial duty lies in the duty of reward. In other words, parents should be repaid for their love. The premise that society and state are extensions of the families legitimises other care-related duties such as respecting older adults in the community and loyalty to the emperor of the state. Because older adults and the king of the state are parental figures, a person should give appropriate care to them (Fan, 2002).

In Confucianism, family is regarded as the private sphere. At the same time, family is the unit of society that forms the public sphere. What is significant is that codes of conduct within the family are the foundation of the codes of conduct in society. Within the boundary of family, a person gives care to parents according to the codes of conduct involved in the practice of filial piety. Outside the boundary of family, care is given to elders in the community. Although caregiving to parents is different from caregiving to other elders in the community, the logic is the same, that is, the benevolence of the junior, the young and the subordinate, to the senior, the elder and the dominant (Herr, 2003).

In terms of care, what needs to be highlighted is the idea that the caregiving of the junior subordinate, to the senior superior, is so natural that there is nothing to be appreciated or rewarded. If a child does not give care to the parents in the appropriate manner, the most crucial duty is not fulfilled therefore a punishment will follow. However, if a child gives care to his parents, the child's behaviour of caregiving is so natural that his parents do not have to appreciate the child's care or give rewards for the care. If parents appreciate their children's care, this is sometimes considered to be unnatural and inappropriate behaviour (Mijung & Chesla, 2007).

Cohabitation of parents with their adult children has been decreasing across the world, even in traditional Confucian societies where elders are viewed as a source of wisdom, like Japan and South Korea (Sundstrom, 1993). According to a study conducted by Yamashita and Amagai (2008), family caregiving is a long-standing tradition in Japanese society, with a foundation in sociocultural and historical norms. Whether or not family caregivers conform to the societal norms may determine the extent of utilisation of the care services. Traditionally, in the Japanese family, daughters and daughters-in-law have been expected to assume a caregiving role for their aged parents or parents-in-law who require care at home. In recent years, however, due to decreased birth rates and nuclear family structure, spouses rather than their children are obliged to care for the partner who requires care at home. Common to the successful caregivers is speaking well about elders and including them in daily routines or other family activities. Seeking help from outside the home is contraindicated as daughters-in-law are expected to conform to the socially ascribed behaviour of functioning as a dutiful daughter-in-law (otherwise, they would be regarded as abandoning their expected filial role; Arai et al., 2002).

As an example of East Asian societies, most children in Korea (especially the eldest son or daughter) plan to live with their parents when the parents become frail (Park & Cho, 1995). At the same time, parents want to be cared for by their children. If children do not take care of their parents, it brings shame to the family (Yang & Rosenblatt, 2001). Moreover, the political concerns about the ageing society have been opportunistic and encourage strengthening the Confucian value related to care given to frail older adults.

Latin America is another example where the relationship between parents and children is culturally of extreme importance. Sotomayor (1989) insists on the value of familism (embracing family as central in life) and its influence on the perception that caregiving is a form of showing loyalty, reciprocity and solidarity to an older relative, an appraisal that seems to buffer against feeling burdened by the caregiving situation. Ethnicity and culture also exert an influence on the structure of the caregiving situation among Latin Americans. Mexican American children, for example, are more likely to care for their older parents, whether the parents are married, widowed or single, whereas non-Latin American white children are more likely to care for a widowed parent (Phillips et al., 2000). Caregiving also tends to be seen as a form of setting an example to younger children and of transmitting cultural values such as respect for older relatives (Neary & Mahoney, 2005). Latin American women are expected to be the primary caregivers of the ageing parents and to care for them at home for as long as possible. Such expectations are based on the cultural norm that women should be self-sacrificing and nurturing.

Islam emphasises kindness to and good treatment of parents. Muslims are obliged to respect, be kind towards, and obey their parents, regardless of faith, with the exception of when parents attempt to lead them away from Islam; this is an Islamic duty. Ageing is viewed in a positive light and as a sign of the overwhelming mercy, justice and power of Allah (Thursby, 1992). Hence the importance of caring for elders is evident and can be observed in more detail from this excerpt of The Koran: 'Whether one of them (the parents) attain old age in thy life, say not to them a word of contempt, nor repel them, but address them in terms of honour' (17; 23 cited in El Azayem & Hedayat-Diba, 1994). Fostering a sense that one has a supportive social and familial network is therefore seen as crucially important in old age for Muslims (Azaiza *et al.*, 2010). In the majority of Muslim countries, the ageing population is increasing at a fast pace. This rate is not limited only to Muslim countries; the number of ageing Muslims living in the USA, Germany, England, Belgium, Holland and France, is also increasing at a fast pace (*Islamic Horizons*, 2006).

Caring for the carer

Regardless of culture, adequate care for elderly people cannot exist without caring for the carer. In the research of one of the authors (AW), family members identified three elements contributing toward quality in caregiving:

- good prior relationships between caregivers and care recipients;
- positive interpretations of the relative's condition;
- utilisation of resources.

The use of health care services for care recipients who are more physically disabled is associated with better caregiver outcomes; whereas the use of home services when the care recipient displays behaviour problems is associated with lower caregiver depression (Bass *et al.*, 1996).

Recently in Ireland carers across the country have received what The Carers Association is calling a 'slap in the face' with the government's announcement that the committed National Carers Strategy, for which the organisation has been lobbying for over 5 years, would not be published. In response to that, the Chief Executive Officer of The Carers Association asserted that:

> We are devastated and appalled that Government have reneged on their promise to develop and publish a National Carers Strategy as committed to under the Social Partnership Agreement – Towards 2016. This is indicative of the complete lack of recognition and value that Government places on family carers and their invaluable work in our society. Government has accepted over 3 million hours of work per week provided by family carers, yet is not even willing to publish a strategy that at the very least, recognises and values carers for their contribution to the state.
>
> (Carers Ireland, 2009: para 1)

Difficulties in residential care

Akin to home care, residential care also faces difficulties. Halldorsdottir (1997) contends that modern day health care has witnessed a separation of competence, that is the delivery of complex technical care, from caring as an affective process; the former being seen as a preserve of the professions and the latter delegated to others. She argues that simply being warm hearted and having common sense are inadequate, and that good care must combine competence with caring if quality is to be maintained. This requires a model of competence that extends beyond the delivery of excellent technical care, to one which is based upon a more sophisticated understanding of the skills required for a person-centred approach. Another issue relates to systemic influences on staff that include such variables as working conditions, rosters, family expectation of staff roles, institutional and personal attitudes and prejudices about older adults and staff self-care policies and practices. Staff may change or rotate as a consequence of these varied and interacting factors and families often realise that there is no continuity of care in their relationships with staff. Feeling that they have lost control over the situation and concern that staff are not providing adequate care can be very distressing to families (Duncan & Morgan, 1994). A more detailed account of residential care provision and associated staff influences is reviewed by Woods (2008).

Lack of education

When caring for someone with dementia or other mental health problems, carers often misinterpret behaviours in ways that lead to greater distress to themselves and to the cared for person, for example, the caregiver may believe that the person with dementia deliberately asks the same questions repeatedly just to cause annoyance. In turn the carer responds with anger and exasperation, which increases the patient's agitation. Better public education campaigns would reduce such misconceptions (Zarit & Edwards, 2008).

Community care

Community and home care services for older adults include a wide variety of out-of-hospital, non-medical community-based residential facilities or support in their homes that provide living arrangements, meals and protective oversight. The aims of such care are to: keep older people at home, promote independence, strengthen primary health and community services and reinforce voluntary and neighbourhood support (GHETS, 2005).

Availability of specialist services

Kovner *et al.* (2002: 84) report that institutions training health care workers responded to 20th-century demographics and embraced the need to prepare workers in paediatrics for example, the authors assert, 'all programs in nursing and medicine . . . have required pediatric rotations, but a similar commitment to geriatrics is yet to emerge'. To quantify the difference, today globally there is approximately 1 paediatrician for every 1,000 children, but only 1 geriatrician for every 2,000 elderly persons will be available by 2030. The authors recommend that every health care professional be trained in geriatrics, to ensure the proper treatment of elderly people.

There is a critical shortage of health care professionals suitably trained in geriatrics. In 2002 globally more than 23 per cent of people who were age 65 and older reported poor or fair health. There is some evidence that care of older adults by health care professionals trained in geriatrics yields improvements in outcomes, such as better physical, functional and psycho-social status without an increase in costs. A recent study found that although frail older patients treated in both inpatient and outpatient geriatric units had the same mortality rates as those treated with usual care, the patients who received specialised geriatric input had sizeable reductions in functional decline and improvements in mental health at no additional cost (Cohen *et al.*, 2002).

Eldercare in Ireland is a mixture of both public and private provision, a large proportion of which is provided by private individuals within the family, together with some voluntary sector provision and private market-based services (Barry, 2010). However, Barry (2010: 4) concludes that 'the most fundamental criticism of the system of eldercare in Ireland is the lack of statutory entitlements within a legislative framework that would under-pin a rights-based approach to the provision of critical services and supports at household, community and institutional levels'. A review of the provision of psychological services on the ground suggests a woeful quantum of service in Ireland and elsewhere.

The role of psychology

A psychologist can be viewed as a source of emotional support for the elderly person and his or her family as well as an expert in normal and abnormal developmental psychological processes. A psychology service may also be used by the health services to inform diagnosis and treatment of a range of complex old-age related issues. Psychologists receive an education in normal developmental psychology that allows them to formulate psycho-logical difficulties in a manner that captures a wide range of variables. They can then apply abnormal or clinical models and theories to generate individualised profiles that can inform appropriate clinical intervention.

The Irish 'Vision for Change Strategy' (Expert Group on Mental Health Policy, 2006) recommended 39 clinical psychology posts for the population of over sixty-fives in Ireland. As stated before, the over sixty-fives age group constitutes 11 per cent of the general population. To date only 7.8 older adult clinical psychologists are in service, which amounts to 1.8 per cent of all HSE psychology posts. This means that 1.8 per cent of all HSE employed clinical psychologists cater for the 11 per cent of the population. In the UK, the British Psychological Society (2006) recommends 1 whole time clinical psychologist per 10,000 older people in secondary mental health services. This figure does not include provision of psychological services in primary care or specialist services such as stroke care or dementia care.

Baty (1998) states that there is limited provision of clinical psychology for older people throughout the world. Acquired cultural beliefs through age stereotypes may have shaped this lack of services (Levy & Langer, 1994). For example, within mainstream American culture, ageism is not frowned upon as much as sexism or, in particular, racism (Levy & Banaji, 2002). Where clinical psychology services have developed, they have focused primarily on younger adults, Ireland being a illuminating example.

Future directions for clinical psychology with older people must include collaborative work with primary care teams that encompass consultancy and training. Such an approach will assist in improving the evidence base on what approaches work for older people who may present with a range of problems that include physical as well as mental health difficulties. Equally important to extending the availability of service delivery to older adults will be ensuring that the quality and content of training of health care professionals in initial professional education works to overcome the many negative attitudes about this particular age group. A key part of this strategy could be to include older adults in the education and training of professionals. This could highlight that older adults do not solely rely on care provided by other members of the society, those in charge of providing services for them and the government. They can and often do care for themselves by themselves.

Do we really not care?

Age is among the top three most rapidly perceived features of another person (Fiske, 1998). Not surprisingly it is therefore a target for attitude bias and prejudice that have been highlighted in various domains in earlier chapters. The prejudices directed to older adults generally revolve around affective responses related to pity and sympathy (Cuddy *et al.*, 2005), which is somewhat ironic given that as seen in the chapters on older adult abuse, when such individuals are discriminated against, it can be in the most appalling manner. However, although it is correct to highlight when individuals or services do not fulfil care duties, there is another perspective to consider when addressing the question raised at the outset of this chapter. As older age becomes a part of the identity of an individual, that part is not necessarily actively internalised into individuals' perception of themselves (Fiske & Taylor, 2008). If society sees older adults as a burden, incompetent physically or psychologically, then an older person is not going to easily accommodate such a negative stereotype into whom they think they are. Resisting the natural progression through the lifespan and its individualised impact is a form of not caring for the self as it can impede decision making related to, for example, lifestyle choices. For example, drivers with dementia, like most other drivers, are reluctant to relinquish their driving privileges, making discussions about driving cessation difficult and of great concern to family members (Adler, 2010).

According to Phillipson (1998) the emergence of a global capitalist economy, based on advances in technology, is beginning to undermine the welfare policies of Western nation states, including public pensions and health care benefits for elderly people. These trends, in combination with declining private pensions, could lead to the unravelling of retirement as an institution established over the last 50 years. When these developments occur, Phillipson believes they will undermine the socioeconomic supports for psychological and cultural identity in old age. The privatisation of these supports will increase insecurity and anxiety among older people and those approaching old age particularly those with limited private means to sustain them. Elderly people may find themselves stranded in a post-modern culture where there are few resources for maintaining a stable core identity, which is necessary to provide the foundation for a coherent life narrative and a sense of experience adding up and culminating in a perception of completion and achieved wisdom. For older people with the resources to protect themselves from the loss of socioeconomic supports, life in a post-modern culture may offer some advantages, including opportunities to experiment with roles and identities made available by the erosion of cultural constraints defining age-appropriate roles and behaviour. This kind of freedom, however, will be beyond the means of many elderly people.

Phillipson notes that this is not 'a rehearsal of an old argument that the problem facing older people is that they lack meaningful roles which tie them to society' (1998: 32). Rather, there is a more complicated argument – namely, that modern living undercuts the construction of a viable identity for living in old age.

An obvious manifestation of older people not being cared for lies in the area of crime and its impact on this cohort. The findings from the first British Crime Survey in 1982 indicated that women, elderly people and those in inner cities felt least safe (Home Office, 2007). This has remained unchanged. According to the 2004/05 survey, women and elderly people were again most likely to feel unsafe walking alone. More serious crime is perpetrated against older adults. For example, Burgess et al. (2000) published 20 cases of proven sexual assault of elderly female nursing home residents in the USA. However, the greatest threat to older adults' sense of safety seems to be their perception that they are more likely to become a victim of crime although there is not universal agreement on this oft reported viewpoint, for example see Ahlf (1994). Stereotypes of elderly people that portray them as rather uniformly and irrationally responding to risks that they do not really face are inconsistent with the research evidence (Sacco & Nakhaie, 2001). A study in the UK by Ball and Fowler (2008) found that sexual offences against women above the age of 60 years were very uncommon amounting to 1.7 per cent of all sexual offences against adult female victims. The question arises as to attributions of not caring and tying these to specific, often high-profile crime incidents or 'discriminatory' economic policies, in order to maintain the myth that simply by being older one must more likely be 'not cared for'.

Conclusion

Caring for older people is increasingly being seen as stressful and demanding. As the population has aged, more people need help often for a prolonged period of time. Modern society has undergone some significant changes and, as a consequence family resources to care for elderly people have declined particularly with the relatively modern phenomenon of one-child families.

Caregiving is often very stressful for families especially in cases of dementia and when need for care persists over a long period of time. Often it may not be possible to improve the elder's condition; however what is frequently present are modifiable aspects of the care situation. For instance building social support and improvement in the management of stress levels can alleviate some of the emotional discomfort. Clinical interventions have a role to play where carers' levels of distress are concerned in order to lower the burden on caregivers and assist them to continue to care for their loved one in the optimal way. This is premised on the need to build a professional services capacity that is free from prejudice and bias with regards older adults, an issue that should be central to education and training programmes across the health professions. When working with older adults it is also important to be cognisant of cultural influences on expectations both of and for the older adult. As highlighted these are many and varied and in deciding when to care and when not to, it is prudent to acknowledge the individual need, desire and capacity to receive care and the potential to reject it.

Notes

1 The professionals approached requested that their names and location remain anonymous.

References

Adler, G. (2010). Driving decision-making in older adults with dementia. *Dementia: The International Journal of Social Research and Practice*, 9(1), 45–60.

Ahlf, E. (1994). [The elderly as victims of violent crime]. *Zeitschrift für Gerontologie*, 27(5), 289–98.

Arai, Y., Zarit, S., Sugiura, M., & Washio, M. (2002). Patterns of outcome of caregiving for the impaired elderly: a longitudinal study in rural Japan. *Aging & Mental Health*, 6(1), 39–46.

Azaiza, F., Ron, P., Shoham, M., & Gigini, I. (2010). Death and dying anxiety among elderly Arab Muslims in Israel. *Death Studies*, 34(4), 351–64.

Balagopal, G. (2009). Access to health care among poor elderly women in India: how far do policies respond to women's realities? *Gender & Development*, 17(3), 481–91.

Ball, H., & Fowler, D. (2008). Sexual offending against older female victims: An empirical study of the prevalence and characteristics of recorded offences in a semi-rural English county. *Journal of Forensic Psychiatry & Psychology*, 19(1), 14–32.

Barry, U. (2010). *Elderly Care in Ireland: Provisions and Providers. UCD School of Social Justice Working Papers Series*. Dublin: University College Dublin. (Retrieved 31 August 2010 from http://irserver.ucd.ie/dspace/bitstream/10197/2083/3/Barry-EGGEIrelandeldercare-2010.pdf)

Bass, D. M., Noelker, L. S., & Saito, Y. (1996). The moderating influence of service use on negative caregiving consequences. *Journals of Gerontology Series B: Psychological Sciences and Social Sciences*, 51, 121–31.

Baty, F. (1998). A clinical psychology service for older adults: the integrated primary care model. *PSIGE Newsletter*, 67, 3–7.

Baumgarten, M. (1989). The health of persons giving care to the demented elderly: a critical review. *Journal of Clinical Epidemiology*, 42, 1137–48.

British Psychological Society. (2006). *Commissioning Clinical Psychology Services for Older People, their Families and Other Carers*. Leicester: BPS.

Brodaty, H., Draper, B., & Low, L.-F. (2003). Nursing home staff attitudes towards residents with dementia: strain and satisfaction with work. *Journal of Advanced Nursing*, 44, 583–90.

Brown, L. J., Potter, J. F., & Foster, B. G. (1990). Caregiver burden should be evaluated during geriatric assessment. *Journal of the American Geriatrics Society*, 38, 455–60.

Burgess, A., Prentky, R., & Dowdell, E. (2000). Sexual predators in nursing homes. *Journal of Psychosocial Nursing and Mental Health Services*, 38(8), 26–35.

Burns, A., & Rabins, P. (2000). Carer burden in dementia. *Journal of Geriatric Psychiatry*, 15, 9–13.

Cambridge International Dictionary of English. Definition of 'Care' and 'Extra'. Cambridge: Cambridge International Dictionary of English. (Retrieved 9 March 2009 from www.dictionary.cambridge.org)

Carers Association. (2008). *Listen to Carers – Report on a Nation-wide Carer Consultation*. Tullamore: Carers Association. (Retrieved 11 March 2009 from www.carersireland.com)

Carers Ireland. (2009). 'Slap in the face' for carers as Government reneges on committed National Carers Strategy. (Retrieved 1 December 2010 from www.carersireland.com/docs/pressreleases/2003_03_04.pdf)

Carers UK. (2009). *Facts about Carers*. London: Carers UK. (Retrieved 1 June 2010 from http://www.carersuk.org/newsandcampaigns/Media/Factsaboutcaring)

Cohen, H. J., Feussner, J. R., Weinberger, M., Carnes, M., Hamdy, R. C., Hsieh, F., *et al.* (2002). A controlled trial of inpatient and outpatient geriatric evaluation and management. *New England Journal of Medicine*, 346(12), 905–12.

Cuddy, A. J. C., Norton, M. I., & Fiske, S. T. (2005). This old stereotype: The pervasiveness and persistence of the elderly stereotype. *Journal of Social Issues*, 61, 267–85.

Duncan, M. T., & Morgan, D. L. (1994). Sharing the caring: family caregivers' views of their relationships with the nursing home staff. *The Gerontologist*, 34, 235–44.

Eggebeen, D. J. (1992). Family structure and intergenerational exchanges. *Research on Aging*, 14, 427–47.

El Azayem, G., & Hedayat-Diba, Z. (1994). The psychological aspects of Islam: Basic principles of Islam and their psychological corollary. *International Journal for the Psychology of Religion*, 4(1), 41–50.

Evans, M., & Harkness, S. (2008). Elderly people in Vietnam: social protection, informal support and poverty. *Benefits: The Journal of Poverty and Social Justice*, 16(3), 245–53.

Expert Group on Mental Health Policy. (2006). *A Vision for Change: Report of the Expert Group on Mental Health Policy*. Dublin: The Stationery Office.

Fan, R. (2002). Reconstructionist Confucianism and health care: An Asian moral account of health care resource allocation. *Journal of Medicine & Philosophy*, 27(6), 675–82.

Farcnik, K., & Persyko, M. S. (2002). Assessment, measures and approaches to easing caregiver burden in Alzheimer's disease. *Drugs & Aging*, 19(3), 203–15.

Fiske, S. (1998). Stereotyping, prejudice, and discrimination. In Gilbert, D. T., Fiske, S. T., & Lindzey, G., eds., *The Handbook of Social Psychology, Vols. 1 and 2, 4th ed.* New York: McGraw-Hill, pp. 357–411.

Fiske, S., & Taylor, S. E. (2008). *Social Cognition: From Brains to Culture*. New York: McGraw-Hill.

Frankel, J., & McCarty, S. (1993). Women's employment and childbearing decisions. In Frankel, J., ed., *The Employed Mother and the Family Context*. New York: Springer Publishing Co, pp. 31–46.

Global Health through Education Training and Service. (2005). *Support for the Development of the Network: TUFH (Towards Unity for Health) Elderly Care Taskforce Community-Based Care for Older Adults Position Paper, November 2005*. (Retrieved 25 March 2009 from www.the-networktufh.org/publications_resources/positionpapers.asp).

Haley, W. E., Levine, E. G., Brown, S. L., & Bertolucci, A. A. (1987). Stress, appraisal, coping and social support as predictors of adaptational outcome among dementia caregivers. *Psychology and Aging*, 2, 323–30.

Halldorsdottir, S. (1997). *Caring and Uncaring Encounters in Nursing and Health Care – Developing a Theory. Linköping University Medical Dissertations No. 493.* Linköping: Department of Caring Sciences, Faculty of Health Sciences Linköping University, Sweden.

Hermanova, H. (1995). Healthy aging in Europe in the 1990s and implications for education and training in the care of the elderly. *Educational Gerontology*, 21, 1–14.

Herr, R. (2003). Is Confucianism compatible with care ethics? A critique. *Philosophy East & West*, 53(4), 471–89.

Hogan, D. P., Eggebeen, D. J., & Clogg, C. C. (1993). The structure of inter-generational exchanges in American families. *American Journal of Sociology*, 98, 1428–58.

Home Office. (2007). *Measuring Crime for 25 Years*. London: Home Office. (Retrieved 4 August 2010 from http://rds.homeoffice.gov.uk/rds/pdfs07/bcs25.pdf)

Islamic Horizons. Aging Muslim in America. *Islamic Horizons*, 36, July/August 2006.

Kovner, C. T., Mezey, M., & Harrington, C. (2002). Who cares for older adults? Workforce implications of an aging society – Geriatrics need to join paediatrics as a required element of training the next generation of healthcare professionals. *Health Affairs*, 21(5), 78–89.

Kramarow, E. (1995). The elderly who live alone in the United States: Historical perspectives on household change. *Demography*, 32(3), 335–52.

Levy, B., & Banaji, M. (2002). Implicit ageism. In Nelson, T. D., ed., *Ageism: Stereotyping and Prejudice Against Older Persons*. Cambridge, MA: The MIT Press, pp. 49–75.

Levy, B., & Langer, E. (1994). Aging free from negative stereotypes: Successful memory in China among the American deaf. *Journal of Personality and Social Psychology*, 66(6), 989–97.

Mattelaer, J. (2005). The aging male in African ethnic cultures. *The Aging Male*, 8(1), 42–7.

Mijung, P., & Chesla, C. (2007). Revisiting Confucianism as a conceptual framework for Asian family study. *Journal of Family Nursing*, 13(3), 293–311.

National Alliance for Caregiving. (2005). *Caregiving in the United States*. Bethesda, MD: NAC. (Retrieved 16 April 2010 from www.caregiving.org/data/04execsumm.pdf)

Navaie-Waliser, M., Feldman, P. H., & Gould, D. A. A. (2001). The experiences and challenges of informal caregivers: Common themes and differences among Whites, Blacks, and Hispanics. *The Gerontologist*, 41, 733–41.

Neary, S. R., & Mahoney, D. F. (2005). Dementia caregiving: The experiences of Hispanic/Latino caregivers. *Journal of Transcultural Nursing*, 26(2), 163–70.

Park, I. H., & Cho, L. J. (1995). Confucianism and the Korean family. *Journal of Comparative Family Studies*, 26, 117–25.

Phillips, L. R., Torres de Ardon, E., Kommenich, P., Killeen, M., & Rusinak, R. (2000). The Mexican American caregiving experience. *Hispanic Journal of Behavioral Sciences*, 22, 296–313.

Phillipson, C. (1998). *Reconstructing Old Age. New Agendas in Social Theory and Practice*. Thousand Oaks, CA: Sage.

Prasad, S. (2007). Does hospitalization make elderly households poor? An examination of the case of Kerala, India. *Social Policy & Administration*, 41(4), 355–71.

Sacco, V., & Nakhaie, M. (2001). Coping with crime: An examination of elderly and nonelderly adaptations. *International Journal of Law and Psychiatry*, 24(2–3), 305–23

Schulz, R., Newsom, J., Mittelmark, M., Burton, L., Hirsch, C., & Jackson, S. (1997). Health effects of caregiving: The caregiver effects study – An ancillary study of the Cardiovascular Health Study. *Annals of Behavioral Medicine*, 19(2), 110–16.

Soldo, B. (1980). America's elderly in the 1980s. *Population Bulletin*, 35, 148.

Sotomayor, M. (1989). The Hispanic elderly and the intergenerational family. *Journal of Children in Contemporary Society*, 20, 55–65.

Sundstrom, G. (1993). Care by families: An overview of trends. In *Caring for Frail Elderly People. Social Policy Studies No. 14*. Paris: OECD.

Tataru, N., & Dicker, A. (2009). S38-03 Ageing – ethical issues and stigma. *European Psychiatry*, 24, S204.

Thorslund, M. (1991). The increasing number of very old people will change the Swedish model of the welfare state. *Social Science & Medicine*, 32, 455–64.

Thursby, G. (1992). Islamic, Hindu, and Buddhist conceptions of aging. In Cole, T. R., Kastenbaum, R., & Ray, R. E., eds., *Handbook of the Humanities and Aging*. New York: Springer Publishing, pp. 175–96.

Woods, B. (2008). Residential care. In Woods, R. T., & Clare, L., eds., *Handbook of the Clinical Psychology of Ageing, 2nd ed*. New York: John Wiley & Sons, pp. 289–309.

Yamashita, M., & Amagai, M. (2008). Family caregiving in dementia in Japan. *Applied Nursing Research*, 21, 227–31.

Yang, S., & Rosenblatt, P. C. (2001). Shame in Korean families. *Journal of Comparative Family Studies*, 32, 361–75.

Zarit, S. H., & Edwards, C. J. (2008). *Mental Disorders in Older Adults, 2nd ed*. New York, Guilford Press.

Chapter 14

The paradox of ageing

Why do older people look so happy when they have nothing to look forward to?

Jutta Roisín Greve, Patrick Ryan and Cian Aherne

Introduction

The question outlined in the proposed paradox of ageing immediately brings to mind two apparent stereotypes/archetypes the 'young' may entertain of the 'older person'. First, the phrase 'old people look so happy' invites an image of the peaceful and wise sage who has lived life to the full and is now enjoying the fruit of her hard labour throughout earlier life-stages and upon reflecting on her life's achievements and disappointments has come to a place of acceptance and deeper understanding of life's mysteries. Second, the phrase 'they have nothing to look forward to' again invites an image, which one may conceive of as being a polar opposite to the image of 'the sage'; namely that of physical frailty, poverty, social isolation and loneliness, depression and imminent death. Both need to be refuted both in terms of their portrayal of an oversimplified and generalised image of older people and the fact that they simply ignore the complexity and broad array of human experience.

In an attempt to unearth whether the paradox referred to here is simply based on myth, or possibly referring to two extremes on a broad spectrum of possible human experiences relevant to individuals who happen to live through to old age, the authors propose to outline relevant epidemiological findings and further explore various theories of ageing with a view to eliciting a more elaborate, both person-centred and contextual, understanding of old age as a developmental stage. It is hoped to do so to inform and ultimately enhance the clinical practice of professionals working with older adults by highlighting the myriad of factors affecting a person who happens to be 'old' in terms of their physical, mental health and general functioning.

As a broader conceptual framework to working with older people, the concept of the 'active ageing paradigm' will be highlighted; a health promotion-/human rights-based concept introduced by the World Health Organization (WHO) in the late 1990s. It is designed to convey an inclusive message and to recognise the factors in addition to health care that affect how individuals and populations age by addressing individual, environmental as well as broader social issues impinging on 'successful ageing' of the increasing older population in industrialised societies (WHO, 2002; Kalache, 2007).

Background to the study of old age

Every culture, past and present has constructed terms and phrases to structure the various life phases. 'Old age' like other aspects of the human condition has inspired men and women alike to attribute a plethora of positive, negative, contradictory, even ambiguous and ambivalent images and ideas, which typically correlate with the processes, problems, challenges as well as opportunities of growing older (Laws, 1996).

From a scientific perspective, however, assumptions held about old age and the older person will inevitably affect the questions researchers will ask about this developmental stage and ultimately guide the conclusions drawn about the nature of life in later years (Kenyon, 1988, as cited in Perlmutter & Hall, 1992; Rempusheski & O'Hara, 2005). Is development after maturity a downhill course, in which ageing means an escalating series of losses? Or do we get better as we get older, so that gains may balance losses? The answers to these questions are extremely important given that the views about the nature of old age determine our attitudes toward older adults and ultimately their place in society (Perlmutter & Hall, 1992; Hayo & Ono, 2010).

Although the process of ageing was initially conceptualised as consisting of age-related changes characterised by losses, namely the decay of structures and deterioration of function (Perlmutter & Hall, 1992) newer perspectives on the ageing process now view late adulthood increasingly as a period of tremendous individual variability rather than one of universal decline (Weaver, 1999, as cited in Bee & Boyd, 2003).

An epidemiological perspective to ageing

It is important to point out the significant differences between various subgroups of the older aged. Gerontologists distinguish between the *young-old* (aged 60–75), the *old-old* (aged 75–85), and the *oldest-old* (aged 85 and over) (Bee & Boyd, 2003). Between 1960 and 1994 for example, the over-65 population in the USA doubled, while the over-85 population tripled (Federal Interagency Forum on Aging-Related Statistics [FIFARS], 2000, as cited in Bee & Boyd, 2003). Similarly to the trend observed in the USA, every industrialised country in the world is experiencing this kind of growth in the older aged population (Century Foundation, 1998, as cited in Bee & Boyd, 2003).

It is the significant growth in the oldest-old, however, which has given rise to a heightened awareness among health professionals of the specific physical challenges accompanying the ageing process. The oldest-old are more likely to suffer from siginificant physical and mental impairments than their younger peers.

Despite variability in health and functioning among older adults, there are several changes in physical functioning that characterise the late adult years for almost everyone. These include gradual changes in various bodily systems, the most obvious being changes to vision, hearing and gradual slowing of both physical and cognitive processes, among other physical functions (Willis, 1996, as cited in Bee & Boyd, 2003; Damián et al., 2008).

Although epidemiological data have mainly refuted common stereotypes of old age as being a period of illness, the proportion of older people with good health is a great deal lower than the equivalent proportions for young and middle-aged adults (FIFARS, 2000) and health services are faced with increasing demands and readjustments in order to meet the changing needs of an ageing population (Nordberg et al., 2007).

Have older people really nothing to look forward to? Physical and mental health indices in old age

There is no doubt that from an objective perspective, old age seems to present individuals with many challenges. Older people have typically retired from paid employment, their friends and close relatives may die, their physical health is declining, and they have reduced opportunities to be involved in society.

Among a myriad of contributing factors, health, in fact, is the single largest factor determining the trajectory of an adult's physical and mental status over the years beyond age 65. Older adults who are already suffering from one or more chronic diseases at 65 show far more rapid declines than those who begin late adulthood with no disease. This, in part, is an effect of the disease processes themselves (Bee & Boyd, 2003). Cardiovascular-related illnesses for example result in, among other things, restricted blood flow to many organs, including the brain, with resultant effects on learning and memory processes. The Seattle Longitudinal Study for example has, in fact, shown that adults with this disease show earlier declines in all mental abilities (Schaie, 1996, as cited in Bee & Boyd, 2003). Those suffering from early stages of Alzheimer's disease, or another disease causing dementia, will experience far more rapid declines in mental abilities compared with their healthy peers (Ricci et al., 2009).

With regard to general cognitive functioning, researchers have found a great deal of variability among older adults (Willis et al., 1992). Studies have indeed shown that memory function as measured by delayed recall of newly learned material is not substantially decreased for most older people (Geffen *et al.*, 1990; Mitrushina *et al.*, 1991; Petersen *et al.*, 1992, as cited in Knopman *et al.*, 2003). Hence, the consistent story from neuropsychology is that typical ageing *per se* does not degrade memory – disease does (Knopman *et al.*, 2003; Bopp & Verhaeghan, 2009; Duverne *et al.*, 2009).

Daily functioning and quality of life

In relation to an older person's ability to engage in day-to day functional activities, gerontologists generally define a disability as a limitation in an individual's ability to perform certain roles and tasks, in particular self-help tasks and other chores of daily living (Jette, 1996, as cited in Bee & Boyd, 2003). Daily tasks are often categorised into: activities of daily living (ADLs), including for example bathing, dressing and using the toilet. Instrumental activities of daily living (IADLs), include tasks such as doing housework, cooking and managing monetary matters (Millán-Calenti *et al.*, 2010).

In this context therefore, disabilites resulting from experiencing difficulties with carrying out some or most of these tasks become more common with growing age. Approximately 50 per cent of those over the age of 85 years report at least some level of difficulty performing some basic daily living activities (Jette, 1996; Fujiwara *et al.*, 2008). This also means however that there is a huge proportion of older people who maintain their independence in this regard, even when faced with physical problems, such as arthritis and/or hypertension.

From an Irish perspective according to the national health document, 'Adding Years to Life and Life to Years' (Department of Health and Children, 1998), the life expectancy for people over 65 does not seem to compare favourably with other European Union countries or the USA. Although there are signs that life expectancy is improving, older Irish people are still in relatively poor health (Fahey, 1995, as cited in Department of Health and Children, 1998). Mortality gives only part of the picture of a population's health status and although many diseases or accidents are not fatal, they may cause considerable disability and reduce quality of life (QoL). A major study of older Irish people in the community found that almost half of the respondents had major health problems (Fahey & Murray, 1994). The study further found that almost one in four people showed significant signs of psychological distress and that the major contributing factor was the onset of poor health and disability rather than old age itself. Trollor *et al.* (2007) found that one in 16 elderly people experienced symptoms consistent with any anxiety or affective disorder in Australia.

Mental health issues relevant to older adults

In relation to mental health problems affecting older adults, the dementias are the best known and incorporate a group of neurological disorders involving problems with memory and thinking that affect an individual's emotional, social and physical functioning. Aside from depression, dementia is the leading cause for institutionalisation of older people in the USA (FIFARS, 2000; Chen *et al.*, 2007; Matthews & Dening, 2002).

With scientists still not having fully understood the normal ageing process, their understanding of the causes of dementia and ways of preventing such illnesses is still very much in its infancy. For example some genetic contributors seem to be important in some, but not in all cases of Alzheimer's disease. Hence, in the absence of any clear knowledge about risk factors and causes for such a debilitating disease, supporting affected individuals and increasingly their carers with the management of the illness seems to be at the forefront in terms of health service involvement at present (Wilks, 2009; Huang *et al.*, 2009; Sørensen *et al.*, 2008; Beard *et al.*, 2009).

There are of course also other types of dementia, caused, for example, by multiple strokes (vascular dementia). In addition, dementia may also be caused by depression, metabolic disturbances, drug intoxication, hypothyroidism and tumours to name but a few. Many of the these causes are clearly treatable and approximately 10 per cent of all patients who are evaluated for dementia turn out to have some reversible problem, which highlights the importance of detailed assessment to ensure careful diagnosis of underlying causes (Bee & Boyd, 2003; Tripathi & Vibha, 2009).

Depression is another prevalent mental health problem affecting many older people. Common physical symptoms accompanying low mood are loss of appetite, sleep disturbances and lack of energy. It is vital to consider that older adults are more likely to report such symptoms no matter what their emotional state and hence may be diagnosed with depression when they are not actually depressed. Further distinctions have been made between depressed mood and clinical depression, in that depressed mood, also called geriatric dysthymia, among older people does not normally progress on to clinical depression and has been found to be more related to ongoing life stressors (Kocsis, 1998, as cited in Bee & Boyd, 2003; Ruppel *et al.*, 2010).

The most prevalent risk factors for depression in an older population relate to a myriad of biopsychosocial issues affecting older adults, such as inadequate social support, inadequate income and emotional loss (deaths of spouse, family or friends). The strongest predictor nonetheless again seems to be related to the actual health status experienced by the older person and hence across all ethnic and socioeconomic groups, the more disabling conditions older adults have the more depressive symptoms they present with (Black *et al.*, 1998, FIFARS, 2000; Lam *et al.*, 1997; Okwumabua *et al.*, 1997, as cited in Bee & Boyd, 2003; Chang-Quan *et al.*, 2010).

Psychosocial theories of ageing

In an attempt then to illucidate reasons for individual variability among older adults in relation to how they cope with some of the common as well as specific health challenges faced by them, a number of theories have been put forward exploring the psychological and behavioural processes involved in the healthy adjustment to ageing. Theories seem to differ in their focus on either the psychological or social challenges that older people may be faced with.

Erikson's theory of personality and social development

Erikson's theory of personality and social development termed the last of his eight life crises the Ego Integrity Versus Despair Stage (Erikson, 1959, as cited in Bee & Boyd, 2003). He proposed that the task of achieving ego integrity, namely the sense that one has lived a useful life, which begins in middle adulthood is the most central developmental challenge in late adulthood. To achieve ego integrity, the older adult must come to terms with who she/he is and has been, how his/her life has been lived, the choices she/he made, and the opportunities gained and lost. Furthermore, the process also involved coming to terms with death and accepting its imminence. Erikson believed that failing to achieve ego integrity in late adulthood would result in feelings of hopelessness and despair because of there being too little time to make changes to one's life before death (Sneed et al., 2006).

Despite the prominence of Erikson's theory, researchers in this field have found no convincing evidence however to suggest that older people are more likely than younger people or middle-aged people to achieve such self-acceptance (Eysenck, 2000). It appears though that adults become more reflective and philosophical in their approach to life as they move through the later adult years. Those older adults who use their growing capacity for philosophical reflection to achieve some degree of self-acceptance tend to be less fearful of death (Prager, 1998, as cited in Bee & Boyd, 2003; Butler & Ciarrochi, 2007). In addition, those older adults singled out by their own peers as 'wise' are more likely to rank high on Erikson's proposed construct of ego integrity and are more likely to show concern for humanity as a whole (Bee & Boyd, 2003).

More recent psychological theories on ageing

Ongoing research has explored other potential psychological constructs contributing to mental well-being in older age. The concept of valuation of life (VOL; Lawton et al., 2001), for example, has been identified as a significant component of quality of life aside from prominent mental and physical health indices. The VOL scale defines an inner state that expresses a mixture of positive mental health, domain-specific quality of life, purpose and determination.

It has been defined as:

> . . . the extent to which the person is attached to his or her present life, for reasons related to a sense not only of enjoyment and the absence of distress, but also hope, futurity, purpose, meaningfulness, persistence, and self-efficacy . . . VOL is not only determined by health and the negative qualities associated with illness or depression. Our umbrella hypothesis is that positive and negative factors act in balance and counterbalance with one another and that people perform a very complex calculus in putting it all together into the concept we mean by VOL. VOL is in some ways an existential concept that is meant to approach the concept of total reason for living.
>
> (Lawton *et al.*, 1999: 407, as cited in Moss *et al.*, 2007)

Based on their findings the authors propose that clinicians aside from acknowledging obvious mental and physical health indices should also recognise the way an older person views his or her use of time and psychological well-being. Such an approach may be a more useful indice of well-being given that a task of ageing is to consider the value of life to date.

In a similar fashion to the above concept is a certain lifespan theory of motivation, namely the *socioemotional selectivity theory*, which proposes that time perspective is the dominating force that structures human motivations and goals throughout life (Carstensen, 1993, 1995; Carstensen & Charles, 1998; Carstensen *et al.*, 1999; St. Jacques *et al.*, 2009). The theory contends that humans have a conscious and subconscious awareness of their time left in life, and that perceived boundaries on time direct attention to emotionally meaningful aspects of life. Among older adults, when time is perceived as limited, emotional experience assumes primacy and people are motivated to monitor and select their environments to optimise emotional meaningfulness and emotional functioning. Consistent with the theory, older age is associated with improved emotional regulation, which is defined as the maintenance of positive affect and decrease of negative affect, and this is a skill shown to improve with age (Carstensen *et al.*, 2000). One study reported that positive affect was higher in older people compared with their younger counterparts (Mroczek & Kolarz, 1998). Further research has started to explore the underlying cognitive processes of this phenomenon and some findings suggest that older adults may process positive and negative information differently in that they attend to and memorise positive information better (Charles *et al.*, 2003). Combined with subjective reports of increased control over emotions (Gross *et al.*, 1997; Lawton *et al.*,

1992), the emerging profile is that older adults appear more effective in regulating their emotions in ways that reduce the impact of negative experiences compared with younger adults (Charles *et al.*, 2003).

Activity versus disengagement theory

Other theories have also tried to acknowledge the impact of changing social roles in adulthood and to determine whether it is normal, necessary, or healthy for older adults to remain active as long as possible or whether some gradual turning inward presents the more adaptive pattern given their changing roles in society.

The activity theory proposed by Havighurst (1964, as cited in Eysenck, 2000) argues that the psychologically and physically healthiest response to old age is to maintain the greatest possible level of activity and involvement in as many roles as is possible. Activity theorists often refer to findings demonstrating that most active older adults report slightly greater satisfaction with themselves or their lives, are healthiest, and have the highest morale (Adelman, 1994; Bryant & Rakowski, 1992; George, 1990; McIntosh & Danigelis, 1995, as cited in Bee & Boyd, 2003; Lobo *et al.*, 2008) even among older people who suffer from disabilities such as arthritis, for whom active social participation may be physically painful (Zimmer *et al.*, 1995, as cited in Bee & Boyd, 2003).

Cumming and Henry (1961, as cited in Eysenck, 2000) proposed disengagement theory, which proposes that there are various reasons why older people become less and less actively involved in society. It proposes three aspects to ageing: the shrinkage of life-space; increased individuality; and the acceptance of these changes. Some of the reasons for disengagement are as a result of factors beyond the control of the individual, such as compulsory retirement, deaths of relatives and friends, and children moving away from home and many older people may choose to reduce the scope of their social lives as the best way of adapting to the realities of old age.

Evidence for both the activity theory and the disegagement theory has been contradictory in terms of applicability. Some studies have shown that older people progressively disengage from society (i.e. Cumming & Henry, 1961, as cited in Eysenck, 2000); in particular those who had always been rather reclusive (Maddox, 1970) or during the last 2 years of life when disengagement, in many cases, was forced on the individuals by ill health (Lieberman & Coplan, 1970, as cited in Eysenck, 2000; Kuo *et al.*, 2004). Studies in the UK and Australia have found that the majority of elderly people remain very socially active through the church or community organisations (Eysenck, 2000; Krause, 2002). Other findings, supporting disengagement theory reported that some of those studied were *disengagers*. These people had chosen to disengage themselves from social activities but were nevertheless happy and in spite of their declining levels of social engagement, less likely than younger people to experience loneliness (Havighurst *et al.*, 1968; Wrosch *et al.*, 2003).

What makes older people happier?

On the whole therefore it can be concluded that the phenomenon of mental well-being and the ability to cope with what old age brings is complex. The level of health and to what extent one may be able to engage in social roles is important in this regard. However, in the absence of good health, which may prevent an older adult from actively engaging in former social roles, psychological resources as proposed by the disengagement theory in the form of acceptance and adjustment to changing roles, may be of particular significance in terms of dealing favourably with the challenges of ageing (Greene & Dunkle, 1992; Wilson, 1997; Butler & Ciarrochi, 2007). Furthermore, the effect of an older person's conscious and subconscious awareness of his or her time left in life and resulting positive changes with regard to emotional regulation and increased valuation of life may also explain why older adults achieve emotional stability (Flint *et al.*, 1983; Chan & Yau, 2009; Moreno *et al.*, 2009). However, further research into individual variability with regards to the processes underlying successful emotional regulation and potential avenues for intervention are certainly needed in this field.

Sociocultural factors relevant to the adjustment to old age

A major limitation of many of the theoretical models lies in their tendency to only focus on individual factors affecting adjustment without also taking into account broader social and contextual factors that may facilitate or inhibit healthy adjustment in this regard (Eysenck, 2000; Leino-Kilpi *et al.*, 2003). Ferris and Bramston (1994, as cited in Eysenck, 2000) and Thanakwang (2009) found that relationships, social networks and good health were the three most important factors having an impact on quality of life. The importance of social support was also observed by Russell and Cuatrona (1991, as cited in Eysenck, 2000) and Yoon (2006). Elderly people with little social support were more likely to develop depressive symptoms over a 1-year period.

Clearly role changes are inevitable in old age, and physical and cognitive changes are responsible for many of them. However, some may also be caused by ageism. Physical appearance (i.e. wrinkles, grey hair) often form the basis for judgement about the competence of older people (Hummert *et al.*, 1997, as cited in Boyd & Bee, 2003), which may result in older adults being unjustly forced out of roles by younger adults, and potentially affecting issues around employment among others. Many old people also have little money, and so financial security is another important factor. Krause *et al.* (1991, as cited in Eysenck, 2000) found in America and in Japan that elderly people with financial problems experienced depression and a sense of worthlessness.

Moreover, sociologists point out that the roles that older adults retain have far less content compared with earlier roles they occupied. For example, most older adults continue their role as parents or become grand-parents, but this role typically becomes less demanding. In a practical sense then, daily routines of many older people are no longer structured by specific social roles. Although some developmentalists see this loss of role definition as carrying with it a significant risk of isolation or alienation, surely this depends again on a myriad of other factors.

Furthermore, cultural differences need to be acknowledged in terms of the role a society may ascribe to its older members. Social perceptions of the value and benefit of older age vary in different cultures. In many traditional societies, typical words that describe older people characterise them 'as persons with knowledge'. In such societies, older people tend to enjoy higher social status and perform more roles in society. They are more likely to live with their adult children and are often involved in childcare, and their opinions on family matters are frequently sought (WHO, 1999; Dening, 2009).

Of particular importance here is the distinction between individualism and collectivism. In Western societies, with their individualistic emphasis on personal achievement, older people with perceived declining powers are likely to be at least, in part, rejected by society. The greater emphasis on cooperation and supportive groups in the collectivist societies of Asia and Africa on the other hand leads to older people remaining more integrated and engaged with society (Triandis, 1994; Tout, 1989, as cited in Eysenck, 2000). However, exceptions also exist in realms of culture. Nomadic people for example, who are frequently moving from one place to the next often show little respect towards their elders because they reduce the mobility of the entire group (Tout, 1989).

The impact of the spread of Western influences today throughout much of the world on social structures surely cannot be denied. This has indeed led to a marked reduction in the extended family with the grandparents at its head in numerous cultures in Africa and Asia. Turnbull (1989, as cited in Eysenck, 2000) has observed a growing tendency towards social exclusion of elderly people in some cultures such as the Ik people of Uganda, who historically were considered more collectivist. On the whole, modernisation of traditional societies has eroded many traditional values, often resulting in loss of esteem for older people and leading to social isolation (WHO, 1999; Hegland *et al.*, 2007).

On the whole it is accepted, however, from studies across all cultures, that social integration and support tend to provide people with emotional and practical resources and that older people, who are more socially integrated overall enjoy better physical and mental health (WHO, 1999; Sun *et al.*, 2007).

Health promotion for older people and the 'active ageing paradigm'

In the face of the myriad of aforementioned challenges faced by older adults and factors contributing to or preventing their adjustment, how can health professionals and society as a whole support older adults in developing or maintaining both their physical, but most importantly their mental health?

The World Health Organization Regional Office for Europe for example has set targets for improving the health of older people. Among the strategies outlined for reaching these goals are the promotion of lifestyle changes, the creation and the provision of supportive environments and appropriate support services for older people (WHO, 2002).

Although it is widely accepted that health promotion for a long, healthy and active life should ideally begin as early as possible during the life course, reviews of the literature on health promotion for older people have revealed that health promotion and preventative care in later life can also improve longevity and benefit health and quality of life (Eurolink Age, 1997, as cited in Department of Health and Children, 1998; Kim *et al.*, 2003; Meng *et al.*, 2007).

Health promotion programmes, for older people and the settings in which they are provided must take account of the physiological, social and economic changes that are associated with ageing and which are often beyond the control of older people themselves as well as the health care sector. Thus, policies in a wide range of areas including pensions, housing and transport need to be acknowledged in terms of their impact on the health and well-being of older people (Department of Health and Children, 1998; Boermal, 2006).

Furthermore, health promotion for older people also has an important role to play in reducing the disabling effects of illness among those who are already ill. Early recognition and treatment of illness is essential in enabling older people to cope with illness and to prevent the onset of psychological distress and possible withdrawal from society. For many older people who are ill, housebound or living in residential care, measures, which enable them to remain mentally and physically active and to participate in their wider community are essential for improving their quality of life (Department of Health and Children, 1998; Shmotkin *et al.*, 2003).

Finally, at a global level the WHO (2002) recently introduced the concept of 'active ageing', which refers to health as encompassing physical, mental and social well-being. If ageing is to be a positive experience, longer life must also be accompanied by continuing opportunities for health, participation and security. Whereas, traditionally, old age has been associated with retirement, illness and dependency, the 'active ageing paradigm' endeavours to shift perspectives to older people as active participants in an age-integrated society and as active contributors as well as beneficiaries of development. This includes recognition of the contribution of older people who are ill, frail and vulnerable by championing their rights to care and security (WHO, 2002).

The active ageing approach also endeavours to take a life course perspective on ageing by recognising that older people are not an homogenous group and that individual diversity tends to increase with age. Individual factors such as lifestyle behaviours and psychological resources that have formed during earlier developmental stages (i.e. formation of secure attachment in infancy) are also acknowledged and addressed as contributing to the healthy adjustment of the individual to old age (Rabinowitz *et al.*, 2007). In addition, social support, opportunities for education and lifelong learning, peace and protection from violence and abuse are addressed in terms of being key factors in the social environment that can enhance the health of an older person (WHO, 2002).

Hence, from a health service perspective, a life-course and multisystemic perspective seems to make most sense in terms of facilitating a healthy and active ageing process by building up physical and psychological capacities of individuals across the lifespan and furthermore building supportive environments for older people, which enables them to continue to participate in society (Wynne & Groves, 1995).

The 'paradox of ageing' revisited – does it actually exist?

In an attempt, therefore, to shed some light on the proposed paradox of ageing, namely the assumption that 'older people are happy even though they have nothing to look forward to', we have endeavoured to create an understanding of older adults that was based on the systematic collation of individual, population and wider systemic realities as identified through scientific exploration and not mere stereotypical myth.

There is no doubt that the ageing process brings with it certain physical, mental and social realities that require immense adjustment on the side of the individual. It can certainly be helpful to identify commonalities of the ageing process, such as the most prevalent health problems and resulting functional and social limitations to be able to address relevant health, social and environmental obstacles at a population level. This would begin to enable older people and relevant carers to continue to be involved in their communities and build the resources for contentment and happiness.

However, individual older adults will undoubtedly experience old age differently; some may be happy, others may not be and, depending on changes in overall health and social status, individuals may shift from being happy to being unhappy or vice versa. Hence, the actual emotional experiences of older people, much like during earlier developmental stages, may fluctuate. Further research on the concepts of resilience and emotional regulation among others and how these contribute to healthy emotional adjustment in ageing may shed further light on individual variability in this context.

On the whole we propose that in order to be able to effectively address *all* of the biopsychosocial factors contributing to good 'quality of life' and mental health in older adults, the life course approach as proposed by WHO (2002) surely needs to be implemented in order to intervene during those 'windows of opportunity' at earlier developmental stages when significant psychological and behavioural patterns relevant to healthy living establish themselves.

References

Adelman, P. K. (1994). Multiple roles and physical health among older adults: Gender and ethnic comparions. *Research on Aging*, 16, 142–166.

Beard, R., Fetterman, D., Wu, B., & Bryant, L. (2009). The two voices of Alzheimer's: attitudes toward brain health by diagnosed individuals and support persons. *The Gerontologist*, 49, S40–9.

Bee, H., & Boyd, D. (2003). *Lifespan Development, 3rd ed.* Boston, MA: Allyn & Bacon.

Black, S., Markides, K., & Miller, T. (1998). Correlates of depressive symptomatology among older community-dwelling Mexican Americans: The Hispanic EPESE. *Journals of Gerontology Series B: Psychological Sciences and Social Sciences*, 53B, S198–208.

Boermel, A. (2006). 'No wasting' and 'empty nesters': 'old age' in Beijing. *Oxford Development Studies*, 34(4), 401–18.

Bopp, K., & Verhaeghen, P. (2009). Working memory and aging: Separating the effects of content and context. *Psychology and Aging*, 24(4), 968–80.

Bryant, S., & Rakowski, W. (1992). Predictors of mortality among elderly African-Americans. *Research on Aging*, 14, 50–67.

Butler, J., & Ciarrochi, J. (2007). Psychological acceptance and quality of life in the elderly. *Quality of Life Research*, 16(4), 607–15.

Carstensen, L. L. (1993). Motivation for social contact across the life span: A theory of socioemotional selectivity. In Jacobs, J., ed., *Nebraska Symposium on Motivation: Vol. 40. Developmental Perspectives on Motivation*. Lincoln: University of Nebraska Press, pp. 209–54.

Carstensen, L. L. (1995). Evidence for a life-span theory of socioemotional selectivity. *Current Directions in Psychological Science*, 4, 151–6.

Carstensen, L. L., & Charles, S. T. (1998). Emotion in the second half of life. *Current Directions*, 7, 144–9.

Carstensen, L. L., Isaacowitz, D. M., & Charles, S. T. (1999). Taking time seriously: A theory of socioemotional selectivity. *American Psychologist*, 54, 165–81.

Carstensen, L. L., Pasupathi, M., Mayr, U., & Nesselroade, J. (2000). Emotional experience in everyday life across the adult life span. *Journal of Personality and Social Psychology*, 79, 644–55.

Century Foundation. (1998). *Social Security Reform: A Century Foundation Guide to the Issues*. Washington, DC: Century Foundation. (Retrieved 22 February 2010 from http://www.tcf.org/)

Chan, C., & Yau, M. (2009). Death preparation among the ethnic Chinese well-elderly in Singapore: an exploratory study. *Omega: Journal of Death and Dying*, 60(3), 225–39.

Chang-Quan, H., Xue-Mei, Z., Bi-Rong, D., Zhen-Chan, L., Ji-Rong, Y., & Qing-Xiu, L. (2010). Health status and risk for depression among the elderly: a meta-analysis of published literature. *Age and Ageing*, 39(1), 23–30.

Charles, S. T., Mather, M., & Carstensen, L. (2003). Aging and emotional memory: the forgettable nature of negative images in older adults. *Journal of Experimental Psychology: General*, 132, 310–24.

Chen, T., Chiu, M., Tang, L., Chiu, Y., Chang, S., Su, C., et al. (2007). Institution type-dependent high prevalence of dementia in long-term care units. *Neuroepidemiology*, 28(3), 142–9.

Cumming, E., & Henry, W. E. (1961). *Growing Old*. New York: Basic Books

Damián, J., Pastor-Barriuso, R., & Valderrama-Gama, E. (2008). Factors associated with self-rated health in older people living in institutions. *BMC Geriatrics*, 8, 5.

Dening, T. (2009). Review of 'Integrated management of depression in the elderly'. *Psychological Medicine: A Journal of Research in Psychiatry and the Allied Sciences*, 39(1), 172.

Department of Health and Children. (1998). *Adding Years to Life and Life to Years – A Health Promotion Strategy for Older People*. Dublin, Ireland.

Duverne, S., Motamedinia, S., & Rugg, M. (2009). Effects of age on the neural correlates of retrieval cue processing are modulated by task demands. *Journal of Cognitive Neuroscience*, 21(1), 1–17.

Erikson, E. H. (1959). *Identity and the Life Cycle*. New York: Norton.

Eurolink Age. (1997). *Adding Life to Years. A Report of the Eurolink Age Workshop, Helsinki 7–9 November 1996*. London: Eurolink Age.

Eysenck, M. W. (2000). *Psychology – A Student's Handbook*. Hove: Psychology Press.

Fahey, T. (1995). *The Health and Social Care Implications of Population Ageing in Ireland, 1991–2011. Report No. 42*. Dublin: National Council for the Elderly.

Fahey, T., & Murray, P. (1994). *Health and Autonomy of Over-65s in Ireland*. Dublin: National Council for the Elderly.

Federal Interagency Forum on Aging-Related Statistics. (2000). *Older Americans 2000: Key Indicators of Well-being*. Hyattsville, MD: Federal Interagency Forum on Aging-Related Statistics.

Ferris, C., & Bramston, P. (1994). Quality of life in the elderly: A contribution to its understanding. *The Australasian Journal of Ageing*, 13, 120–3.

Flint, G., Gayton, W., & Ozmon, K. (1983). Relationship between life satisfaction and acceptance of death by elderly persons. *Psychological Reports*, 53(1), 290.

Fujiwara, Y., Yoshida, H., Amano, H., Fukaya, T., Liang, J., Uchida, H., *et al.* (2008). Predictors of improvement or decline in instrumental activities of daily living among community-dwelling older Japanese. *Gerontology*, 54(6), 373–80.

Geffen, G., Moar, K. J., O'Hanlon, A. P., Clark, C. R., & Geffen, L. B. (1990). Performance measures of 16- to 86-year-old males and females on the Auditory Verbal Learning Test. *The Clinical Neuropsychologist*, 4, 45–63.

George, L. K. (1990). Social structure, social processes, and social-psychological states. In Binstock, R. H., & George, L. K., eds., *Handbook of Aging and the Social Sciences, 3rd ed.* San Diego, CA: Academic Press, pp. 186–204.

Greene, R., & Dunkle, R. (1992). Is the elderly patient's denial of long term care adversive to later adjustment to placement? *Physical & Occupational Therapy in Geriatrics*, 10(4), 59–75.

Gross, J. J., Carstensen, L. L., Pasupathi, M., Tsai, J., Skorpen, C. G., & Hsu, A. Y. C. (1997). Emotion and aging: Experience, expression, and control. *Psychology and Aging*, 12, 590–9.

Havighurst, R. J. (1964). Stages of vocational development. In Borrow, H., ed., *Man in a World of Work*. Boston, MA: Houghton Mifflin.

Havighurst, R. J., Neugarten, B. L. A., & Tobin, S. S. C. (1968). Disengagement and patterns of aging. In Neugarten, B. L., ed., *Middle Age and Aging*. Chicago, IL: University of Chicago Press.

Hayo, B., & Ono, H. (2010). Comparing public attitudes toward providing for the livelihood of the elderly in two aging societies: Germany and Japan. *Journal of Socio-Economics*, 39(1), 72–80.

Hegland, M., Sarraf, Z., & Shahbazi, M. (2007). Modernisation and social change: The impact on Iranian elderly social networks and care systems. *Anthropology of the Middle East*, 2(2), 55–73.

Huang, C. Y., Sousa, V., Perng, S. J., Hwang, M. Y., Tsai, C. C., Huang, M. H., *et al.* (2009). Stressors, social support, depressive symptoms and general health status of Taiwanese caregivers of persons with stroke or Alzheimer's disease. *Journal of Clinical Nursing*, 18(4), 502–11.

Hummert, M., Garstka, T., & Shaner, J. (1997). Stereotyping of older adults: The role of target facial cues and perceiver characteristics. *Psychology and Aging*, 12, 107–14.

Jette, A. M. (1996). Disability trends and transitions. In Binstock, R. H., & George, L. K., eds., *Handbook of Aging and the Social Sciences, 4th ed.* San Diego, CA: Academic Press, pp. 94–116.

Kalache, A. (2007). The World Health Organization and global ageing. In Robinson, M., Novelli, W., Pearson, C., & Norris, L., eds., *Global Health and Global Ageing*. San Francisco, CA: Jossey-Bass, pp. 31–46.

Kenyon, G. M. (1988). Basic assumptions in theories of of human aging. In Birren, J. E., & Bengston, V. L., eds., *Emergent Theories of Aging*. New York: Springer.

Kim, C., June, K., & Song, R. (2003). Effects of a health-promotion program on cardiovascular risk factors, health behaviors, and life satisfaction in institutionalized elderly women. *International Journal of Nursing Studies*, 40(4), 375.

Knopman, D. S., Boeve, B. F., & Petersen, R. C. (2003). Essentials of the proper diagnoses of mild cognitive impairment, dementia, and major subtypes of dementia. *Mayo Clinic Proceedings*, 78, 1290–308.

Kocsis, J. (1998). Geriatric dysthymia. *Journal of Clinical Psychiatry*, 59, 13–15.

Krause, N. (2002). Church-based social support and health in old age: exploring variations by race. *Journals of Gerontology Series B: Psychological Sciences and Social Sciences*, 57B(6), S332–47.

Krause, N., Jay, G., & Liang, J. (1991). Financial strain and psychological well-being among the American and Japanese elderly. *Psychology and Aging*, 6, 170–81.

Kuo, Y F., Raji, M., Peek, M., & Goodwin, J. (2004). Health-related social disengagement in elderly diabetic patients. *Diabetes Care*, 27(7), 1630–7.

Lam, R., Pacala, J., & Smith, S. (1997). Factors related to depressive symptoms in an elderly Chinese American sample. *The Gerontologist*, 17, 57–70.

Laws, G. (1996). 'A shot of economic adrenalin': Reconstructing 'the elderly' in the retiree-based economic development literature. *Journal of Aging Studies*, 10(3), 171–88.

Lawton, M. P., Kleban, M. H., Rajagopal, D., & Dean, J. (1992). The dimensions of affective experience in three age groups. *Psychology and Aging*, 7, 171–84.

Lawton, M., Moss, M., Hoffman, C., Kleban, M., Ruckdeschel, K., & Winter, L. (2001). Valuation of life: A concept and a scale. *Journal of Aging and Health*, 13(1), 3–31.

Leino-Kilpi, H., Välimäki, M., Dassen, T., Gasull, M., Lemonidou, C., Schopp, A., et al. (2003). Perceptions of autonomy, privacy and informed consent in the care of elderly people in five European countries: general overview. *Nursing Ethics*, 10(1), 18–27.

Lieberman, M., & Coplan, A. (1970). Distance from death as a variable in the study of aging. *Developmental Psychology*, 2(1), 71–84.

Lobo, A., Santos, P., Carvalho, J., & Mota, J. (2008). Relationship between intensity of physical activity and health-related quality of life in Portuguese institutionalized elderly. *Geriatrics & Gerontology International*, 8(4), 284–290.

McIntosh, B. R., & Danigelis, N. L. (1995). Race, gender, and the relevance of productive activity for elders' affect. *Journals of Gerontology: Social Sciences*, 50B, S229–39.

Maddox, G. L. (1970). Persistence of life style among the elderly. In Palmore, E., ed., *Normal Aging*. Durham, NC: Duke University Press.

Matthews, F., & Dening, T. (2002). Prevalence of dementia in institutional care. *Lancet*, 360(9328), 225.

Meng, H., Wamsley, B., Eggert, G., & Van Nostrand, J. (2007). Impact of a health promotion nurse intervention on disability and health care costs among elderly adults with heart conditions. *The Journal of Rural Health*, 23(4), 322–31.

Millán-Calenti, J., Tubío, J., Pita-Fernández, S., González-Abraldes, I., Lorenzo, T., Fernández-Arruty, T., et al. (2010). Prevalence of functional disability in activities of daily living (ADL), instrumental activities of daily living (IADL) and associated factors, as predictors of morbidity and mortality. *Archives of Gerontology and Geriatrics*, 50(3), 306–10.

Mitrushina, M., Satz, P., Chervinsky, A., & D'Elia, L. (1991). Performance of four age groups of normal elderly on the Rey Auditory-Verbal Learning Test. *Journal of Clinical Psychology*, 47, 351–7.

Moreno, R., De La Fuente Solana, E., Rico, M., & Fernández, L. (2009). Death anxiety in institutionalized and non-institutionalized elderly people in Spain. *Omega: Journal of Death and Dying*, 58(1), 61–76.

Moss, M. S., Hoffman, C. J., Mossey, J., & Rovine, M. (2007). Changes over 4 years in health, quality of life, mental health and valuation of life. *Journal of Aging and Health*, 19, 1025–44.

Mroczek, D. K., & Kolarz, C. M. (1998). The effect of age on positive and negative affect: A developmental perspective on happiness. *Journal of Personality and Social Psychology*, 75, 1333–49.

Nordberg, G., Wimo, A., Jönsson, L., Kåreholt, I., Sjölund, B., Lagergren, M., *et al.* (2007). Time use and costs of institutionalised elderly persons with or without dementia: results from the Nordanstig cohort in the Kungsholmen Project—a population based study in Sweden. *International Journal of Geriatric Psychiatry*, 22(7), 639–48.

Okwumabua, J., Baker, F., Wong, S., & Pilgram, B. (1997). Characteristics of depressive symptoms in elderly urban and rural African Americans. *Journal of Gerontology*, 52A, M241–46.

Perlmutter, M., & Hall, E. (1992). *Adult Development and Aging.* New York: John Wiley & Sons.

Petersen, R. C., Smith, G., Kokmen, E., Ivnik, R. J., & Tangalos, E. G. (1992). Memory function in normal aging. *Neurology*, 42, 396–401.

Prager, E. (1998). Men and meaning in later life. *Journal of Clinical Geropsychology*, 4, 191–203.

Rabinowitz, Y., Mausbach, B., Thompson, L., & Gallagher-Thompson, D. (2007). The relationship between self-efficacy and cumulative health risk associated with health behavior patterns female caregivers of elderly relatives with Alzheimer's dementia. *Journal of Aging and Health*, 19(6), 946–64.

Rempusheski, V., & O'Hara, C. (2005). Psychometric properties of the Grandparent Perceptions of Family Scale (GPFS). *Nursing Research*, 54(6), 419–27.

Ricci, M., Guidoni, S., Sepe-Monti, M., Bomboi, G., Antonini, G., Blundo, C., *et al.* (2009). Clinical findings, functional abilities and caregiver distress in the early stage of dementia with Lewy bodies (DLB) and Alzheimer's disease (AD). *Archives of Gerontology and Geriatrics*, 49(2), 101–4.

Ruppel, S., Jenkins, W., Griffin, J., & Kizer, J. (2010). Are they depressed or just old? A study of perceptions about the elderly suffering from depression. *North American Journal of Psychology*, 12(1), 31–42.

Russell, D. W., & Cuatrona, C. E. (1991). Social support, stress, and depressive symptoms among the elderly: Test of a process model. *Psychology and Aging*, 6, 190–201.

Schaie, K. W. (1996). Intellectual development in adulthood. In Birren, J. E., & Schaie, K. W., eds., *Handbook of the Psychology of Aging, 4th ed.* San Diego, CA: Academic Press, pp. 266–86.

Shmotkin, D., Blumstein, T., & Modan, B. (2003). Beyond keeping active: Concomitants of being a volunteer in old-old age. *Psychology and Aging*, 18(3), 602–7.

Sneed, J., Whitbourne, S., & Culang, M. (2006). Trust, identity, and ego integrity: modeling Erikson's core stages over 34 years. *Journal of Adult Development*, 13(3/4), 148–57.

Sørensen, L., Waldorff, F., & Waldemar, G. (2008). Early counselling and support for patients with mild Alzheimer's disease and their caregivers: A qualitative study on outcome. *Aging & Mental Health*, 12(4), 444–50.

St. Jacques, P., Dolcos, F., & Cabeza, R. (2009). Effects of aging on functional connectivity of the amygdala for subsequent memory of negative pictures: A network analysis of functional magnetic resonance imageing data. *Psychological Science*, 20(1), 74–84.

Sun, W., Watanabe, M., Tanimoto, Y., Shibutani, T., Kono, R., Saito, M., *et al.* (2007). Factors associated with good self-rated health of non-disabled elderly living alone in Japan: a cross-sectional study. *BMC Public Health*, 7, 297–9.

Thanakwang, K. (2009). Social relationships influencing positive perceived health among Thai older persons: A secondary data analysis using the National Elderly Survey. *Nursing & Health Sciences*, 11(2), 144–9.

Tout, K. (1989). *Ageing in Developing Countries*. Oxford: Oxford University Press.

Triandis, H. C. (1994). *Culture and Social Behavior*. New York: McGraw-Hill.

Tripathi, M., & Vibha, D. (2009). Reversible dementias. *Indian Journal of Psychiatry*, 51, 52–5.

Trollor, J., Anderson, T., Sachdev, P., Brodaty, H., & Andrews, G. (2007). Age shall not weary them: mental health in the middle-aged and the elderly. *Australian and New Zealand Journal of Psychiatry*, 41(7), 581–9.

Turnbull, C. M. (1989). *The Mountain People*. London: London: Paladin.

Weaver, J. (1999). Gerontology education: A new paradigm for the 21st century. *Educational Gerontology*, 25, 479–90.

Wilks, S. (2009). Support for Alzheimer's caregivers: psychometric evaluation of familial and friend support measures. *Research on Social Work Practice*, 19(6), 722–9.

Willis, S. L. (1996). Everyday problem solving. In Birren, J. E., & Schaie, K. W., eds., *Handbook of Psychology of Aging, 4th ed.* San Diego, CA: Academic Press, pp. 287– 307.

Willis, S. L., Jay, G. M., Diehl, M., & Marsiske, M. (1992). Longitudinal change and prediction of everyday task competence in the elderly. *Research on Aging*, 14, 68–91.

Wilson, S. (1997). The transition to nursing home life: a comparison of planned and unplanned admissions. *Journal of Advanced Nursing*, 26(5), 864–71.

World Health Organization. (1999). *A Life Course Perspective of Maintaining Independence in Older Age. Ageing and Health.* Geneva, WHO.

World Health Organization. (2002). *Active Ageing: A Policy Framework.* Geneva, WHO.

Wrosch, C., Scheier, M. F., Carver, C. S., & Schulz, R. (2003). The importance of goal disengagement in adaptive self-regulation: When giving up is beneficial. *Self and Identity*, 2, 1–20.

Wynne, R., & Groves, D. (1995). Life span approach to understanding coping styles of the elderly. *Education*, 115(3), 448.

Yoon, D. P. (2006). Factors affecting subjective well-being for rural elderly individuals: The importance of spirituality, religiousness, and social support. *Journal of Religion & Spirituality in Social Work*, 25(2), 59–75.

Zimmer, Z., Hickey, T., & Searle, M. S. (1995). Activity participation and well-being among older people with arthritis. *The Gerontologist*, 35(4), 463–71.

Chapter 15

Older adults

Key to the success of younger generations

Patrick Ryan, Claire O'Sullivan and Mairead Smyth

Introduction

How successful an individual is in his/her life can be defined in multiple ways, through multiple lenses and from multiple perspectives. In short, success is many different things to many different people. It can be defined by tangibles such as material wealth, educational qualifications, creation of a family home and successful relationships. It can also comprise of things less obvious – the gift of wisdom, sensations of pleasure and happiness or simply the joy in being alive. Success is also not a fixed variable in the life of an individual – it varies across the developmental phases, can be built on cumulatively or be replaced with alternatives as the personality of the individual evolves.

In psychological terms, and for the purposes of this chapter, a large component of what success is defined as derives from the existence of relationships and the experience of relating that an individual generates in his/her life. This is largely to do with the fact that much psychological research is driven by the desire to either reduce unhappiness or increase happiness in people's lives by understanding the individual in relation to the environment in which she/he operates and in particular the relating and relationship environment that she/he builds.

Lifespan relating

Success at operating usefully and meaningfully in the relating world determines experiences of success for the person in that core psychological needs are fulfilled. Such needs – connection, love, belonging, challenge, reciprocity – evolve with the development of a person but those outlined above are required from birth to old age. Children's physical, social, emotional and intellectual needs must all be met if they are to develop to their full potential and become fulfilled adolescents, adults and older adults who contribute to society. The caregiving that children receive is a cornerstone for the development of their physical, social, emotional, intellectual and interpersonal well-being. Caregiving generally occurs within the context of families. The family has been described as a unique social system found in all societies that unites individuals into cooperative groups that oversee the bearing and raising of children. Families can also be described as being built on kinship, a social bond based on blood, adoption, fostering or marriage that joins and unites individuals into families.

A narrow definition of the family or what constituted the 'traditional' or 'nuclear' family is no longer useful or reflective of families today due to significant changes in many societies caused by divorce, separation, remarriage, single-parenthood as well as fostering and adoption. A family can be thought of as consisting of people who love and care for one another (Carrington, 1999) or as a network of people in a child's psychosocial field (Carr, 2006). The family has its own life-cycle model (Carter & McGoldrick, 1999) that shows the ways in which the family meets the needs of the child. It also shows the ways in which families put demands on children and other members of the family at varying stages of the life cycle. The model begins with the family of origin experiences, progresses to a family with young children and finishes the cycle with the stage of later life.

Older adults, seniors or elders are the terms attributed to individuals who are over 65 years old, those adults who are at the last stage of Carter and McGoldrick's (1999) family life-cycle model. According to Erikson's stages of the psychosocial life cycle (1968), these individuals are in the stage of integrity versus despair and isolation. Erikson's life-cycle model describes eight stages of the life cycle that are defined as periods when the person is in a state of increased vulnerability. When the person resolves this crisis period they progress and move on to the next stage. Development is continuous through the stages and individuals may regress to an earlier stage. Erikson describes the stage that older adults experience as the conflict between integrity, the sense of satisfaction that one feels in reflecting on a life productively lived, and despair and isolation, the sense that life has had little purpose or meaning. Erikson (1950) maintained that healthy children will not fear life if their parents and elders have integrity enough not to fear death. In making sense of this, older adults who experience late adulthood as a time of contentment, who have acceptance of their place in life and in the family life cycle, who believe that their life has had meaning, act as positive role models for younger generations. Erikson argued that growing old requires active preparation that begins at an earlier stage in life and as some societies may not be prepared to meet the needs of the older adult, they themselves must take responsibility for ensuring that these needs are successfully met. Younger people progressing through the earlier stages of the life cycle will evolve their beliefs about life based on how their elders experienced and perceive older age and pass their beliefs on. They may also observe the active preparation and responsibility needed and progress from the earlier stages into integrity without crises or psychopathology as this engagement with preparation is transmitted through the generations. Thus, Erikson's stages of the life cycle indicate how older people may influence the younger generations as positive role models.

Attachment theory (Bowlby, 1969/1982, 1973, 1980) provides a lens through which to understand human development from the cradle to the grave. Human attachment relationships according to Bowlby (1979) are regulated by a behavioural–motivational system that develops in infancy and that is shared with others. The biological function of attachment behaviour is protection and survival. The attachment system monitors the physical proximity and psychological availability of a 'stronger and wiser' attachment figure and activates attachment towards that figure. This figure is generally the biological mother where available. Bowlby (1969/1982) states that almost from the beginning, many children have more than one figure to whom they direct attachment behaviour. Ainsworth (1967) adds that the majority of children will become attached to more than one familiar person during the first year. In most societies this means the biological parents, older siblings, aunts, uncles and grandparents (Cassidy & Shaver, 1999).

Impact of grand parenting

Grandparent-provided child care is an important component of family support. Although the proportion of children living with grandparents appears to have remained relatively stable over time, families in which grandparents raise their grandchildren became an increasingly prevalent family structure during the 1900s (Hayslip & Kaminski, 2005; Mutchler & Baker, 2004). In the USA in 2000, 5.7 million grandparents lived with their grandchildren (Bryson, 2001; US Bureau of the Census, 2001) and approximately 2.4 million were raising their grandchildren. In New Zealand the 2001 census reported that over 4,000 grandparents had taken on the role of parent to their grandchildren (Statistics New Zealand, 2002). Considerable changes within the Irish family have occurred over the last 25 years with married women in the labour force becoming the norm rather than the exception (Larragy, 2001) and 32 per cent of all children in Ireland in 2004 being born outside of marriage (Fahey & Russell, 2001). Healthier ageing and greater longevity especially among women (Fahey & Murray, 1994; Bengston & Lowenstein, 2003) has also increased the percentage of older adults in the population. The number of separated and divorced people in Ireland increased by over a half between 1996 and 2002, reflecting the legalisation of divorce in Ireland in 1997 (Browne, 2003). These changes in Irish society are reflected internationally and have made older adults, grandparents, caring for and generally being involved in the lives of their grandchildren increasingly common (Lundstrom, 2001). Grandparents are providing informal care to their grandchildren for the working week taking over the traditional maternal caring role. Grandparents also find themselves in the position of full-time carers for various reasons including the death of a parent, alcoholism, mental health difficulties, parental drug abuse, domestic abuse and parental abandonment. In addition to grandparents who look after or are living with their grandchildren, an increasing number have taken on a custodial role as grandparents. These grandparents have the legal and physical custody of their grandchildren and are responsible for their daily care. A study conducted by Hank and Buber (2007) examined grandparent care-providing in ten European countries finding high levels of support with regards to prevalence and intensity of child care provided by grandparents reflecting that of other recent studies (Hank, 2007; Yi & Farrell, 2006).

Older adults as mentors rather than minders

That older adults and especially grandparents are significant in the lives of the younger cohorts seems apparent but begs the question as to how this caregiving is influencing younger people. The quality of attachment relationships has implications for an individual's later social and emotional development. Ainsworth (1967, 1973) proposed that differences in the security of attachment may have significant long-term implications for future self-understanding, intimate relationships and psychopathology. Bowlby's (1980, 1988) concept of the 'internal working model' of self is also key to the predictive formulations of attachment security. Bowlby proposed that early experiences of care contribute to the growth of broader representations relating to a caregiver's accessibility and responsiveness as well as to the beliefs about one's worthiness of receiving such care. A secure or insecure attachment can shape many aspects of developing personality including sociability, independence, self-esteem, trust and emotional being (Cassidy & Shaver, 1999).

It is clear that attachment between grandparents and younger generations is fundamental to their overall development with a secure attachment providing young people with all of the essential components to meet their developing needs ensuring future success within society. A number of studies have looked at the attachment between grandparents and children such as Myers and colleagues (1987). They examined attachment behaviours of young children during a play separation situation and found that grandmothers can function as attachment figures that play important roles in children's social development. Tinsely and Parke (1987) observed play with each parent and maternal and paternal grandparents and found that despite the different roles operationalised by each generation, significant correlations existed between the grandparents' and the parents' behavioural interactions with the child. It is important to look at intergenerational transmission within the context of social learning theory. Simons and colleagues (1991) examined the transmission of harsh parenting across three generations. Their results showed that parents who had received this type of parenting were more likely to use similar practices with their own children.

Howes (1999) highlighted that the majority of grandparents raising grandchildren measure up as attachment figures over the child's parents because they are the people who are providing emotional and physical care, and are consistent people in the child's life (Poehlmann, 2003). Studies focusing on the well-being of children raised by grandparents found that previously maltreated children living in kinship care with grandparents are less likely to display clinically significant behaviour problems than those children placed in foster care (Brooks & Barth, 1998; Heflinger et al., 2000). These studies comparing kinship versus foster care are significant for the future of young people and have implications for social policies and practices. Grandparents can serve as positive role models for children whose parents are physically or emotionally absent. In these cases children exhibit improved school performance, are more likely to excel academically and are as likely to succeed in school as children from single-parent families and exhibit less behaviour problems (Solomon & Marx, 1995).

Grandparents as moderators of adversity

An additional area of caregiving where older adults as grandparents influence and benefit the younger generations are families with children with developmental disabilities. Research indicated that support and care from grandparents is more important to adaptation to the crises period within the family than from professionals (Prudoe & Peters, 1995; Sandler et al., 1995). It is therefore important that professionals including psychologists are aware of the positive influence of older adults on both family dynamics and the child with a disability (Gowen et al., 1989). It is reasonable to conclude that systemic intervention that includes grandparents as significant others and embracing them in the child's treatment programme can make good use of this positive contribution from the older generation. A study by Katz and Kessel (2002) looked at the involvement of grandparents in the life of their grandchild with disability as well as their relationship with the child and family. They found that grandparents provided emotional support, financial aid, and were involved in medical care, respite care and participative in decision making. A number of studies have found that the maternal grandmother tends to be the most involved and supportive with children who have special needs (Vadasy et al., 1986). A review of the literature conducted by Seligman (1991) shows that grandparents of children with disabilities provide emotional and instrumental support and contribute to the mother's psychological well-being and perceived adjustment. The emotional and practical support that grandparents offer and provide for the younger generations helps parents meet the needs of the child with disability better as they tend to have more time, energy, financial resources and emotional resources.

Grand parenting can also be fraught with complexities such as social and economic difficulties, increased stress and role strain (Burton & deVries, 1993), role overload and role confusion (Emick & Hayslip, 1999) financial strain, as well as poorer physical and mental health than non-caregivers (Strawbridge *et al.*, 1997). The costs or negative aspects of older adults as caregivers are well documented in the literature but these costs seem to be outweighed by the positive influences and benefits of the older adult on the young person. In addition, the gain is not a one-way system. Close social support between older persons and their children, their grandchildren, their siblings and relatives will enhance subjective well-being, in addition to improving their immune system functioning (Peterson, 2000).

Cultural variation

The meaning of grandparenthood varies from society to society and from family to family and includes a plethora of varying roles. In this way older adults and grandparents influence younger generations in varying ways and levels of intensity. Western culture tends to see the growing number of older people more as a demographic problem than a demographic reward. Older people are spoken of as a group of highly dependent people putting a strain on financial resources such as pensions and health care. Many countries share this evolving perception of older adults. The relationship between the generations is documented to have changed in Botswana and specifically that between grandparents and grandchildren. In an account of the generations, elderly Botswana people speak about an idealised past where the young had respect for elders (Ingstad, 2004).

Other cultures have maintained this respect and value for their elders. Within African kinships their proverbs reflect the societal value they place on elders or 'opanyin'. 'Unlucky the house that does not have an old person living in it' (Geest, 2004: 47). Geest (2004) asked young people and older generations to describe the relationship between the young and old in a Ghanaian community. They believe that elders have lived long and have a wealth of experience so they are entitled to the respect and attention of their children, grandchildren and of youth in general. Another African proverb 'Opanyin ano sen obosom', translates as 'the mouth of an elder is stronger than god' and highlights the value placed on the wisdom and life experience of an elder.

Wisdom has been long being defined in many Asian, African and Western cultures. Some of these accounts of wisdom include:

- wisdom addresses important and difficult questions about the conduct and meaning of life;

- wisdom represents a truly superior level of knowledge, judgement and advice;
- wisdom represents knowledge used for the good or well-being of oneself and that of others (Baltes, 1993; Baltes & Smith, 1990; Baltes & Staudinger, 2000).

Interest in the concept of wisdom emerged as a result of a one-sided focus on the negative in terms of the gerontological research in the 1960s and 1970s (Baltes & Smith, 1990). At that time there were few aspects of ageing that were examined positively with the exception of Erikson's (1968) framework on generativity and wisdom as central tasks to adult life (Snyder & Lopez, 2005). The main reasons for generating a psychological theory of wisdom were to understand what may be positive in ageing. African cultures believe that wisdom enables the old to anticipate misfortune and to tell the younger generations how they can prevent it from happening. One African said that "young people just begin to act without thinking"', 'the wisdom and capacity to look ahead endows the old person with power' (Geest, 2004: 52). The role of adviser and helper were strongly expressed in the accounts of the younger people of the older adults as were the tales and stories they were told. Within indigenous communities in America and Canada the role of elders is to maintain and propagate rituals, disseminate traditional values and teachings and provide guidance and assistance to younger generations (Barusch & Tenbarge, 2003; Cook, 1999). Within Australian culture elders are respected within their communities with old age referring less to actual age and more to status (Pollitt, 1997). Aboriginal culture also reflects different elements to the sense of belonging of elders in a community that differ from western culture (Dudgeon et al., 2002). A study by Warburton and McLaughlin (2007: 52–6), focused on the accounts of many older adults and their role in cultural maintenance and highlights the following attitudes.

- 'We the older are the fountain of information that they pass on to younger people . . . its learning and educating role we play'.
- 'Without the older person, the younger person wouldn't learn the culture', 'culture . . . it's handed down from generation to generation'.
- 'Your elders have to be role models within the community'.
- 'The relationship between old and young is particularly important because older people are able to pass on the cultural traditions down the generations'.

Many indigenous elders spoke about the role that they have in 'putting troubled kids on the right track' and how they were on the panels of courts and were involved in prison visitations and the development of employment and support programmes for younger people (Warburton & McLaughlin, 2007: 52–6).

Within some societies, culture and social knowledge is passed down through observation (Gillision, 1997). This is seen in India in the Gimi culture where the tradition of the presenting of the 'sacred flutes' is transmitted to young men of the community during initiation rituals. Similarly the Kashinawa culture in Peru passes down rituals such as weaving and trance performances. In India, the Jenu Kurumba has a very specific death ritual that is carried out within the whole community. Cultural meaning and concepts of society and community are obtained through the visual with older generations introducing the youth to the key behaviours that communicate important societal concepts. Knowledge in this way is transmitted through visual perception and a visual understanding, a system of how things are seen and how what is seen is interpreted (Morphy, 1994).

Cohen (2005) has explored the positive potential of the mature mind in the context of developmental intelligence. Such intelligence allows for a range of biopsychosocial variables to amalgamate in a synergistic process that ultimately generates a positive developmental outcome for the individual. Cohen's model supports the ongoing development of adaptability, stability, creativity and well-being and dovetails with the work of Staudinger (1999) on the development of wisdom in old age. The implications for these theories are that wisdom cannot be acquired without having progressed through a number of life stages and accumulating tacit knowledge (acquired through personal experience and modelling, not through instruction). Thus wisdom may be an aspect of cognition and a trump card for the older person, one which is developed in late adulthood and cannot inherently be developed by younger individuals.

Guardians of spiritual and religious belief systems

Religion represents one of the other several intergenerational threads that older generations pass down to the younger generations. Relationships with grandchildren facilitate religious grandparents to pass down religious beliefs, values and practices to younger generations within both the family and within a wider community setting. Older adults can transmit their beliefs in many ways; by the direct instruction of beliefs to children, by role-modelling practices of faith, by observational learning of rituals that illustrates the required outcome for children or by status inheritance by which grandparents place the younger generations in specific social and economic contexts that influence specific sets of values. Many rituals or sacraments of Christianity complete the lifespan from baptism to anointing of the sick before death. A study by Copen and Silverstein (2008) found that grandmothers are important transmitters of religious beliefs to their grandchildren and that the influence of the older generations on the religiosity of the young is greatest when both grandmothers and mothers share consistent strong beliefs. They also found that parental divorce weakens the intergenerational transmission of beliefs.

Educators and teachers

Older adults also play a role in directly educating the younger generations. Older adults who have taken on a custodial role are required to communicate continually with schools. Grandparents are increasingly participative in children's educational school programmes with many schools having developed programmes and strategies to support grandparents. Many schools are now inviting grandparents to school ceremonies and parties, involving them in school activities, have professional contact in the case of problems with the child and invite grandparents to regular school meetings (Findler, 2007). Findler (2007) also found that teachers rate grandparents as a stable and significant component of the families' support network.

Older adults also act as potential role models with respect to higher order values. Take for example, forgiveness. By nature our inclination to avoid and more so to retaliate or seek revenge post insult or victimisation is deeply ingrained in our biological, psychological and cultural make-up (Newberg *et al.*, 2000, cited in Snyder & Lopez, 2005). Forgiveness is an approach whereby we can quell our natural negative responses to transgressors and become more motivated to engage in positive behaviour towards them. Within the context of mental health, research by Mauger *et al.* (1996) found that people who are forgiving report less negative affect such as anxiety, depression and hostility and are less ruminative and exploitative. Girard and Mullet (1997) found that older adults (65–96 years) were more inclined to forgive across a variety of transgression scenarios in comparison to adults or adolescents. They also found that older adults were more disposed to forgive in comparison with young adults.

Thus there appears to be an increase in ones propensity to forgive as one progresses across the lifespan. Certainly, other factors such as personality, health, social units (marriage, organisations) and the character of transgressions and their context also influence forgiveness, however 'ageing' as a process appears to be a protective and predisposing factor that can facilitate the development of forgiveness within an individual.

Research by Wuthnow (2000) reported that among groups that explicitly fostered forgiveness, 61 per cent of participants reported an ability to forgive, while others reported greater self-report attempts and successes in overcoming guilt, addiction and perceiving encouragement when feeling discouraged.

Empirical research into forgiveness is still in its infancy relative to other psychological theories and concepts. Notwithstanding this theory's limitations by virtue of its stage of development, these findings highlight the strengths in older people and provide the psychological architecture for the prevention of mental ill health within this population.

Resilience

The relationship between older generations and young is fundamental to the well-being of youth. The concept of individual resilience in the face of adversity is marked in myths, fairy tales, art and literature over the centuries in people illustrated as heroes and heroines (Snyder & Lopez, 2005). Resilience has being defined as: 'the result of negotiations between individuals and their environment to maintain a self definition as healthy' (Ungar, 2004: 24); 'the self righting capacity for healthy growth and development' (Benard, 2006: 198). Resilience can be seen in the achievement of normal psychosocial development and life success by young people in the face of multiple risks and adversity. There are many documented factors accounting for young people's resilience including close attachment relationships with caregiving adults, positive family climate, organised family climate, and close relationships to competent, prosocial and supportive adults (Snyder & Lopez, 2005). There are many protective factors that underlie the resilience and success of young people, in which older adults within the family as grandparents and within the wider community and society play a part.

Many studies have reported that resident grandparents help younger generations through adjustment difficulties (DeLeire & Kalil, 2002). A study by Ruiz and Silverstein (2007) of grandparents not co-residing explored whether social and emotional cohesion with grandparents affected the psychological well-being of late adolescents and young adults. The study found that close relationships with grandparents reduced depressive symptoms and that grandparents act as functional substitutes in reducing distress among young adults and improving their self-esteem. Similarly Yi et al. (2006) found that family kin relations in Taiwan are a significant factor in explaining adolescents' depression.

Older adults: one key that can fit many locks

It is clear that in many cultures the role of elders is varied, many view themselves as having an important role in maintaining and promoting the culture and in some cultures elders are valued not only as the most important person in the family but in the wider community. Elders are seen as contributing to society and adding value to the broader community life. Older people from diverse backgrounds and cultures advise and guide young people, ensure sustainable and strong communities as well as improving intergenerational relationships. Elders serve roles such as historian, providing a link with the cultural and familial past, a mentor to the young, a storyteller passing tales and fables on, and a caregiver and nurturer. Within the majority of cultures, older adults enjoy passing down these stories. Through narratives the younger generations develop a deeper understanding of the social world, how other people think and behave; and the consequences people's behaviour and actions hold for others. Narratives transmit cultural knowledge; values and beliefs and are a significant instrument for socialisation of the younger generations (Miller *et al.*, 1997).

It is apparent that within some cultures the gap between young and old is wider than others. This 'generation gap', denotes the wide differences in cultural norms between members of a younger generation and their elders. It also symbolises a disconnection between one significant cohort and another in the general population. It can be argued that this 'generation gap' occurs when older and younger people do not understand each other because of their different experiences, opinions and behaviours. Within many societies efforts are being made to bridge this gap between young and old. The end result may not be as important as the process that brings it about. Educating cohorts about each other, delineating similarities, understanding differences and maintaining links between them may all be skills that help to improve the general lot of a society regardless of the final outcome. Within the Japanese culture, 'the dancing granny', a logo of a 'happy granny dancing merrily with a group of children' has become a symbol of Kotoen's commitment to generation re-engagement (Thang, 1999). Recognition for the need for interaction between young and old has led to the establishment of a number of intergenerational programmes such as providing services for young and elderly people within the same compound, and setting up programmes where children visit elderly homes and clubs. A number of countries have recognised this need and implemented intergenerational programmes. Programmes in America include the Retired Senior Volunteer Program, the Foster Grandparent Program, the Senior Community Service Program and more problem-focused programmes like intergenerational At-Risk Youths and Intergenerational Arts for At-Risk School Age Children (Newman & Brummel, 1989).

All programmes deliberately designed to enhance either the quality of life of older adults or to promote the health and well-being of the younger generations have one significant thread in common. They are designed from the premise that connection between the cohorts is crucially important. The essence of how older adults are the key to the success of younger generations is the relationship that is allowed to be built between young and old. When that happens, the qualitative experiences as outlined by one of this chapter's authors (MS) below can result.

- Grandma lived about 100 yards from my home and this meant I was free to run up and down the lane to see her any hour of the day or night, and I did.

- Grandma was fantastic at providing Cadbury's Rolos, one for each hand, and always giving you a slice of white coconut cake with the tea.
- She helped in teaching me how to read, write and how to remember my maths times tables.
- She showed me values such as the importance of family through her stories and her ways with us.
- She taught me how to love and be loved.

It seems to come back to basic needs being fulfilled and to the fact that 'We are born with the expectation of being met as a person' (Sutherland, 1993, cited in McCloskey, 2005: 1).

References

Ainsworth, M. D. S. (1967). *Infancy in Uganda: Infant Care and the Growth of Love.* Baltimore, MD: Johns Hopkins University Press.

Ainsworth, M. D. S. (1973). The development of the infant mother attachment. In Caldwell, B., & Ricciuti, H., eds., *Review of Child Development Research, Vol. 3.* Chicago, IL: University of Chicago Press, pp. 1–94.

Baltes, P. B. (1993). The aging mind: potential and limits. *The Gerontologist,* 33, 580–94.

Baltes, P. B., & Smith, J. (1990). Toward a psychology of wisdom and its ontogenesis. In Sternberg, R. J., ed., *Wisdom: Its Nature, Origins and Development.* New York: Cambridge University Press, pp. 87–120.

Baltes, P. B., & Staudinger, U. M. (2000). Wisdom: A metaheuristic (pragmatic) to orchestrate mind and virtue toward excellence. *American Psychologist,* 55, 122–36.

Barusch, A., & Tenbarge, C. (2003). Indigenous elders in rural America. *Journal of Gerontological Social Work,* 41, 121–36.

Benard, B. (2006). Using strengths-based practice to tap the resilience of families. In Saleebey, D., ed., *The Strengths Perspective in Social Work Practice, 4th ed.* Boston, MD: Allyn & Bacon, pp. 197–220.

Bengston, V., & Lowenstein, A. (2003). *Global Aging and Challenges to Families.* New York: Aldine de Gruyter.

Bowlby, J. (1973). *Attachment and Loss: Vol. 2. Separation: Anxiety and Anger.* New York: Basic Books.

Bowlby, J. (1979). *The Making and Breaking of Affectional Bonds.* London: Tavistock.

Bowlby, J. (1980). *Attachment and Loss: Vol. 3. Loss: Sadness and Depression.* New York: Basic Books.

Bowlby, J. (1982). *Attachment and Loss: Vol. 1. Attachment, 2nd ed.* New York: Basic Books. Original publication 1969.

Bowlby, J. (1988). Attachment, communication, and the therapeutic process. In *A Secure Base: Clinical Applications of Attachment Theory.* London. Routledge.

Brooks, D., & Barth, R. P. (1998). Characteristics and outcomes of drug-exposed and non drug-exposed children in kinship and non-relative foster care. *Children and Youth Services Review*, 20, 475–501.

Browne, M. (2003). *Family Matters Ten Years On*. Dublin: Comhairle. (Retrieved 5 August 2010 from http://www.citizensinformationboard.ie/publications/social/downloads/FamilyMattersTenYearsOnReport2005.pdf)

Bryson, K. (2001). *New Census Bureau Data on Grandparents Raising Grandchildren*. Paper presented at the Annual Scientific Meeting of the Gerontological Society of America, Chicago, Illinois, USA.

Burton, L. M., & deVries, C. (1993). Challenges and rewards: African American grandparents as surrogate parents. In Burton, L., ed., *Families and Aging*. San Francisco, CA: Baywood Press, pp. 101–8.

Carr, A. (2006). *Handbook of Child and Adolescent Clinical Psychology, A Contextual Approach*. London: Routledge.

Carrington, C. (1999). *No Place Like Home: Relationships and Family Life Among Lesbians and Gay Men*. Chicago, IL: University of Chicago Press.

Carter, B., & McGoldrick, M. (1999). *The Expanded Family Life Cycle. Individual, Family and Social Perspectives, 3rd ed*. Boston, MD: Allyn & Bacon.

Cassidy, J., & Shaver, P. (1999). *Handbook of Attachment, Theory, Research and Clinical Applications*. New York: Guilford Press.

Cohen, G. (2005). *The Mature Mind: The Positive Power of the Aging Brain*. New York: Basic Books.

Cook P. (1999). Capacity-building partnerships between indigenous youth and elders. *Child & Youth Services*, 20, 189–202.

Copen, C., & Silverstein, M. (2008). The transmission of religious beliefs across generations: do grandparents matter? *Journal of Comparative Family Studies*, 38, 497–510.

DeLeire, T., & Kalil, A. (2002). Good things come in threes: Single parent multigenerational family structure and adolescent adjustment. *Demography*, 39, 393–412.

Dudgeon, P., Mallard, J., Oxenham, D., & Fielder, J. (2002). Contemporary Aboriginal perceptions of community. In Fisher, A. T., Sonn, C. C., & Bishop, B. J., eds., *Psychological Sense of Community Research, Applications and Implications*. New York: Kluwer, 247–67.

Emick, M. A., & Hayslip, B. (1999). Custodial grandparenting: stresses, coping skills and relationships with grandchildren. *International Journal of Aging & Human Development*, 48, 35–61.

Erikson, E. (1950). *Childhood and Society*. New York: W. W. Norton.

Erikson, E. (1968). *Identity, Youth and Crises*. New York: W. W. Norton.

Fahey, T., & Murray, P. (1994). *Health and Autonomy Among the Over 65's in Ireland*. Dublin: National Council for the Elderly.

Fahey, T., & Russell, H. (2001). *Family Formation in Ireland: Trends, Data Needs and Implications: Report to Family Affairs Unit, Department of Social, Community and Family Affairs*. Dublin: ERSI.

Findler, L. (2007). Grandparents – the overlooked potential partners: perceptions and practice of teachers in special and regular education. *European Journal of Special Needs Education*, 22, 199–216.

Geest, S. Van Der (2004). Grandparents and grandchildren in Kwahu, Ghana: the performance of respect. *Africa*, 74(1), 47–61.

Gillision, G. (1997). To see or not to see: Looking as an object of exchange in the New Guinea Highlands. In Banks, M., & Murphy, H., eds., *Rethinking Visual Anthropology*. New Haven, CT: Yale University, pp. 170–185.

Girard, M., & Mullet, E. (1997). Propensity to forgive in adolescents, young adults, older adults, and elderly people. *Journal of Adult Development*, 4, 209–20.

Gowen, J. W., Johnson-Martin, N., Goldman, B. D., & Appelbaum, M. (1989). Feelings of depression and parenting competence of mothers of handicapped and non-handicapped infants: A longitudinal study. *American Journal on Mental Retardation*, 94, 259–71.

Hank, K. (2007). Proximity and contacts between older parents and their children: A European comparison. *Journal of Marriage and Family*, 69, 157–73.

Hank, K., & Buber, I. (2007). *Grandparents Caring for their Grandchildren: Findings from the 2004 Survey of Health, Ageing, and Retirement in Europe*. Mannheim: Mannheim Research Institute for the Economics of Ageing.

Hayslip, B., & Kaminski, P. L. (2005). Grandparents raising their grandchildren: A review of the literature and suggestions for practice. *The Gerontologist*, 45, 262–9.

Heflinger, C. A., Simpkins, C. G., & Combs-Orme, T. (2000). Using the CBCL to determine the clinical status of children in state custody. *Children and Youth Services Review*, 22, 55–73.

Howes, C. (1999). Attachment relationships in the context of multiple caregivers. In Cassidy, J., & Shaver, P. R., eds., *Handbook of Attachment: Theory, Research and Clinical Applications*. New York: Guilford. pp. 671–87.

Ingstad, B. (2004). The value of grandchildren: Changing relations between generations in Botswana. *Africa*, 1, 62–75.

Katz, S., & Kessel, L. (2002). Grandparents of children with developmental disabilities: Perceptions, beliefs, and involvement in their care. *Issues in Comprehensive Pediatric Nursing*, 25, 113–28.

Larragy, J. (2001). *Ireland's Economic Turnaround – Origins and Implications for Social Policy*. Paper presented to the COST A15 Action, Group 4, Employment Policies and Welfare Reform, Berlin.

Lundstrom, F. (2001). *Grandparenthood in Modern Ireland*. Dublin: Age Action Ireland.

McCloskey, U. (2005) *To Be Met as a Person: The Dynamics of Attachment in Professional Encounters*. London: Hobbs.

Mauger, P. A., Saxon, A., Hamill, C., & Pannell, M. (1996). *The Relationship of Forgiveness to Interpersonal Behaviour*. Paper presented at the Annual Convention of the Southeastern Psychological Association, Norfolk.

Miller, P. J., Wiley, A. R., Fung, H., & Liang, C. (1997). Personal story-telling as a medium for socialization in Chinese and American families. *Child Development*, 68, 557–68.

Morphy, H. (1994). The interpretation of ritual: reflections from film on anthropological practice. *Man*, 29, 117–46.

Mutchler, J. E., & Baker, L. A. (2004). A demographic examination of grandparent caregivers in the Census 2000 Supplementary Survey. *Population Research and Policy Review*, 23, 359–77.

Myers, B. J., Jarvis, P. A., & Creasey, G. L. (1987). Infants' behavior with their mothers and grandmothers. *Infant Behavior & Development*, 10, 245–59.

Newman, S., & Brummel, S. (1989). *Intergenerational Programs: Imperatives, Strategies, Impacts, Trends.* New York: Hayworth Press.

Peterson, C. (2000). The future of optimism. *American Psychologist,* 55, 44–55.

Poehlmann, J. (2003). An attachment perspective on grandparents raising their very young grandchildren: implications from intervention and research. *Infant Mental Health Journal,* 24, 149–73.

Pollitt, P. A. (1997). The problem of dementia in Australian Aboriginal and Torres Strait Islander communities: An overview. *International Journal of Geriatric Psychiatry,* 12, 155–63.

Prudoe, C. M., & Peters, D. L. (1995). Social support of parents and grandparents in the neonatal intensive care unit. *Pediatric Nursing,* 21, 140–6.

Ruiz, S., & Silverstein, M. (2007). Relationships with grandparents and the emotional wellbeing of late adolescent and young adult grandchildren. *Journal of Social Issues,* 4, 793–808.

Sandler, A. G., Warren, S. H., & Raver, S. A. (1995). Grandparents as a source of support for parents of children with disabilities: A brief report. *Mental Retardation,* 33, 248–50.

Seligman, M. (1991). *Learned Optimism.* New York: Knopf.

Simons, R. L., Whitbeck, L. B., Conger, R. D., & Wu, C. (1991). Intergenerational transmission of harsh parenting. *Developmental Psychology,* 27, 159–71.

Snyder, C. R., & Lopez, S. J. (2005). *Handbook of Positive Psychology.* Oxford: Oxford University Press.

Solomon, J. C., & Marx, J. (1995). "To grandmothers house we go": health and school adjustment of children raised solely by grandparents. *The Gerontologist,* 35, 386–94.

Statistics New Zealand (2002). *2001 Census of Population and Dwellings: Families and Households.* Auckland: Statistics New Zealand.

Staudinger, U. (1999). Older and wiser? Integrating results on the relationship between age and wisdom-related performance. *International Journal of Behavioral Development,* 23(3), 641–4.

Strawbridge, W. J., Wallhagen, M. I., Shema, S. J., & Kaplan, G. A. (1997). New burdens or more of the same? Comparing grandparent, spouse, and adult–child caregivers. *The Gerontologist,* 37, 505–10.

Sutherland, J. D. (1993). *The Interpersonal World of the Infant.* New York: Basic Books.

Thang, L. L. (1999). The dancing Granny: linking the generations in a Japanese age-integrated welfare centre. *Japanese Studies,* 19, 151–62.

Tinsely, B. J., & Parke, R. D. (1987). Grandparents as interactive and social support agents for families with young infants. *International Journal of Aging & Human Development,* 25, 259–77.

Ungar, M. (2004). The importance of parents and other caregivers to the resilience of high risk adolescents. *Family Process,* 43, 23–41.

US Bureau of the Census. (2001). *Co-resident Grandparents and Grandchildren.* Washington, DC: US Bureau of the Census. (Retrieved 4 August 2010 from http://www.Census.gov)

Vadasy, P. F., Fewell, R. R., & Meyer, D. J. (1986). Grandparents of children with special needs: Insights into their experiences and concerns. *Journal of Early Intervention,* 10, 36–44.

Warburton, J., & McLaughlin, D. (2007). Passing on our culture: how older Australians from diverse cultural backgrounds contribute to civil society. *Journal of Cross Cultural Gerontology*, 22, 47–60.

Wuthnow, R. (2000). How religious groups promote forgiving: A national study. *Journal for the Scientific Study of Religion*, 36, 124–37.

Yi, C., & Farrell, M. (2006). Globalization and the intergenerational relation: cross-cultural perspectives on support and interaction patterns. *Journal of Family Issues*, 27, 1035–41.

Yi, C. C., Wu, C., & Chang, Y. H. (2006). *Youth Development in Taiwan: An Analysis of the Taiwan Youth Project, 2000–2005*. Paper presented at the 16th ISA World Congress of Sociology, RC06 Session 1, Durban, South Africa.

Index

Girard, M. and Mullet, E. 256
Glendenning, F. 168
Global Health through Education
Training and Service (GHETS),
Kenya 217
goal planning, appropriate 57
Goismann, R. M. 72
Goldwasser, A. *et al.* 101
Gotlib, I. and Hammen, C. 132, 135
Gott, M. and Hinchliff, S. 202
grandparents: attachment between
younger generations and 251–2;
cultural variation in meaning of
grandparenthood and elders 253–5;
as educators and teachers 256–7;
and the encouragement of resilience
257; as guardians of spiritual and
religious belief systems 255–6;
impact of grandparenting 250–1; as
mentors rather than minders 251–2;
as moderators of adversity 252–3;
multiple roles of elders and 257–9;
and the well-being of children 252,
257
Granholm, E. *et al.* 69
grief: definitions 110; grief work
viewpoints and theories 116–18;
management, in older adults
112–14; older adult's experience of
loss, bereavement and 109–20
Grimley Evans, J. 27; and Tallis, R. C.
39
Gueli, N. *et al.* 7
guilt 215, 256; survivor guilt 206–7
Guirani, F. and Hansen, M. 160

Halldorsdottir, S. 221
Hamilton Rating Scale for Depression
(HRSD) 136
Hamilton, W. D. 26
Hancock, G. A. *et al.* 59
Hank, K. and Buber, I. 251
Hansson, R. O. and Strobe, M. S.
112
happiness 183, 238; and the paradox of
ageing 230–42; Utilitarianism and
the 'Greatest-Happiness Principle'
37–8
Harding, K. *et al.* 57
Harris, L. and Wier, M. 207
Harwood, D. 72
Harwood, J. *et al.* 199

Havighurst, R. J. 13; *et al.* 12–13;
lifespan approach to ageing 17–18
Hayek, F. A. 38
Hayflick, L. 7
health indices in old age 232–3
Health of the Nation targets 58
health promotion for older people
240–1
Health Service Executive (HSE) 143–4,
149, 150, 162, 223
health service provision 38–9, 40, 59;
discrimination in 38–9, 75–6
Heaphy, B. *et al.* 205
hearing loss/difficulties 7, 55, 111, 145,
214, 232
Help the Aged 43
Hinchliff, S. and Gott, M. 195, 201,
202–3
Hirsch, R. and Vollhardt, B. 163
HIV 207
Hogan, R. 195
homosexual older people 205–7
Hörl, J. 162
hormone replacement therapy (HRT) 31
Horn, J. and Stankov, L. 9–10
Horwitz, A. *et al.* 55
Howes, C. 252
HRT (hormone replacement therapy)
31
HSE (Health Service Executive) 143–4,
149, 150, 162, 223
humiliation 77
Husband, H. 99
hypertension 27, 97; effects of alpha
blockers on sexual desire 197
hypnotic drugs 73–4
hysterectomy 197

IADLs (instrumental activities of daily
living) 233
ICD (International Classification of
Diseases) 93, 128
identity threat, through multiple losses
111
illness: and the biology of ageing 26–8;
disease *see* disease
immunological theory of ageing 6
incontinence 27
independent living 166
individualism 239
insomnia 73–4, 113 (*see also* sleep
problems)